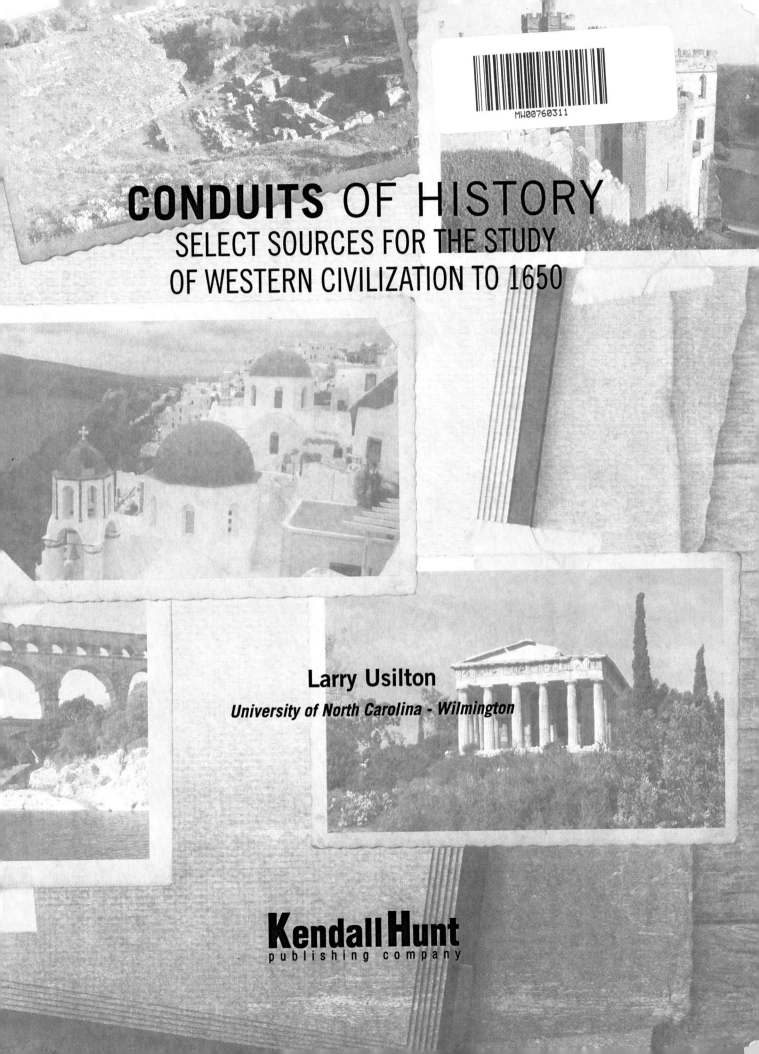

CONDUITS OF HISTORY
SELECT SOURCES FOR THE STUDY
OF WESTERN CIVILIZATION TO 1650

Larry Usilton
University of North Carolina - Wilmington

Kendall Hunt
publishing company

Cover images provided by Larry Usilton.

www.kendallhunt.com
Send all inquiries to:
4050 Westmark Drive
Dubuque, IA 52004-1840

Printed in the United States of America

For my loving mother, Agnes L. Usilton, by the grace of God,
now in the ninth decade of her life.

TABLE OF CONTENTS

The Ancient Near East

Civilization first developed in the Near East around 3500 BCE in the river valleys of Mesopotamia (modern-day Iraq) and Egypt. Here, the rivers each year flooded their banks leaving silt deposits, which renewed the land. The early inhabitants soon discovered that they could put down permanent roots and abandon the nomadic ways of the past. There were, however, significant differences between these two civilizations. In Mesopotamia, the flood waters of the Tigris and Euphrates were less predictable and potentially more destructive than those of the Nile. Those who lived "between the rivers," to use the early Greek name for the area, had to learn how to dig short canals to make efficient use of the flood waters. Mesopotamia also lacked abundant resources. There was little wood and stone and few precious mineral resources, which limited the size, shape, and scope of Mesopotamian architecture, sculpture, and painting. What the Mesopotamians did have in great abundance was clay that was used to construct their cities, temples, homes, pottery, and the tablets on which they wrote.

Current research suggests that a people called the Sumerians either brought the first civilization to Mesopotamia or reached that state shortly after they arrived in the fourth millennium BCE. Within their walled cities in the southernmost part of the Valley, the Sumerians built majestic temples called ziggurats, invented math and astronomy, and kept detailed written records in a cuneiform script. The latter invention was especially important as it allowed the Sumerians to keep business records and in their leisure time to fashion stories about the gods and creation, catastrophic floods, and great heroes such as Gilgamesh who spent his days looking for the secret to eternal life. The Sumerian influence was felt both within and beyond Mesopotamia. When Sargon of Akkad conquered the Sumerian states ca. 2300 BCE, the ingredients of civilization were quickly absorbed and eventually transmitted to others. Akkadian rule, though, was short-lived. As other groups pressed into the Valley, the Sumerians under the leadership of the kings of Ur regained their independence and, in doing so, entered the last great phase of their history. During the so-called Sumerian Renaissance (ca. 2100–2000 BCE), the most powerful king of the period, Ur-Nammu, built the largest of all ziggurats and issued one of the earliest law codes in history. Sumer, though, was no more fortunate than the Valley's other ephemeral kingdoms. When a fresh wave of invaders, chiefly the Elamites, entered the Valley, Sumer ceased to exist as a political entity and was eventually forgotten until rediscovered in the last years of the nineteenth century of the Modern Era.

Two centuries of chaos ensued before some semblance of order was restored by the Amorite king Hammurabi (1792–1750 BCE). One of the most important figures in the annals of the history of the

Ancient Near East, Hammurabi reunited the Valley, established Babylon as his political capital, and then issued a great law code. Although the code guaranteed important rights to all levels of society and promised severe penalties for infractions of the law, it also gave the disparate groups that made up the empire a political identity. Babylonia, as the area came to be known, reached its peak under Hammurabi, but declined under his less capable successors as other groups, most notably the Hittites and Kassites, entered the area.

In the meantime, civilization had also taken root in Egypt. Here, too, geography played an important role. In addition to the life-giving flood waters of the Nile, Egypt possessed innumerable other resources—large quantities of stone that enabled its kings, called pharaohs, to construct great tombs, temples, obelisks, and other monuments to commemorate their achievements, papyri on which the scribes kept written records in an hieroglyphic script, and defensible boundaries which, after unification, ensured political continuity.

Tradition tells us that it was an Upper Egyptian king named Menes who first brought the country together under his rule ca. 3100 BCE. By the Old Kingdom Period (2700–2200 BCE), Egypt was firmly united under pharaohs who traced their descent from the gods, most notably the sun god Ra or Re. So powerful were the pharaohs of the Fourth Dynasty that, during the flood season, they could summon the Egyptian peasantry to construct pyramids and great structures within the Valley. One of these, the so-called Great Pyramid of Khufu or Cheops at Giza, is numbered among the great wonders of the ancient world. Egypt, though, was not immune to the problems that afflicted her neighbors. On two occasions, internal friction between pharaoh's rule and the great nobles of the country and the priesthood plunged the country into anarchy. During one of these periods, Egypt was invaded and conquered by the warlike Hyksos. Egypt recovered, though, thanks to the rulers of Thebes who, ca. 1575 BCE, expelled the Hyksos and founded the Eighteenth Dynasty. Under the first nine pharaohs of this Dynasty, which reached its peak under the rule of a woman named Hatshepsut and her stepson Thutmose III, a great empire was created which stretched eastward to the Euphrates. However, the gains made by these pharaohs were seriously threatened when, in the middle of the fourteenth-century BCE, the enigmatic Amenhotep IV, better known as Akhenaton, came to power. Akhenaton's obsession with the sun god from which his name is derived, the Aton, alienated the priesthood and people of Egypt and left him precious little time for governmental business and the defense of the realm. Following his demise, Egypt limped through the short, pathetic reigns of two family members, including the boy king Tutankhamon, before it was rescued by the pharaohs of the Nineteenth and Twentieth Dynasties. The strongest of these pharaohs, Ramses II, claims to have triumphed over the Hittites of Asia Minor, built great monuments to attest to the glory of his long reign, and fathered well over a hundred children. Ramses III, the last significant pharaoh of the New Kingdom Period, saved Egypt from the Sea Peoples, but eventually succumbed to an attempt on his life as the country slipped into a period of quiescence from which it would never emerge.

Egypt's demise ushered in a politically fragmented age dominated by a number of smaller kingdoms. The Phoenicians, situated along the eastern Mediterranean coast in modern-day Lebanon, developed a number of important coastal cities such as Tyre, Sidon, Beirut, and Byblos from which their ships, the finest of the era, sailed to distant lands. Colonies and trading posts were founded throughout the Mediterranean area and beyond. Carthage, one of these colonies, would eventually become powerful enough to challenge the Romans for supremacy in the ancient world. Situated to the east of the Phoenician settlements were the Aramaean communities of Palmyra, Damascus, and Kadesh.

The Aramaeans, a landlocked people, became famous for their overland trade, which took them along all of the important trade routes of the Near East. The most important of these groups, though, were the Jewish settlements of Palestine. According to the Old Testament of the Bible, the Jews, originally situated in Mesopotamia, made their way to the land of Canaan (later Palestine) and from there, possibly during a famine, down into Egypt where they were eventually enslaved and put to work building pharaoh's cities and monuments. Under Moses, the Jews, or Hebrews as they are often called, regained their independence and, after a long sojourn in the desert, eventually returned to Palestine. Here, for a short period, they fell under the domination of the warlike Philistines. Under the leadership of Saul, David, and Solomon, the Jews overcame the Philistines and others to create a formidable small kingdom with a capital at Jerusalem. Unfortunately, internal dissension shattered Jewish unity and led to the creation of two kingdoms, those of Judah and Israel.

By about 700 BCE, the independence of these small states was seriously threatened by the emergence of a new empire—that of the Assyrians. Under a long succession of very warlike kings, the Assyrians, a Semitic people originally situated in the upper reaches of the Tigris–Euphrates River Valley, were poised to take control of the Near East. Their army, the finest of its day, defeated armies in the field, razed cities, and inflicted horrible atrocities on the captured. Although their chief occupation was warfare, the Assyrians kept good written records and were unsurpassed in the field of relief sculpture. Ashurbanipal, the last significant ruler of this Empire, created a great library in his palace at Nineveh, which he stocked with thousands of cuneiform texts, including a copy of the creation story and the Epic of Gilgamesh.

By the latter part of the seventh century, however, the Assyrian Empire was at an end. The size of the Empire, the loss of irreplaceable warriors in battle, and the intense hatred generated among the conquered rendered its fall inevitable. In 612 BCE, the Chaldeans and Medes united to take and destroy the Assyrian capital of Nineveh. With the Empire's collapse, a number of smaller kingdoms emerged. Under the leadership of the Chaldean king Nebuchadnezzar, Babylonia experienced a brief revival. A competent captain, Nebuchadnezzar destroyed Jerusalem and carried the Jews off into the famous "Babylonian Captivity." During more peaceful times, he worked hard to beautify Babylon, constructing the Ishtar Gate and the fabled Hanging Gardens. In Asia Minor, the Lydians, an Indo-European people, capitalized on their location near busy trade routes to become one of the wealthiest kingdoms of the ancient world. Under the leadership of Croesus, the Lydians minted gold coins, the first nation of antiquity to do so, and established important ties with the Greek states along the coast of Asia Minor.

Once again, though, the independence of these small kingdoms was extinguished by the emergence of a new empire. Under Cyrus the Great, the Persian tribes of Elam were united into a powerful fighting force, which conquered, among others, the Medes, the Lydians, and the Babylonians. The "King of Kings," as Persian rulers sometimes styled themselves in official correspondence, reigned over many different lands and people from great palaces in cities such as Ecbatana, Susa, Persepolis, and Babylon. If the Persians were somewhat more successful than the Assyrians in the unification and governance of the Near East, it is because the rulers early on adopted a policy that allowed the conquered some degree of political autonomy and respect for their local traditions, including even the gods they worshipped. Under Cyrus' successors, the Persians marched to the shores of the Aegean Sea and, in doing so, precipitated a confrontation with the states of the Greek world. By the turn of the fifth century BCE, the Persian Empire, militarily and geographically, was at its peak.

RECOMMENDED READINGS

Aldred, Cyril. *The Egyptians*. 1998.

Hallo, William W. and William K. Simpson. *The Ancient Near East: A History*. 1998. Revised edition.

Kuhrt, Amelie. *The Ancient Near East, c. 3000–330 B.C.* 2 vols. 1995.

Pritchard, James B., ed. *Ancient Near Eastern Texts Relating to the Old Testament*. 1969.

Saggs, H.W.F. *Babylonians*. 1995.

Snell, Daniel C. *Life in the Ancient Near East, 3100–332 B.C.E.* 1997.

Van De Mieroop, Marc. *A History of the Ancient Near East ca. 3000–323 B.C.* 2006.

QUESTIONS

1. Why is the Epic of Gilgamesh important in our understanding of Babylonian Fatalism?
2. What rights did women and slaves have under Hammurapi's law code?
3. What factors aided Joseph in his rise from rags to riches in Egypt?
4. What similarities are there between Akhenaton's *Hymn to the Aten* and Psalm 104 in the Bible?
5. What did Solomon do to ensure that he would become one of the great figures in the history of the Ancient Near East?

THE EPIC OF GILGAMESH
N. K. Sandars

THE SEARCH FOR EVERLASTING LIFE

BITTERLY Gilgamesh wept for his friend Enkidu; he wandered over the wilderness as a hunter, he roamed over the plains; in his bitterness he cried, 'How can I rest, how can I be at peace? Despair is in my heart. What my brother is now, that shall I be when I am dead. Because I am afraid of death I will go as best I can to find Utnapishtim whom they call the Faraway, for he has entered the assembly of the gods.' So Gilgamesh travelled over the wilderness, he wandered over the grasslands, a long journey, in search of Utnapishtim, whom the gods took after the deluge; and they set him to live in the land of Dilmun, in the garden of the sun; and to him alone of men they gave everlasting life.

At night when he came to the mountain passes Gilgamesh prayed: 'In these mountain passes long ago I saw lions, I was afraid and I lifted my eyes to the moon; I prayed and my prayers went up to the gods, so now, O moon god Sin, protect me.' When he had prayed he lay down to sleep, until he was woken from out of a dream. He saw the lions round him glorying in life; then he took his axe in his hand, he drew his sword from his belt, and he fell upon them like an arrow from the string, and struck and destroyed and scattered them.

So at length Gilgamesh came to Mashu, the great mountains about which he had heard many things, which guard the rising and the setting sun. Its twin peaks are as high as the wall of heaven and its paps reach down to the underworld. At its gate the Scorpions stand guard, half man and half dragon; their glory is terrifying, their stare strikes death into men, their shimmering halo sweeps the mountains that guard the rising sun. When Gilgamesh saw them he shielded his eyes for the length of a moment only; then he took courage and approached. When they saw him so undismayed the Man-Scorpion called to his mate, 'This one who comes to us now is flesh of the gods.' The mate of the Man-Scorpion answered, 'Two thirds is god but one third is man.'

Then he called to the man Gilgamesh, he called to the child of the gods; 'Why have you come so great a journey; for what have you travelled so far, crossing the dangerous waters; tell me the reason for your coming?' Gilgamesh answered, 'For Enkidu; I loved him dearly, together we endured all kinds of hardships; on his account I have come, for the common lot of man has taken him. I have wept for him day and night, I would not give up his body for burial, I thought my friend would come back because of my weeping. Since he went, my life is nothing; that is why I have travelled here in search of Utnapishtim my father; for men say he has entered the assembly of the gods, and has found everlasting life. I have a desire to question him concerning the living and the dead.' The Man-Scorpion opened his mouth and said, speaking to Gilgamesh, 'No man born of woman has done what you have asked, no mortal man has gone into the mountain; the length of it is twelve leagues of darkness; in it there is no light, but the heart is oppressed with darkness. From the rising of the sun to the setting of the sun there is no light.' Gilgamesh said, 'Although I should go in sorrow and in pain, with sighing and with weeping, still I must go. Open the gate of the mountain.' And the Man-Scorpion said, 'Go, Gilgamesh, I permit you to pass through the mountain of Mashu and through the high ranges;

may your feet carry you safely home. The gate of the mountain is open.'

When Gilgamesh heard this he did as the Man-Scorpion had said, he followed the sun's road to his rising, through the mountain. When he had gone one league the darkness became thick around him, for there was no light, he could see nothing ahead and nothing behind him. After two leagues the darkness was thick and there was no light, he could see nothing ahead and nothing behind him. After three leagues the darkness was thick, and there was no light, he could see nothing ahead and nothing behind him. After four leagues the darkness was thick and there was no light, he could see nothing ahead and nothing behind him. At the end of five leagues the darkness was thick and there was no light, he could see nothing ahead and nothing behind him. At the end of six leagues the darkness was thick and there was no light, he could see nothing ahead and nothing behind him. When he had gone seven leagues the darkness was thick and there was no light, he could see nothing ahead and nothing behind him. When he had gone eight leagues Gilgamesh gave a great cry, for the darkness was thick and he could see nothing ahead and nothing behind him. After nine leagues he felt the north wind on his face, but the darkness was thick and there was no light, he could see nothing ahead and nothing behind him. After ten leagues the end was near. After eleven leagues the dawn light appeared. At the end of twelve leagues the sun streamed out.

There was the garden of the gods; all round him stood bushes bearing gems. Seeing it he went down at once, for there was fruit of carnelian with the vine hanging from it, beautiful to look at; lapis lazuli leaves hung thick with fruit, sweet to see. For thorns and thistles there were haematite and rare stones, agate, and pearls from out of the sea. While Gilgamesh walked in the garden by the edge of the sea Shamash saw him, and he saw that he was dressed in the skins of animals and ate their flesh. He was distressed, and he spoke and said,

'No mortal man has gone this way before, nor will, as long as the winds drive over the sea.' And to Gilgamesh he said, 'You will never find the life for which you are searching.' Gilgamesh said to glorious Shamash, 'Now that I have toiled and strayed so far over the wilderness, am I to sleep, and let the earth cover my head for ever? Let my eyes see the sun until they are dazzled with looking. Although I am no better than a dead man, still let me see the light of the sun.'

Beside the sea she lives, the woman of the vine, the maker of wine; Siduri sits in the garden at the edge of the sea, with the golden bowl and the golden vats that the gods gave her. She is covered with a veil; and where she sits she sees Gilgamesh coming towards her, wearing skins, the flesh of the gods in his body, but despair in his heart, and his face like the face of one who has made a long journey. She looked, and as she scanned the distance she said in her own heart, 'Surely this is some felon; where is he going now?' And she barred her gate against him with the cross-bar and shot home the bolt. But Gilgamesh, hearing the sound of the bolt, threw up his head and lodged his foot in the gate; he called to her, 'Young woman, maker of wine, why do you bolt your door; what did you see that made you bar your gate? I will break in your door and burst in your gate, for I am Gilgamesh who seized and killed the Bull of Heaven, I killed the watchman of the cedar forest, I overthrew Humbaba who lived in the forest, and I killed the lions in the passes of the mountain.'

Then Siduri said to him, 'If you are that Gilgamesh who seized and killed the Bull of Heaven, who killed the watchman of the cedar forest, who overthrew Humbaba that lived in the forest, and killed the lions in the passes of the mountain, why are your cheeks so starved and why is your face so drawn? Why is despair in your heart and your face like the face of one who has made a long journey? Yes, why is your face burned from heat and cold, and why do you come here wandering over the pastures in search of the wind?'

Gilgamesh answered her, 'And why should not my cheeks be starved and my face drawn? Despair is in my heart and my face is the face of one who has made a long journey, it was burned with heat and with cold. Why should I not wander over the pastures in search of the wind? My friend, my younger brother, he who hunted the wild ass of the wilderness and the panther of the plains, my friend, my younger brother who seized and killed the Bull of Heaven and overthrew Humbaba in the cedar forest, my friend who was very dear to me and who endured dangers beside me, Enkidu my brother, whom I loved, the end of mortality has overtaken him. I wept for him seven days and nights till the worm fastened on him. Because of my brother I am afraid of death, because of my brother I stray through the wilderness and cannot rest. But now, young woman, maker of wine, since I have seen your face do not let me see the face of death which I dread so much.'

She answered, 'Gilgamesh, where are you hurrying to? You will never find that life for which you are looking. When the gods created man they allotted to him death, but life they retained in their own keeping. As for you, Gilgamesh, fill your belly with good things; day and night, night and day, dance and be merry, feast and rejoice. Let your clothes be fresh, bathe yourself in water, cherish the little child that holds your hand, and make your wife happy in your embrace; for this too is the lot of man.'

But Gilgamesh said to Siduri, the young woman, 'How can I be silent, how can I rest, when Enkidu whom I love is dust, and I too shall die and be laid in the earth. You live by the sea-shore and look into the heart of it; young woman, tell me now, which is the way to Utnapishtim, the son of Ubara-Tutu? What directions are there for the passage; give me, oh, give me directions. I will cross the Ocean if it is possible; if it is not I will wander still farther in the wilderness.' The wine-maker said to him, 'Gilgamesh, there is no crossing the Ocean; whoever has come, since the days of old, has not been able to pass that sea. The Sun in his glory crosses the Ocean, but who beside Shamash has ever crossed it? The place and the passage are difficult, and the waters of death are deep which flow between. Gilgamesh, how will you cross the Ocean? When you come to the waters of death what will you do? But Gilgamesh, down in the woods you will find Urshanabi, the ferryman of Utnapishtim; with him are the holy things, the things of stone. He is fashioning the serpent prow of the boat. Look at him well, and if it is possible, perhaps you will cross the waters with him; but if it is not possible, then you must go back.'

When Gilgamesh heard this he was seized with anger. He took his axe in his hand, and his dagger from his belt. He crept forward and he fell on them like a javelin. Then he went into the forest and sat down. Urshanabi saw the dagger flash and heard the axe, and he beat his head, for Gilgamesh had shattered the tackle of the boat in his rage. Urshanabi said to him, 'Tell me, what is your name? I am Urshanabi, the ferryman of Utnapishtim the Faraway.' He replied to him, 'Gilgamesh is my name, I am from Uruk, from the house of Anu.' Then Urshanabi said to him, 'Why are your cheeks so starved and your face drawn? Why is despair in your heart and your face like the face of one who has made a long journey; yes, why is your face burned with heat and with cold, and why do you come here wandering over the pastures in search of the wind?'

Gilgamesh said to him, 'Why should not my cheeks be starved and my face drawn? Despair is in my heart, and my face is the face of one who has made a long journey. I was burned with heat and with cold. Why should I not wander over the pastures? My friend, my younger brother who seized and killed the Bull of Heaven, and overthrew Humbaba in the cedar forest, my friend who was very dear to me, and who endured dangers beside me, Enkidu my brother whom I loved, the end of mortality has overtaken him. I wept for him seven days and nights till the worm fastened on him. Because of my brother I am afraid of death, because of my brother I stray through the wilderness. His fate lies heavy upon me. How can I be silent, how can I rest? He is dust and I too shall die and be laid in the earth for ever. I am afraid of death, therefore, Urshanabi, tell me which is the road to Utnapishtim? If it is possible I will cross the waters of death; if not I will wander still farther through the wilderness.'

Urshanabi said to him, 'Gilgamesh, your own hands have prevented you from crossing the Ocean; when you destroyed the tackle of the boat you destroyed its safety.' Then the two of them talked it over and Gilgamesh said, 'Why are you so angry with me, Urshanabi, for you yourself cross the sea by day and night, at all seasons you cross it.' 'Gilgamesh, those things you destroyed, their property is to carry me over the water, to prevent the waters of death from touching me. It was for this reason that I preserved them, but you have destroyed them, and the *urnu* snakes with them. But now, go into the forest, Gilgamesh; with your axe cut poles, one hundred and twenty, cut them sixty cubits long, paint them with bitumen, set on them ferrules and bring them back.'

When Gilgamesh heard this he went into the forest, he cut poles one hundred and twenty; he cut them sixty cubits long, he painted them with bitumen, he set on them ferrules, and he brought them to Urshanabi. Then they boarded the boat, Gilgamesh and Urshanabi together, launching it out on the waves of Ocean. For three days they ran on as it were a journey of a month and fifteen days, and at last Urshanabi brought the boat to the waters of death. Then Urshanabi said to Gilgamesh, 'Press on, take a pole and thrust it in, but do not let your hands touch the waters. Gilgamesh, take a second pole, take a third, take a fourth pole. Now, Gilgamesh, take a fifth, take a sixth and seventh pole. Gilgamesh, take an eighth, and ninth, a tenth pole. Gilgamesh, take an eleventh, take a twelfth pole.' After one hundred and twenty thrusts Gilgamesh had used the last pole. Then he stripped himself, he held up his arms for a mast and his covering for a sail. So Urshanabi the ferryman brought Gilgamesh to Utnapishtim, whom they call the Faraway, who lives in Dilmun at the place of the sun's transit, eastward of the mountain.

To him alone of men the gods had given everlasting life.

Now Utnapishtim, where he lay at ease, looked into the distance and he said in his heart, musing to himself, 'Why does the boat sail here without tackle and mast; why are the sacred stones destroyed, and why does the master not sail the boat? That man who comes is none of mine; where I look I see a man whose body is covered with skins of beasts. Who is this who walks up the shore behind Urshanabi, for surely he is no man of mine?' So Utnapishtim looked at him and said, 'What is your name, you who come here wearing the skins of beasts, with your cheeks starved and your face drawn? Where are you hurrying to now? For what reason have you made this great journey, crossing the seas whose passage is difficult? Tell me the reason for your coming.'

He replied, 'Gilgamesh is my name. I am from Uruk, from the house of Anu.' Then Utnapishtim said to him, 'If you are Gilgamesh, why are your cheeks so starved and your face drawn? Why is despair in your heart and your face like the face of one who has made a long journey? Yes, why is your face burned with heat and cold; and why do you come here, wandering over the wilderness in search of the wind?'

Gilgamesh said to him, 'Why should not my cheeks be starved and my face drawn? Despair is in my heart and my face is the face of one who has made a long journey. It was burned with heat and with cold. Why should I not wander over the pastures? My friend, my younger brother who seized and killed the Bull of Heaven and overthrew Humbaba in the cedar forest, my friend who was very dear to me and endured dangers beside me, Enkidu, my brother whom I loved, the end of mortality has overtaken him. I wept for him seven days and nights till the worm fastened on him. Because of my brother I am afraid of death; because of my brother I stray through the wilderness. His fate lies heavy upon me. How can I be silent, how can I rest? He is dust and I shall die also and be laid in the earth for ever.' Again Gilgamesh said, speaking to Utnapishtim,

'It is to see Utnapishtim whom we call the Faraway that I have come this journey. For this I have wandered over the world, I have crossed many difficult ranges, I have crossed the seas, I have wearied myself with travelling; my joints are aching, and I have lost acquaintance with sleep which is sweet. My clothes were worn out before I came to the house of Siduri. I have killed the bear and hyena, the lion and panther, the tiger, the stag and the ibex, all sorts of wild game and the small creatures of the pastures. 1 ate their flesh and I wore their skins; and that was how I came to the gate of the young woman, the maker of wine, who barred her gate of pitch and bitumen against me. But from her I had news of the journey; so then I came to Urshanabi the ferryman, and with him I crossed over the waters of death. Oh, father Utnapishtim, you who have entered the assembly of the gods, I wish to question you concerning the living and the dead, how shall I find the life for which I am searching?'

Utnapishtim said, 'There is no permanence. Do we build a house to stand for ever, do we seal a contract to hold for all time? Do brothers divide an inheritance to keep for ever, docs the flood-time of rivers endure? It is only the nymph of the dragon-fly who sheds her larva and sees the sun in his glory. From the days of old there is no permanence. The sleeping and the dead, how alike they are, they are like a painted death. What is there between the master and the servant when both have fulfilled their doom? When the Anunnaki, the judges, come together, and Mammetun the mother of destinies, together they decree the fates of men. Life and death they allot but the day of death they do not disclose.'

Then Gilgamesh said to Utnapishtim the Faraway, 'I look at you now, Utnapishtim, and your appearance is no different from mine; there is nothing strange in your features. I thought I should find you like a hero prepared for battle, but you lie here taking your ease on your back. Tell me truly, how was it that you came to enter the company of the gods and to possess everlasting life?' Utnapishtim said to Gilgamesh, 'I will reveal to you a mystery, I will tell you a secret of the gods.'

THE STORY OF THE FLOOD

'You know the city Shurrupak, it stands on the banks of Euphrates? That city grew old and the gods that were in it were old. There was Anu, lord of the firmament, their father, and warrior Enlil their counsellor, Ninurta the helper, and Ennugi watcher over canals; and with them also was Ea. In those days the world teemed, the people multiplied, the world bellowed like a wild bull, and the great god was aroused by the clamour. Enlil heard the clamour and he said to the gods in council, "The uproar of mankind is intolerable and sleep is no longer possible by reason of the babel." So the gods agreed to exterminate mankind. Enlil did this, but Ea because of his oath warned me in a dream. He whispered their words to my house of reeds, "Reed-house, reed-house! Wall, O wall, hearken reed-house, wall reflect; O man of Shurrupak, son of Ubara-Tutu; tear down your house and build a boat, abandon possessions and look for life, despise worldly goods and save your soul alive. Tear down your house, I say, and build a boat. These are the measurements of the barque as you shall build her: let her beam equal her length, let her deck be roofed like the vault that covers the abyss; then take up into the boat the seed of all living creatures."

'When I had understood I said to my lord, "Behold, what you have commanded I will honour and perform, but how shall I answer the people, the city, the elders?" Then Ea opened his mouth and said to me, his servant, "Tell them this: I have learnt that Enlil is wrathful against me, I dare no longer walk in his land nor live in his city; I will go down to the Gulf to dwell with Ea my lord. But on you he will rain down abundance, rare fish and shy wild-fowl, a rich harvest-tide. In the evening the rider of the storm will bring you wheat in torrents."

'In the first light of dawn all my household gathered round me, the children brought pitch and the men whatever was necessary. On the fifth day I laid the keel and the ribs, then I made fast the planking. The ground-space was one acre, each side of the deck measured one hundred and twenty cubits, making a square. I built six decks below, seven in all, I divided them into nine sections with bulkheads between. I drove in wedges where needed, I saw to the punt-poles, and laid in supplies. The carriers brought oil in baskets, I poured pitch into the furnace and asphalt and oil; more oil was consumed in caulking, and more again the master of the boat took into his stores. I slaughtered bullocks for the people and every day I killed sheep. I gave the shipwrights wine to drink as though it were river water, raw wine and red wine and oil and white wine. There was feasting then as there is at the time of the New Year's festival; I myself anointed my head. On the seventh day the boat was complete.

'Then was the launching full of difficulty; there was shifting of ballast above and below till two thirds was submerged. I loaded into her all that I had of gold and of living things, my family, my kin, the beast of the field both wild and tame, and all the craftsmen. I sent them on board, for the time that Shamash had ordained was already fulfilled when he said, "In the evening, when the rider of the storm sends down the destroying rain, enter the boat and batten her down." The time was fulfilled, the evening came, the rider of the storm sent down the rain, I looked out at the weather and it was terrible, so I too boarded the boat and battened her down. All was now complete, the battening and the caulking; so I handed the tiller to Puzur-Amurri the steersman, with the navigation and the care of the whole boat.

'With the first light of dawn a black cloud came from the horizon; it thundered within where Adad, lord of the storm was riding. In front over hill and plain Shullat and Hanish, heralds of the storm, led on. Then the gods of the abyss rose up; Nergal pulled out the dams of the nether waters, Ninurta the war-lord threw down the dykes, and the seven judges of hell, the Annunaki, raised their torches, lighting the land with their livid flame. A stupor of despair went up to heaven when the god of the storm turned daylight to darkness, when he

smashed the land like a cup. One whole day the tempest raged, gathering fury as it went, it poured over the people like the tides of battle; a man could not see his brother nor the people be seen from heaven. Even the gods were terrified at the flood, they fled to the highest heaven, the firmament of Anu; they crouched against the walls, cowering like curs. Then Ishtar the sweet-voiced Queen of Heaven cried out like a woman in travail: "Alas the days of old are turned to dust because I commanded evil; why did I command this evil in the council of all the gods? I commanded wars to destroy the people, but are they not my people, for I brought them forth? Now like the spawn of fish they float in the ocean." The great gods of heaven and of hell wept, they covered their mouths.

'For six days and six nights the winds blew, torrent and tempest and flood overwhelmed the world, tempest and flood raged together like warring hosts. When the seventh day dawned the storm from the south subsided, the sea grew calm, the flood was stilled; I looked at the face of the world and there was silence, all mankind was turned to clay. The surface of the sea stretched as flat as a roof-top; I opened a hatch and the light fell on my face. Then I bowed low, I sat down and I wept, the tears streamed down my face, for on every side was the waste of water. I looked for land in vain, but fourteen leagues distant there appeared a mountain, and there the boat grounded; on the mountain of Nisir the boat held fast, she held fast and did not budge. One day she held, and a second day on the mountain of Nisir she held fast and did not budge. A third day, and a fourth day she held fast on the mountain and did not budge; a fifth day and a sixth day she held fast on the mountain. When the seventh day dawned I loosed a dove and let her go. She flew away, but finding no resting-place she returned. Then I loosed a swallow, and she flew away but finding no resting-place she returned. I loosed a raven, she saw that the waters had retreated, she ate, she flew around, she cawed, and she did not come back. Then I threw everything open to the four winds, I made a sacrifice and poured out a libation on the mountain top. Seven and again seven cauldrons I set up on their stands, I heaped up wood and cane and cedar and myrtle. When the gods smelled the sweet savour, they gathered like flies over the sacrifice. Then, at last, Ishtar also came, she lifted her necklace with the jewels of heaven that once Anu had made to please her. "O you gods here present, by the lapis lazuli round my neck I shall remember these days as I remember the jewels of my throat; these last days I shall not forget. Let all the gods gather round the sacrifice, except Enlil. He shall not approach this offering, for without reflection he brought the flood; he consigned my people to destruction."

'When Enlil had come, when he saw the boat, he was wrath and swelled with anger at the gods, the host of heaven, "Has any of these mortals escaped? Not one was to have survived the destruction." Then the god of the wells and canals Ninurta opened his mouth and said to the warrior Enlil, "Who is there of the gods that can devise without Ea? It is Ea alone who knows all things." Then Ea opened his mouth and spoke to warrior Enlil, "Wisest of gods, hero Enlil, how could you so senselessly bring down the flood?

> Lay upon the sinner his sin,
> Lay upon the transgressor his transgression,
> Punish him a little when he breaks loose,
> Do not drive him too hard or he perishes;
> Would that a lion had ravaged mankind
> Rather than the flood,
> Would that a wolf had ravaged mankind
> Rather than the flood,
> Would that famine had wasted the world
> Rather than the flood,
> Would that pestilence had wasted mankind
> Rather than the flood.

It was not I that revealed the secret of the gods; the wise man learned it in a dream. Now take your counsel what shall be done with him."

'Then Enlil went up into the boat, he took me by the hand and my wife and made us enter the boat and kneel down on either side, he standing between us. He touched our foreheads to bless us saying," In time past Utnapishtim was a mortal man; henceforth he and his wife shall live in the distance at the mouth of the rivers." Thus it was that the gods took me and placed me here to live in the distance, at the mouth of the rivers.'

THE RETURN

UTNAPISHTIM said, 'As for you, Gilgamesh, who will assemble the gods for your sake, so that you may find that life for which you are searching? But if you wish, come and put it to the test: only prevail against sleep for six days and seven nights.' But while Gilgamesh sat there resting on his haunches, a mist of sleep like soft wool teased from the fleece drifted over him, and Utnapishtim said to his wife, 'Look at him now, the strong man who would have everlasting life, even now the mists of sleep are drifting over him.' His wife replied, 'Touch the man to wake him, so that he may return to his own land in peace, going back through the gate by which he came.' Utnapishtim said to his wife, 'All men are deceivers, even you he will attempt to deceive; therefore bake loaves of bread, each day one loaf, and put it beside his head; and make a mark on the wall to number the days he has slept.'

So she baked loaves of bread, each day one loaf, and put it beside his head, and she marked on the wall the days that he slept; and there came a day when the first loaf was hard, the second loaf was like leather, the third was soggy, the crust of the fourth had mould, the fifth was mildewed, the sixth was fresh, and the seventh was still on the embers. Then Utnapishtim touched him and he woke. Gilgamesh said to Utnapishtim the Faraway, 'I hardly slept when you touched and roused me.' But Utnapishtim said, 'Count these loaves and learn how many days you slept, for your first is hard, your second like leather, your third is soggy, the crust of your fourth has mould, your fifth is mildewed, your sixth is fresh and your seventh was still over the glowing embers when I touched and woke you.' Gilgamesh said, 'What shall I do, O Utnapishtim, where shall I go?

Already the thief in the night has hold of my limbs, death inhabits my room; wherever my foot rests, there I find death.'

Then Utnapishtim spoke to Urshanabi the ferryman: 'Woe to you Urshanabi, now and for ever more you have become hateful to this harbourage; it is not for you, nor for you are the crossings of this sea. Go now, banished from the shore. But this man before whom you walked, bringing him here, whose body is covered with foulness and the grace of whose limbs has been spoiled by wild skins, take him to the washing-place. There he shall wash his long hair clean as snow in the water, he shall throw off his skins and let the sea carry them away, and the beauty of his body shall be shown, the fillet on his forehead shall be renewed, and he shall be given clothcs to cover his nakedness. Till he reaches his own city and his journey is accomplished, these clothes will show no sign of age, they will wear like a new garment.' So Urshanabi took Gilgamesh and led him to the washing-place, he washed his long hair as clean as snow in the water, he threw off his skins, which the sea carried away, and showed the beauty of his body. He renewed the fillet on his forehead, and to cover his nakedness gave him clothes which would show no sign of age, but would wear like a new garment till he reached his own city, and his journey was accomplished.

Then Gilgamesh and Urshanabi launched the boat on to the water and boarded it, and they made ready to sail away; but the wife of Utnapishtim the Faraway said to him, 'Gilgamesh came here wearied out, he is worn out; what will you give him to carry him back to his own country?' So Utnapishtim spoke, and Gilgamesh took a pole and brought the boat in to the bank. 'Gilgamesh, you came here a man wearied out, you have worn yourself out; what shall I give you to carry you back to your own country? Gilgamesh, I shall reveal a secret thing, it is a mystery of the gods that I am telling you. There is a plant that grows under the water, it has a prickle like a thorn, like a rose; it will wound your hands, but if you succeed in taking it, then your

hands will hold that which restores his lost youth to a man.'

When Gilgamesh heard this he opened the sluices so that a sweet-water current might carry him out to the deepest channel; he tied heavy stones to his feet and they dragged him down to the water-bed. There he saw the plant growing; although it pricked him he took it in his hands; then he cut the heavy stones from his feet, and the sea carried him and threw him on to the shore. Gilgamesh said to Urshanabi the ferryman, 'Come here, and see this marvellous plant. By its virtue a man may win back all his former strength. I will take it to Uruk of the strong walls; there I will give it to the old men to eat. Its name shall be "The Old Men Are Young Again"; and at last I shall eat it myself and have back all my lost youth.' So Gilgamesh returned by the gate through which he had come, Gilgamesh and Urshanabi went together. They travelled their twenty leagues and then they broke their fast; after thirty leagues they stopped for the night.

Gilgamesh saw a well of cool water and he went down and bathed; but deep in the pool there was lying a serpent, and the serpent sensed the sweetness of the flower. It rose out of the water and snatched it away, and immediately it sloughed its skin and returned to the well. Then Gilgamesh sat down and wept, the tears ran down his face, and he took the hand of Urshanabi; 'O Urshanabi, was it for this that I toiled with my hands, is it for this I have wrung out my heart's blood? For myself I have gained nothing; not I, but the beast of the earth has joy of it now. Already the stream has carried it twenty leagues back to the channels where I found it. I found a sign and now I have lost it. Let us leave the boat on the bank and go.'

After twenty leagues they broke their fast, after thirty leagues they stopped for the night; in three days they had walked as much as a journey of a month and fifteen days. When the journey was accomplished they arrived at Uruk, the strong-walled city. Gilgamesh spoke to him, to Urshanabi the ferryman, 'Urshanabi, climb up on to the wall of

Uruk, inspect its foundation terrace, and examine well the brickwork; see if it is not of burnt bricks; and did not the seven wise men lay these foundations? One third of the whole is city, one third is garden, and one third is field, with the precinct of the goddess Ishtar. These parts and the precinct are all Uruk.'

This too was the work of Gilgamesh, the king, who knew the countries of the world. He was wise, he saw mysteries and knew secret things, he brought us a tale of the days before the flood. He went a long journey, was weary, worn out with labour, and returning engraved on a stone the whole story.

HAMMURABI'S CODE OF LAWS
(circa 1780 B.C.)
Translated by L. W. King

When Anu the Sublime, King of the Anunaki, and Bel, the lord of Heaven and earth, who decreed the fate of the land, assigned to Marduk, the over-ruling son of Ea, God of righteousness, dominion over earthly man, and made him great among the Igigi, they called Babylon by his illustrious name, made it great on earth, and founded an everlasting kingdom in it, whose foundations are laid so solidly as those of heaven and earth; then Anu and Bel called by name me, Hammurabi, the exalted prince, who feared God, to bring about the rule of righteousness in the land, to destroy the wicked and the evil-doers; so that the strong should not harm the weak; so that I should rule over the black-headed people like Shamash, and enlighten the land, to further the well-being of mankind.

Hammurabi, the prince, called of Bel am I, making riches and increase, enriching Nippur and Dur-ilu beyond compare, sublime patron of E-kur; who reestablished Eridu and purified the worship of E-apsu; who conquered the four quarters of the world, made great the name of Babylon, rejoiced the heart of Marduk, his lord who daily pays his devotions in Saggil; the royal scion whom Sin made; who enriched Ur; the humble, the reverent, who brings wealth to Gish-shir-gal; the white king, heard of Shamash, the mighty, who again laid the foundations of Sippara; who clothed the gravestones of Malkat with green; who made E-babbar great, which is like the heavens, the warrior who guarded Larsa and renewed E-babbar, with Shamash as his helper; the lord who granted new life to Uruk, who brought plenteous water to its inhabitants, raised the head of E-anna, and perfected the beauty of Anu and Nana; shield of the land, who reunited the scattered inhabitants of Isin; who richly endowed E-gal-mach; the protecting king of the city, brother of the god Zamama; who firmly founded the farms of Kish, crowned E-me-te-ursag with glory, redoubled the great holy treasures of Nana, managed the temple of Harsag-kalama; the grave of the enemy, whose help brought about the victory; who increased the power of Cuthah; made all glorious in E-shidlam, the black steer, who gored the enemy; beloved of the god Nebo, who rejoiced the inhabitants of Borsippa, the Sublime; who is indefatigable for E-zida; the divine king of the city; the White, Wise; who broadened the fields of Dilbat, who heaped up the harvests for Urash; the Mighty, the lord to whom come scepter and crown, with which he clothes himself; the Elect of Ma-ma; who fixed the temple bounds of Kesh, who made rich the holy feasts of Nin-tu; the provident, solicitous, who provided food and drink for Lagash and Girsu, who provided large sacrificial offerings for the temple of Ningirsu; who captured the enemy, the Elect of the oracle who fulfilled the prediction of Hallab, who rejoiced the heart of Anunit; the pure prince, whose prayer is accepted by Adad; who satisfied the heart of Adad, the warrior, in Karkar, who restored the vessels for worship in E-ud-gal-gal; the king who granted life to the city of Adab; the guide of E-mach; the princely king of the city, the irresistible warrior, who granted life to the inhabitants of Mashkanshabri, and brought abundance to the temple of Shidlam; the White, Potent, who penetrated the secret cave of the bandits, saved the inhabitants of Malka from misfortune, and fixed their home fast in wealth; who established pure sacrificial gifts for Ea and Dam-gal-nun-na, who made his kingdom everlastingly great; the princely king of the city, who subjected the districts on the Ud-kib-nun-na Canal to the sway of Dagon, his Creator; who spared the inhabitants of Mera and Tutul; the sublime prince, who makes the face of Ninni shine; who presents holy meals to the divinity of Nin-a-zu, who cared for its inhabitants in their need, provided a portion for them in Babylon in peace; the shepherd of the oppressed and of the slaves; whose deeds find favor before Anunit, who provided for Anunit in the temple of Dumash in the suburb of Agade; who recognizes the right, who rules by law; who gave back to the city of Ashur its protecting god; who let the name of Ishtar of Nineveh remain in E-mish-mish; the Sublime, who humbles himself before the great gods; successor of Sumula-il; the mighty son of Sin-muballit; the royal scion of Eternity; the mighty monarch, the sun of Babylon, whose rays shed light over the land of Sumer and Akkad; the king, obeyed by the four quarters of the world; Beloved of Ninni, am I.

When Marduk sent me to rule over men, to give the protection of right to the land, I did right and right-eousness in . . . , and brought about the well-being of the oppressed.

CODE OF LAWS

1. If any one ensnare another, putting a ban upon him, but he can not prove it, then he that ensnared him shall be put to death.

2. If any one bring an accusation against a man, and the accused go to the river and leap into the river, if he sink in the river his accuser shall take possession of his house. But if the river prove that the accused is not guilty, and he escape unhurt, then he who had brought the accusation shall be put to death, while he who leaped into the river shall take possession of the house that had belonged to his accuser.

3. If any one bring an accusation of any crime before the elders, and does not prove what he has charged, he shall, if it be a capital offense charged, be put to death.

4. If he satisfy the elders to impose a fine of grain or money, he shall receive the fine that the action produces.

5. If a judge try a case, reach a decision, and present his judgment in writing; if later error shall appear in his decision, and it be through his own fault, then he shall pay twelve times the fine set by him in the case, and he shall be publicly removed from the judge's bench, and never again shall he sit there to render judgement.

6. If any one steal the property of a temple or of the court, he shall be put to death, and also the one who receives the stolen thing from him shall be put to death.

7. If any one buy from the son or the slave of another man, without witnesses or a contract, silver or gold, a male or female slave, an ox or a sheep, an ass or anything, or if he take it in charge, he is considered a thief and shall be put to death.

8. If any one steal cattle or sheep, or an ass, or a pig or a goat, if it belong to a god or to the court, the thief shall pay thirtyfold therefor; if they belonged to a freed man of the king he shall pay tenfold; if the thief has nothing with which to pay he shall be put to death.

9. If any one lose an article, and find it in the possession of another: if the person in whose possession the thing is found say "A merchant sold it to me, I paid for it before witnesses," and if the owner of the thing say, "I will bring witnesses who know my property," then shall the purchaser bring the merchant who sold it to him, and the witnesses before whom he bought it, and the owner shall bring witnesses who can identify his property. The judge shall examine their testimony—both of the witnesses before whom the price was paid, and of the witnesses who identify the lost article on oath. The merchant is then proved to be a thief and shall be put to death. The owner of the lost article receives his property, and he who bought it receives the money he paid from the estate of the merchant.

10. If the purchaser does not bring the merchant and the witnesses before whom he bought the article, but its owner bring witnesses who identify it, then the buyer is the thief and shall be put to death, and the owner receives the lost article.

11. If the owner do not bring witnesses to identify the lost article, he is an evil-doer, he has traduced, and shall be put to death.

12. If the witnesses be not at hand, then shall the judge set a limit, at the expiration of six months. If his witnesses have not appeared within the six months, he is an evil-doer, and shall bear the fine of the pending case. [editor's note: there is no 13th law in the code, 13 being considered and unlucky and evil number]

14. If any one steal the minor son of another, he shall be put to death.

15. If any one take a male or female slave of the court, or a male or female slave of a freed man, outside the city gates, he shall be put to death.

16. If any one receive into his house a runaway male or female slave of the court, or of a freedman, and does not bring it out at the public proclamation of the major domus, the master of the house shall be put to death.

17. If any one find runaway male or female slaves in the open country and bring them to their masters, the master of the slaves shall pay him two shekels of silver.

18. If the slave will not give the name of the master, the finder shall bring him to the palace; a further investigation must follow, and the slave shall be returned to his master.

19. If he hold the slaves in his house, and they are caught there, he shall be put to death.

20. If the slave that he caught run away from him, then shall he swear to the owners of the slave, and he is free of all blame.

21. If any one break a hole into a house (break in to steal), he shall be put to death before that hole and be buried.

22. If any one is committing a robbery and is caught, then he shall be put to death.

23. If the robber is not caught, then shall he who was robbed claim under oath the amount of his loss; then shall the community, and . . . on whose ground and territory and in whose domain it was compensate him for the goods stolen.

24. If persons are stolen, then shall the community and . . . pay one mina of silver to their relatives.

25. If fire break out in a house, and some one who comes to put it out cast his eye upon the property of the owner of the house, and take the property of the master of the house, he shall be thrown into that self-same fire.

26. If a chieftain or a man (common soldier), who has been ordered to go upon the king's highway for war does not go, but hires a mercenary, if he withholds the compensation, then shall this officer or man be put to death, and he who represented him shall take possession of his house.

27. If a chieftain or man be caught in the misfortune of the king (captured in battle), and if his fields and garden be given to another and he take possession, if he return and reaches his place, his field and garden shall be returned to him, he shall take it over again.

28. If a chieftain or a man be caught in the misfortune of a king, if his son is able to enter into possession, then the field and garden shall be given to him, he shall take over the fee of his father.

29. If his son is still young, and can not take possession, a third of the field and garden shall be given to his mother, and she shall bring him up.

30. If a chieftain or a man leave his house, garden, and field and hires it out, and some one else takes possession of his house, garden, and field and uses it for three years: if the first owner return and claims his house, garden, and field, it shall not be given to him, but he who has taken possession of it and used it shall continue to use it.

31. If he hire it out for one year and then return, the house, garden, and field shall be given back to him, and he shall take it over again.

32. If a chieftain or a man is captured on the "Way of the King" (in war), and a merchant buy him free, and bring him back to his place; if he have the means in his house to buy his freedom, he shall buy himself free: if he have nothing in his house with which to buy himself free, he shall be bought free by the temple

of his community; if there be nothing in the temple with which to buy him free, the court shall buy his freedom. His field, garden, and house shall not be given for the purchase of his freedom.

33. If a . . . or a . . . enter himself as withdrawn from the "Way of the King," and send a mercenary as substitute, but withdraw him, then the . . . or . . . shall be put to death.

34. If a . . . or a . . . harm the property of a captain, injure the captain, or take away from the captain a gift presented to him by the king, then the . . . or . . . shall be put to death.

35. If any one buy the cattle or sheep which the king has given to chieftains from him, he loses his money.

36. The field, garden, and house of a chieftain, of a man, or of one subject to quit-rent, can not be sold.

37. If any one buy the field, garden, and house of a chieftain, man, or one subject to quit-rent, his contract tablet of sale shall be broken (declared invalid) and he loses his money. The field, garden, and house return to their owners.

38. A chieftain, man, or one subject to quit-rent can not assign his tenure of field, house, and garden to his wife or daughter, nor can he assign it for a debt.

39. He may, however, assign a field, garden, or house which he has bought, and holds as property, to his wife or daughter or give it for debt.

40. He may sell field, garden, and house to a merchant (royal agents) or to any other public official, the buyer holding field, house, and garden for its usufruct.

41. If any one fence in the field, garden, and house of a chieftain, man, or one subject to quit-rent, furnishing the palings therefor; if the chieftain, man, or one subject to quit-rent return to field, garden, and house, the palings which were given to him become his property.

42. If any one take over a field to till it, and obtain no harvest therefrom, it must be proved that he did no work on the field, and he must deliver grain, just as his neighbor raised, to the owner of the field.

43. If he do not till the field, but let it lie fallow, he shall give grain like his neighbor's to the owner of the field, and the field which he let lie fallow he must plow and sow and return to its owner.

44. If any one take over a waste-lying field to make it arable, but is lazy, and does not make it arable, he shall plow the fallow field in the fourth year, harrow it and till it, and give it back to its owner, and for each ten gan (a measure of area) ten gur of grain shall be paid.

45. If a man rent his field for tillage for a fixed rental, and receive the rent of his field, but bad weather come and destroy the harvest, the injury falls upon the tiller of the soil.

46. If he do not receive a fixed rental for his field, but lets it on half or third shares of the harvest, the grain on the field shall be divided proportionately between the tiller and the owner.

47. If the tiller, because he did not succeed in the first year, has had the soil tilled by others, the owner may raise no objection; the field has been cultivated and he receives the harvest according to agreement.

48. If any one owe a debt for a loan, and a storm prostrates the grain, or the harvest fail, or the grain does not grow for lack of water; in that year he need not give his creditor any grain, he washes his debt-tablet in water and pays no rent for this year.

49. If any one take money from a merchant, and give the merchant a field tillable for corn or sesame and order him to plant corn or sesame in the field, and to harvest the crop; if the cultivator plant corn or sesame in the field, at the harvest the corn or sesame that is in the field shall belong to the owner of the field and he shall pay corn as rent, for the money he received from the merchant, and the livelihood of the cultivator shall he give to the merchant.

50. If he give a cultivated corn-field or a cultivated sesame-field, the corn or sesame in the field

shall belong to the owner of the field, and he shall return the money to the merchant as rent.

51. If he have no money to repay, then he shall pay in corn or sesame in place of the money as rent for what he received from the merchant, according to the royal tariff.

52. If the cultivator do not plant corn or sesame in the field, the debtor's contract is not weakened.

53. If any one be too lazy to keep his dam in proper condition, and does not so keep it; if then the dam break and all the fields be flooded, then shall he in whose dam the break occurred be sold for money, and the money shall replace the corn which he has caused to be ruined.

54. If he be not able to replace the corn, then he and his possessions shall be divided among the farmers whose corn he has flooded.

55. If any one open his ditches to water his crop, but is careless, and the water flood the field of his neighbor, then he shall pay his neighbor corn for his loss.

56. If a man let in the water, and the water overflow the plantation of his neighbor, he shall pay ten gur of corn for every ten gan of land.

57. If a shepherd, without the permission of the owner of the field, and without the knowledge of the owner of the sheep, lets the sheep into a field to graze, then the owner of the field shall harvest his crop, and the shepherd, who had pastured his flock there without permission of the owner of the field, shall pay to the owner twenty gur of corn for every ten gan.

58. If after the flocks have left the pasture and been shut up in the common fold at the city gate, any shepherd let them into a field and they graze there, this shepherd shall take possession of the field which he has allowed to be grazed on, and at the harvest he must pay sixty gur of corn for every ten gan.

59. If any man, without the knowledge of the owner of a garden, fell a tree in a garden he shall pay half a mina in money.

60. If any one give over a field to a gardener, for him to plant it as a garden, if he work at it, and care for it for four years, in the fifth year

the owner and the gardener shall divide it, the owner taking his part in charge.

61. If the gardener has not completed the planting of the field, leaving one part unused, this shall be assigned to him as his.

62. If he do not plant the field that was given over to him as a garden, if it be arable land (for corn or sesame) the gardener shall pay the owner the produce of the field for the years that he let it lie fallow, according to the product of neighboring fields, put the field in arable condition and return it to its owner.

63. If he transform waste land into arable fields and return it to its owner, the latter shall pay him for one year ten gur for ten gan.

64. If any one hand over his garden to a gardener to work, the gardener shall pay to its owner two-thirds of the produce of the garden, for so long as he has it in possession, and the other third shall he keep.

65. If the gardener do not work in the garden and the product fall off, the gardener shall pay in proportion to other neighboring gardens. [Here a portion of the text is missing, apparently comprising thirty-four paragraphs.]

100. . . . interest for the money, as much as he has received, he shall give a note therefor, and on the day, when they settle, pay to the merchant.

101. If there are no mercantile arrangements in the place whither he went, he shall leave the entire amount of money which he received with the broker to give to the merchant.

102. If a merchant entrust money to an agent (broker) for some investment, and the broker suffer a loss in the place to which he goes, he shall make good the capital to the merchant.

103. If, while on the journey, an enemy take away from him anything that he had, the broker shall swear by God and be free of obligation.

104. If a merchant give an agent corn, wool, oil, or any other goods to transport, the agent shall give a receipt for the amount, and compensate the merchant therefor. Then he shall obtain a receipt form the merchant for the money that he gives the merchant.

105. If the agent is careless, and does not take a receipt for the money which he gave the merchant, he can not consider the unreceipted money as his own.

106. If the agent accept money from the merchant, but have a quarrel with the merchant (denying the receipt), then shall the merchant swear before God and witnesses that he has given this money to the agent, and the agent shall pay him three times the sum.

107. If the merchant cheat the agent, in that as the latter has returned to him all that had been given him, but the merchant denies the receipt of what had been returned to him, then shall this agent convict the merchant before God and the judges, and if he still deny receiving what the agent had given him shall pay six times the sum to the agent.

108. If a tavern-keeper (feminine) does not accept corn according to gross weight in payment of drink, but takes money, and the price of the drink is less than that of the corn, she shall be convicted and thrown into the water.

109. If conspirators meet in the house of a tavern-keeper, and these conspirators are not captured and delivered to the court, the tavern-keeper shall be put to death.

110. If a "sister of a god" open a tavern, or enter a tavern to drink, then shall this woman be burned to death.

111. If an inn-keeper furnish sixty ka of usakani-drink to . . . she shall receive fifty ka of corn at the harvest.

112. If any one be on a journey and entrust silver, gold, precious stones, or any movable property to another, and wish to recover it from him; if the latter do not bring all of the property to the appointed place, but appropriate it to his own use, then shall this man, who did not bring the property to hand it over, be convicted, and he shall pay fivefold for all that had been entrusted to him.

113. If any one have consignment of corn or money, and he take from the granary or box without the knowledge of the owner, then shall he who took corn without the knowledge of the owner out of the granary or money out of the box be legally convicted, and repay the corn he has taken. And he shall lose whatever commission was paid to him, or due him.

114. If a man have no claim on another for corn and money, and try to demand it by force, he shall pay one-third of a mina of silver in every case.

115. If any one have a claim for corn or money upon another and imprison him; if the prisoner die in prison a natural death, the case shall go no further.

116. If the prisoner die in prison from blows or maltreatment, the master of the prisoner shall convict the merchant before the judge. If he was a free-born man, the son of the merchant shall be put to death; if it was a slave, he shall pay one-third of a mina of gold, and all that the master of the prisoner gave he shall forfeit.

117. If any one fail to meet a claim for debt, and sell himself, his wife, his son, and daughter for money or give them away to forced labor: they shall work for three years in the house of the man who bought them, or the proprietor, and in the fourth year they shall be set free.

118. If he give a male or female slave away for forced labor, and the merchant sublease them, or sell them for money, no objection can be raised.

119. If any one fail to meet a claim for debt, and he sell the maid servant who has borne him children, for money, the money which the merchant has paid shall be repaid to him by the owner of the slave and she shall be freed.

120. If any one store corn for safe keeping in another person's house, and any harm happen to the corn in storage, or if the owner of the house open the granary and take some of the corn, or if especially he deny that the corn was stored in his house: then the owner of the corn shall claim his corn before God (on oath), and the owner of the house shall pay its owner for all of the corn that he took.

121. If any one store corn in another man's house he shall pay him storage at the rate of one gur for every five ka of corn per year.

122. If any one give another silver, gold, or anything else to keep, he shall show everything to some witness, draw up a contract, and then hand it over for safe keeping.

123. If he turn it over for safe keeping without witness or contract, and if he to whom it was given deny it, then he has no legitimate claim.

124. If any one deliver silver, gold, or anything else to another for safe keeping, before a witness, but he deny it, he shall be brought before a judge, and all that he has denied he shall pay in full.

125. If any one place his property with another for safe keeping, and there, either through thieves or robbers, his property and the property of the other man be lost, the owner of the house, through whose neglect the loss took place, shall compensate the owner for all that was given to him in charge. But the owner of the house shall try to follow up and recover his property, and take it away from the thief.

126. If any one who has not lost his goods state that they have been lost, and make false claims: if he claim his goods and amount of injury before God, even though he has not lost them, he shall be fully compensated for all his loss claimed. (I.e., the oath is all that is needed.)

127. If any one "point the finger" (slander) at a sister of a god or the wife of any one, and can not prove it, this man shall be taken before the judges and his brow shall be marked. (by cutting the skin, or perhaps hair.)

128. If a man take a woman to wife, but have no intercourse with her, this woman is no wife to him.

129. If a man's wife be surprised (in flagrante delicto) with another man, both shall be tied and thrown into the water, but the husband may pardon his wife and the king his slaves.

130. If a man violate the wife (betrothed or child-wife) of another man, who has never known a man, and still lives in her father's house, and sleep with her and be surprised, this man shall be put to death, but the wife is blameless.

131. If a man bring a charge against one's wife, but she is not surprised with another man, she must take an oath and then may return to her house.

132. If the "finger is pointed" at a man's wife about another man, but she is not caught sleeping with the other man, she shall jump into the river for her husband.

133. If a man is taken prisoner in war, and there is a sustenance in his house, but his wife leave house and court, and go to another house: because this wife did not keep her court, and went to another house, she shall be judicially condemned and thrown into the water.

134. If any one be captured in war and there is not sustenance in his house, if then his wife go to another house this woman shall be held blameless.

135. If a man be taken prisoner in war and there be no sustenance in his house and his wife go to another house and bear children; and if later her husband return and come to his home: then this wife shall return to her husband, but the children follow their father.

136. If any one leave his house, run away, and then his wife go to another house, if then he return, and wishes to take his wife back: because he fled from his home and ran away, the wife of this runaway shall not return to her husband.

137. If a man wish to separate from a woman who has borne him children, or from his wife who has borne him children: then he shall give that wife her dowry, and a part of the usufruct of field, garden, and property, so that she can rear her children. When she has brought up her children, a portion of all that is given to the children, equal as that of one son, shall be given to her. She may then marry the man of her heart.

138. If a man wishes to separate from his wife who has borne him no children, he shall give her the amount of her purchase money and the dowry which she brought from her father's house, and let her go.

139. If there was no purchase price he shall give her one mina of gold as a gift of release.

140. If he be a freed man he shall give her one-third of a mina of gold.

141. If a man's wife, who lives in his house, wishes to leave it, plunges into debt, tries to ruin her house, neglects her husband, and is judicially convicted: if her husband offer her release, she may go on her way, and he gives her nothing as a gift of release. If her husband does not wish to release her, and if he take another wife, she shall remain as servant in her husband's house.

142. If a woman quarrel with her husband, and say: "You are not congenial to me," the reasons for her prejudice must be presented. If she is guiltless, and there is no fault on her part, but he leaves and neglects her, then no guilt attaches to this woman, she shall take her dowry and go back to her father's house.

143. If she is not innocent, but leaves her husband, and ruins her house, neglecting her husband, this woman shall be cast into the water.

144. If a man take a wife and this woman give her husband a maid-servant, and she bear him children, but this man wishes to take another wife, this shall not be permitted to him; he shall not take a second wife.

145. If a man take a wife, and she bear him no children, and he intend to take another wife: if he take this second wife, and bring her into the house, this second wife shall not be allowed equality with his wife.

146. If a man take a wife and she give this man a maid-servant as wife and she bear him children, and then this maid assume equality with the wife: because she has borne him children her master shall not sell her for money, but he may keep her as a slave, reckoning her among the maid-servants.

147. If she have not borne him children, then her mistress may sell her for money.

148. If a man take a wife, and she be seized by disease, if he then desire to take a second wife he shall not put away his wife, who has been attacked by disease, but he shall keep her in the house which he has built and support her so long as she lives.

149. If this woman does not wish to remain in her husband's house, then he shall compensate her for the dowry that she brought with her from her father's house, and she may go.

150. If a man give his wife a field, garden, and house and a deed therefor, if then after the death of her husband the sons raise no claim, then the mother may bequeath all to one of her sons whom she prefers, and need leave nothing to his brothers.

151. If a woman who lived in a man's house made an agreement with her husband, that no creditor can arrest her, and has given a document therefor: if that man, before he married that woman, had a debt, the creditor can not hold the woman for it. But if the woman, before she entered the man's house, had contracted a debt, her creditor can not arrest her husband therefor.

152. If after the woman had entered the man's house, both contracted a debt, both must pay the merchant.

153. If the wife of one man on account of another man has their mates (her husband and the other man's wife) murdered, both of them shall be impaled.

154. If a man be guilty of incest with his daughter, he shall be driven from the place (exiled).

155. If a man betroth a girl to his son, and his son have intercourse with her, but he (the father) afterward defile her, and be surprised, then he shall be bound and cast into the water (drowned).

Rape

156. If a man betroth a girl to his son, but his son has not known her, and if then he defile her, he shall pay her half a gold mina, and compensate her for all that she brought out of her father's house. She may marry the man of her heart.

157. If any one be guilty of incest with his mother after his father, both shall be burned.

158. If any one be surprised after his father with his chief wife, who has borne children, he shall be driven out of his father's house.

159. If any one, who has brought chattels into his father-in-law's house, and has paid the purchase-money, looks for another wife, and says to his father-in-law: "I do not want your

daughter," the girl's father may keep all that he had brought.

160. If a man bring chattels into the house of his father-in-law, and pay the "purchase price" (for his wife): if then the father of the girl say: "I will not give you my daughter," he shall give him back all that he brought with him.

161. If a man bring chattels into his father-in-law's house and pay the "purchase price," if then his friend slander him, and his father-in-law say to the young husband: "You shall not marry my daughter," the he shall give back to him undiminished all that he had brought with him; but his wife shall not be married to the friend.

162. If a man marry a woman, and she bear sons to him; if then this woman die, then shall her father have no claim on her dowry; this belongs to her sons.

163. If a man marry a woman and she bear him no sons; if then this woman die, if the "purchase price" which he had paid into the house of his father-in-law is repaid to him, her husband shall have no claim upon the dowry of this woman; it belongs to her father's house.

164. If his father-in-law do not pay back to him the amount of the "purchase price" he may subtract the amount of the "Purchase price" from the dowry, and then pay the remainder to her father's house.

165. If a man give to one of his sons whom he prefers a field, garden, and house, and a deed therefor: if later the father die, and the brothers divide the estate, then they shall first give him the present of his father, and he shall accept it; and the rest of the paternal property shall they divide.

166. If a man take wives for his son, but take no wife for his minor son, and if then he die: if the sons divide the estate, they shall set aside besides his portion the money for the "purchase price" for the minor brother who had taken no wife as yet, and secure a wife for him.

167. If a man marry a wife and she bear him children: if this wife die and he then take another wife and she bear him children: if then the father die, the sons must not partition the estate according to the mothers, they shall divide the dowries of their mothers only in this way; the paternal estate they shall divide equally with one another.

168. If a man wish to put his son out of his house, and declare before the judge: "I want to put my son out," then the judge shall examine into his reasons. If the son be guilty of no great fault, for which he can be rightfully put out, the father shall not put him out.

169. If he be guilty of a grave fault, which should rightfully deprive him of the filial relationship, the father shall forgive him the first time; but if he be guilty of a grave fault a second time the father may deprive his son of all filial relation.

170. If his wife bear sons to a man, or his maid-servant have borne sons, and the father while still living says to the children whom his maid-servant has borne: "My sons," and he count them with the sons of his wife; if then the father die, then the sons of the wife and of the maid-servant shall divide the paternal property in common. The son of the wife is to partition and choose.

171. If, however, the father while still living did not say to the sons of the maid-servant: "My sons," and then the father dies, then the sons of the maid-servant shall not share with the sons of the wife, but the freedom of the maid and her sons shall be granted. The sons of the wife shall have no right to enslave the sons of the maid; the wife shall take her dowry (from her father), and the gift that her husband gave her and deeded to her (separate from dowry, or the purchase-money paid her father), and live in the home of her husband: so long as she lives she shall use it, it shall not be sold for money. Whatever she leaves shall belong to her children.

172. If her husband made her no gift, she shall be compensated for her gift, and she shall receive a portion from the estate of her husband, equal to that of one child. If her sons oppress her, to force her out of the house, the judge shall examine into the matter, and if the sons are at fault the woman shall not leave her husband's

house. If the woman desire to leave the house, she must leave to her sons the gift which her husband gave her, but she may take the dowry of her father's house. Then she may marry the man of her heart.

173. If this woman bear sons to her second husband, in the place to which she went, and then die, her earlier and later sons shall divide the dowry between them.

174. If she bear no sons to her second husband, the sons of her first husband shall have the dowry.

175. If a State slave or the slave of a freed man marry the daughter of a free man, and children are born, the master of the slave shall have no right to enslave the children of the free.

176. If, however, a State slave or the slave of a freed man marry a man's daughter, and after he marries her she bring a dowry from a father's house, if then they both enjoy it and found a household, and accumulate means, if then the slave die, then she who was free born may take her dowry, and all that her husband and she had earned; she shall divide them into two parts, one-half the master for the slave shall take, and the other half shall the free-born woman take for her children. If the free-born woman had no gift she shall take all that her husband and she had earned and divide it into two parts; and the master of the slave shall take one-half and she shall take the other for her children.

177. If a widow, whose children are not grown, wishes to enter another house (remarry), she shall not enter it without the knowledge of the judge. If she enter another house the judge shall examine the state of the house of her first husband. Then the house of her first husband shall be entrusted to the second husband and the woman herself as managers. And a record must be made thereof. She shall keep the house in order, bring up the children, and not sell the house-hold utensils. He who buys the utensils of the children of a widow shall lose his money, and the goods shall return to their owners.

178. If a "devoted woman" or a prostitute to whom her father has given a dowry and a deed therefor, but if in this deed it is not stated that she may bequeath it as she pleases, and has not explicitly stated that she has the right of disposal; if then her father die, then her brothers shall hold her field and garden, and give her corn, oil, and milk according to her portion, and satisfy her. If her brothers do not give her corn, oil, and milk according to her share, then her field and garden shall support her. She shall have the usufruct of field and garden and all that her father gave her so long as she lives, but she can not sell or assign it to others. Her position of inheritance belongs to her brothers.

179. If a "sister of a god," or a prostitute, receive a gift from her father, and a deed in which it has been explicitly stated that she may dispose of it as she pleases, and give her complete disposition thereof: if then her father die, then she may leave her property to whomsoever she pleases. Her brothers can raise no claim thereto.

180. If a father give a present to his daughter—either marriageable or a prostitute (unmarriageable)—and then die, then she is to receive a portion as a child from the paternal estate, and enjoy its usufruct so long as she lives. Her estate belongs to her brothers.

181. If a father devote a temple-maid or temple-virgin to God and give her no present: if then the father die, she shall receive the third of a child's portion from the inheritance of her father's house, and enjoy its usufruct so long as she lives. Her estate belongs to her brothers.

182. If a father devote his daughter as a wife of Mardi of Babylon (as in 181), and give her no present, nor a deed; if then her father die, then shall she receive one-third of her portion as a child of her father's house from her brothers, but Marduk may leave her estate to whomsoever she wishes.

183. If a man give his daughter by a concubine a dowry, and a husband, and a deed; if then her

father die, she shall receive no portion from the paternal estate.

184. If a man do not give a dowry to his daughter by a concubine, and no husband; if then her father die, her brother shall give her a dowry according to her father's wealth and secure a husband for her.

185. If a man adopt a child and to his name as son, and rear him, this grown son can not be demanded back again.

186. If a man adopt a son, and if after he has taken him he injure his foster father and mother, then this adopted son shall return to his father's house.

187. The son of a paramour in the palace service, or of a prostitute, can not be demanded back.

188. If an artizan has undertaken to rear a child and teaches him his craft, he can not be demanded back.

189. If he has not taught him his craft, this adopted son may return to his father's house.

190. If a man does not maintain a child that he has adopted as a son and reared with his other children, then his adopted son may return to his father's house.

191. If a man, who had adopted a son and reared him, founded a household, and had children, wish to put this adopted son out, then this son shall not simply go his way. His adoptive father shall give him of his wealth one-third of a child's portion, and then he may go. He shall not give him of the field, garden, and house.

192. If a son of a paramour or a prostitute say to his adoptive father or mother: "You are not my father, or my mother," his tongue shall be cut off.

193. If the son of a paramour or a prostitute desire his father's house, and desert his adoptive father and adoptive mother, and goes to his father's house, then shall his eye be put out.

194. If a man give his child to a nurse and the child die in her hands, but the nurse unbeknown to the father and mother nurse another child, then they shall convict her of having nursed another child without the knowledge of the father and mother and her breasts shall be cut off.

195. If a son strike his father, his hands shall be hewn off.

196. If a man put out the eye of another man, his eye shall be put out. [An eye for an eye]

197. If he break another man's bone, his bone shall be broken.

198. If he put out the eye of a freed man, or break the bone of a freed man, he shall pay one gold mina.

199. If he put out the eye of a man's slave, or break the bone of a man's slave, he shall pay one-half of its value.

200. If a man knock out the teeth of his equal, his teeth shall be knocked out. [A tooth for a tooth]

201. If he knock out the teeth of a freed man, he shall pay one-third of a gold mina.

202. If any one strike the body of a man higher in rank than he, he shall receive sixty blows with an ox-whip in public.

203. If a free-born man strike the body of another free-born man or equal rank, he shall pay one gold mina.

204. If a freed man strike the body of another freed man, he shall pay ten shekels in money.

205. If the slave of a freed man strike the body of a freed man, his ear shall be cut off.

206. If during a quarrel one man strike another and wound him, then he shall swear, "I did not injure him wittingly," and pay the physicians.

207. If the man die of his wound, he shall swear similarly, and if he (the deceased) was a free-born man, he shall pay half a mina in money.

208. If he was a freed man, he shall pay one-third of a mina.

209. If a man strike a free-born woman so that she lose her unborn child, he shall pay ten shekels for her loss.

210. If the woman die, his daughter shall be put to death.

211. If a woman of the free class lose her child by a blow, he shall pay five shekels in money.

212. If this woman die, he shall pay half a mina.

213. If he strike the maid-servant of a man, and she lose her child, he shall pay two shekels in money.

214. If this maid-servant die, he shall pay one-third of a mina.

215. If a physician make a large incision with an operating knife and cure it, or if he open a tumor (over the eye) with an operating knife, and saves the eye, he shall receive ten shekels in money.

216. If the patient be a freed man, he receives five shekels.

217. If he be the slave of some one, his owner shall give the physician two shekels.

218. If a physician make a large incision with the operating knife, and kill him, or open a tumor with the operating knife, and cut out the eye, his hands shall be cut off.

219. If a physician make a large incision in the slave of a freed man, and kill him, he shall replace the slave with another slave.

220. If he had opened a tumor with the operating knife, and put out his eye, he shall pay half his value.

221. If a physician heal the broken bone or diseased soft part of a man, the patient shall pay the physician five shekels in money.

222. If he were a freed man he shall pay three shekels.

223. If he were a slave his owner shall pay the physician two shekels.

224. If a veterinary surgeon perform a serious operation on an ass or an ox, and cure it, the owner shall pay the surgeon one-sixth of a shekel as a fee.

225. If he perform a serious operation on an ass or ox, and kill it, he shall pay the owner one-fourth of its value.

226. If a barber, without the knowledge of his master, cut the sign of a slave on a slave not to be sold, the hands of this barber shall be cut off.

227. If any one deceive a barber, and have him mark a slave not for sale with the sign of a slave, he shall be put to death, and buried in his house. The barber shall swear: "I did not mark him wittingly," and shall be guiltless.

228. If a builder build a house for some one and complete it, he shall give him a fee of two shekels in money for each sar of surface.

229. If a builder build a house for some one, and does not construct it properly, and the house which he built fall in and kill its owner, then that builder shall be put to death.

230. If it kill the son of the owner the son of that builder shall be put to death.

231. If it kill a slave of the owner, then he shall pay slave for slave to the owner of the house.

232. If it ruin goods, he shall make compensation for all that has been ruined, and inasmuch as he did not construct properly this house which he built and it fell, he shall re-erect the house from his own means.

233. If a builder build a house for some one, even though he has not yet completed it; if then the walls seem toppling, the builder must make the walls solid from his own means.

234. If a shipbuilder build a boat of sixty gur for a man, he shall pay him a fee of two shekels in money.

235. If a shipbuilder build a boat for some one, and do not make it tight, if during that same year that boat is sent away and suffers injury, the shipbuilder shall take the boat apart and put it together tight at his own expense. The tight boat he shall give to the boat owner.

236. If a man rent his boat to a sailor, and the sailor is careless, and the boat is wrecked or goes aground, the sailor shall give the owner of the boat another boat as compensation.

237. If a man hire a sailor and his boat, and provide it with corn, clothing, oil and dates, and other things of the kind needed for fitting it: if the sailor is careless, the boat is wrecked, and its contents ruined, then the sailor shall compensate for the boat which was wrecked and all in it that he ruined.

238. If a sailor wreck any one's ship, but saves it, he shall pay the half of its value in money.

239. If a man hire a sailor, he shall pay him six gur of corn per year.

240. If a merchantman run against a ferryboat, and wreck it, the master of the ship that was wrecked shall seek justice before God; the master of the merchantman, which wrecked the ferryboat, must compensate the owner for the boat and all that he ruined.

241. If any one impresses an ox for forced labor, he shall pay one-third of a mina in money.

242. If any one hire oxen for a year, he shall pay four gur of corn for plow-oxen.

243. As rent of herd cattle he shall pay three gur of corn to the owner.

244. If any one hire an ox or an ass, and a lion kill it in the field, the loss is upon its owner.

245. If any one hire oxen, and kill them by bad treatment or blows, he shall compensate the owner, oxen for oxen.

246. If a man hire an ox, and he break its leg or cut the ligament of its neck, he shall compensate the owner with ox for ox.

247. If any one hire an ox, and put out its eye, he shall pay the owner one-half of its value.

248. If any one hire an ox, and break off a horn, or cut off its tail, or hurt its muzzle, he shall pay one-fourth of its value in money.

249. If any one hire an ox, and God strike it that it die, the man who hired it shall swear by God and be considered guiltless.

250. If while an ox is passing on the street (market) some one push it, and kill it, the owner can set up no claim in the suit (against the hirer).

251. If an ox be a goring ox, and it shown that he is a gorer, and he do not bind his horns, or fasten the ox up, and the ox gore a free-born man and kill him, the owner shall pay one-half a mina in money.

252. If he kill a man's slave, he shall pay one-third of a mina.

253. If any one agree with another to tend his field, give him seed, entrust a yoke of oxen to him, and bind him to cultivate the field, if he steal the corn or plants, and take them for himself, his hands shall be hewn off.

254. If he take the seed-corn for himself, and do not use the yoke of oxen, he shall compensate him for the amount of the seed-corn.

255. If he sublet the man's yoke of oxen or steal the seed-corn, planting nothing in the field, he shall be convicted, and for each one hundred gan he shall pay sixty gur of corn.

256. If his community will not pay for him, then he shall be placed in that field with the cattle (at work).

257. If any one hire a field laborer, he shall pay him eight gur of corn per year.

258. If any one hire an ox-driver, he shall pay him six gur of corn per year.

259. If any one steal a water-wheel from the field, he shall pay five shekels in money to its owner.

260. If any one steal a shadduf (used to draw water from the river or canal) or a plow, he shall pay three shekels in money.

261. If any one hire a herdsman for cattle or sheep, he shall pay him eight gur of corn per annum.

262. If any one, a cow or a sheep . . .

263. If he kill the cattle or sheep that were given to him, he shall compensate the owner with cattle for cattle and sheep for sheep.

264. If a herdsman, to whom cattle or sheep have been entrusted for watching over, and who has received his wages as agreed upon, and is satisfied, diminish the number of the cattle or sheep, or make the increase by birth less, he shall make good the increase or profit which was lost in the terms of settlement.

265. If a herdsman, to whose care cattle or sheep have been entrusted, be guilty of fraud and make false returns of the natural increase, or sell them for money, then shall he be convicted and pay the owner ten times the loss.

266. If the animal be killed in the stable by God (an accident), or if a lion kill it, the herdsman shall declare his innocence before God, and the owner bears the accident in the stable.

267. If the herdsman overlook something, and an accident happen in the stable, then the herdsman is at fault for the accident which he has caused in the stable, and he must compensate the owner for the cattle or sheep.

268. If any one hire an ox for threshing, the amount of the hire is twenty ka of corn.

269. If he hire an ass for threshing, the hire is twenty ka of corn.

270. If he hire a young animal for threshing, the hire is ten ka of corn.

271. If any one hire oxen, cart and driver, he shall pay one hundred and eighty ka of corn per day.

272. If any one hire a cart alone, he shall pay forty ka of corn per day.

273. If any one hire a day laborer, he shall pay him from the New Year until the fifth month (April to August, when days are long and the work hard) six gerahs in money per day; from the sixth month to the end of the year he shall give him five gerahs per day.

274. If any one hire a skilled artizan, he shall pay as wages of the . . . five gerahs, as wages of the potter five gerahs, of a tailor five gerahs, of . . . gerahs, . . . of a ropemaker four gerahs, of . . . gerahs, of a mason . . . gerahs per day.

275. If any one hire a ferryboat, he shall pay three gerahs in money per day.

276. If he hire a freight-boat, he shall pay two and one-half gerahs per day.

277. If any one hire a ship of sixty gur, he shall pay one-sixth of a shekel in money as its hire per day.

278. If any one buy a male or female slave, and before a month has elapsed the benu-disease be developed, he shall return the slave to the seller, and receive the money which he had paid.

279. If any one by a male or female slave, and a third party claim it, the seller is liable for the claim.

280. If while in a foreign country a man buy a male or female slave belonging to another of his own country; if when he return home the owner of the male or female slave recognize it: if the male or female slave be a native of the country, he shall give them back without any money.

281. If they are from another country, the buyer shall declare the amount of money paid therefor to the merchant, and keep the male or female slave.

282. If a slave say to his master: "You are not my master," if they convict him his master shall cut off his ear.

THE EPILOGUE

LAWS of justice which Hammurabi, the wise king, established. A righteous law, and pious statute did he teach the land. Hammurabi, the protecting king am I. I have not withdrawn myself from the men, whom Bel gave to me, the rule over whom Marduk gave to me, I was not negligent, but I made them a peaceful abiding-place. I expounded all great difficulties, I made the light shine upon them. With the mighty weapons which Zamama and Ishtar entrusted to me, with the keen vision with which Ea endowed me, with the wisdom that Marduk gave me, I have uprooted the enemy above and below (in north and south), subdued the earth, brought prosperity to the land, guaranteed security to the inhabitants in their homes; a disturber was not permitted. The great gods have called me, I am the salvation-bearing shepherd, whose staff is straight, the good shadow that is spread over my city; on my breast I cherish the inhabitants of the land of Sumer and Akkad; in my shelter I have let them repose in peace; in my deep wisdom have I enclosed them. That the strong might not injure the weak, in order to protect the widows and orphans, I have in Babylon the city where Anu and Bel raise high their head, in E-Sagil, the Temple, whose foundations stand firm as heaven and earth, in order to bespeak justice in the land, to settle all disputes, and heal all injuries, set up these my precious words, written upon my memorial stone, before the image of me, as king of righteousness.

The king who ruleth among the kings of the cities am I. My words are well considered; there is no wisdom like unto mine. By the command of Shamash, the great judge of heaven and earth, let righteousness go forth in the land: by the order of Marduk, my lord, let no destruction befall my monument. In E-Sagil, which I love, let my name be ever repeated; let the oppressed, who has a case at law, come and stand before this my image as king of righteousness; let him read the inscription, and understand my precious words: the inscription will explain his case to him; he will find out what is just, and his heart will be glad, so that he will say:

"Hammurabi is a ruler, who is as a father to his subjects, who holds the words of Marduk in reverence, who has achieved conquest for Marduk over the north and south, who rejoices the heart of Marduk, his lord, who has bestowed benefits for ever and ever on his subjects, and has established order in the land."

When he reads the record, let him pray with full heart to Marduk, my lord, and Zarpanit, my lady; and then shall the protecting deities and the gods, who frequent E-Sagil, graciously grant the desires daily presented before Marduk, my lord, and Zarpanit, my lady.

In future time, through all coming generations, let the king, who may be in the land, observe the words of righteousness which I have written on my monument; let him not alter the law of the land which I have given, the edicts which I have enacted; my monument let him not mar. If such a ruler have wisdom, and be able to keep his land in order, he shall observe the words which I have written in this inscription; the rule, statute, and law of the land which I have given; the decisions which I have made will this inscription show him; let him rule his subjects accordingly, speak justice to them, give right decisions, root out the miscreants and criminals from this land, and grant prosperity to his subjects.

Hammurabi, the king of righteousness, on whom Shamash has conferred right (or law) am I. My words are well considered; my deeds are not equaled; to bring low those that were high; to humble the proud, to expel insolence. If a succeeding ruler considers my words, which I have written in this my inscription, if he do not annul my law, nor corrupt my words, nor change my monument, then may Shamash lengthen that king's reign, as he has that of me, the king of righteousness, that he may reign in righteousness over his subjects. If this ruler do not esteem my words, which I have written in my inscription, if he despise my curses, and fear not the curse of God, if he destroy the law which I have given, corrupt my words, change my monument, efface my name, write his name there, or on account of the curses commission another so to do, that man, whether king or ruler, patesi, or commoner, no matter what he be, may the great God (Anu), the Father of the gods, who has ordered my rule, withdraw from him the glory of royalty, break his scepter, curse his destiny. May Bel, the lord, who fixeth destiny, whose command can not be altered, who has made my kingdom great, order a rebellion which his hand can not control; may he let the wind of the overthrow of his habitation blow, may he ordain the years of his rule in groaning, years of scarcity, years of famine, darkness without light, death with seeing eyes be fated to him; may he (Bel) order with his potent mouth the destruction of his city, the dispersion of his subjects, the cutting off of his rule, the removal of his name and memory from the land. May Belit, the great Mother, whose command is potent in E-Kur (the Babylonian Olympus), the Mistress, who harkens graciously to my petitions, in the seat of judgment and decision (where Bel fixes destiny), turn his affairs evil before Bel, and put the devastation of his land, the destruction of his subjects, the pouring out of his life like water into the mouth of King Bel. May Ea, the great ruler, whose fated decrees come to pass, the thinker of the gods, the omniscient, who maketh long the days of my life, withdraw understanding and wisdom from him, lead him to forgetfulness, shut up his rivers at their sources, and not allow corn or sustenance for man to grow in his land. May Shamash, the great Judge of heaven and earth, who supporteth all means of livelihood, Lord of life-courage, shatter his dominion, annul his law, destroy his way, make vain the march of his troops, send him in his visions forecasts of the uprooting of the foundations of his throne and of the destruction of his land. May the condemnation of Shamash overtake him forthwith; may he be deprived of water above among the living, and his spirit below in the earth. May Sin (the Moon-god), the Lord of Heaven, the divine father, whose crescent gives light among the gods, take away the crown and regal throne from him; may he put upon him heavy guilt, great decay, that nothing may be lower than he. May he destine him as fated, days, months and years of dominion filled with sighing and tears, increase of the burden of dominion, a life that is like unto death. May Adad, the lord of fruitfulness, ruler of heaven and earth, my helper, withhold from him rain from heaven, and the flood of water from the springs, destroying his land by famine and want; may he rage mightily over his city, and make his land into flood-hills (heaps of ruined cities). May Zamama, the great warrior, the first-born son of E-Kur, who goeth at my right hand, shatter his weapons on the field of battle, turn day into night for him, and let his foe triumph over him. May Ishtar, the goddess of fighting and war, who unfetters my weapons, my gracious protecting spirit, who loveth my dominion, curse his kingdom in her angry heart; in her great wrath, change his grace into evil, and shatter his weapons on the place of fighting and war. May she create disorder and sedition for him, strike down his warriors, that the earth may drink their blood, and throw down the piles of corpses of his warriors on the field; may

she not grant him a life of mercy, deliver him into the hands of his enemies, and imprison him in the land of his enemies. May Nergal, the might among the gods, whose contest is irresistible, who grants me victory, in his great might burn up his subjects like a slender reedstalk, cut off his limbs with his mighty weapons, and shatter him like an earthen image. May Nin-tu, the sublime mistress of the lands, the fruitful mother, deny him a son, vouchsafe him no name, give him no successor among men. May Nin-karak, the daughter of Anu, who adjudges grace to me, cause to come upon his members in E-kur high fever, severe wounds, that can not be healed, whose nature the physician does not understand, which he can not treat with dressing, which, like the bite of death, can not be removed, until they have sapped away his life.

May he lament the loss of his life-power, and may the great gods of heaven and earth, the Anunaki, altogether inflict a curse and evil upon the confines of the temple, the walls of this E-barra (the Sun temple of Sippara), upon his dominion, his land, his warriors, his subjects, and his troops. May Bel curse him with the potent curses of his mouth that can not be altered, and may they come upon him forthwith.

AKHENATON: THE HYMN TO THE ATON

The Pharaoh Amen-hotep IV broke with the established religion of Egypt and instituted the worship of the Aton, the sun disc as the source of life. "The Amarna Revolution" attempted a distinct break with Egypt's traditional and static ways of life in religion, politics, art, and literature. Pharaoh changed his name to Akh-en-Aton (perhaps "He Who Is Serviceable to the Aton") and moved his capital from Thebes to Tell el-Amarna. Pharaoh's own attitude to the god is expressed in the famous hymn which follows. Beyond doubt, the hymn shows the universality and beneficence of the creating and re-creating sun disc. A similarity of spirit and wording to the 104th Psalm has often been noted, and a direct relation between the two has been argued.[1] Because Akh-en-Aton was devoted lo this god alone, the Amarna religion has been called monotheistic. This is a debatable question, and a reserved attitude would note that only Akh-en-Aton and his family worshiped the Aton, Akh-en-Aton's courtiers worshiped Akh-en-Aton himself, and the great majority of Egyptians was ignorant of or hostile to the new faith.

This is the "long hymn" to the Aton, from the tomb of Eye at Tell el-Amarna. Akh-en-Aton's reign was about 1380 to 1362 B.C. The best copy of the text is that of N. de G. Davies, *The Rock Tombs of El Amarna*, VI (London, 1908), Pl. XXVII. Translations will be found in Erman, *LAE*, 288–91, and in J. H. Breasted, *The Dawn of Conscience* (New York, 1933), 281–86.

[2]The number "seventy," which contained the sounds *safekh* is carried over in a pun to the beginning and end of the stanza, with the words *safekh* "dissolve," and *khesef* "oppose."

[3]The role of Fate was powerful at this period, but not immutable if the god intervened.

[4]From the context, this continues the idea of Amon at a soothing breeze against more violent winds.

Praise of Re Har-akhti, Rejoicing on the Horizon, in His Name as Shu Who Is in the Aton-disc,[2] living forever and ever; the living great Aton who is in jubilee, lord of all that the Aton encircles, lord of heaven, lord of earth, lord of the House of Aton in Akhet-Aton;[3] (and praise of) the King of Upper and Lower Egypt, who lives on truth, the Lord of the Two Lands: Nefer-kheperu-Re Wa-en-Re; the Son of Re, who lives on truth, the Lord of Diadems: Akh-en-Aton, long in his lifetime; (and praise of) the Chief Wife of the King, his beloved, the Lady of the Two Lands: Nefer-neferu-Aton Nefert-iti, living, healthy, and youthful forever and ever; (by) the Fan-Bearer on the Right Hand of the King . . . Eye. He says:

> Thou appearest beautifully on the horizon of heaven,
> Thou living Aton, the beginning of life!
> When thou art risen on the eastern horizon,
> Thou hast filled every land with thy beauty.
> Thou art gracious, great, glistening, and high over every land;
> Thy rays encompass the lands to the limit of all that thou hast made:
> As thou art Re, thou reachest to the end of them;[4]
> (Thou) subduest them (for) thy beloved son.[5]

---

1 As in Breasted, *op. cit.*, 366–70.
2 The Aton had a dogmatic name written within a royal cartouche and including the three old solar deities, Re, Har-of-the-Horizon, and Shu.
3 Akhet-Aton was the name of the capital at Tell el-Amarna.
4 Pun: *Ra* "Re," and *er-ra* "to the end."
5 Akh-en-Aton.

Though thou art far away, thy rays are on earth;
Though thou art in *their* faces, *no one knows thy*
going.

When thou settest in the western horizon,
The land is in darkness, in the manner of death.
They sleep in a room, with heads wrapped up,
Nor sees one eye the other.
All their goods which are under their heads might
be stolen,
(But) they would not perceive (it).
Every lion is come forth from his den;
All creeping things, they sting.
Darkness *is a shroud*, and the earth is in stillness,
For he who made them rests in his horizon.[6]

At daybreak, when thou arisest on the horizon,
When thou shinest as the Aton by day,
Thou drivest away the darkness and givest thy rays.
The Two Lands are in festivity *every day*,
Awake and standing upon (their) feet,
For thou hast raised them up.
Washing their bodies, taking (their) clothing,   (5)
Their arms are (raised) in praise at thy appearance.
All the world, they do their work.[7]

All beasts are content with their pasturage;
Trees and plants are flourishing.
The birds which fly from their nests,
Their wings are (stretched out) in praise to thy *ka*.
All beasts spring upon (their) feet.
Whatever flies and alights,
They live when thou hast risen (for) them.[8]
The ships are sailing north and south as well,
For every way is open at thy appearance.
The fish in the river dart before thy face;
Thy rays are in the midst of the great green sea.[9]

Creator of seed in women,
Thou who makest fluid into man,
Who maintainest the son in the womb of his mother,
Who soothest him with that which stills his weeping,

Thou nurse (even) in the womb,
Who givest breath to sustain all that he has made!
When he descends from the womb to *breathe*
On the day when he is born,
Thou openest his mouth completely,
Thou suppliest his necessities.
When the chick in the egg speaks within the shell,
Thou givest him breath within it to maintain him.
When thou hast made him his fulfillment within
the egg, to break it,
He comes forth from the egg to speak at his com-
pleted (time);
He walks upon his legs when he comes forth from it.

How manifold it is, what thou hast made!
They are hidden from the face (of man).
O sole god, like whom there is no other!
Thou didst create the world according to thy desire,
Whilst thou were alone:[10]
All men, cattle, and wild beasts,
Whatever is on earth, going upon (its) feet,
And what is on high, flying with its wings.

The countries of Syria and Nubia, the *land* of
Egypt,
Thou settest every man in his place,
Thou suppliest their necessities:
Everyone has his food, and his time of life is
reckoned.[11]
Their tongues are separate in speech,
And their natures as well;
Their skins are distinguished,
As thou distinguishest the foreign peoples.
Thou makest a Nile in the underworld,
Thou bringest it forth as thou desirest
To maintain the people (of Egypt)[12]
According as thou madest them for thyself,
The lord of all of them, wearying (himself) with
them,
The lord of every land, rising for them,
The Aton of the day, great of majesty.

---

6 cf. Ps. 104:20–21.
7 cf. Ps. 104:22–23.
8 cf. Ps. 104:11–14.
9 cf. Ps. 104:25–26.
10 cf. Ps. 104:24.
11 cf. Ps. 104:27.
12 The Egyptians believed that their Nile came from the waters under the earth, called by them Nun.

All distant foreign countries, thou makest their life (also),
For thou hast set a Nile in heaven,
That it may descend for them and make waves upon the mountains,[13]   (10)
Like the great green sea,
To water their fields in their towns.[14]
How effective they are, thy plans, O lord of eternity!
The Nile in heaven, it is for the foreign peoples
And for the beasts of every desert that go upon (their) feet;
(While the true) Nile comes from the underworld for Egypt.

Thy rays suckle every meadow.
When thou risest, they live, they grow for thee.
Thou makest the seasons in order to rear all that thou hast made,
The winter to cool them,
And the heat that *they* may taste thee.
Thou hast made the distant sky in order to rise therein,
In order to see all that thou dost make.
Whilst thou wert alone,
Rising in thy form as the living Aton,
Appearing, shining, *withdrawing or approaching,*

Thou madest millions of forms of thyself alone.
Cities, towns, fields, road, and river—
Every eye beholds thee over against them,
For thou art the Aton of the day over *the earth.* . . .

Thou art in my heart,
And there is no other that knows thee
Save thy son Nefer-kheperu-Re Wa-en-Re,[15]
For thou hast made him well-versed in thy plans and in thy strength.[16]
The world came into being by thy hand,
According as thou hast made them.
When thou hast risen they live,
When thou settest they die.
Thou art lifetime thy own self,
For one lives (only) through thee.
Eyes are (fixed) on beauty until thou settest.
All work is laid aside when thou settest in the west.
(But) when (thou) risest (again),
[*Everything is*] made to flourish for the king, . . .
Since thou didst found the earth
And raise them up for thy son,
Who came forth from thy body:
the King of Upper and Lower Egypt, . . . Akh-en-Aton, . . . and the Chief Wife of the King . . . Nefert-iti, living and youthful forever and ever.

---

13 cf. Ps. 104:6, 10.
14 The rain of foreign countries is like the Nile of rainless Egypt.
15 For though the hymn was recited by the official Eye, he states that Akh-en-Aton alone knows the Aton.
16 Pharaoh was the official intermediary between the Egyptians and their [[??]]. The Amarna religion did not change this dogma.

PSALM 104

PSALM 104

[1]Praise the LORD, my soul.

LORD my God, you are very great;
you are clothed with splendor and majesty.

[2] The LORD wraps himself in light as with a garment;
he stretches out the heavens like a tent and lays the
beams of his upper chambers on their waters.

[3] He makes the clouds his chariot
and rides on the wings of the wind.

[4] He makes winds his messengers,[a]
flames of fire his servants.

[5] He set the earth on its foundations;
it can never be moved.

[6] You covered it with the watery depths as with a
garment; the waters stood above the mountains.

[7] But at your rebuke the waters fled,
at the sound of your thunder they took to flight;

[8] they flowed over the mountains, they went down
into the valleys,to the place you assigned for them.

[9] You set a boundary they cannot cross;
never again will they cover the earth.

[10] He makes springs pour water into the ravines;
it flows between the mountains.

[11] They give water to all the beasts of the field;
the wild donkeys quench their thirst.

[12] The birds of the sky nest by the waters;
they sing among the branches.

[13] He waters the mountains from his upper chambers;
the land is satisfied by the fruit of his work.

[14] He makes grass grow for the cattle,
and plants for people to cultivate—
bringing forth food from the earth:

[15] wine that gladdens human hearts,
oil to make their faces shine,
and bread that sustains their hearts.

[16] The trees of the LORD are well watered,
the cedars of Lebanon that he planted.

[17] There the birds make their nests;
the stork has its home in the junipers.

[18] The high mountains belong to the wild goats;
the crags are a refuge for the hyrax.

[19] He made the moon to mark the seasons,
and the sun knows when to go down.

[20] You bring darkness, it becomes night,
and all the beasts of the forest prowl.

[21] The lions roar for their prey
and seek their food from God.

[22] The sun rises, and they steal away;
they return and lie down in their dens.

[23] Then people go out to their work,
to their labor until evening.

[24] How many are your works, LORD! In wisdom you
made them all; the earth is full of your creatures.

[25] There is the sea, vast and spacious,
teeming with creatures beyond number—
living things both large and small.

[26] There the ships go to and fro,
and Leviathan, which you formed to frolic there.

[27] All creatures look to you
to give them their food at the proper time.

[28] When you give it to them,
they gather it up;
when you open your hand,
they are satisfied with good things.

[29] When you hide your face,
they are terrified;

---

a   Psalm 104:4 Or *angels*

New International Version (NIV)

when you take away their breath,
they die and return to the dust.

30 When you send your Spirit,
they are created,
and you renew the face of the ground.

31 May the glory of the LORD endure forever;
may the LORD rejoice in his works—

32 he who looks at the earth, and it trembles,
who touches the mountains, and they smoke.

33 I will sing to the LORD all my life;
I will sing praise to my God as long as I live.

34 May my meditation be pleasing to him,
as I rejoice in the LORD.

35 But may sinners vanish from the earth
and the wicked be no more.

Praise the LORD, my soul.

Praise the LORD.[b]

---

b   Psalm 104:35 Hebrew *Hallelu Yah*; in the Septuagint this line stands at the beginning of Psalm 105.

GENESIS: CHAPTERS 37, 39–41
(Story of Joseph)

37 Jacob settled in the land where his father had lived as an alien, the land of Canaan. ²This is the story of the family of Jacob.

Joseph, being seventeen years old, was shepherding the flock with his brothers; he was a helper to the sons of Bilhah and Zilpah, his father's wives; and Joseph brought a bad report of them to their father. ³Now Israel loved Joseph more than any other of his children, because he was the son of his old age; and he had made him a long robe with sleeves. ⁴But when his brothers saw that their father loved him more than all his brothers, they hated him, and could not speak peaceably to him.

5 Once Joseph had a dream, and when he told it to his brothers, they hated him even more. ⁶He said to them, 'Listen to this dream that I dreamed. ⁷There we were, binding sheaves in the field. Suddenly my sheaf rose and stood upright; then your sheaves gathered around it, and bowed down to my sheaf.' ⁸His brothers said to him, 'Are you indeed to reign over us? Are you indeed to have dominion over us?' So they hated him even more because of his dreams and his words.

9 He had another dream, and told it to his brothers, saying, 'Look, I have had another dream: the sun, the moon, and eleven stars were bowing down to me.' ¹⁰But when he told it to his father and to his brothers, his father rebuked him, and said to him, 'What kind of dream is this that you have had? Shall we indeed come, I and your mother and your brothers, and bow to the ground before you?' ¹¹So his brothers were jealous of him, but his father kept the matter in mind.

12 Now his brothers went to pasture their father's flock near Shechem. ¹³And Israel said to Joseph, 'Are not your brothers pasturing the flock at Shechem? Come, I will send you to them.' He answered, 'Here I am.' ¹⁴So he said to him, 'Go now, see if it is well with your brothers and with the flock; and bring word back to me.' So he sent him from the valley of Hebron.

He came to Shechem, ¹⁵and a man found him wandering in the fields; the man asked him, 'What are you seeking?' ¹⁶'I am seeking my brothers,' he said; 'tell me, please, where they are pasturing the flock.' ¹⁷The man said, 'They have gone away, for I heard them say, "Let us go to Dothan."' So Joseph went after his brothers, and found them at Dothan. ¹⁸They saw him from a distance, and before he came near to them, they conspired to kill him. ¹⁹They said to one another, 'Here comes this dreamer. ²⁰Come now, let us kill him and throw him into one of the pits; then we shall say that a wild animal has devoured him, and we shall see what will become of his dreams.' ²¹But when Reuben heard it, he delivered him out of their hands, saying, 'Let us not take his life.' ²²Reuben said to them, 'Shed no blood; throw him into this pit here in the wilderness, but lay no hand on him'—that he might rescue him out of their hand and restore him to his father. ²³So when Joseph came to his brothers, they stripped him of his robe, the long robe with sleeves 'that he wore; ²⁴and they took him and threw him into a pit. The pit was empty; there was no water in it.

25 Then they sat down to eat; and looking up they saw a caravan of Ishmaelites coming from Gilead, with their camels carrying gum, balm, and resin, on their way to carry it down to Egypt. ²⁶Then Judah said to his brothers, 'What profit is there if we kill our brother and conceal his blood? ²⁷Come, let us sell him to the Ishmaelites, and not lay our hands on him, for he is our brother, our own flesh.' And his brothers agreed. ²⁸When some Midianite traders passed by, they drew Joseph up, lifting him out of the pit, and sold him to the Ishmaelites for twenty pieces of silver. And they took Joseph to Egypt.

29 When Reuben returned to the pit and saw that Joseph was not in the pit, he tore his clothes. ³⁰He returned to his brothers, and said, 'The boy is gone; and I, where can I turn?' ³¹Then they took Joseph's robe, slaughtered a goat, and dipped the robe in the blood. ³²They had the long robe with sleeves 'taken to

their father, and they said, 'This we have found; see now whether it is your son's robe or not.' [33]He recognized it, and said, 'It is my son's robe! A wild animal has devoured him; Joseph is without doubt torn to pieces.' [34]Then Jacob tore his garments, and put sackcloth on his loins, and mourned for his son for many days. [35]All his sons and all his daughters sought to comfort him; but he refused to be comforted, and said, 'No, I shall go down to Sheol to my son, mourning.' Thus his father bewailed him. [36]Meanwhile the Midianites had sold him in Egypt to Potiphar, one of Pharaoh's officials, the captain of the guard.

GENESIS 39

39 Now Joseph was taken down to Egypt, and Potiphar, an officer of Pharaoh, the captain of the guard, an Egyptian, bought him from the Ishmaelites who had brought him down there. [2]The LORD was with Joseph, and he became a successful man; he was in the house of his Egyptian master. [3]His master saw that the LORD was with him, and that the LORD caused all that he did to prosper in his hands. [4]So Joseph found favour in his sight and attended him; he made him overseer of his house and put him in charge of all that he had. [5]From the time that he made him overseer in his house and over all that he had, the LORD blessed the Egyptian's house for Joseph's sake; the blessing of the LORD was on all that he had, in house and field. [6]So he left all that he had in Joseph's charge; and, with him there, he had no concern for anything but the food that he ate.

Now Joseph was handsome and good-looking. [7]And after a time his master's wife cast her eyes on Joseph and said, 'Lie with me.' [8]But he refused and said to his master's wife, 'Look, with me here, my master has no concern about anything in the house, and he has put everything that he has in my hand. [9]He is not greater in this house than I am, nor has he kept back anything from me except yourself, because you are his wife. How then could I do this great wickedness, and sin against God?' [10]And although she spoke to Joseph day after day, he would not consent to lie beside her or to be with her. [11]One day, however, when he went into the house to do his work, and while no one else was in the house, [12]she caught hold of his garment, saying, 'Lie with me!' But he left his garment in her hand, and

fled and ran outside. [13]When she saw that he had left his garment in her hand and had fled outside, [14]she called out to the members of her household and said to them, 'See, my husband' has brought among us a Hebrew to insult us! He came in to me to lie with me, and I cried out with a loud voice; [15]and when he heard me raise my voice and cry out, he left his garment beside me, and fled outside.' [16]Then she kept his garment by her until his master came home, [17]and she told him the same story, saying, 'The Hebrew servant, whom you have brought among us, came in to me to insult me; [18]but as soon as I raised my voice and cried out, he left his garment beside me, and fled outside.'

19 When his master heard the words that his wife spoke to him, saying, 'This is the way your servant treated me', he became enraged. [20]And Joseph's master took him and put him into the prison, the place where the king's prisoners were confined; he remained there in prison. [21]But the LORD was with Joseph and showed him steadfast love; he gave him favour in the sight of the chief jailer. [22]The chief jailer committed to Joseph's care all the prisoners who were in the prison, and whatever was done there, he was the one who did it. [23]The chief jailer paid no heed to anything that was in Joseph's care, because the LORD was with him; and whatever he did, the LORD made it prosper.

GENESIS 40

40 Some time after this, the cupbearer of the king of Egypt and his baker offended their lord the king of Egypt. [2]Pharaoh was angry with his two officers, the chief cupbearer and the chief baker, [3]and he put them in custody in the house of the captain of the guard, in the prison where Joseph was confined. [4]The captain of the guard charged Joseph with them, and he waited on them; and they continued for some time in custody. [5]One night they both dreamed—the cupbearer and the baker of the king of Egypt, who were confined in the prison—each his own dream, and each dream with its own meaning. [6]When Joseph came to them in the morning, he saw that they were troubled. [7]So he asked Pharaoh's officers, who were with him in custody in his master's house, 'Why are your faces downcast today?' [8]They said to him, 'We have had dreams, and there is no one to interpret them.'

And Joseph said to them, 'Do not interpretations belong to God? Please tell them to me.'

9 So the chief cupbearer told his dream to Joseph, and said to him, 'In my dream there was a vine before me, ¹⁰and on the vine there were three branches. As soon as it budded, its blossoms came out and the clusters ripened into grapes. ¹¹Pharaoh's cup was in my hand; and I took the grapes and pressed them into Pharaoh's cup, and placed the cup in Pharaoh's hand.' ¹²Then Joseph said to him, 'This is its interpretation: the three branches are three days; ¹³within three days Pharaoh will lift up your head and restore you to your office; and you shall place Pharaoh's cup in his hand, just as you used to do when you were his cupbearer. ¹⁴But remember me when it is well with you; please do me the kindness to make mention of me to Pharaoh, and so get me out of this place. ¹⁵For in fact I was stolen out of the land of the Hebrews; and here also I have done nothing that they should have put me into the dungeon.'

16 When the chief baker saw that the interpretation was favourable, he said to Joseph, 'I also had a dream: there were three cake baskets on my head, ¹⁷and in the uppermost basket there were all sorts of baked food for Pharaoh, but the birds were eating it out of the basket on my head.' ¹⁸And Joseph answered, 'This is its interpretation: the three baskets are three days; ¹⁹within three days Pharaoh will lift up your head—from you!—and hang you on a pole; and the birds will eat the flesh from you.'

20 On the third day, which was Pharaoh's birthday, he made a feast for all his servants, and lifted up the head of the chief cupbearer and the head of the chief baker among his servants. ²¹He restored the chief cupbearer to his cupbearing, and he placed the cup in Pharaoh's hand; ²²but the chief baker he hanged, just as Joseph had interpreted to them. ²³Yet the chief cupbearer did not remember Joseph, but forgot him.

GENESIS 41

41 After two whole years, Pharaoh dreamed that he was standing by the Nile, ²and there came up out of the Nile seven sleek and fat cows, and they grazed in the reed grass. ³Then seven other cows, ugly and thin, came up out of the Nile after them, and stood by the other cows on the bank of the Nile. ⁴The ugly and thin cows ate up the seven sleek and fat cows. And Pharaoh awoke. ⁵Then he fell asleep and dreamed a second time; seven ears of grain, plump and good, were growing on one stalk. ⁶Then seven ears, thin and blighted by the east wind, sprouted after them. ⁷The thin ears swallowed up the seven plump and full ears. Pharaoh awoke, and it was a dream. ⁸In the morning his spirit was troubled; so he sent and called for all the magicians of Egypt and all its wise men. Pharaoh told them his dreams, but there was no one who could interpret them to Pharaoh.

9 Then the chief cupbearer said to Pharaoh, 'I remember my faults today. ¹⁰Once Pharaoh was angry with his servants, and put me and the chief baker in custody in the house of the captain of the guard. ¹¹We dreamed on the same night, he and I, each having a dream with its own meaning. ¹²A young Hebrew was there with us, a servant of the captain of the guard. When we told him, he interpreted our dreams to us, giving an interpretation to each according to his dream. ¹³As he interpreted to us, so it turned out; I was restored to my office, and the baker was hanged.'

14 Then Pharaoh sent for Joseph, and he was hurriedly brought out of the dungeon. When he had shaved himself and changed his clothes, he came in before Pharaoh. ¹⁵And Pharaoh said to Joseph, 'I have had a dream, and there is no one who can interpret it. I have heard it said of you that when you hear a dream you can interpret it.' ¹⁶Joseph answered Pharaoh, 'It is not I; God will give Pharaoh a favourable answer.' ¹⁷Then Pharaoh said to Joseph, 'In my dream I was standing on the banks of the Nile; ¹⁸and seven cows, fat and sleek, came up out of the Nile and fed in the reed grass. ¹⁹Then seven other cows came up after them, poor, very ugly, and thin. Never had I seen such ugly ones in all the land of Egypt. ²⁰The thin and ugly cows ate up the first seven fat cows, ²¹but when they had eaten them no one would have known that they had done so, for they were still as ugly as before. Then I awoke. ²²I fell asleep a second time' and I saw in my dream seven ears of grain, full and good, growing on one stalk, ²³and seven ears, withered, thin, and blighted by the east wind, sprouting after them; ²⁴and the thin ears swallowed up the seven good ears. But when I told it to the magicians, there was no one who could explain it to me.'

25 Then Joseph said to Pharaoh, 'Pharaoh's dreams are one and the same; God has revealed to Pharaoh what he is about to do. ²⁶The seven good cows are seven years, and the seven good ears are seven years; the dreams are one. ²⁷The seven lean and ugly cows that came up after them are seven years, as are the seven empty ears blighted by the east wind. They are seven years of famine. ²⁸It is as I told Pharaoh; God has shown to Pharaoh what he is about to do. ²⁹There will come seven years of great plenty throughout all the land of Egypt. ³⁰After them there will arise seven years of famine, and all the plenty will be forgotten in the land of Egypt; the famine will consume the land. ³¹The plenty will no longer be known in the land because of the famine that will follow, for it will be very grievous. ³²And the doubling of Pharaoh's dream means that the thing is fixed by God, and God will shortly bring it about. ³³Now therefore let Pharaoh select a man who is discerning and wise, and set him over the land of Egypt. ³⁴Let Pharaoh proceed to appoint overseers over the land, and take one-fifth of the produce of the land of Egypt during the seven plenteous years. ³⁵Let them gather all the food of these good years that are coming, and lay up grain under the authority of Pharaoh for food in the cities, and let them keep it. ³⁶That food shall be a reserve for the land against the seven years of famine that are to befall the land of Egypt, so that the land may not perish through the famine.'

37 The proposal pleased Pharaoh and all his servants. ³⁸Pharaoh said to his servants, 'Can we find anyone else like this—one in whom is the spirit of God?' ³⁹So Pharaoh said to Joseph, 'Since God has shown you all this, there is no one so discerning and wise as you. ⁴⁰You shall be over my house, and all my people shall order themselves as you command; only with regard to the throne will I be greater than you.' ⁴¹And Pharaoh said to Joseph, 'See, I have set you over all the land of Egypt.' ⁴²Removing his signet ring from his hand, Pharaoh put it on Joseph's hand; he arrayed him in garments of fine linen, and put a gold chain around his neck. ⁴³He had him ride in the chariot of his second-in-command; and they cried out in front of him, 'Bow the knee!' Thus he set him over all the land of Egypt. ⁴⁴Moreover, Pharaoh said to Joseph, 'I am Pharaoh, and without your consent no one shall lift up hand or foot in all the land of Egypt.' ⁴⁵Pharaoh gave Joseph the name Zaphenath-paneah; and he gave him Asenath daughter of Potiphera, priest of On, as his wife. Thus Joseph gained authority over the land of Egypt.

46 Joseph was thirty years old when he entered the service of Pharaoh king of Egypt. And Joseph went out from the presence of Pharaoh, and went through all the land of Egypt. ⁴⁷During the seven plenteous years the earth produced abundantly. ⁴⁸He gathered up all the food of the seven years when there was plenty˙ in the land of Egypt, and stored up food in the cities; he stored up in every city the food from the fields around it. ⁴⁹So Joseph stored up grain in such abundance—like the sand of the sea—that he stopped measuring it; it was beyond measure.

50 Before the years of famine came, Joseph had two sons, whom Asenath daughter of Potiphera, priest of On, bore to him. ⁵¹Joseph named the firstborn Manasseh,˙ 'For', he said, 'God has made me forget all my hardship and all my father's house.' ⁵²The second he named Ephraim,˙ 'For God has made me fruitful in the land of my misfortunes.'

53 The seven years of plenty that prevailed in the land of Egypt came to an end; ⁵⁴and the seven years of famine began to come, just as Joseph had said. There was famine in every country, but throughout the land of Egypt there was bread. ⁵⁵When all the land of Egypt was famished, the people cried to Pharaoh for bread. Pharaoh said to all the Egyptians, 'Go to Joseph; what he says to you, do.' ⁵⁶And since the famine had spread over all the land, Joseph opened all the storehouses,˙ and sold to the Egyptians, for the famine was severe in the land of Egypt. ⁵⁷Moreover, all the world came to Joseph in Egypt to buy grain, because the famine became severe throughout the world.

1 KINGS: CHAPTER 3: 1–28
(The Wisdom of Solomon)

1 KINGS 3

3 Solomon made a marriage alliance with Pharaoh king of Egypt; he took Pharaoh's daughter and brought her into the city of David, until he had finished building his own house and the house of the LORD and the wall around Jerusalem. ²The people were sacrificing at the high places, however, because no house had yet been built for the name of the LORD.

3 Solomon loved the LORD, walking in the statutes of his father David; only, he sacrificed and offered incense at the high places. ⁴The king went to Gibeon to sacrifice there, for that was the principal high place; Solomon used to offer a thousand burnt-offerings on that altar. ⁵At Gibeon the LORD appeared to Solomon in a dream by night; and God said, 'Ask what I should give you.' ⁶And Solomon said, 'You have shown great and steadfast love to your servant my father David, because he walked before you in faithfulness, in righteousness, and in uprightness of heart towards you; and you have kept for him this great and steadfast love, and have given him a son to sit on his throne today. ⁷And now, O LORD my God, you have made your servant king in place of my father David, although I am only a little child; I do not know how to go out or come in. ⁸And your servant is in the midst of the people whom you have chosen, a great people, so numerous they cannot be numbered or counted. ⁹Give your servant therefore an understanding mind to govern your people, able to discern between good and evil; for who can govern this your great people?'

10 It pleased the Lord that Solomon had asked this. ¹¹God said to him, 'Because you have asked this, and have not asked for yourself long life or riches, or for the life of your enemies, but have asked for yourself understanding to discern what is right, 12 I now do according to your word. Indeed I give you a wise and discerning mind; no one like you has been before you and no one like you shall arise after you. ¹³I give you also what you have not asked, both riches and honour all your life; no other king shall compare with you. ¹⁴If you will walk in my ways, keeping my statutes and my commandments, as your father David walked, then I will lengthen your life.'

15 Then Solomon awoke; it had been a dream. He came to Jerusalem, where he stood before the ark of the covenant of the LORD. He offered up burnt-offerings and offerings of well-being, and provided a feast for all his servants.

16 Later, two women who were prostitutes came to the king and stood before him. ¹⁷One woman said, 'Please, my lord, this woman and I live in the same house; and I gave birth while she was in the house. ¹⁸Then on the third day after I gave birth, this woman also gave birth. We were together; there was no one else with us in the house, only the two of us were in the house. ¹⁹Then this woman's son died in the night, because she lay on him. ²⁰She got up in the middle of the night and took my son from beside me while your servant slept. She laid him at her breast, and laid her dead son at my breast. ²¹When I rose in the morning to nurse my son, I saw that he was dead; but when I looked at him closely in the morning, clearly it was not the son I had borne.' ²²But the other woman said, 'No, the living son is mine, and the dead son is yours.' The first said, 'No, the dead son is yours, and the living son is mine.' So they argued before the king.

23 Then the king said, 'One says, "This is my son that is alive, and your son is dead"; while the other says, "Not so! Your son is dead, and my son is the living one." ' ²⁴So the king said, 'Bring me a sword', and they

brought a sword before the king. [25]The king said, 'Divide the living boy in two; then give half to one, and half to the other.' [26]But the woman whose son was alive said to the king—because compassion for her son burned within her—'Please, my lord, give her the living boy; certainly do not kill him!' The other said, 'It shall be neither mine nor yours; divide it.' [27]Then the king responded: 'Give the first woman the living boy; do not kill him. She is his mother.' [28]All Israel heard of the judgement that the king had rendered; and they stood in awe of the king, because they perceived that the wisdom of God was in him, to execute justice.

KINGS 1: CHAPTER 6: 1-38
(Solomon and the Temple)

I KINGS 6

6 In the four hundred and eightieth year after the Israelites came out of the land of Egypt, in the fourth year of Solomon's reign over Israel, in the month of Ziv, which is the second month, he began to build the house of the LORD. ²The house that King Solomon built for the LORD was sixty cubits long, twenty cubits wide, and thirty cubits high. ³The vestibule in front of the nave of the house was twenty cubits wide, across the width of the house. Its depth was ten cubits in front of the house. ⁴For the house he made windows with recessed frames.* ⁵He also built a structure against the wall of the house, running around the walls of the house, both the nave and the inner sanctuary; and he made side chambers all round. ⁶The lowest story* was five cubits wide, the middle one was six cubits wide, and the third was seven cubits wide; for round the outside of the house he made offsets on the wall in order that the supporting beams should not be inserted into the walls of the house.

7 The house was built with stone finished at the quarry, so that neither hammer nor axe nor any tool of iron was heard in the temple while it was being built.

8 The entrance for the middle story was on the south side of the house: one went up by winding stairs to the middle story, and from the middle story to the third. ⁹So he built the house, and finished it; he roofed the house with beams and planks of cedar. ¹⁰He built the structure against the whole house, each story* five cubits high, and it was joined to the house with timbers of cedar.

11 Now the word of the LORD came to Solomon, ¹²'Concerning this house that you are building, if you will walk in my statutes, obey my ordinances, and keep all my commandments by walking in them, then I will establish my promise with you, which I made to your father David. ¹³I will dwell among the children of Israel, and will not forsake my people Israel.'

14 So Solomon built the house, and finished it. ¹⁵He lined the walls of the house on the inside with boards of cedar; from the floor of the house to the rafters of the ceiling, he covered them on the inside with wood; and he covered the floor of the house with boards of cypress. ¹⁶He built twenty cubits of the rear of the house with boards of cedar from the floor to the rafters, and he built this within as an inner sanctuary, as the most holy place. ¹⁷The house, that is, the nave in front of the inner sanctuary, was forty cubits long. ¹⁸The cedar within the house had carvings of gourds and open flowers; all was cedar, no stone was seen. ¹⁹The inner sanctuary he prepared in the innermost part of the house, to set there the ark of the covenant of the Lord. ²⁰The interior of the inner sanctuary was twenty cubits long, twenty cubits wide, and twenty cubits high; he overlaid it with pure gold. He also overlaid the altar with cedar.* ²¹Solomon overlaid the inside of the house with pure gold, then he drew chains of gold across, in front of the inner sanctuary, and overlaid it with gold. ²²Next he overlaid the whole house with gold, in order that the whole house might be perfect; even the whole altar that belonged to the inner sanctuary he overlaid with gold.

23 In the inner sanctuary he made two cherubim of olive wood, each ten cubits high. ²⁴Five cubits was the length of one wing of the cherub, and five cubits the length of the other wing of the cherub; it was ten cubits from the tip of one wing to the tip of the other. ²⁵The other cherub also measured ten cubits; both cherubim had the same measure and the same form. ²⁶The height of one cherub was ten cubits, and so was that of the other cherub. ²⁷He put the cherubim in the innermost part of the house; the wings of the cherubim were spread out so that

a wing of one was touching one wall, and a wing of the other cherub was touching the other wall; their other wings towards the centre of the house were touching wing to wing. [28]He also overlaid the cherubim with gold.

29 He carved the walls of the house all round about with carved engravings of cherubim, palm trees, and open flowers, in the inner and outer rooms. [30]The floor of the house he overlaid with gold, in the inner and outer rooms.

31 For the entrance to the inner sanctuary he made doors of olive wood; the lintel and the doorposts were five-sided. [32]He covered the two doors of olive wood with carvings of cherubim, palm trees, and open flowers; he overlaid them with gold, and spread gold on the cherubim and on the palm trees.

33 So also he made for the entrance to the nave doorposts of olive wood, each four-sided, [34]and two doors of cypress wood; the two leaves of one door were folding, and the two leaves of the other door were folding. [35]He carved cherubim, palm trees, and open flowers, overlaying them with gold evenly applied upon the carved work. [36]He built the inner court with three courses of dressed stone to one course of cedar beams.

37 In the fourth year the foundation of the house of the LORD was laid, in the month of Ziv. [38]In the eleventh year, in the month of Bul, which is the eighth month, the house was finished in all its parts, and according to all its specifications. He was seven years in building it.

CHAPTER TWO

Ancient Greece

The Greek world began to take shape in the second millennium BCE with the emergence of two great civilizations. The first of these, termed Minoan after a legendary Cretan king mentioned in Homer, was centered in great palaces, such as those of Knossos and Phaistos, on the island of Crete. Within these palaces, scribes kept written records, artists decorated the walls with beautiful frescoes, and potters fashioned giant *pithoi* for the storage of grain and olive oil. The impact of this Atlantian-like civilization would be felt throughout the Aegean area and beyond. After 1500 BCE, Minoan civilization declined owing, in part, to natural disasters such as earthquakes and a massive volcanic eruption on the island of Thera, but also to the invasion of a very warlike people from the Greek mainland. The Mycenaeans, as they are known in the modern era from their principal site at Mycenae in the Peloponnesus, were the first Greek-speaking people to inhabit the mainland. Situated within great hilltop fortresses such as those as Mycenae, Pylos, Tiryns, and elsewhere, the Mycenaeans not only invaded and conquered Crete, but shortly after 1200 BCE laid siege to and eventually took the important commercial city of Troy near the coast of Asia Minor. Centuries later, this particular event provided information for Homer's two epic poems, the *Iliad* and the *Odyssey* Although their principal interest appears to have been warfare, within their fortresses, the Mycenaeans developed a flourishing civilization, kept good written records in the Linear B script, an adaptation of an earlier form of Minoan writing, built great structures with columns called Megarons, and interred their dead kings in rock-lined tombs in the hillside. Unfortunately, Mycenaean hegemony was short-lived. At some point in the twelfth century, fierce Indo-Europeans traditionally known as the Dorians swept over the Greek mainland destroying the Mycenaean fortresses. With little interest in anything but the spoils of war, the Dorians plunged the Greek world into a period of darkness from which it would not emerge for centuries.

By the eighth century, the Greek world had recovered. In the period that followed—often called the Archaic era (750–500 BCE)—the Greek world assumed its traditional form. Hundreds, if not thousands, of city states (*poleis*), many of them quite small, dotted the mainland and islands of the Aegean area. Most of these states emerged from the Dark Ages with kings who were soon eliminated in favor of governments run by oligarchs and, in some instances, by tyrants. Athens, the largest and most culturally brilliant of these states, at times flourished, but also experienced much political and social unrest under such rulers which prompted reformers such as Solon and Cleisthenes to seek remedies and bring about greater participation on the part of the masses in the government. Herein were the seeds of Athenian democracy.

Athenian development during this early period was, perhaps, the norm, but not all states followed this model. Sparta's development was truly unique. Situated in the Peloponnesus, far removed from the cultural influences that enveloped Athens, Sparta, ringed by enemies, was forced to fight for its very existence. A legendary lawgiver by the name of Lycurgus is often credited with the reforms by which Sparta became a veritable military machine. Unlike most other Greek *poleis,* Sparta retained its monarchy and developed a way of life for its people, which emphasized physical training, political stability, and service to the state. To accomplish these things, Sparta had to cut itself off from the outside world. Although Sparta would become the most feared state on the Greek mainland, one of the consequences of its isolation was that it would forever remain culturally and economically backward.

Despite the differences between the city–states of Greece, by the turn of the fifth century, the so-called Classical era, forces were at work, which would bring these states together to fight a common enemy. The Persian Empire had, through conquest, reached the shores of the Aegean Sea. Conflict was inevitable. Herodotus of Halicarnassus, the so-called "father of history," has left a vivid account of the long war that followed in his *Histories.* Although Herodotus had a penchant for exaggeration and gave the gods ample room to operate within the realm of human affairs, there is no reason to doubt the validity of the broad brush strokes of his work. In the battles that followed, Greek generals—Leonidas of Sparta, Miltiades, and Themistocles of Athens among others—fought valiantly at Marathon, Thermopylae, Salamis, and Plataea to eventually bring the war to a successful conclusion.

In the years that followed, Classical Greece reached its zenith. Athens, destroyed by the Persians following the battle at Thermopylae, was rebuilt. Architects and sculptors erected majestic temples and colossal statuary to adorn the Acropolis, while philosophers, dramatists, and others exchanged ideas within the Agora. Under Pericles, Athens' most gifted leader, democracy reached its peak. On the high seas, Athens, buoyed by its victories in the war and now in possession of a powerful navy, became more and more imperialistic. Sparta, ever the isolationist, could only see such growth as a threat to its suzerainty within the Peloponnesus. Thucydides, an exiled Athenian general, has left a notably objective chronicle of the struggle which followed. From the outset, Athens struggled, first with a great plague that claimed thousands of lives including that of Pericles, and later from the inept leadership of demagogues who tempted the army and navy into a number of foolhardy schemes. After Sparta formed an alliance with the Persians to build a navy, the outcome became a foregone conclusion. Blockaded by land and sea, Athens fell to the Spartans in 404 BCE. Sparta's victory, though, proved ephemeral. The attempt to establish hegemony over the other states of Greece was an utter failure. In 371 BCE, the Spartans suffered a crushing defeat at the hands of Thebes at the Battle of Leuctra. Thereafter, Sparta became a second rate power. By the mid-fourth century, mainland Greece remained a politically fragmented area—easy prey for a new enemy to the north.

Under the leadership of Philip II, Macedonia had become a major power. For over thirty years, Philip, a competent captain and a shrewd politician, had moved slowly, but inexorably, toward the conquest of Greece. In 338 BCE, Philip and his young son Alexander defeated a coalition of Greek forces at Chaeronea. As a result, the Greek states hastened to render homage to its new leader. With the resources of the Greek world at his disposal, Philip turned his attention to an old enemy—the Persian Empire. Inspired, perhaps, by Xenophon's story of the 10,000 Greek mercenaries who, after many trials and tribulations, fought their way out of hostile territory, Philip formed the League of Corinth to renew the conflict. Unfortunately, Philip's premature death in 336 BCE at the hands of an assassin left the mission to his son and heir Alexander, now twenty years of age. With the might of Macedonia and Greece at his back, Alexander invaded Asia Minor in 334 BCE. Over the next eleven years, Alexander, convinced that his destiny was to rule the ancient world, defeated the Persians and their allies in a number of battles, most notably at Gaugamela in 331 BCE. By the time of his death eight years later, Alexander had expanded the borders of the Greek world to India.

While historians, novelists, and filmmakers have focused on Alexander's military accomplishments, it is important to remember that the political unity of his empire was quickly lost after his death amid the squabbling of his generals. What endured for centuries were the cultural and economic bonds forged between Greece and the Near East in the aftermath of his conquests. This new world—termed Hellenistic—was at once culturally brilliant and politically chaotic. Wherever Alexander marched, new cities and colonies were founded. Alexandria in Egypt became one of the ancient world's greatest cities, especially renowned for its library. Archimedes of Syracuse, Aristarchus of Samos, Euclid and others made significant contributions in math and science, while philosophers such as Epicurus, Zeno, and Diogenes sought answers to difficult questions in a world which, to their way of thinking, had become unstable and chaotic. At the same time, to the West, a new empire was in the making, one which would bring unity and order to the ancient world.

RECOMMENDED READINGS

Castleden, Rodney. *Minoans: Life in Bronze Age Crete.* 1993.

Chadwick, John. *The Mycenaean World.* 1976.

Forest, William G. *A History of Sparta: 950–192 B.C.* 1968.

Green, Peter. *The Greco-Persian Wars.* 1996.

Kagan, Donald. *The Peloponnesian War.* 2003.

Meiggs, Russell. *The Athenian Empire.* 1972.

Osborne, Robin. *Greece in the Making 1200–479 B.C.* 1996.

Stoneman, Richard. *Alexander the Great.* 1997.

QUESTIONS

1. What can be learned from the funeral games staged by Achilles for his fallen comrade Patroclus which would give us a better understanding of Greek sport and recreation?
2. How did the reforms of Lycurgus help to transform Sparta from a fairly ordinary state into a military power?
3. How did the death of 300 Spartans and their colleagues at Thermopylae contribute to the eventual Greek victory in the Persian Wars?
4. Who was Pericles and what sort of contrast did he draw between Athens and Sparta in his Funeral Oration?
5. How did the plague which hit Athens in the early years of the Peloponnesian War contribute to the overall outcome of the conflict with Sparta?

THE ILIAD
Homer

BOOK XXIII

The funeral of Patroclus, and the funeral games.

Thus did they make their moan throughout the city, while the Achaeans when they reached the Hellespont went back every man to his own ship. But Achilles would not let the Myrmidons go, and spoke to his brave comrades saying, "Myrmidons, famed horsemen and my own trusted friends, not yet, forsooth, let us unyoke, but with horse and chariot draw near to the body and mourn Patroclus, in due honour to the dead. When we have had full comfort of lamentation we will unyoke our horses and take supper all of us here."

On this they all joined in a cry of wailing and Achilles led them in their lament. Thrice did they drive their chariots all sorrowing round the body, and Thetis stirred within them a still deeper yearning. The sands of the seashore and the men's armour were wet with their weeping, so great a minister of fear was he whom they had lost. Chief in all their mourning was the son of Peleus: he laid his bloodstained hand on the breast of his friend. "Fare well," he cried, "Patroclus, even in the house of Hades. I will now do all that I erewhile promised you; I will drag Hector hither and let dogs devour him raw; twelve noble sons of Trojans will I also slay before your pyre to avenge you."

As he spoke he treated the body of noble Hector with contumely, laying it at full length in the dust beside the bier of Patroclus. The others then put off every man his armour, took the horses from their chariots, and seated themselves in great multitude by the ship of the fleet descendant of Aeacus, who thereon feasted them with an abundant funeral banquet. Many a goodly ox, with many a sheep and bleating goat did they butcher and cut up; many a tusked boar moreover, fat and well-fed, did they singe and set to roast in the flames of Vulcan; and rivulets of blood flowed all round the place where the body was lying.

Then the princes of the Achaeans took the son of Peleus to Agamemnon, but hardly could they persuade him to come with them, so wroth was he for the death of his comrade. As soon as they reached Agamemnon's tent they told the serving-men to set a large tripod over the fire in case they might persuade the son of Peleus to wash the clotted gore from this body, but he denied them sternly, and swore it with a solemn oath, saying, "Nay, by King Jove, first and mightiest of all gods, it is not meet that water should touch my body, till I have laid Patroclus on the flames, have built him a barrow, and shaved my head—for so long as I live no such second sorrow shall ever draw nigh me. Now, therefore, let us do all that this sad festival demands, but at break of day, King Agamemnon, bid your men bring wood, and provide all else that the dead may duly take into the realm of darkness; the fire shall thus burn him out of our sight the sooner, and the people shall turn again to their own labours."

Thus did he speak, and they did even as he had said. They made haste to prepare the meal, they ate, and every man had his full share so that all were satisfied. As soon as they had had enough to eat and drink, the others went to their rest each in his own tent, but the son of Peleus lay grieving among his Myrmidons by the shore of the sounding sea, in an open place where the waves came surging in one after another. Here a very deep slumber took hold upon him and eased the burden of his sorrows, for his limbs were weary with chasing Hector round windy Ilius. Presently the sad spirit of Patroclus drew near him, like what he had been in stature, voice, and the light of his beaming eyes, clad, too, as he had been clad in life. The spirit hovered over his head and said—

"You sleep, Achilles, and have forgotten me; you loved me living, but now that I am dead you think for me no further. Bury me with all speed that I may pass the gates of Hades; the ghosts, vain shadows of men that can labour no more, drive me away from them; they will not yet suffer me to join those that are beyond the river, and I wander all desolate by the wide gates of the house of Hades. Give me now your hand I pray you, for when you have once given me my dues of fire, never shall I again come forth out of the house of Hades. Nevermore shall we sit apart and take sweet counsel among the living; the cruel fate which was my birth-right has yawned its wide jaws around me—nay, you too Achilles, peer of gods, are doomed to die beneath the wall of the noble Trojans.

"One prayer more will I make you, if you will grant it; let not my bones be laid apart from yours, Achilles, but with them; even as we were brought up together in your own home, what time Menoetius brought me to you as a child from Opoeis because by a sad spite I had killed the son of Amphidamas—not of set purpose, but in childish quarrel over the dice. The knight Peleus took me into his house, entreated me kindly, and named me to be your squire; therefore let our bones lie in but a single urn, the two-handled golden vase given to you by your mother."

And Achilles answered, "Why, true heart, are you come hither to lay these charges upon me? I will of my own self do all as you have bidden me. Draw closer to me, let us once more throw our arms around one another, and find sad comfort in the sharing of our sorrows."

He opened his arms towards him as he spoke and would have clasped him in them, but there was nothing, and the spirit vanished as a vapour, gibbering and whining into the earth. Achilles sprang to his feet, smote his two hands, and made lamentation saying, "Of a truth even in the house of Hades there are ghosts and phantoms that have no life in them; all night long the sad spirit of Patroclus has hovered over head making piteous moan, telling me what I am to do for him, and looking wondrously like himself."

Thus did he speak and his words set them all weeping and mourning about the poor dumb dead, till rosy-fingered morn appeared. Then King Agamemnon sent men and mules from all parts of the camp, to bring wood, and Meriones, squire to Idomeneus, was in charge over them. They went out with woodmen's axes and strong ropes in their hands, and before them went the mules. Up hill and down dale did they go, by straight ways and crooked, and when they reached the heights of many-fountained Ida, they laid their axes to the roots of many a tall branching oak that came thundering down as they felled it. They split the trees and bound them behind the mules, which then wended their way as they best could through the thick brushwood on to the plain. All who had been cutting wood bore logs, for so Meriones squire to Idomeneus had bidden them, and they threw them down in a line upon the seashore at the place where Achilles would make a mighty monument for Patroclus and for himself.

When they had thrown down their great logs of wood over the whole ground, they stayed all of them where they were, but Achilles ordered his brave Myrmidons to gird on their armour, and to yoke each man his horses; they therefore rose, girded on their armour and mounted each his chariot—they and their charioteers with them. The chariots went before, and they that were on foot followed as a cloud in their tens of thousands after. In the midst of them his comrades bore Patroclus and covered him with the locks of their hair which they cut off and threw upon his body. Last came Achilles with his head bowed for sorrow, so noble a comrade was he taking to the house of Hades.

When they came to the place of which Achilles had told them they laid the body down and built up the wood. Achilles then bethought him of another matter. He went a space away from the pyre, and cut off the yellow lock which he had let grow for the river Spercheius. He looked all sorrowfully out upon the dark sea, and said, "Spercheius, in vain did my father Peleus vow to you that when I returned home to my loved native land I should cut off this lock and offer you a holy hecatomb; fifty she-goats was I to sacrifice to you there at your springs, where is your grove and your altar fragrant with burnt-offerings. Thus did my father vow, but you have not fulfilled his prayer; now, therefore, that I shall see my home no more, I give this lock as a keepsake to the hero Patroclus."

As he spoke he placed the lock in the hands of his dear comrade, and all who stood by were filled with yearning and lamentation. The sun would have gone down upon their mourning had not Achilles presently said to Agamemnon, "Son of Atreus, for it is to you that the people will give ear, there is a time to mourn and a time to cease from mourning; bid the people now leave the pyre and set about getting their dinners: we, to whom the dead is dearest, will see to what is wanted here, and let the other princes also stay by me."

When King Agamemnon heard this he dismissed the people to their ships, but those who were about the dead heaped up wood and built a pyre a hundred feet this way and that; then they laid the dead all sorrowfully upon the top of it. They flayed and dressed many fat sheep and oxen before the pyre, and Achilles took fat from all of them and wrapped the body therein from head to foot, heaping the flayed carcases all round it. Against the bier he leaned two-handled jars of honey and unguents; four proud horses did he then cast upon the pyre, groaning the while he did so. The dead hero had had house-dogs; two of them did Achilles slay and threw upon the pyre; he also put twelve brave sons of noble Trojans to the sword and laid them with the rest, for he was full of bitterness and fury. Then he committed all to the resistless and devouring might of the fire; he groaned aloud and called on his dead comrade by name. "Fare well," he cried, "Patroclus, even in the house of Hades; I am now doing all that I have promised you. Twelve brave sons of noble Trojans shall the flames consume along with yourself, but dogs, not fire, shall devour the flesh of Hector son of Priam."

Thus did he vaunt, but the dogs came not about the body of Hector, for Jove's daughter Venus kept them off him night and day, and anointed him with ambrosial oil of roses that his flesh might not be torn when Achilles was dragging him about. Phoebus Apollo moreover sent a dark cloud from heaven to earth, which gave shade to the whole place where Hector lay, that the heat of the sun might not parch his body.

Now the pyre about dead Patroclus would not kindle. Achilles therefore bethought him of another matter; he went apart and prayed to the two winds Boreas and Zephyrus vowing them goodly offerings. He made them many drink-offerings from the golden cup and besought them to come and help him that the wood might make haste to kindle and

the dead bodies be consumed. Fleet Iris heard him praying and started off to fetch the winds. They were holding high feast in the house of boisterous Zephyrus when Iris came running up to the stone threshold of the house and stood there, but as soon as they set eyes on her they all came towards her and each of them called her to him, but Iris would not sit down. "I cannot stay," she said, "I must go back to the streams of Oceanus and the land of the Ethiopians who are offering hecatombs to the immortals, and I would have my share; but Achilles prays that Boreas and shrill Zephyrus will come to him, and he vows them goodly offerings; he would have you blow upon the pyre of Patroclus for whom all the Achaeans are lamenting."

With this she left them, and the two winds rose with a cry that rent the air and swept the clouds before them. They blew on and on until they came to the sea, and the waves rose high beneath them, but when they reached Troy they fell upon the pyre till the mighty flames roared under the blast that they blew. All night long did they blow hard and beat upon the fire, and all night long did Achilles grasp his double cup, drawing wine from a mixing-bowl of gold, and calling upon the spirit of dead Patroclus as he poured it upon the ground until the earth was drenched. As a father mourns when he is burning the bones of his bridegroom son whose death has wrung the hearts of his parents, even so did Achilles mourn while burning the body of his comrade, pacing round the bier with piteous groaning and lamentation.

At length as the Morning Star was beginning to herald the light which saffron-mantled Dawn was soon to suffuse over the sea, the flames fell and the fire began to die. The winds then went home beyond the Thracian sea, which roared and boiled as they swept over it. The son of Peleus now turned away from the pyre and lay down, overcome with toil, till he fell into a sweet slumber. Presently they who were about the son of Atreus drew near in a body, and roused him with the noise and tramp of their coming. He sat upright and said, "Son of Atreus, and all other princes of the Achaeans, first pour red wine everywhere upon the fire and quench it; let us then gather the bones of Patroclus son of Menoetius, singling them out with care; they are easily found, for they lie in the middle of the pyre, while all else, both men and horses, has been thrown in a heap and burned at the outer edge. We will lay the bones in a golden urn, in two layers of fat, against the time when I shall myself go down into the house of Hades. As for the barrow, labour not to raise a great one now, but such as is reasonable. Afterwards, let those Achaeans who may be left at the ships when I am gone, build it both broad and high."

Thus he spoke and they obeyed the word of the son of Peleus. First they poured red wine upon the thick layer of ashes and quenched the fire. With many tears they singled out the whitened bones of their loved comrade and laid them within a golden urn in two layers of fat: they then covered the urn with a linen cloth and took it inside the tent. They marked off the circle where the barrow should be, made a foundation for it about the pyre, and forthwith heaped up the earth. When they had thus raised a mound they were going away, but Achilles stayed the people and made them sit in assembly. He brought prizes from the ships—cauldrons, tripods, horses and mules, noble oxen, women with fair girdles, and swart iron.

The first prize he offered was for the chariot races—a woman skilled in all useful arts, and a three-legged cauldron that had ears for handles, and would hold twenty-two measures. This was for the man who came in first. For the second there was a six-year old mare, unbroken, and in foal to a he-ass; the third was to have a goodly cauldron that had never yet been on the fire; it was still bright as when it left the maker, and would hold four measures. The fourth prize was two talents of gold, and the fifth a two-handled urn as yet unsoiled by smoke. Then he stood up and spoke among the Argives saying—

"Son of Atreus, and all other Achaeans, these are the prizes that lie waiting the winners of the chariot races. At any other time I should carry off the first prize and take it to my own tent; you know how far my steeds excel all others—for they are immortal; Neptune gave them to my father Peleus, who in his turn gave them to myself; but I shall hold aloof, I and my steeds that have lost their brave and kind driver, who many a time has washed them in clear water and anointed their manes with oil. See how they stand weeping here, with their manes trailing on the ground in the extremity of their sorrow. But do you others set yourselves in order throughout the host, whosoever has confidence in his horses and in the strength of his chariot."

Thus spoke the son of Peleus and the drivers of chariots bestirred themselves. First among them all uprose Eumelus, king of men, son of Admetus, a man excellent in horsemanship. Next to him rose mighty Diomed son of Tydeus; he yoked the Trojan horses which he had taken from Aeneas, when Apollo bore him out of the fight. Next to him, yellow-haired Menelaus son of Atreus rose and yoked his fleet horses, Agamemnon's mare Aethe, and his own horse Podargus. The mare had been given to Agamemnon by Echepolus son of Anchises, that he might not have to follow him to Ilius, but might stay at home and take his ease; for Jove had endowed him with great wealth and he lived in spacious Sicyon. This mare, all eager for the race, did Menelaus put under the yoke.

Fourth in order Antilochus, son to noble Nestor son of Neleus, made ready his horses. These were bred in Pylos, and his father came up to him to give him good advice of which, however, he stood in but little need. "Antilochus," said Nestor, "you are young, but Jove and Neptune have loved you well, and have made you an excellent horseman. I need not therefore say much by way of instruction. You are skilful at wheeling your horses round the post, but the horses themselves are very slow, and it is this that will, I fear, mar your chances. The other drivers know less than you do, but their horses are fleeter; therefore, my dear son, see if you cannot hit upon some artifice whereby you may insure that the prize shall not slip through your fingers. The woodman does more by skill than by brute force; by skill the pilot guides his storm-tossed barque over the sea, and so by skill one driver can beat another. If a man go wide in rounding this way and that, whereas a man who knows what he is doing may have worse horses, but he will keep them well in hand when he sees the doubling-post; he knows the precise moment at which to pull the rein, and keeps his eye well on the man in front of him. I will give you this certain token which cannot escape your notice. There is a stump of a dead tree—oak or pine as it may be—some six feet above the ground, and not yet rotted away by rain; it stands at the fork of the road; it has two white stones set one on each side, and there is a clear course all round it. It may have been a monument to some one long since dead, or it may have been used as a doubling-post in days gone by; now, however, it has been fixed on by Achilles as the mark round which the chariots shall turn; hug it as close as you can, but as you stand in your chariot lean over a little to the left; urge on your right-hand horse with voice and lash, and give him a loose rein, but let the left-hand horse keep so close in, that the nave of your wheel shall almost graze the post; but mind the stone, or you will wound your horses and break your chariot in pieces, which would be sport for others but confusion for yourself. Therefore, my dear son, mind well what you are about, for if you can be first to round the post there is no chance of any one giving you the go-by later, not even though you had Adrestus's horse Arion behind you—a horse which is of divine race—or those of Laomedon, which are the noblest in this country."

When Nestor had made an end of counselling his son he sat down in his place, and fifth in order Meriones got ready his horses. They then all mounted their chariots and cast lots. Achilles shook the helmet, and the lot of Antilochus son of Nestor fell out first; next came that of King Eumelus, and after his, those of Menelaus son of Atreus and of Meriones. The last place fell to the lot of Diomed son of Tydeus, who was the best man of them all. They took their places in line; Achilles showed them the doubling-post round which they were to turn, some way off upon the plain; here he stationed his father's follower Phoenix as umpire, to note the running, and report truly.

At the same instant they all of them lashed their horses, struck them with the reins, and shouted at them with all their might. They flew full speed over the plain away from the ships, the dust rose from under them as it were a cloud or whirlwind, and their manes were all flying in the wind. At one moment the chariots seemed to touch the ground, and then again they bounded into the air; the drivers stood erect, and their hearts beat fast and furious in their lust of victory. Each kept calling on his horses, and the horses scoured the plain amid the clouds of dust that they raised.

It was when they were doing the last part of the course on their way back towards the sea that their pace was strained to the utmost and it was seen what each could do. The horses of the descendant of Pheres now took the lead, and close behind them came the Trojan stallions of Diomed. They seemed as if about to mount Eumelus's chariot, and he could feel their warm breath on his back and on his broad shoulders, for their heads were close to him as they flew over the course. Diomed would have now passed him, or there would have been a dead heat, but Phoebus Apollo to spite him made him drop his whip. Tears of anger fell from his eyes as he saw the mares going on faster than ever, while his own horses lost ground through his having no whip. Minerva saw the trick which Apollo had played the son of Tydeus, so she brought him his whip and put spirit into his horses; moreover she went after the son of Admetus in a rage and broke his yoke for him; the mares went one to one side of the course, and the other to the other, and the pole was broken against the ground. Eumelus was thrown from his chariot close to the wheel; his elbows, mouth, and nostrils were all torn, and his forehead was bruised above his eyebrows; his eyes filled with tears and he could find no utterance. But the son of Tydeus turned his horses aside and shot far ahead, for Minerva put fresh strength into them and covered Diomed himself with glory.

Menelaus son of Atreus came next behind him, but Antilochus called to his father's horses. "On with you both," he cried, "and do your very utmost. I do not bid you try to beat the steeds of the son of Tydeus, for Minerva has put running into them, and has covered Diomed with glory; but you must overtake the horses of the son of Atreus and not be left behind, or Aethe who is so fleet will taunt you. Why, my good fellows, are you lagging? I tell you, and it shall surely be—Nestor will keep neither of you, but will put both of you to the sword, if we win any the worse a prize through your carelessness. Fly after them at your utmost speed; I will hit on a plan for passing them in a narrow part of the way, and it shall not fail me."

They feared the rebuke of their master, and for a short space went quicker. Presently Antilochus saw a narrow place where the road had sunk. The ground was broken, for the winter's rain had gathered and had worn the road so that the whole place was deepened. Menelaus was making towards it so as to get there first, for fear of a foul, but Antilochus turned his horses out of the way, and followed him a little on one side. The son of Atreus was afraid and shouted out, "Antilochus, you are driving recklessly; rein in your horses; the road is too narrow here, it will be wider soon, and you can pass me then; if you foul my chariot you may bring both of us to a mischief."

But Antilochus plied his whip, and drove faster, as though he had not heard him. They went side by side for about as far as a young man can hurl a disc from his shoulder when he is trying his strength, and then Menelaus's mares drew behind, for he left off driving for fear the horses should foul one another and upset the chariots; thus, while pressing on in quest of victory, they might both come headlong to the ground. Menelaus then upbraided Antilochus and said, "There is no greater trickster living than you are; go, and bad luck go with you; the Achaeans say not well that you have understanding, and come what may you shall not bear away the prize without sworn protest on my part."

Then he called on his horses and said to them, "Keep your pace, and slacken not; the limbs of the other horses will weary sooner than yours, for they are neither of them young."

The horses feared the rebuke of their master, and went faster, so that they were soon nearly up with the others.

Meanwhile the Achaeans from their seats were watching how the horses went, as they scoured the plain amid clouds of their own dust. Idomeneus captain of the Cretans was first to make out the running, for he was not in the thick of the crowd, but stood on the most commanding part of the ground. The driver was a long way off, but Idomeneus could hear him shouting, and could see the foremost horse quite plainly—a chestnut with a round white star, like the moon, on its forehead. He stood up and said among the Argives, "My friends, princes and counsellors of the Argives, can you see the running as well as I can? There seems to be another pair in front now, and another driver; those that led off at the start must have been disabled out on the

plain. I saw them at first making their way round the doubling-post, but now, though I search the plain of Troy, I cannot find them. Perhaps the reins fell from the driver's hand so that he lost command of his horses at the doubling-post, and could not turn it. I suppose he must have been thrown out there, and broken his chariot, while his mares have left the course and gone off wildly in a panic. Come up and see for yourselves, I cannot make out for certain, but the driver seems an Aetolian by descent, ruler over the Argives, brave Diomed the son of Tydeus."

Ajax the son of Oileus took him up rudely and said, "Idomeneus, why should you be in such a hurry to tell us all about it, when the mares are still so far out upon the plain? You are none of the youngest, nor your eyes none of the sharpest, but you are always laying down the law. You have no right to do so, for there are better men here than you are. Eumelus's horses are in front now, as they always have been, and he is on the chariot holding the reins."

The captain of the Cretans was angry, and answered, "Ajax you are an excellent railer, but you have no judgement, and are wanting in much else as well, for you have a vile temper. I will wager you a tripod or cauldron, and Agamemnon son of Atreus shall decide whose horses are first. You will then know to your cost."

Ajax son of Oileus was for making him an angry answer, and there would have been yet further brawling between them, had not Achilles risen in his place and said, "Cease your railing, Ajax and Idomeneus; it is not seemly; you would be scandalised if you saw any one else do the like: sit down and keep your eyes on the horses; they are speeding towards the winning-post and will be here directly. You will then both of you know whose horses are first, and whose come after."

As he was speaking, the son of Tydeus came driving in, plying his whip lustily from his shoulder, and his horses stepping high as they flew over the course. The sand and grit rained thick on the driver, and the chariot inlaid with gold and tin ran close behind his fleet horses. There was little trace of wheel-marks in the fine dust, and the horses came flying in at their utmost speed. Diomed stayed them in the middle of the crowd, and the sweat from their manes and chests fell in streams on to the ground. Forthwith he sprang from his goodly chariot, and leaned his whip against his horses' yoke; brave Sthenelus now lost no time, but at once brought on the prize, and gave the woman and the ear-handled cauldron to his comrades to take away. Then he unyoked the horses.

Next after him came in Antilochus of the race of Neleus, who had passed Menelaus by a trick and not by the fleetness of his horses; but even so Menelaus came in as close behind him as the wheel is to the horse that draws both the chariot and its master. The end hairs of a horse's tail touch the tyre of the wheel, and there is never much space between wheel and horse when the chariot is going; Menelaus was no further than this behind Antilochus, though at first he had been a full disc's throw behind him. He had soon caught him up again, for Agamemnon's mare Aethe kept pulling stronger and stronger, so that if the course had been longer he would have passed him, and there would not even have been a dead heat. Idomeneus's brave squire Meriones was about a spear's cast behind Menelaus. His horses were slowest of all, and he was the worst driver. Last of them all came the son of Admetus, dragging his chariot and driving his horses on in front. When Achilles saw him he was sorry, and stood up among the Argives saying, "The best man is coming in last. Let us give him a prize for it is reasonable. He shall have the second, but the first must go to the son of Tydeus."

Thus did he speak and the others all of them applauded his saying, and were for doing as he had said, but Nestor's son Antilochus stood up and claimed his rights from the son of Peleus. "Achilles," said he, "I shall take it much amiss if you do this thing; you would rob me of my prize, because you think Eumelus's chariot and horses were thrown out, and himself too, good man that he is. He should have prayed duly to the immortals; he would not have come in last if he had done so. If you are sorry for him and so choose, you have much gold in your tents, with bronze, sheep, cattle and horses. Take something from this store if you would have the Achaeans speak well of you, and give him a better prize even than that which you have now offered; but

I will not give up the mare, and he that will fight me for her, let him come on."

Achilles smiled as he heard this, and was pleased with Antilochus, who was one of his dearest comrades. So he said—

"Antilochus, if you would have me find Eumelus another prize, I will give him the bronze breast-plate with a rim of tin running all round it which I took from Asteropaeus. It will be worth much money to him."

He bade his comrade Automedon bring the breast-plate from his tent, and he did so. Achilles then gave it over to Eumelus, who received it gladly.

But Menelaus got up in a rage, furiously angry with Antilochus. An attendant placed his staff in his hands and bade the Argives keep silence: the hero then addressed them. "Antilochus," said he, "what is this from you who have been so far blameless? You have made me cut a poor figure and baulked my horses by flinging your own in front of them, though yours are much worse than mine are; there-fore, O princes and counsellors of the Argives, judge between us and show no favour, lest one of the Achaeans say, 'Menelaus has got the mare through lying and corruption; his horses were far inferior to Antilochus's, but he has greater weight and influ-ence.' Nay, I will determine the matter myself, and no man will blame me, for I shall do what is just. Come here, Antilochus, and stand, as our custom is, whip in hand before your chariot and horses; lay your hand on your steeds, and swear by earth-encircling Neptune that you did not purposely and guilefully get in the way of my horses."

And Antilochus answered, "Forgive me; I am much younger, King Menelaus, than you are; you stand higher than I do and are the better man of the two; you know how easily young men are betrayed into indiscretion; their tempers are more hasty and they have less judgement; make due allowances there-fore, and bear with me; I will of my own accord give up the mare that I have won, and if you claim any further chattel from my own possessions, I would rather yield it to you, at once, than fall from your good graces henceforth, and do wrong in the sight of heaven."

The son of Nestor then took the mare and gave her over to Menelaus, whose anger was thus appeased; as when dew falls upon a field of ripening corn, and the lands are bristling with the harvest—even so, O Menelaus, was your heart made glad within you. He turned to Antilochus and said, "Now, Antilochus, angry though I have been, I can give way to you of my own free will; you have never been headstrong nor ill-disposed hitherto, but this time your youth has got the better of your judgement; be careful how you outwit your betters in future; no one else could have brought me round so easily, but your good father, your brother, and yourself have all of you had infinite trouble on my behalf; I therefore yield to your entreaty, and will give up the mare to you, mine though it indeed be; the people will thus see that I am neither harsh nor vindictive."

With this he gave the mare over to Antilochus's comrade Noemon, and then took the cauldron. Meriones, who had come in fourth, carried off the two talents of gold, and the fifth prize, the two-handled urn, being unawarded, Achilles gave it to Nestor, going up to him among the assembled Argives and saying, "Take this, my good old friend, as an heirloom and memorial of the funeral of Patroclus—for you shall see him no more among the Argives. I give you this prize though you cannot win one; you can now neither wrestle nor fight, and cannot enter for the javelin-match nor foot-races, for the hand of age has been laid heavily upon you."

So saying he gave the urn over to Nestor, who received it gladly and answered, "My son, all that you have said is true; there is no strength now in my legs and feet, nor can I hit out with my hands from either shoulder. Would that I were still young and strong as when the Epeans were burying King Amarynceus in Buprasium, and his sons offered prizes in his honour. There was then none that could vie with me neither of the Epeans nor the Pylians themselves nor the Aetolians. In boxing I overcame Clytomedes son of Enops, and in wrestling, Ancaeus of Pleuron who had come forward against me. Iphiclus was a good runner, but I beat him, and threw farther with my spear than either Phyleus or Polydorus. In chariot-racing alone did the two sons of Actor surpass me by crowding their horses in front of me, for they were angry at the way victory had gone, and at the greater part of the prizes remaining in the place in which they had been offered. They were twins, and the one kept on holding the reins, and holding the reins, while the other plied the whip. Such was I then, but now I must leave these matters to younger men; I must bow before the weight of years, but in those days I was eminent among heroes. And now, sir, go on with the funeral contests in honour of your comrade: gladly do I accept this urn, and my heart rejoices that you do not forget me but are ever mindful of my goodwill towards you, and of the respect due to me from the Achaeans. For all which may the grace of heaven be vouchsafed you in great abundance."

Thereon the son of Peleus, when he had listened to all the thanks of Nestor, went about among the concourse of the Achaeans, and presently offered prizes for skill in the painful art of boxing. He brought out a strong mule, and made it fast in the middle of the crowd—a she-mule never yet broken, but six years old—when it is hardest of all to break them: this was for the victor, and for the vanquished he offered a double cup. Then he stood up and said among the Argives, "Son of Atreus, and all other Achaeans, I invite our two champion boxers to lay about them lustily and compete for these prizes. He to whom Apollo vouchsafes the greater endurance, and whom the Achaeans acknowledge as victor, shall take the mule back with him to his own tent, while he that is vanquished shall have the double cup."

As he spoke there stood up a champion both brave and of great stature, a skilful boxer, Epeus, son of Panopeus. He laid his hand on the mule and said, "Let the man who is to have the cup come hither, for none but myself will take the mule. I am the best boxer of all here present, and none can beat me. Is it not enough that I should fall short of you in actual fighting? Still, no man can be good at everything. I tell you plainly, and it shall come true; if any man will box with me I will bruise his body and break his bones; therefore let his friends stay here in a body and be at hand to take him away when I have done with him."

They all held their peace, and no man rose save Euryalus son of Mecisteus, who was son of Talaus. Mecisteus went once to Thebes after the fall of

Oedipus, to attend his funeral, and he beat all the people of Cadmus. The son of Tydeus was Euryalus's second, cheering him on and hoping heartily that he would win. First he put a waistband round him and then he gave him some well-cut thongs of ox-hide; the two men being now girt went into the middle of the ring, and immediately fell to; heavily indeed did they punish one another and lay about them with their brawny fists. One could hear the horrid crashing of their jaws, and they sweated from every pore of their skin. Presently Epeus came on and gave Euryalus a blow on the jaw as he was looking round; Euryalus could not keep his legs; they gave way under him in a moment and he sprang up with a bound, as a fish leaps into the air near some shore that is all bestrewn with sea-wrack, when Boreas furs the top of the waves, and then falls back into deep water. But noble Epeus caught hold of him and raised him up; his comrades also came round him and led him from the ring, unsteady in his gait, his head hanging on one side, and spitting great clots of gore. They set him down in a swoon and then went to fetch the double cup.

The son of Peleus now brought out the prizes for the third contest and showed them to the Argives. These were for the painful art of wrestling. For the winner there was a great tripod ready for setting upon the fire, and the Achaeans valued it among themselves at twelve oxen. For the loser he brought out a woman skilled in all manner of arts, and they valued her at four oxen. He rose and said among the Argives, "Stand forward, you who will essay this contest."

Forthwith uprose great Ajax the son of Telamon, and crafty Ulysses, full of wiles, rose also. The two girded themselves and went into the middle of the ring. They gripped each other in their strong hands like the rafters which some master-builder frames for the roof of a high house to keep the wind out. Their backbones cracked as they tugged at one another with their mighty arms—and sweat rained from them in torrents. Many a bloody weal sprang up on their sides and shoulders, but they kept on striving with might and main for victory and to win the tripod. Ulysses could not throw Ajax, nor Ajax him; Ulysses was too strong for him; but when the Achaeans began to tire of watching them, Ajax said to Ulysses, "Ulysses, noble son of Laertes, you shall either lift me, or I you, and let Jove settle it between us."

He lifted him from the ground as he spoke, but Ulysses did not forget his cunning. He hit Ajax in the hollow at back of his knee, so that he could not keep his feet, but fell on his back with Ulysses lying upon his chest, and all who saw it marvelled. Then Ulysses in turn lifted Ajax and stirred him a little from the ground but could not lift him right off it, his knee sank under him, and the two fell side by side on the ground and were all begrimed with dust. They now sprang towards one another and were for wrestling yet a third time, but Achilles rose and stayed them. "Put not each other further," said he, "to such cruel suffering; the victory is with both alike, take each of you an equal prize, and let the other Achaeans now compete."

Thus did he speak and they did even as he had said, and put on their shirts again after wiping the dust from off their bodies.

The son of Peleus then offered prizes for speed in running—a mixing-bowl beautifully wrought, of pure silver. It would hold six measures, and far exceeded all others in the whole world for beauty; it was the work of cunning artificers in Sidon, and had been brought into port by Phoenicians from beyond the sea, who had made a present of it to Thoas. Eueneus son of Jason had given it to Patroclus in ransom of Priam's son Lycaon, and Achilles now offered it as a prize in honour of his comrade to him who should be the swiftest runner. For the second prize he offered a large ox, well fattened, while for the last there was to be half a talent of gold. He then rose and said among the Argives, "Stand forward, you who will essay this contest."

Forthwith uprose fleet Ajax son of Oileus, with cunning Ulysses, and Nestor's son Antilochus, the fastest runner among all the youth of his time. They stood side by side and Achilles showed them the goal. The course was set out for them from the starting-post, and the son of Oileus took the lead at once, with Ulysses as close behind him as the shuttle is to a woman's bosom when she throws the woof across the warp and holds it close up to her; even so close behind him was Ulysses—treading in his footprints before the dust could settle there, and Ajax could feel his breath on the back of his head as he ran swiftly on. The Achaeans all shouted applause as they saw him straining his utmost, and cheered him as he shot past them; but when they were now nearing the end of the course Ulysses prayed inwardly to Minerva. "Hear me," he cried, "and help my feet, O goddess." Thus did he pray, and Pallas Minerva heard his prayer; she made his hands and his feet feel light, and when the runners were at the point of pouncing upon the prize, Ajax, through Minerva's spite slipped upon some offal that was lying there from the cattle which Achilles had slaughtered in honour of Patroclus, and his mouth and nostrils were all filled with cow dung. Ulysses therefore carried off the mixing-bowl, for he got before Ajax and came in first. But Ajax took the ox and stood with his hand on one of its horns, spitting the dung out of his mouth. Then he said to the Argives, "Alas, the goddess has spoiled my running; she watches over Ulysses and stands by him as though she were his own mother." Thus did he speak and they all of them laughed heartily.

Antilochus carried off the last prize and smiled as he said to the bystanders, "You all see, my friends, that now too the gods have shown their respect for seniority. Ajax is somewhat older than I am, and as for Ulysses, he belongs to an earlier generation, but he is hale in spite of his years, and no man of the Achaeans can run against him save only Achilles."

He said this to pay a compliment to the son of Peleus, and Achilles answered, "Antilochus, you shall not have praised me to no purpose; I shall give you an additional half talent of gold." He then gave the half talent to Antilochus, who received it gladly.

Then the son of Peleus brought out the spear, helmet and shield that had been borne by Sarpedon, and were taken from him by Patroclus. He stood up and said among the Argives, "We bid two champions put on their armour, take their keen blades, and make trial of one another in the presence of the multitude; whichever of them can first wound the flesh of the other, cut through his armour, and draw blood, to him will I give this goodly Thracian sword inlaid with silver, which I took

from Asteropaeus, but the armour let both hold in partnership, and I will give each of them a hearty meal in my own tent."

Forthwith uprose great Ajax the son of Telamon, as also mighty Diomed son of Tydeus. When they had put on their armour each on his own side of the ring, they both went into the middle eager to engage, and with fire flashing from their eyes. The Achaeans marvelled as they beheld them, and when the two were now close up with one another, thrice did they spring forward and thrice try to strike each other in close combat. Ajax pierced Diomed's round shield, but did not draw blood, for the cuirass beneath the shield protected him; thereon the son of Tydeus from over his huge shield kept aiming continually at Ajax's neck with the point of his spear, and the Achaeans alarmed for his safety bade them leave off fighting and divide the prize between them. Achilles then gave the great sword to the son of Tydeus, with its scabbard, and the leathern belt with which to hang it.

Achilles next offered the massive iron quoit which mighty Eetion had erewhile been used to hurl, until Achilles had slain him and carried it off in his ships along with other spoils. He stood up and said among the Argives, "Stand forward, you who would essay this contest. He who wins it will have a store of iron that will last him five years as they go rolling round, and if his fair fields lie far from a town his shepherd or ploughman will not have to make a journey to buy iron, for he will have a stock of it on his own premises."

Then uprose the two mighty men Polypoetes and Leonteus, with Ajax son of Telamon and noble Epeus. They stood up one after the other and Epeus took the quoit, whirled it, and flung it from him, which set all the Achaeans laughing. After him threw Leonteus of the race of Mars. Ajax son of Telamon threw third, and sent the quoit beyond any mark that had been made yet, but when mighty Polypoetes took the quoit he hurled it as though it had been a stockman's stick which he sends flying about among his cattle when he is driving them, so far did his throw out-distance those of the others. All who saw it roared applause, and his comrades carried the prize for him and set it on board his ship.

Achilles next offered a prize of iron for archery—ten double-edged axes and ten with single edges: he set up a ship's mast, some way off upon the sands, and with a fine string tied a pigeon to it by the foot; this was what they were to aim at. "Whoever," he said, "can hit the pigeon shall have all the axes and take them away with him; he who hits the string without hitting the bird will have taken a worse aim and shall have the single-edged axes."

Then uprose King Teucer, and Meriones the stalwart squire of Idomeneus rose also, They cast lots in a bronze helmet and the lot of Teucer fell first. He let fly with his arrow forthwith, but he did not promise hecatombs of firstling lambs to King Apollo, and missed his bird, for Apollo foiled his aim; but he hit the string with which the bird was tied, near its foot; the arrow cut the string clean through so that it hung down towards the ground, while the bird flew up into the sky, and the Achaeans shouted applause. Meriones, who had his arrow ready while Teucer was aiming, snatched the bow out of his hand, and at once promised that he would sacrifice a hecatomb of firstling lambs to Apollo lord of the bow; then espying the pigeon high up under the clouds, he hit her in the middle of the wing as she was circling upwards; the arrow went clean through the wing and fixed itself in the ground at Meriones' feet, but the bird perched on the ship's mast hanging her head and with all her feathers drooping; the life went out of her, and she fell heavily from the mast. Meriones, therefore, took all ten double-edged axes, while Teucer bore off the single-edged ones to his ships.

Then the son of Peleus brought in a spear and a cauldron that had never been on the fire; it was worth an ox, and was chased with a pattern of flowers; and those that throw the javelin stood up—to wit the son of Atreus, king of men Agamemnon, and Meriones, stalwart squire of Idomeneus. But Achilles spoke saying, "Son of Atreus, we know how far you excel all others both in power and in throwing the javelin; take the cauldron back with you to your ships, but if it so please you, let us give the spear to Meriones; this at least is what I should myself wish."

King Agamemnon assented. So he gave the bronze spear to Meriones, and handed the goodly cauldron to Talthybius his esquire.

THE HISTORY OF HERODOTUS
Translated by G. C. Macaulay, [1890]

HERODOTUS BOOK 7: POLYMNIA [200]

200. There is also another river called Phoinix, to the South of the Asopos, of no great size, which flowing from these mountains runs out into the Asopos; and at the river Phoinix is the narrowest place, for here has been constructed a road with a single wheel-track only. Then from the river Phoinix it is a distance of fifteen furlongs to Thermopylai; and in the space between the river Phoinix and Thermopylai there is a village called Anthela, by which the river Asopos flows, and so runs out into the sea; and about this village there is a wide space in which is set up a temple dedicated to Demeter of the Amphictyons, and there are seats for the Amphictyonic councillors and a temple dedicated to Amphictyon himself.

201. King Xerxes, I say, was encamped within the region of Trachis in the land of the Malians, and the Hellenes within the pass. This place is called by the Hellenes in general Thermopylai, but by the natives of the place and those who dwell in the country round it is called Pylai. Both sides then were encamped hereabout, and the one had command of all that lies beyond Trachis in the direction of the North Wind, and the others of that which tends towards the South Wind and the mid-day on this side of the continent.

202. These were the Hellenes who awaited the attack of the Persian in this place:—of the Spartans three hundred hoplites; of the men of Tegea and Mantineia a thousand, half from each place, from Orchomenos in Arcadia a hundred and twenty, and from the rest of Arcadia a thousand,—of the Arcadians so many; from Corinth four hundred, from Phlius two hundred, and of the men of Mykene eighty: these were they who came from the Peloponnese; and from the Bœotians seven hundred of the Thespians, and of the Thebans four hundred.

203. In addition to these the Locrians of Opus had been summoned to come in their full force, and of the Phokians a thousand: for the Hellenes had of themselves sent a summons to them, saying by messengers that they had come as forerunners of the others, that the rest of the allies were to be expected every day, that their sea was safely guarded, being watched by the Athenians and the Eginetans and by those who had been appointed to serve in the fleet, and that they need fear nothing: for he was not a god, they said, who was coming to attack Hellas, but a man; and there was no mortal, nor would be any, with those fortunes evil had not been mingled at his very birth, and the greatest evils for the greatest men; therefore he also who was marching against them, being mortal, would be destined to fail of his expectation. They accordingly, hearing this, came to the assistance of the others at Trachis.

204. Of these troops, although there were other commanders also according to the State to which each belonged, yet he who was most held in regard and who was leader of the whole army was the Lacedemonian Leonidas son of Anaxandrides, son of Leon, son of Eurycratides, son of Anaxander, son of Eurycrates, son of Polydoros, son of Alcamenes, son of Teleclos, son of Archelaos, son of Hegesilaos, son of Doryssos, son of Leobotes, son of Echestratos, son of Agis, son of Eurysthenes, son of Aristodemos, son of Aristomachos, son of Cleodaios, son of Hyllos, son of Heracles; who had obtained the kingdom of Sparta contrary to expectation.

205. For as he had two brothers each older than himself, namely Cleomenes and Dorieos, he had been far removed from the thought of becoming king. Since however Cleomenes had died without male child, and Dorieos was then no longer alive, but he also had brought his life to an end

in Sicily, thus the kingdom came to Leonidas, both because was of elder birth than Cleombrotos (for Cleombrotos was the youngest of the sons of Anaxandrides) and also because he had in marriage the daughter of Cleomenes. He then at this time went to Thermopylai, having chosen arrived, those Thebans whom I mentioned when I reckoned them in the number of the troops, of whom the commander was Leontiades the son of Eurymachos: and for this reason Leonidas was anxious to take up these with him of all the Hellenes, namely because accusations had been strongly brought against them that they were taking the side of the Medes; therefore he summoned them to the war, desiring to know whether they would send troops with them or whether they would openly renounce the alliance of the Hellenes; and they sent men, having other thoughts in their mind the while.

206. These with Leonidas the Spartans had sent out first, in order that seeing them the other allies might join in the campaign, and for fear that they also might take the side of the Medes, if they heard that the Spartans were putting off their action. Afterwards, however, when they had kept the festival, (for the festival of the Carneia stood in their way), they intended then to leave a garrison in Sparta and to come to help in full force with speed: and just so also the rest of the allies had thought of doing themselves; for it chanced that the Olympic festival fell at the same time as these events. Accordingly, since they did not suppose that the fighting in Thermopylai would so soon be decided, they sent only the forerunners of their force.

207. These, I say, had intended to do thus: and meanwhile the Hellenes at Thermopylai, when the Persian had come near to the pass, were in dread, and deliberated about making retreat from their position. To the rest of the Peloponnesians then it seemed best that they should go to the Peloponnese and hold the Isthmus in guard; but Leonidas, when the Phokians and Locrians were indignant at this opinion, gave his vote for remaining there, and for sending at the same time messengers to the several States bidding them to come up to help them, since they were but few to repel the army of the Medes.

208. As they were thus deliberating, Xerxes sent a scout on horseback to see how many they were in number and what they were doing; for he had heard while he was yet in Thessaly that there had ἡγεμόνας been assembled in this place a small force, and that the leaders of it were Lacedemonians together with Leonidas, who was of the race of Heracles. And when the horseman had ridden up towards their camp, he looked upon them and had a view not indeed of the whole of their army, for of those which were posted within the wall, which they had repaired and were keeping a guard, it was not possible to have a view, but he observed those who were outside, whose station was in front of the wall; and it chanced at that time that the Lacedemonians were they who were posted outside. So then he saw some of the men practising athletic exercises and some combing their long hair: and as he looked upon these things he marvelled, and at the same time he observed their number: and when he had observed all exactly, he rode back unmolested, for no one attempted to pursue him and he found himself treated with much indifference. And when he returned he reported to Xerxes all that which he had seen.

209. Hearing this Xerxes was not able to conjecture the truth about the matter, namely that they were preparing themselves to die and to deal death to the enemy so far as they might; but it seemed to him that they were acting in a manner merely ridiculous; and therefore he sent for Demaratos the son of Ariston, who was in his camp, and when he came, Xerxes asked him of these things severally, desiring to discover what this was which the Lacedemonians were doing: and he said: "Thou didst hear from my mouth at a former time, when we were setting forth to go against Hellas, the things concerning these men; and having heard them thou madest me an object of laughter, because I told thee of these things which I perceived would come to pass; for to me it is the greatest of all ends to speak the truth continually before thee, O king. Hear then now also: these men have come to fight with us for the passage, and this is it that they are preparing to do; for they have a custom which is as follows;—whenever they are about to put their lives in peril, then they attend to the arrangement of their hair. Be assured however, that if thou shalt subdue these and the rest of them

which remain behind in Sparta, there is no other race of men which will await thy onset, O king, or will raise hands against thee: for now thou art about to fight against the noblest kingdom and city of those which are among the Hellenes, and the best men." To Xerxes that which was said seemed to be utterly incredible, and he asked again a second time in what manner being so few they would fight with his host. He said; "O king, deal with me as with a liar, if thou find not that these things come to pass as I say."

210. Thus saying he did not convince Xerxes, who let four days go by, expecting always that they would take to flight; but on the fifth day, when they did not depart but remained, being obstinate, as he thought, in impudence and folly, he was enraged and sent against them the Medes and the Kissians, charging them to take the men alive and bring them into his presence. Then when the Medes moved forward and attacked the Hellenes, there fell many of them, and others kept coming up continually, and they were not driven back, though suffering great loss: and they made it evident to every man, and to the king himself not least of all, that human beings are many but men are few. This combat went on throughout the day:

211. and when the Medes were being roughly handled, then these retired from the battle, and the Persians, those namely whom the king called "Immortals," of whom Hydarnes was commander, took their place and came to the attack, supposing that they at least would easily overcome the enemy. When however these also engaged in combat with the Hellenes, they gained no more success than the Median troops but the same as they, seeing that they were fighting in a place with a narrow passage, using shorter spears than the Hellenes, and not being able to take advantage of their superior numbers. The Lacedemonians meanwhile were fighting in a memorable fashion, and besides other things of which they made display, being men perfectly skilled in fighting opposed to men who were unskilled, they would turn their backs to the enemy and make a pretence of taking to flight; and the Barbarians, seeing them thus taking a flight, would follow after them with shouting and clashing of arms: then the Lacedemonians, when they were these times a few of the Spartans themselves.

So, as the Persians were not able to obtain any success by making trial of the entrance and attacking it by divisions and every way, they retired back.

212. And during these onsets it is said that the king, looking on, three times leapt up from his seat, struck with fear for his army. Thus they contended then: and on the following day the Barbarians strove with no better success; for because the men opposed to them were few in number, they engaged in battle with the expectation that they would be found to be disabled and would not be capable any longer of raising their hands against them in fight. The Hellenes however were ordered by companies as well as by nations, and they fought successively each in turn, excepting the Phokians, for these were posted upon the mountain to guard the path. So the Persians, finding nothing different from that which they had seen on the former day, retired back from the fight.

213. Then when the king was in a strait as to what he should do in the matter before him, Epialtes the son of Eurydemos, a Malian, came to speech with him, supposing that he would win a very great reward from the king; and this man told him of the path which leads over the mountain to Thermopylai, and brought about the destruction of those Hellenes who remained in that place. Afterwards from fear of the Lacedemonians he fled to Thessaly, and when he had fled, a price was proclaimed for his life by the Deputies, when the Amphictyons met for their assembly at Pylai. Then some time afterwards having returned to Antikyra he was slain by Athenades a man of Trachis. Now this Athenades killed Epialtes for another cause, which I shall set forth in the following part of the history, but he was honoured for it none the less by the Lacedemonians.

214. Thus Epialtes after these events was slain: there is however another tale told, that Onetes the son of Phanagoras, a man of Carystos, and Corydallos of Antikyra were those who showed the Persians the way round the mountain; but this I can by no means accept: for first we must judge by this fact, namely that the Deputies of the Hellenes did not proclaim a price for the lives of Onetes and Corydallos, but for that of Epialtes the Trachinian, having surely obtained the most exact information of the matter;

and secondly we know that Epialtes was an exile from his country to avoid this charge. True it is indeed that Onetes might know of this path, even though he were not a Malian, if he had had much intercourse with the country; but Epialtes it was who led them round the mountain by the path, and him therefore I write down as the guilty man.

215. Xerxes accordingly, being pleased by that which Epialtes engaged to accomplish, at once with great joy proceeded to send Hydarnes and the men of whom Hydarnes was commander; and they set forth from the camp about the time when the lamps are lit. This path of which we speak had been discovered by the Malians who dwell in that land, and having discovered it they led the Thessalians by it against the Phokians, at the time when the Phokians had fenced the pass with a wall and thus were sheltered from the attacks upon them: so long ago as this had the pass been proved by the Malians to be of no value.

216. And this path lies as follows:—it begins from the river Asopos, which flows through the cleft, and the name of this mountain and of the path is the same, namely Anopaia; and this Anopaia stretches over the ridge of the mountain and ends by the town of Alpenos, which is the first town of the Locrians towards Malis, and by the stone called Black Buttocks and the seats of the Kercopes, where is the very narrowest part.

217. By this path thus situated the Persians after crossing over the Asopos proceeded all through the night, having on their right hand the mountains of the Oitaians and on the left those of the Trachinians: and when dawn appeared, they had reached the summit of the mountain. In this part of the mountain there were, as I have before shown, a thousand hoplites of the Phokians keeping guard, to protect their own country and to keep the path: for while the pass below was guarded by those whom I have mentioned, the path over the mountain was guarded by the Phokians, who had undertaken the business for Leonidas by their own offer.

218. While the Persians were ascending they were concealed from these, since all the mountain was covered with oak-trees; and the Phokians became aware of them after they had made the ascent as follows:—the day was calm, and not a little noise was made by the Persians, as was likely when leaves were lying spread upon the ground under their feet; upon which the Phokians started up and began to put on their arms, and by this time the Barbarians were close upon them. These, when they saw men arming themselves, fell into wonder, for they were expecting that no one would appear to oppose them, and instead of that they had met with an armed force. Then Hydarnes, seized with fear lest the Phokians should be Lacedemonians, asked Epialtes of what people the force was; and being accurately informed he set the Persians in order for battle. The Phokians however, when they were hit by the arrows of the enemy, which flew thickly, fled and got away at once to the topmost peak of the mountain, fully assured that it was against them that the enemy had designed to come, and here they were ready to meet death. These, I say, were in this mind; but the Persians meanwhile with Epialtes and Hydarnes made no account of the Phokians, but descended the mountain with all speed.

219. To the Hellenes who were in Thermopylai first the soothsayer Megistias, after looking into the victims which were sacrificed, declared the death which was to come to them at dawn of day; and afterwards deserters brought the report of the Persians having gone round. These signified it to them while it was yet night, and thirdly came the day-watchers, who had run down from the heights when day was already dawning. Then the Hellenes deliberated, and their opinions were divided; for some urged that they should not desert their post, while others opposed this counsel. After this they departed from their assembly, and some went away and dispersed each to their several cities, while others of them were ready to remain there together with Leonidas.

220. However it is reported also that Leonidas himself sent them away, having a care that they might not perish, but thinking that it was not seemly for himself and for the Spartans who were present to leave the post to which they had come at first to keep guard there. I am inclined rather to be of this latter opinion, namely that because Leonidas perceived that the allies were out of heart and did not desire to face the danger with him to the end, he ordered them to depart, but held that for himself to go away

was not honourable, whereas if he remained, a great fame of him would be left behind, and the prosperity of Sparta would not be blotted out: for an oracle had been given by the Pythian prophetess to the Spartans, when they consulted about this war at the time when it was being first set on foot, to the effect that either Lacedemon must be destroyed by the Barbarians, or their king must lose his life. This reply the prophetess gave them in hexameter verses, and it ran thus:

"But as for you, ye men who in wide-spaced Sparta inhabit, Either your glorious city is sacked by the children of Perses, Or, if it be not so, then a king of the stock Heracleian Dead shall be mourned for by all in the boundaries of broad Lacedemon. Him nor the might of bulls nor the raging of lions shall hinder; For he hath might as of Zeus; and I say he shall not be restrained, Till one of the other of these he have utterly torn and divided."

I am of opinion that Leonidas considering these things and desiring to lay up for himself glory above all the other Spartans, dismissed the allies, rather than that those who departed did so in such disorderly fashion, because they were divided in opinion.

221. Of this the following has been to my mind a proof as convincing as any other, namely that Leonidas is known to have endeavoured to dismiss the soothsayer also who accompanied this army, Megistias the Acarnanian, who was said to be descended from Melampus, that he might not perish with them after he had declared from the victims that which was about to come to pass for them. He however when he was bidden to go would not himself depart, but sent away his son who was with him in the army, besides whom he had no other child.

222. The allies then who were dismissed departed and went away, obeying the word of Leonidas, and only the Thespians and the Thebans remained behind with the Lacedemonians. Of these the Thebans stayed against their will and not because they desired it, for Leonidas kept them, counting them as hostages; but the Thespians very willingly, for they said that they would not depart and leave Leonidas and those with him, but they stayed behind and died with them. The commander of these was Demophilos the son of Diadromes.

223. Xerxes meanwhile, having made libations at sunrise, stayed for some time, until about the hour when the market fills, and then made an advance upon them; for thus it had been enjoined by Epialtes, seeing that the descent of the mountain is shorter and the space to be passed over much less than the going round and the ascent. The Barbarians accordingly with Xerxes were advancing to the attack; and the Hellenes with Leonidas, feeling that they were going forth to death, now advanced out much further than at first into the broader part of the defile; for when the fence of the wall was being guarded, they on the former days fought retiring before the enemy into the narrow part of the pass; but now they engaged with them outside the narrows, and very many of the Barbarians fell: for behind them the leaders of the divisions with scourges in their hands were striking each man, ever urging them on to the front. Many of them then were driven into the sea and perished, and many more still were trodden down while yet alive by one another, and there was no reckoning of the number that perished: for knowing the death which was about to come upon them by reason of those who were going round the mountain, they displayed upon the Barbarians all the strength which they had, to its greatest extent, disregarding danger and acting as if possessed by a spirit of recklessness.

224. Now by this time the spears of the greater number of them were broken, so it chanced, in this combat, and they were slaying the Persians with their swords; and in this fighting fell Leonidas, having proved himself a very good man, and others also of the Spartans with him, men of note, of whose names I was informed as of men who had proved themselves worthy, and indeed I was told also the names of all the three hundred. Moreover of the Persians there fell here, besides many others of note, especially two sons of Dareios, Abrocomes and Hyperanthes, born to Dareios of Phratagune the daughter of Artanes: now

Artanes was the brother of king Dareios and the son of Hystaspes, the son of Arsames; and he in giving his daughter in marriage to Dareios gave also with her all his substance, because she was his only child.

225. Two brothers of Xerxes, I say, fell here fighting; and meanwhile over the body of Leonidas there arose a great struggle between the Persians and the Lacedemonians, until the Hellenes by valour dragged this away from the enemy and turned their opponents to flight four times. This conflict continued until those who had gone with Epialtes came up; and when the Hellenes learnt that these had come, from that moment the nature of the combat was changed; for they retired backwards to the narrow part of the way, and having passed by the wall they went and placed themselves upon the hillock, all in a body together except only the Thebans: now this hillock is in the entrance, where now the stone lion is placed for Leonidas. On this spot while defending themselves with daggers, that is those who still had them left, and also with hands and with teeth, they were overwhelmed by the missiles of the Barbarians, some of these having followed directly after them and destroyed the fence of the wall, while others had come round and stood about them on all sides.

226. Such were the proofs of valour given by the Lacedemonians and Thespians; yet the Spartan Dienekes is said to have proved himself the best man of all, the same who, as they report, uttered this saying before they engaged battle with the Medes:—being informed by one of the men of Trachis that when the Barbarians discharged their arrows they obscured the light of the sun by the multitude of the arrows, so great was the number of their host, he was not dismayed by this, but making small account of the number of the Medes, he said that their guest from Trachis brought them very good news, for if the Medes obscured the light of the sun, the battle against them would be in the shade and not in the sun.

227. This and other sayings of this kind they report that Dienekes the Lacedemonian left as memorials of himself; and after him the bravest they say of the Lacedemonians were two brothers Alpheos and Maron, sons of Orsiphantos. Of the Thespians the man who gained most honour was named Dithyrambos son of Harmatides.

228. The men were buried were they fell; and for these, as well as for those who were slain before being sent away by Leonidas, there is an inscription which runs thus:

"Here once, facing in fight three hundred myriads of foemen, Thousands four did contend, men of the Peloponnese."

This is the inscription for the whole body; and for the Spartans separately there is this:

"Stranger, report this word, we pray, to the Spartans, that lying Here in this spot we remain, faithfully keeping their laws."

This, I say, for the Lacedemonians; and for the soothsayer as follows:

"This is the tomb of Megistias renowned, whom the Median foemen, Where Sperchios doth flow, slew when they forded the stream; Soothsayer he, who then knowing clearly the fates that were coming, Did not endure in the fray Sparta's good leaders to leave."

The Amphictyons it was who honoured them with inscriptions and memorial pillars, excepting only in the case of the inscription to the soothsayer; but that of the soothsayer Megistias was inscribed by Simonides the son of Leoprepes on account of guest-friendship.

THE HISTORY OF THE PELOPONNESIAN WAR
Thucydides 431 BC
Translated by Richard Crawley

BOOK II

CHAPTER VI

In the same winter the Athenians gave a funeral at the public cost to those who had first fallen in this war. It was a custom of their ancestors, and the manner of it is as follows. Three days before the ceremony, the bones of the dead are laid out in a tent which has been erected; and their friends bring to their relatives such offerings as they please. In the funeral procession cypress coffins are borne in cars, one for each tribe; the bones of the deceased being placed in the coffin of their tribe. Among these is carried one empty bier decked for the missing, that is, for those whose bodies could not be recovered. Any citizen or stranger who pleases, joins in the procession: and the female relatives are there to wail at the burial. The dead are laid in the public sepulchre in the Beautiful suburb of the city, in which those who fall in war are always buried; with the exception of those slain at Marathon, who for their singular and extraordinary valour were interred on the spot where they fell. After the bodies have been laid in the earth, a man chosen by the state, of approved wisdom and eminent reputation, pronounces over them an appropriate panegyric; after which all retire. Such is the manner of the burying; and throughout the whole of the war, whenever the occasion arose, the established custom was observed. Meanwhile these were the first that had fallen, and Pericles, son of Xanthippus, was chosen to pronounce their eulogium. When the proper time arrived, he advanced from the sepulchre to an elevated platform in order to be heard by as many of the crowd as possible, and spoke as follows:

"Most of my predecessors in this place have commended him who made this speech part of the law, telling us that it is well that it should be delivered at the burial of those who fall in battle. For myself, I should have thought that the worth which had displayed itself in deeds would be sufficiently rewarded by honours also shown by deeds; such as you now see in this funeral prepared at the people's cost. And I could have wished that the reputations of many brave men were not to be imperilled in the mouth of a single individual, to stand or fall according as he spoke well or ill. For it is hard to speak properly upon a subject where it is even difficult to convince your hearers that you are speaking the truth. On the one hand, the friend who is familiar with every fact of the story may think that some point has not been set forth with that fullness which he wishes and knows it to deserve; on the other, he who is a stranger to the matter may be led by envy to suspect exaggeration if he hears anything above his own nature. For men can endure to hear others praised only so long as they can severally persuade themselves of their own ability to equal the actions recounted: when this point is passed, envy comes in and with it incredulity. However, since our ancestors have stamped this custom with their approval, it becomes my duty to obey the law and to try to satisfy your several wishes and opinions as best I may.

"I shall begin with our ancestors: it is both just and proper that they should have the honour of the first mention on an occasion like the present. They dwelt in the country without break in the succession from generation to generation, and handed it down free to the present time by their valour. And if our more remote ancestors deserve praise, much more do our own fathers, who added to their inheritance the empire which we now possess, and spared no pains to be able to leave their acquisitions to us of the present generation. Lastly, there are few parts of our dominions that have not been augmented by those of us here, who are still more or less in the vigour of life; while the mother country has been furnished by us with everything that can enable her to depend on her own resources whether for war or for peace. That part of our history which tells of the military achievements which gave us our several possessions, or of the ready valour with which either we or our fathers stemmed the tide of Hellenic or foreign aggression, is a theme too familiar to my hearers for me to dilate on, and I shall therefore pass it by. But what was the road by which we reached our position, what the form of government under which our greatness grew, what the national habits out of which it sprang; these are questions which I may try to solve before I proceed to my panegyric upon these men; since I think this to be a subject upon which on the present occasion a speaker may properly dwell, and to which the whole assemblage, whether citizens or foreigners, may listen with advantage.

"Our constitution does not copy the laws of neighbouring states; we are rather a pattern to others than imitators ourselves. Its administration favours the many instead of the few; this is why it is called a democracy. If we look to the laws, they afford equal justice to all in their private differences; if no social standing, advancement in public life falls to reputation for capacity, class considerations not being allowed to interfere with merit; nor again does poverty bar the way, if a man is able to serve the state, he is not hindered by the obscurity of his condition. The freedom which we enjoy in our government extends also to our ordinary life. There, far from exercising a jealous surveillance over each other, we do not feel called upon to be angry with our neighbour for doing what he likes, or even to indulge in those injurious looks which cannot fail to be offensive, although they inflict no positive penalty. But all this ease in our private relations does not make us lawless as citizens. Against this fear is our chief safeguard, teaching us to obey the magistrates and the laws, particularly such as regard the protection of the injured, whether they are actually on the statute book, or belong to that code which, although unwritten, yet cannot be broken without acknowledged disgrace.

"Further, we provide plenty of means for the mind to refresh itself from business. We celebrate games and sacrifices all the year round, and the elegance of our private establishments forms a daily source of pleasure and helps to banish the spleen; while the magnitude of our city draws the produce of the world into our harbour, so that to the Athenian the fruits of other countries are as familiar a luxury as those of his own.

"If we turn to our military policy, there also we differ from our antagonists. We throw open our city to the world, and never by alien acts exclude foreigners from any opportunity of learning or observing, although the eyes of an enemy may occasionally profit by our liberality; trusting less in system and policy than to the native spirit of our citizens; while in education, where our rivals from their very cradles by a painful discipline seek after manliness, at Athens we live exactly as we please, and yet are just as ready to encounter every legitimate danger. In proof of this it may be noticed that the Lacedaemonians do not invade our country alone, but bring with them all their confederates; while we Athenians advance unsupported into the territory of a neighbour, and fighting upon a foreign soil usually vanquish with ease men who are defending their homes. Our united force was never yet encountered by any enemy, because we have at once to attend to our marine and to dispatch our citizens by land upon a hundred different services; so that, wherever they engage with some such fraction of our strength, a success against a detachment is magnified into a victory over the nation, and a defeat into a reverse suffered at the hands of our entire people. And yet if with habits not of labour but of ease, and courage not of art but of nature, we are still willing to encounter danger, we have the double advantage of escaping the experience of hardships in anticipation and of facing them in the hour of need as fearlessly as those who are never free from them.

"Nor are these the only points in which our city is worthy of admiration. We cultivate refinement without extravagance and knowledge without effeminacy; wealth we employ more for use than for show, and place the real disgrace of poverty not in owning to the fact but in declining the struggle against it. Our public men have, besides politics, their private affairs to attend to, and our ordinary citizens, though occupied with the pursuits of industry, are still fair judges of public matters; for, unlike any other nation, regarding him who takes no part in these duties not as unambitious but as useless, we Athenians are able to judge at all events if we cannot originate, and, instead of looking on discussion as a stumbling-block in the way of action, we think it an indispensable preliminary to any wise action at all. Again, in our enterprises we present the singular spectacle of daring and deliberation, each carried to its highest point, and both united in the same persons; although usually decision is the fruit of ignorance, hesitation of reflection. But the palm of courage will surely be adjudged most justly to those, who best know the difference between hardship and pleasure and yet are never tempted to shrink from danger. In generosity we are equally singular, acquiring our friends by conferring, not by receiving, favours. Yet, of course, the doer of the favour is the firmer friend of the two, in order by continued kindness to keep the recipient in his debt; while the debtor feels less keenly from the very consciousness that the return he makes will be a payment, not a free gift. And it is only the Athenians, who, fearless of consequences, confer their benefits not from calculations of expediency, but in the confidence of liberality.

"In short, I say that as a city we are the school of Hellas, while I doubt if the world can produce a man who, where he has only himself to depend upon, is equal to so many emergencies, and graced by so happy a versatility, as the Athenian. And that this is no mere boast thrown out for the occasion, but plain matter of fact, the power of the state acquired by these habits proves. For Athens alone of her contemporaries is found when tested to be greater than her reputation, and alone gives no occasion to her assailants to blush at the antagonist by whom they have been worsted, or to her subjects to question her title by merit to rule. Rather, the admiration of the present and succeeding ages will be ours, since we have not left our power without witness, but have shown it by mighty proofs; and far from needing a Homer for our panegyrist, or other of his craft whose verses might charm for the moment only for the impression which they gave to melt at the touch of fact, we have forced every sea and land to be the highway of our daring, and everywhere, whether for evil or for good, have left imperishable monuments behind us. Such is the Athens for which these men, in the assertion of their resolve not to lose her, nobly fought and died; and well may every one of their survivors be ready to suffer in her cause.

"Indeed if I have dwelt at some length upon the character of our country, it has been to show that our stake in the struggle is not the same as theirs who have no such blessings to lose, and also that the panegyric of the men over whom I am now speaking might be by definite proofs established. That panegyric is now in a great measure complete; for the Athens that I have celebrated is only what the heroism of these and their like have made her, men whose fame, unlike that of most Hellenes, will be found to be only commensurate with their deserts. And if a test of worth be wanted, it is to be found in their closing scene, and this not only in cases in which it set the final seal upon their merit, but also in those in which it gave the first intimation of their having any. For there is justice in the claim that steadfastness in his country's battles should be as a cloak to cover a man's other imperfections; since the good action has blotted out the bad, and his merit as a citizen more than outweighed his demerits as an individual. But none of these allowed either wealth with its prospect of future enjoyment to unnerve his spirit, or poverty with its hope of a day of freedom and riches to tempt him to shrink from danger. No, holding that vengeance upon their enemies was more to be desired than any personal blessings, and reckoning this to be the most glorious of hazards, they joyfully determined to accept the risk, to make sure of their vengeance, and to let their wishes wait; and while committing to hope the uncertainty of final success, in the business before them they thought fit to act boldly and trust in themselves. Thus choosing to die resisting, rather than to live submitting, they fled only from dishonour, but met danger face to face, and after one brief moment, while at the summit of their fortune, escaped, not from their fear, but from their glory.

"So died these men as became Athenians. You, their survivors, must determine to have as unfaltering a resolution in the field, though you may pray that it may have a happier issue. And not contented with ideas derived only from words of the advantages which are bound up with the defence of your country, though these would furnish a valuable text to a speaker even before an audience so alive to them as the present, you must yourselves realize the power of Athens, and feed your eyes upon her from day to day, till love of her fills your hearts; and then, when all her greatness shall break upon you, you must reflect that it was by courage, sense of duty, and a keen feeling of honour in action that men were enabled to win all this, and that no personal failure in an enterprise could make them consent to deprive their country of their valour, but they laid it at her feet as the most glorious contribution that they could offer. For this offering of their lives made in common by them all they each of them individually received that renown which never grows old, and for a sepulchre, not so much that in which their bones have been deposited, but that noblest of shrines wherein their glory is laid up to be eternally remembered upon every occasion on which deed or story shall call for its commemoration. For heroes have the whole earth for their tomb; and in lands far from their own, where the column with its epitaph declares it, there is enshrined in every breast a record unwritten with no tablet to preserve it, except that of the heart. These take as your model and, judging happiness to be the fruit of freedom and freedom of valour, never decline the dangers of war. For it is not the miserable that would most justly be unsparing of their lives; these have nothing to hope for: it is rather they to whom continued life may bring reverses as yet unknown, and to whom a fall, if it came, would be most tremendous in its consequences. And surely, to a man of spirit, the degradation of cowardice must be immeasurably more grievous than the unfelt death which strikes him in the midst of his strength and patriotism!

"Comfort, therefore, not condolence, is what I have to offer to the parents of the dead who may be here. Numberless are the chances to which, as they know, the life of man is subject; but fortunate indeed are they who draw for their lot a death so glorious as that which has caused your mourning, and to whom life has been so exactly measured as to terminate in the happiness in which it has been passed. Still

I know that this is a hard saying, especially when those are in question of whom you will constantly be reminded by seeing in the homes of others blessings of which once you also boasted: for grief is felt not so much for the want of what we have never known, as for the loss of that to which we have been long accustomed. Yet you who are still of an age to beget children must bear up in the hope of having others in their stead; not only will they help you to forget those whom you have lost, but will be to the state at once a reinforcement and a security; for never can a fair or just policy be expected of the citizen who does not, like his fellows, bring to the decision the interests and apprehensions of a father. While those of you who have passed your prime must congratulate yourselves with the thought that the best part of your life was fortunate, and that the brief span that remains will be cheered by the fame of the departed. For it is only the love of honour that never grows old; and honour it is, not gain, as some would have it, that rejoices the heart of age and helplessness.

"Turning to the sons or brothers of the dead, I see an arduous struggle before you. When a man is gone, all are wont to praise him, and should your merit be ever so transcendent, you will still find it difficult not merely to overtake, but even to approach their renown. The living have envy to contend with, while those who are no longer in our path are honoured with a goodwill into which rivalry does not enter. On the other hand, if I must say anything on the subject of female excellence to those of you who will now be in widowhood, it will be all comprised in this brief exhortation. Great will be your glory in not falling short of your natural character; and greatest will be hers who is least talked of among the men, whether for good or for bad.

"My task is now finished. I have performed it to the best of my ability, and in word, at least, the requirements of the law are now satisfied. If deeds be in question, those who are here interred have received part of their honours already, and for the rest, their children will be brought up till manhood at the public expense: the state thus offers a valuable prize, as the garland of victory in this race of valour, for the reward both of those who have fallen and their survivors. And where the rewards for merit are greatest, there are found the best citizens.

"And now that you have brought to a close your lamentations for your relatives, you may depart."

CHAPTER VII

Second Year of the War—The Plague of Athens— Position and Policy of Pericles—Fall of Potidaea

Such was the funeral that took place during this winter, with which the first year of the war came to an end. In the first days of summer the Lacedaemonians and their allies, with two-thirds of their forces as before, invaded Attica, under the command of Archidamus, son of Zeuxidamus, King of Lacedaemon, and sat down and laid waste the country. Not many days after their arrival in Attica the plague first began to show itself among the Athenians. It was said that it had broken out in many places previously in the neighbourhood of Lemnos and elsewhere; but a pestilence of such extent and mortality was nowhere remembered. Neither were the physicians at first of any service, ignorant as they were of the proper way to treat it, but they died themselves the most thickly, as they visited the sick most often; nor did any human art succeed any better. Supplications in the temples, divinations, and so forth were found equally futile, till the overwhelming nature of the disaster at last put a stop to them altogether.

It first began, it is said, in the parts of Ethiopia above Egypt, and thence descended into Egypt and Libya and into most of the King's country. Suddenly falling upon Athens, it first attacked the population in Piraeus—which was the occasion of their saying that the Peloponnesians had poisoned the reservoirs, there being as yet no wells there—and afterwards appeared in the upper city, when the deaths became much more frequent. All speculation as to its origin and its causes, if causes can be found adequate to produce so great a disturbance, I leave to other writers, whether lay or professional; for myself, I shall simply set down its nature, and explain the symptoms by which perhaps it may be recognized by the student, if it should ever break out again. This I can the better do, as I had the disease myself, and watched its operation in the case of others.

That year then is admitted to have been otherwise unprecedentedly free from sickness; and such few cases as occurred all determined in this. As a rule, however, there was no ostensible cause; but people in good health were all of a sudden attacked by violent heats in the head, and redness and inflammation in the eyes, the inward parts, such as the throat or tongue, becoming bloody and emitting an unnatural and fetid breath. These symptoms were followed by sneezing and hoarseness, after which the pain soon reached the chest, and produced a hard cough. When it fixed in the stomach, it upset it; and discharges of bile of every kind named by physicians ensued, accompanied by very great distress. In most cases also an ineffectual retching followed, producing violent spasms, which in some cases ceased soon after, in others much later. Externally the body was not very hot to the touch, nor pale in its appearance, but reddish, livid, and breaking out into small pustules and ulcers. But internally it burned so that the patient could not bear to have on him clothing or linen even of the very lightest description; or indeed to be otherwise than stark naked. What they would have liked best would have been to throw themselves into cold water; as indeed was done by some of the neglected sick, who plunged into the rain-tanks in their agonies of unquenchable thirst; though it made no difference whether they drank little or much. Besides this, the miserable feeling of not being able to rest or sleep never ceased to torment them. The body meanwhile did not waste away so long as the distemper was at its height, but held out to a marvel against its ravages; so that when they succumbed, as in most cases, on the seventh or eighth day to the internal inflammation, they had still some strength in them. But if they passed this stage, and the disease descended further into the bowels, inducing a violent ulceration there accompanied by severe diarrhoea, this brought on a weakness which was generally fatal. For the disorder first settled in the head, ran its course from thence through the whole of the body, and, even where it did not prove mortal, it still left its mark on the extremities; for it settled in the privy parts, the fingers and the toes, and many escaped with the loss of these, some too with that of their eyes. Others again were seized with an entire loss of memory on their first recovery, and did not know either themselves or their friends.

But while the nature of the distemper was such as to baffle all description, and its attacks almost too grievous for human nature to endure, it was still in the following circumstance that its difference from all ordinary disorders was most clearly shown. All the birds and beasts that prey upon human bodies, either abstained from touching them (though there were many lying unburied), or died after tasting them. In proof of this, it was noticed that birds of this kind actually disappeared; they were not about the bodies, or indeed to be seen at all. But of course the effects which I have mentioned could best be studied in a domestic animal like the dog.

Such then, if we pass over the varieties of particular cases which were many and peculiar, were the general features of the distemper. Meanwhile the town enjoyed an immunity from all the ordinary disorders; or if any case occurred, it ended in this. Some died in neglect, others in the midst of every attention. No remedy was found that could be used as a specific; for what did good in one case, did harm in another. Strong and weak constitutions proved equally incapable of resistance, all alike being swept away, although dieted with the utmost precaution. By far the most terrible feature in the malady was the dejection which ensued when any one felt himself sickening, for the despair into which they instantly fell took away their power of resistance, and left them a much easier prey to the disorder; besides which, there was the awful spectacle of men dying like sheep, through having caught the infection in nursing each other. This caused the greatest mortality. On the one hand, if they were afraid to visit each other, they perished from neglect; indeed many houses were emptied of their inmates for want of a nurse: on the other, if they ventured to do so, death was the consequence. This was especially the case with such as made any pretensions to goodness: honour made them unsparing of themselves in their attendance in their friends' houses, where even the members of the family were at last worn out by the moans of the dying, and succumbed to the force of the disaster. Yet it was with those who had recovered from the disease that the sick and the dying found most compassion.

These knew what it was from experience, and had now no fear for themselves; for the same man was never attacked twice—never at least fatally. And such persons not only received the congratulations of others, but themselves also, in the elation of the moment, half entertained the vain hope that they were for the future safe from any disease whatsoever.

An aggravation of the existing calamity was the influx from the country into the city, and this was especially felt by the new arrivals. As there were no houses to receive them, they had to be lodged at the hot season of the year in stifling cabins, where the mortality raged without restraint. The bodies of dying men lay one upon another, and half-dead creatures reeled about the streets and gathered round all the fountains in their longing for water. The sacred places also in which they had quartered themselves were full of corpses of persons that had died there, just as they were; for as the disaster passed all bounds, men, not knowing what was to become of them, became utterly careless of everything, whether sacred or profane. All the burial rites before in use were entirely upset, and they buried the bodies as best they could. Many from want of the proper appliances, through so many of their friends having died already, had recourse to the most shameless sepultures: sometimes getting the start of those who had raised a pile, they threw their own dead body upon the stranger's pyre and ignited it; sometimes they tossed the corpse which they were carrying on the top of another that was burning, and so went off.

Nor was this the only form of lawless extravagance which owed its origin to the plague. Men now coolly ventured on what they had formerly done in a corner, and not just as they pleased, seeing the rapid transitions produced by persons in prosperity suddenly dying and those who before had nothing succeeding to their property. So they resolved to spend quickly and enjoy themselves, regarding their lives and riches as alike things of a day. Perseverance in what men called honour was popular with none, it was so uncertain whether they would be spared to attain the object; but it was settled that present enjoyment, and all that contributed to it, was both honourable and useful. Fear of gods or law of man there was none to restrain them. As for the first, they judged it to be just the same whether they worshipped them or not, as they saw all alike perishing; and for the last, no one expected to live to be brought to trial for his offences, but each felt that a far severer sentence had been already passed upon them all and hung ever over their heads, and before this fell it was only reasonable to enjoy life a little.

Such was the nature of the calamity, and heavily did it weigh on the Athenians; death raging within the city and devastation without. Among other things which they remembered in their distress was, very naturally, the following verse which the old men said had long ago been uttered:

A Dorian war shall come and with it death.

So a dispute arose as to whether dearth and not death had not been the word in the verse; but at the present juncture, it was of course decided in favour of the latter; for the people made their recollection fit in with their sufferings. I fancy, however, that if another Dorian war should ever afterwards come upon us, and a dearth should happen to accompany it, the verse will probably be read accordingly. The oracle also which had been given to the Lacedaemonians was now remembered by those who knew of it. When the god was asked whether they should go to war, he answered that if they put their might into it, victory would be theirs, and that he would himself be with them. With this oracle events were supposed to tally. For the plague broke out as soon as the Peloponnesians invaded Attica, and never entering Peloponnese (not at least to an extent worth noticing), committed its worst ravages at Athens, and next to Athens, at the most populous of the other towns. Such was the history of the plague.

After ravaging the plain, the Peloponnesians advanced into the Paralian region as far as Laurium, where the Athenian silver mines are, and first laid waste the side looking towards Peloponnese, next that which faces Euboea and Andros. But Pericles, who was still general, held the same opinion as in the former invasion, and would not let the Athenians march out against them.

However, while they were still in the plain, and had not yet entered the Paralian land, he had prepared

an armament of a hundred ships for Peloponnese, and when all was ready put out to sea. On board the ships he took four thousand Athenian heavy infantry, and three hundred cavalry in horse transports, and then for the first time made out of old galleys; fifty Chian and Lesbian vessels also joining in the expedition. When this Athenian armament put out to sea, they left the Peloponnesians in Attica in the Paralian region. Arriving at Epidaurus in Peloponnese they ravaged most of the territory, and even had hopes of taking the town by an assault: in this however they were not successful. Putting out from Epidaurus, they laid waste the territory of Troezen, Halieis, and Hermione, all towns on the coast of Peloponnese, and thence sailing to Prasiai, a maritime town in Laconia, ravaged part of its territory, and took and sacked the place itself; after which they returned home, but found the Peloponnesians gone and no longer in Attica.

During the whole time that the Peloponnesians were in Attica and the Athenians on the expedition in their ships, men kept dying of the plague both in the armament and in Athens. Indeed it was actually asserted that the departure of the Peloponnesians was hastened by fear of the disorder; as they heard from deserters that it was in the city, and also could see the burials going on. Yet in this invasion they remained longer than in any other, and ravaged the whole country, for they were about forty days in Attica.

The same summer Hagnon, son of Nicias, and Cleopompus, son of Clinias, the colleagues of Pericles, took the armament of which he had lately made use, and went off upon an expedition against the Chalcidians in the direction of Thrace and Potidaea, which was still under siege. As soon as they arrived, they brought up their engines against Potidaea and tried every means of taking it, but did not succeed either in capturing the city or in doing anything else worthy of their preparations. For the plague attacked them here also, and committed such havoc as to cripple them completely, even the previously healthy soldiers of the former expedition catching the infection from Hagnon's troops; while Phormio and the sixteen hundred men whom he commanded only escaped by being no longer in the neighbourhood of the Chalcidians. The end of it was that Hagnon returned with his ships to Athens, having lost one thousand and fifty out of four thousand heavy infantry in about forty days; though the soldiers stationed there before remained in the country and carried on the siege of Potidaea.

After the second invasion of the Peloponnesians a change came over the spirit of the Athenians. Their land had now been twice laid waste; and war and pestilence at once pressed heavy upon them. They began to find fault with Pericles, as the author of the war and the cause of all their misfortunes, and became eager to come to terms with Lacedaemon, and actually sent ambassadors thither, who did not however succeed in their mission. Their despair was now complete and all vented itself upon Pericles. When he saw them exasperated at the present turn of affairs and acting exactly as he had anticipated, he called an assembly, being (it must be remembered) still general, with the double object of restoring confidence and of leading them from these angry feelings to a calmer and more hopeful state of mind. He accordingly came forward and spoke as follows:

"I was not unprepared for the indignation of which I have been the object, as I know its causes; and I have called an assembly for the purpose of reminding you upon certain points, and of protesting against your being unreasonably irritated with me, or cowed by your sufferings. I am of opinion that national greatness is more for the advantage of private citizens, than any individual well-being coupled with public humiliation. A man may be personally ever so well off, and yet if his country be ruined he must be ruined with it; whereas a flourishing commonwealth always affords chances of salvation to unfortunate individuals. Since then a state can support the misfortunes of private citizens, while they cannot support hers, it is surely the duty of every one to be forward in her defence, and not like you to be so confounded with your domestic afflictions as to give up all thoughts of the common safety, and to blame me for having counselled war and yourselves for having voted it. And yet if you are angry with me, it is with one who, as I believe, is second to no man either in knowledge of the proper policy, or in the ability to expound it, and who is moreover not only a patriot but an honest one. A man possessing that knowledge without

that faculty of exposition might as well have no idea at all on the matter: if he had both these gifts, but no love for his country, he would be but a cold advocate for her interests; while were his patriotism not proof against bribery, everything would go for a price. So that if you thought that I was even moderately distinguished for these qualities when you took my advice and went to war, there is certainly no reason now why I should be charged with having done wrong.

"For those of course who have a free choice in the matter and whose fortunes are not at stake, war is the greatest of follies. But if the only choice was between submission with loss of independence, and danger with the hope of preserving that independence, in such a case it is he who will not accept the risk that deserves blame, not he who will. I am the same man and do not alter, it is you who change, since in fact you took my advice while unhurt, and waited for misfortune to repent of it; and the apparent error of my policy lies in the infirmity of your resolution, since the suffering that it entails is being felt by every one among you, while its advantage is still remote and obscure to all, and a great and sudden reverse having befallen you, your mind is too much depressed to persevere in your resolves. For before what is sudden, unexpected, and least within calculation, the spirit quails; and putting all else aside, the plague has certainly been an emergency of this kind. Born, however, as you are, citizens of a great state, and brought up, as you have been, with habits equal to your birth, you should be ready to face the greatest disasters and still to keep unimpaired the lustre of your name. For the judgment of mankind is as relentless to the weakness that falls short of a recognized renown, as it is jealous of the arrogance that aspires higher than its due. Cease then to grieve for your private afflictions, and address yourselves instead to the safety of the commonwealth.

"If you shrink before the exertions which the war makes necessary, and fear that after all they may not have a happy result, you know the reasons by which I have often demonstrated to you the groundlessness of your apprehensions. If those are not enough, I will now reveal an advantage arising from the greatness of your dominion, which I think has never yet suggested itself to you, which I never mentioned in my previous speeches, and which has so bold a sound that I should scarce adventure it now, were it not for the unnatural depression which I see around me. You perhaps think that your empire extends only over your allies; I will declare to you the truth. The visible field of action has two parts, land and sea. In the whole of one of these you are completely supreme, not merely as far as you use it at present, but also to what further extent you may think fit: in fine, your naval resources are such that your vessels may go where they please, without the King or any other nation on earth being able to stop them. So that although you may think it a great privation to lose the use of your land and houses, still you must see that this power is something widely different; and instead of fretting on their account, you should really regard them in the light of the gardens and other accessories that embellish a great fortune, and as, in comparison, of little moment. You should know too that liberty preserved by your efforts will easily recover for us what we have lost, while, the knee once bowed, even what you have will pass from you. Your fathers receiving these possessions not from others, but from themselves, did not let slip what their labour had acquired, but delivered them safe to you; and in this respect at least you must prove yourselves their equals, remembering that to lose what one has got is more disgraceful than to be balked in getting, and you must confront your enemies not merely with spirit but with disdain. Confidence indeed a blissful ignorance can impart, ay, even to a coward's breast, but disdain is the privilege of those who, like us, have been assured by reflection of their superiority to their adversary. And where the chances are the same, knowledge fortifies courage by the contempt which is its consequence, its trust being placed, not in hope, which is the prop of the desperate, but in a judgment grounded upon existing resources, whose anticipations are more to be depended upon.

"Again, your country has a right to your services in sustaining the glories of her position. These are a common source of pride to you all, and you cannot decline the burdens of empire and still expect to share its honours. You should remember also that what you are fighting against is not merely slavery as an exchange for independence, but also loss of empire and danger from the animosities incurred in

its exercise. Besides, to recede is no longer possible, if indeed any of you in the alarm of the moment has become enamoured of the honesty of such an unambitious part. For what you hold is, to speak somewhat plainly, a tyranny; to take it perhaps was wrong, but to let it go is unsafe. And men of these retiring views, making converts of others, would quickly ruin a state; indeed the result would be the same if they could live independent by themselves; for the retiring and unambitious are never secure without vigorous protectors at their side; in fine, such qualities are useless to an imperial city, though they may help a dependency to an unmolested servitude.

"But you must not be seduced by citizens like these or angry with me—who, if I voted for war, only did as you did yourselves—in spite of the enemy having invaded your country and done what you could be certain that he would do, if you refused to comply with his demands; and although besides what we counted for, the plague has come upon us—the only point indeed at which our calculation has been at fault. It is this, I know, that has had a large share in making me more unpopular than I should otherwise have been—quite undeservedly, unless you are also prepared to give me the credit of any success with which chance may present you. Besides, the hand of heaven must be borne with resignation, that of the enemy with fortitude; this was the old way at Athens, and do not you prevent it being so still. Remember, too, that if your country has the greatest name in all the world, it is because she never bent before disaster; because she has expended more life and effort in war than any other city, and has won for herself a power greater than any hitherto known, the memory of which will descend to the latest posterity; even if now, in obedience to the general law of decay, we should ever be forced to yield, still it will be remembered that we held rule over more Hellenes than any other Hellenic state, that we sustained the greatest wars against their united or separate powers, and inhabited a city unrivalled by any other in resources or magnitude. These glories may incur the censure of the slow and unambitious; but in the breast of energy they will awake emulation, and in those who must remain without them an envious regret. Hatred and unpopularity at the moment have fallen to the lot of all who have aspired to rule others; but where odium must be incurred, true wisdom incurs it for the highest objects. Hatred also is short-lived; but that which makes the splendour of the present and the glory of the future remains for ever unforgotten. Make your decision, therefore, for glory then and honour now, and attain both objects by instant and zealous effort: do not send heralds to Lacedaemon, and do not betray any sign of being oppressed by your present sufferings, since they whose minds are least sensitive to calamity, and whose hands are most quick to meet it, are the greatest men and the greatest communities."

Such were the arguments by which Pericles tried to cure the Athenians of their anger against him and to divert their thoughts from their immediate afflictions. As a community he succeeded in convincing them; they not only gave up all idea of sending to Lacedaemon, but applied themselves with increased energy to the war; still as private individuals they could not help smarting under their sufferings, the common people having been deprived of the little that they were possessed, while the higher orders had lost fine properties with costly establishments and buildings in the country, and, worst of all, had war instead of peace. In fact, the public feeling against him did not subside until he had been fined. Not long afterwards, however, according to the way of the multitude, they again elected him general and committed all their affairs to his hands, having now become less sensitive to their private and domestic afflictions, and understanding that he was the best man of all for the public necessities. For as long as he was at the head of the state during the peace, he pursued a moderate and conservative policy; and in his time its greatness was at its height. When the war broke out, here also he seems to have rightly gauged the power of his country. He outlived its commencement two years and six months, and the correctness of his previsions respecting it became better known by his death. He told them to wait quietly, to pay attention to their marine, to attempt no new conquests, and to expose the city to no hazards during the war, and doing this, promised them a favourable result. What they did was the very contrary, allowing private ambitions and private interests, in matters apparently quite foreign to the war, to lead them into projects unjust both to themselves and to their

allies—projects whose success would only conduce to the honour and advantage of private persons, and whose failure entailed certain disaster on the country in the war. The causes of this are not far to seek. Pericles indeed, by his rank, ability, and known integrity, was enabled to exercise an independent control over the multitude—in short, to lead them instead of being led by them; for as he never sought power by improper means, he was never compelled to flatter them, but, on the contrary, enjoyed so high an estimation that he could afford to anger them by contradiction. Whenever he saw them unseasonably and insolently elated, he would with a word reduce them to alarm; on the other hand, if they fell victims to a panic, he could at once restore them to confidence. In short, what was nominally a democracy became in his hands government by the first citizen. With his successors it was different. More on a level with one another, and each grasping at supremacy, they ended by committing even the conduct of state affairs to the whims of the multitude. This, as might have been expected in a great and sovereign state, produced a host of blunders, and amongst them the Sicilian expedition; though this failed not so much through a miscalculation of the power of those against whom it was sent, as through a fault in the senders in not taking the best measures afterwards to assist those who had gone out, but choosing rather to occupy themselves with private cabals for the leadership of the commons, by which they not only paralysed operations in the field, but also first introduced civil discord at home. Yet after losing most of their fleet besides other forces in Sicily, and with faction already dominant in the city, they could still for three years make head against their original adversaries, joined not only by the Sicilians, but also by their own allies nearly all in revolt, and at last by the King's son, Cyrus, who furnished the funds for the Peloponnesian navy. Nor did they finally succumb till they fell the victims of their own intestine disorders. So superfluously abundant were the resources from which the genius of Pericles foresaw an easy triumph in the war over the unaided forces of the Peloponnesians.

During the same summer the Lacedaemonians and their allies made an expedition with a hundred ships against Zacynthus, an island lying off the coast of Elis, peopled by a colony of Achaeans from Peloponnese, and in alliance with Athens. There were a thousand Lacedaemonian heavy infantry on board, and Cnemus, a Spartan, as admiral. They made a descent from their ships, and ravaged most of the country; but as the inhabitants would not submit, they sailed back home.

At the end of the same summer the Corinthian Aristeus, Aneristus, Nicolaus, and Stratodemus, envoys from Lacedaemon, Timagoras, a Tegean, and a private individual named Pollis from Argos, on their way to Asia to persuade the King to supply funds and join in the war, came to Sitalces, son of Teres in Thrace, with the idea of inducing him, if possible, to forsake the alliance of Athens and to march on Potidaea then besieged by an Athenian force, and also of getting conveyed by his means to their destination across the Hellespont to Pharnabazus, who was to send them up the country to the King. But there chanced to be with Sitalces some Athenian ambassadors—Learchus, son of Callimachus, and Ameiniades, son of Philemon—who persuaded Sitalces' son, Sadocus, the new Athenian citizen, to put the men into their hands and thus prevent their crossing over to the King and doing their part to injure the country of his choice. He accordingly had them seized, as they were travelling through Thrace to the vessel in which they were to cross the Hellespont, by a party whom he had sent on with Learchus and Ameiniades, and gave orders for their delivery to the Athenian ambassadors, by whom they were brought to Athens. On their arrival, the Athenians, afraid that Aristeus, who had been notably the prime mover in the previous affairs of Potidaea and their Thracian possessions, might live to do them still more mischief if he escaped, slew them all the same day, without giving them a trial or hearing the defence which they wished to offer, and cast their bodies into a pit; thinking themselves justified in using in retaliation the same mode of warfare which the Lacedaemonians had begun, when they slew and cast into pits all the Athenian and allied traders whom they caught on board the merchantmen round Peloponnese. Indeed, at the outset of the war, the Lacedaemonians butchered as enemies all whom they took on the sea, whether allies of Athens or neutrals.

About the same time towards the close of the summer, the Ambraciot forces, with a number of barbarians that they had raised, marched against the Amphilochian Argos and the rest of that country. The origin of their enmity against the Argives was this. This Argos and the rest of Amphilochia were colonized by Amphilochus, son of Amphiaraus. Dissatisfied with the state of affairs at home on his return thither after the Trojan War, he built this city in the Ambracian Gulf, and named it Argos after his own country. This was the largest town in Amphilochia, and its inhabitants the most powerful. Under the pressure of misfortune many generations afterwards, they called in the Ambraciots, their neighbours on the Amphilochian border, to join their colony; and it was by this union with the Ambraciots that they learnt their present Hellenic speech, the rest of the Amphilochians being barbarians. After a time the Ambraciots expelled the Argives and held the city themselves. Upon this the Amphilochians gave themselves over to the Acarnanians; and the two together called the Athenians, who sent them Phormio as general and thirty ships; upon whose arrival they took Argos by storm, and made slaves of the Ambraciots; and the Amphilochians and Acarnanians inhabited the town in common. After this began the alliance between the Athenians and Acarnanians. The enmity of the Ambraciots against the Argives thus commenced with the enslavement of their citizens; and afterwards during the war they collected this armament among themselves and the Chaonians, and other of the neighbouring barbarians. Arrived before Argos, they became masters of the country; but not being successful in their attacks upon the town, returned home and dispersed among their different peoples.

Such were the events of the summer. The ensuing winter the Athenians sent twenty ships round Peloponnese, under the command of Phormio, who stationed himself at Naupactus and kept watch against any one sailing in or out of Corinth and the Crissaean Gulf. Six others went to Caria and Lycia under Melesander, to collect tribute in those parts, and also to prevent the Peloponnesian privateers from taking up their station in those waters and molesting the passage of the merchantmen from Phaselis and Phoenicia and the adjoining continent. However, Melesander, going up the country into Lycia with a force of Athenians from the ships and the allies, was defeated and killed in battle, with the loss of a number of his troops.

The same winter the Potidaeans at length found themselves no longer able to hold out against their besiegers. The inroads of the Peloponnesians into Attica had not had the desired effect of making the Athenians raise the siege. Provisions there were none left; and so far had distress for food gone in Potidaea that, besides a number of other horrors, instances had even occurred of the people having eaten one another. In this extremity they at last made proposals for capitulating to the Athenian generals in command against them—Xenophon, son of Euripides, Hestiodorus, son of Aristocleides, and Phanomachus, son of Callimachus. The generals accepted their proposals, seeing the sufferings of the army in so exposed a position; besides which the state had already spent two thousand talents upon the siege. The terms of the capitulation were as follows: a free passage out for themselves, their children, wives and auxiliaries, with one garment apiece, the women with two, and a fixed sum of money for their journey. Under this treaty they went out to Chalcidice and other places, according as was their power. The Athenians, however, blamed the generals for granting terms without instructions from home, being of opinion that the place would have had to surrender at discretion. They afterwards sent settlers of their own to Potidaea, and colonized it. Such were the events of the winter, and so ended the second year of this war of which Thucydides was the historian.

PLUTARCH, THE PARALLEL LIVES

5 [1]The Lacedaemonians missed Lycurgus sorely, and sent for him many times. They felt that their kings were such in name and station merely, but in everything else were nothing better than their subjects, while in him there was a nature fitted to lead, and a power to make men follow him. However, not even the kings were averse to having him at home, but hoped that in his presence their subjects would treat them with less insolence. [2]Returning, then, to a people thus disposed, he at once undertook to revolutionize the civil polity. He was convinced that a partial change of the laws would be of no avail whatsoever, but that he must proceed as a physician would with a patient who was debilitated and full of all sorts of diseases; he must reduce and alter the existing temperament by means of drugs and purges, and introduce a new and different regimen. [3]Full of this determination, he first made a journey to Delphi, and after sacrificing to the god and consulting the oracle, he returned with that famous response in which the Pythian priestess addressed him as "beloved of the gods, and rather god than man," and said that the god had granted p219 his prayer for good laws, and promised him a constitution which should be the best in the world.

[4]Thus encouraged, he tried to bring the chief men of Sparta over to his side, and exhorted them to put their hands to the work with him, explaining his designs secretly to his friends at first, then little by little engaging more and uniting them to attempt the task. And when the time for action came, he ordered thirty of the chief men to go armed into the marketplace at break of day, to strike consternation and terror into those of the opposite party. The names of twenty of the most eminent among them have been recorded by Hermippus; but the man who had the largest share in all the undertakings of Lycurgus and co-operated with him in the enactment of his laws, bore the name of Arthmiadas. [5]When the tumult began, King Charilaüs, fearing that the whole affair was a conspiracy against himself, fled for refuge to the Brazen House;[5] but he was soon convinced of his error, and having exacted oaths for his safety from the agitators, left his place of refuge, and even joined them in their enterprise, being of a gentle and yielding disposition, so much so, indeed, that Archelaüs, his royal colleague, is said to have remarked to those who were extolling the young king, "How can Charilaüs be a good man, when he has no severity even for the bad?"

[6]Among the many innovations which Lycurgus made, the first and most important was his institution of a senate, or Council of Elders, which, as Plato says,[6] by being blended with the "feverish" government of the kings, and by having an equal vote with them in matters of the highest importance, p221 brought safety and due moderation into counsels of state. For before this the civil polity was veering and unsteady, inclining at one time to follow the kings towards tyranny, and at another to follow the multitude towards democracy; [7]but now, by making the power of the senate a sort of ballast for the ship of state and putting her on a steady keel, it achieved the safest and the most orderly arrangement, since the twenty-eight senators always took the side of the kings when it was a question of curbing democracy, and, on the other hand, always strengthened the people to withstand the encroachments of tyranny. The number of the senators was fixed at twenty-eight because, according to Aristotle, two of the thirty original associates of Lycurgus abandoned the enterprise from lack of courage. [8]But Sphaerus says that this was originally the number of those who shared the confidence of Lycurgus. Possibly there is some virtue in this number being made up of seven multiplied by four, apart from the fact that, being equal to the sum of its own factors, it is the next perfect number after

six. But in my own opinion, Lycurgus made the senators of just that number in order that the total might be thirty 43 when the two kings were added to the eight and twenty.

6 ¹So eager was Lycurgus for the establishment of this form of government, that he obtained an oracle from Delphi about it, which they call a "rhetra." And this is the way it runs: "When thou hast built a temple to Zeus Syllanius and Athena Syllania, divided the people into 'phylai' and into 'obai,' and established a senate of thirty members, including the 'archagetai,' then from time to time p223 'appellazein' between Babyca⁷ᵃ and Cnacion,⁷ᵇ and there introduce and rescind measures; but the people must have the deciding voice and the power." ²In these clauses, the "phylai" and the "obai" refer to divisions and distributions of the people into *clans* and *phratries*, or *brotherhoods*; by "archagetai" the *kings* are designated, and "appellazein" means *to assemble* the people, with a reference to *Apollo*, the Pythian god, who was the source and author of the polity. The Babyca is now called Cheimarrus, and the Cnacion Oenus; but Aristotle says that Cnacion is a river, and Babyca a bridge. ³Between these they held their assemblies, having neither halls nor any other kind of building for the purpose. For by such things Lycurgus thought good counsel was not promoted, but rather discouraged, since the serious purposes of an assembly were rendered foolish and futile by vain thoughts, as they gazed upon statues and paintings, or scenic embellishments, or extravagantly decorated roofs of council halls. When the multitude was thus assembled, no one of them was permitted to make a motion, but the motion laid before them by the senators and kings could be accepted or rejected by the people. ⁴Afterwards, however, when the people by additions and subtractions perverted and distorted the sense of motions laid before them, Kings Polydorus and Theopompus inserted this clause into the rhetra: "But if the people should adopt a distorted motion, the senators and kings shall have power of adjournment"; that is, should not ratify the vote, but dismiss outright and dissolve the session, on the p225 ground that it was perverting and changing the motion contrary to the best interests of the state. ⁵And they were actually able to persuade the city that the god authorized

this addition to the rhetra, as Tyrtaeus reminds us in these verses:—

> "Phoebus Apollo's the mandate was which they brought from Pytho, Voicing the will of the god, nor were his words unfulfilled: Sway in the council and honours divine belong to the princes Under whose care has been set Sparta's city of charm; Second to them are the elders, and next come the men of the people Duly confirming by vote unperverted decrees."

7 ¹Although Lycurgus thus tempered his civil polity, nevertheless the oligarchical element in it was still unmixed and dominant, and his successors, seeing it "swelling and foaming," as Plato says,⁸ "imposed as it were a curb upon it, namely, the power of the ephors." It was about a hundred and thirty years after Lycurgus that the first ephors, Elatus and his colleagues, were appointed, in the reign of Theopompus. ²This king, they say, on being reviled by his wife because the royal power, when he handed it over to his sons, would be less than when he received it, said: "Nay, but greater, in that it will last longer." And in fact, by renouncing excessive claims and freeing itself from jealous hate, royalty at Sparta escaped its perils, so that the Spartan kings did not experience the fate which the p227 Messenians and Argives inflicted upon their kings, who were unwilling to yield at all or remit their power in favour of the people. And this brings into the clearest light the wisdom and foresight of Lycurgus, when we contrast the factions and misgovernment of the peoples and kings of Messenia and Argos, who were kinsmen and neighbours of the Spartans. ³They were on an equality with the Spartans in the beginning, and in the allotment of territory were thought to be even better off than they, and yet their prosperity did not last long, but what with the insolent temper of their kings and the unreasonableness of their peoples, their established institutions were confounded, 44and they made it clear that it was in very truth a divine blessing which the Spartans had enjoyed in the man who framed and tempered their civil polity for them. These events, however, were of later date.

8 ¹A second, and a very bold political measure of Lycurgus, isº his redistribution of the land. For there was a dreadful inequality in this regard, the city was

heavily burdened with indigent and helpless people, and wealth was wholly concentrated in the hands of a few. Determined, therefore, to banish insolence and envy and crime and luxury, and those yet more deep-seated and afflictive diseases of the state, poverty and wealth, [2]he persuaded his fellow-citizens to make one parcel of all their territory and divide it up anew, and to live with one another on a basis of entire uniformity and equality in the means of subsistence, seeking preëminence through virtue alone, assured that there was no other difference or inequality between man p229 and man than that which was established by blame for base actions and praise for good ones.

[3]Suiting the deed to the word, he distributed the rest of the Laconian land among the "perioeci," or free provincials, in thirty thousand lots, and that which belonged to the city of Sparta, in nine thousand lots, to as many genuine Spartans. But some say that Lycurgus distributed only six thousand lots among the Spartans, and that three thousand were afterwards added by Polydorus; others still, that Polydorus added half of the nine thousand to the half distributed by Lycurgus. [4]The lot of each was large enough to produce annually seventy bushels of barley for a man and twelve for his wife, with a proportionate amount of wine and oil. Lycurgus thought that a lot of this size would be sufficient for them, since they needed sustenance enough to promote vigour and health of body, and nothing else. And it is said that on returning from a journey some time afterwards, as he traversed the land just after the harvest, and saw the heaps of grain standing parallel and equal to one another, he smiled, and said to them that were by: "All Laconia looks like a family estate newly divided among many brothers."

9 [1]Next, he undertook to divide up their movable property also, in order that every vestige of unevenness and inequality might be removed; and when he saw that they could not bear to have it taken from them directly, he took another course, and overcame their avarice by political devices. In the first place, he withdrew all gold and silver money from currency, and ordained the use of iron money only.[a] Then to a great weight and mass of this he gave a trifling p231 value, so that ten minas' worth[9] required a large store-room in the house, and a yoke of cattle to transport it. [2]When this money obtained currency, many sorts of iniquity went into exile from Lacedaemon. For who would steal, or receive as a bribe, or rob, or plunder that which could neither be concealed, nor possessed with satisfaction, nay, nor even cut to pieces with any profit? For vinegar was used, as we are told, to quench the red-hot iron, robbing it of its temper and making it worthless for any other purpose, when once it had become brittle and hard to work.

[3]In the next place, he banished the unnecessary and superfluous arts. And even without such banishment most of them would have departed with the old coinage, since there was no sale for their products. For the iron money could not be carried into the rest of Greece, nor had it any value there, but was rather held in ridicule. It was not possible, therefore, to buy any foreign wares or bric-à-brac; no merchant-seamen brought freight into their harbours; no rhetoric teacher set foot on Laconian soil, no vagabond soothsayer, no keeper of harlots, no gold- or silver-smith, since there was no money there. [4]But luxury, thus gradually deprived of that which stimulated and supported it, died away of itself, 45 and men of large possessions had no advantage over the poor, because their wealth found no public outlet, but had to be stored up at home in idleness. In this way it came about that such common and necessary utensils as bedsteads, chairs, and tables were most excellently made among them, and the Laconian "kothon," or drinking-cup, was in very high repute p233 for usefulness among soldiers in active service, as Critias tells us. [5]For its colour concealed the disagreeable appearance of the water which they were often compelled to drink, and its curving lips caught the muddy sediment and held it inside, so that only the purer part reached the mouth of the drinker. For all this they had to thank their lawgiver; since their artisans were now freed from useless tasks, and displayed the beauty of their workmanship in objects of constant and necessary use.

10 [1]With a view to attack luxury still more and remove the thirst for wealth, he introduced his third and most exquisite political device, namely, the institution of common messes, so that they might eat with

one another in companies, of common and specified foods, and not take their meals at home, reclining on costly couches at costly tables, delivering themselves into the hands of servants and cooks to be fattened in the dark, like voracious animals, ²and ruining not only their characters but also their bodies, by surrendering them to every desire and all sorts of surfeit, which call for long sleeps, hot baths, abundant rest, and, as it were, daily nursing and tending. This was surely a great achievement, but it was a still greater one to make wealth "an object of no desire," as Theophrastus says, and even "unwealth,"¹⁰ by this community of meals and simplicity of diet. ³For the rich man could neither use nor enjoy nor even see or display his abundant means, when he went to the same meal as the poor man; so that it was in Sparta alone, of all the cities under the sun, that men could have that far-famed sight, a Plutus blind, and lying as lifeless p235 and motionless as a picture. For the rich could not even dine beforehand at home and then go to the common mess with full stomachs, but the rest kept careful watch of him who did not eat and drink with them, and reviled him as a weakling, and one too effeminate for the common diet.

11 ¹It was due, therefore, to this last political device above all, that the wealthy citizens were incensed against Lycurgus, and banding together against him, denounced him publicly with angry shouts and cries; finally many pelted him with stones, so that he ran from the market-place. He succeeded in reaching sanctuary before the rest laid hands on him; but one young man, Alcander, otherwise no mean nature, but hasty and passionate, pressed hard upon him, and put out one of his eyes. ²Lycurgus, however, was far from yielding in consequence of this calamity, but confronted his countrymen, and showed them his face besmeared with blood and his eye destroyed. Whereupon they were so filled with shame and sorrow at the sight, that they placed Alcander in his hands, and conducted him to his house with sympathetic indignation. Lycurgus commended them for their conduct, and dismissed them, but took Alcander into the house with him, where he did the youth no harm by word or deed, but after sending away his customary servants and attendants, ordered him to minister to his wants. ³The youth, who was

of a noble disposition, did as he was commanded, without any words, and abiding thus with Lycurgus, and sharing his daily life, he came to know the gentleness of the man, the calmness of his spirit, the rigid simplicity of his habits, and his p237 unwearied industry. He thus became a devoted follower of Lycurgus, and used to tell his intimates and friends that the man was not harsh nor self-willed, as he had supposed, 46but the mildest and gentlest of them all. ⁴Such, then, was the chastisement of this young man, and such the penalty laid upon him, namely, to become, instead of a wild and impetuous youth, a most decorous and discreet man. Lycurgus, moreover, in memory of his misfortune, built a temple to Athena Optilitis, so called from "optilus," which is the local Doric word for *eye*. Some writers, however, of whom one is Dioscorides, who wrote a treatise on the Spartan civil polity, say that although Lycurgus was struck in the eye, his eye was not blinded, but he built the temple to the goddess as a thank-offering for its healing. Be that as it may, the Spartan practice of carrying staves into their assemblies was abandoned after this unfortunate accident.

12 ¹As for the public messes, the Cretans call them "andreia," but the Lacedaemonians, "phiditia," either because they are conducive to *friendship* and friendliness, "phiditia" being equivalent to "philitia"; or, because they accustom men to simplicity and *thrift*, for which their word is "pheido." But it is quite possible, as some say, that the first letter of the word "phiditia" has been added to it, making "phiditia" out of "editia," which refers merely to meals and *eating*. ²They met in companies of fifteen, a few more or less, and each one of the mess-mates contributed monthly a bushel of barley-meal, eight gallons of wine, five pounds of cheese, two and a half pounds of figs, and in addition to this, a very small sum of money for such relishes as flesh and fish. Besides this, whenever any one made a p239 sacrifice of first fruits, or brought home game from the hunt, he sent a portion to his mess. For whenever any one was belated by a sacrifice or the chase, he was allowed to sup at home, but the rest had to be at the mess. ³For a long time this custom of eating at common mess-tables was rigidly observed. For instance, when King Agis, on returning from an expedition in which he

had been victorious over the Athenians, wished to sup at home with his wife, and sent for his rations, the polemarchs[11] refused to send them to him; and when on the following day his anger led him to omit the customary sacrifice, they laid a fine upon him.

[4]Boys also used to come to these public messes, as if they were attending schools of sobriety; there they would listen to political discussions and see instructive models of liberal breeding. There they themselves also became accustomed to sport and jest without scurrility, and to endure jesting without displeasure. Indeed, it seems to have been especially characteristic of a Spartan to endure jesting; but if any one could not bear up under it, he had only to ask it, and the jester ceased. [5]As each one came in, the eldest of the company pointed to the door and said to him: "Through that door no word goes forth outside." And they say that a candidate for membership in one of these messes underwent the following ordeal. Each of the mess-mates took in his hand a bit of soft bread, and when a servant came along with a bowl upon his head, then they cast it into this without a word, like a ballot, leaving it just as it was if he approved of the candidate, but if he disapproved, squeezing it tight in his hand first. [6]For the flattened piece p241 of bread had the force of a perforated, or negative, ballot. And if one such is found in the bowl, the candidate is not admitted to the mess, because they wish all its members to be congenial. The candidate thus rejected is said to have been "caddished," for "caddichus"[12] is the name of the bowl into which they cast the pieces of bread. Of their dishes, the black broth is held in the highest esteem, so that the elderly men do not even ask for a bit of meat, but leave it for the young men, while they themselves have the broth poured out for their meals. [7]And it is said that one of the kings of Pontus actually bought a Spartan cook for the sake of having this broth, and then, when he tasted it, disliked it; whereupon the cooks said: "O King, those who relish this broth must first have bathed in the river Eurotas." After drinking moderately, they go off home without a torch; for they are not allowed to walk with a light, either on this or any other occasion, that they may accustom themselves to marching boldly and without fear in the darkness of night. Such, then, is the fashion of their common messes.

13 [1]None of his laws were put into writing by Lycurgus, indeed, one of the so-called "rhetras" forbids it. For he thought that if the most important and binding principles which conduce to the prosperity and virtue of a city were implanted in the habits and training of its citizens, they would remain unchanged and secure, having a stronger bond than compulsion in the fixed purposes imparted to the young by education, which performs the office of a law-giver for every one of them. [2]And as for minor p243 matters, such as business contracts, and cases where the needs vary from time to time, it was better, as he thought, not to hamper them by written constraints or fixed usages, but to suffer them, as occasion demanded, to receive such modifications as educated men should determine. Indeed, he assigned the function of law-making wholly and entirely to education.

[3]One of his rhetras accordingly, as I have said, prohibited the use of written laws. Another was directed against extravagance, ordaining that every house should have its roof fashioned by the axe, and its doors by the saw only, and by no other tool. For, as in later times Epaminondas is reported to have said at his own table, that such a meal did not comport with treachery, so Lycurgus was the first to see clearly that such a house does not comport with luxury and extravagance. [4]Nor is any man so vulgar and senseless as to introduce into a simple and common house silver-footed couches, purple coverlets, gold drinking-cups, and all the extravagance which goes along with these, but one must of necessity adapt and proportion his couch to his house, his coverlets to the couch, and to this the rest of his supplies and equipment. [5]It was because he was used to this simplicity that Leotychides the Elder, as we are told, when he was dining in Corinth, and saw the roof of the house adorned with costly panellings, asked his host if trees grew square in that country.

A third rhetra of Lycurgus is mentioned, which forbids making frequent expeditions against the same p245 enemies, in order not to accustom such enemies to frequent defence of themselves, which would make them warlike. [6]And this was the special grievance which they had against King Agesilaüs in later times, namely, that by his continual and frequent incursions and expeditions into Boeotia he rendered the Thebans a match for the Lacedaemonians. And therefore, when Antalcidas saw the king wounded, he said: "This is a fine tuition-fee which thou art getting from the Thebans, for teaching them how to fight, when they did not wish to do it, and did not know how." Such ordinances as these were called "rhetras" by Lycurgus, implying that they came from the god and were oracles.

14 [1]In the matter of education, which he regarded as the greatest and noblest task of the law-giver, he began at the very source, by carefully regulating marriages and births. For it is not true that, as Aristotle says,[13] he tried to bring the women under proper restraint, but desisted, because he could not overcome the great licence and power which the women enjoyed on account of the many expeditions in which their husbands were engaged. During these the men were indeed obliged to leave their wives in sole control at home, and for this reason paid them greater deference than was their due, and gave them the title of Mistress. But even to the women Lycurgus paid all possible attention. [2]He made the maidens exercise their bodies in running, wrestling, casting the discus, and hurling the javelin, in order that the fruit of their wombs might have vigorous root in vigorous bodies and come to better maturity, and that they themselves p247 might come with vigour to the fulness of their times, and struggle successfully and easily with the pangs of child-birth. He freed them from softness and delicacy and all effeminacy by accustoming the maidens no less than the youths to wear tunics only in processions, 48and at certain festivals to dance and sing when the young men were present as spectators. [3]There they sometimes even mocked and railed good-naturedly at any youth who had misbehaved himself; and again they would sing the praises of those who had shown themselves worthy, and so inspire the young men with great ambition and ardour. For he who was thus extolled for his valour and held in honour among the maidens, went away exalted by their praises; while the sting of their playful raillery was no less sharp than that of serious admonitions, especially as the kings and senators, together with the rest of the citizens, were all present at the spectacle.

[4]Nor was there anything disgraceful in this scant clothing of the maidens, for modesty attended them,

and wantonness was banished; nay, rather, it produced in them habits of simplicity and an ardent desire for health and beauty of body. It gave also to woman-kind a taste of lofty sentiment, for they felt that they too had a place in the arena of bravery and ambition. Wherefore they were led to think and speak as Gorgo, the wife of Leonidas, is said to have done. When some foreign woman, as it would seem, said to her: "You Spartan women are the only ones who rule their men," she answered: "Yes, we are the only ones that give birth to men."

15 [1]Moreover, there were incentives to marriage in these things, — I mean such things as the appearance p249 of the maidens without much clothing in processions and athletic contests where young men were looking on, for these were drawn on by necessity, "not geometrical, but the sort of necessity which lovers know," as Plato says.[14] Nor was this all; Lycurgus also put a kind of public stigma upon confirmed bachelors. They were excluded from the sight of the young men and maidens at their exercises, and in winter the magistrates ordered them to march round the market-place in their tunics only,[2] and as they marched, they sang a certain song about themselves, and its burden was that they were justly punished for disobeying the laws. Besides this, they were deprived of the honour and gracious attentions which the young men habitually paid to their elders. Therefore there was no one to find fault with what was said to Dercyllidas, reputable general though he was. As he entered a company, namely, one of the younger men would not offer him his seat, but said: "Indeed, thou hast begotten no son who will one day give his seat to me."

[3]For their marriages the women were carried off by force, not when they were small and unfit for wed-lock, but when they were in full bloom and wholly ripe. After the woman was thus carried off, the bride's-maid, so called, took her in charge, cut her hair off close to the head, put a man's cloak and san-dals on her, and laid her down on a pallet, on the floor, alone, in the dark. Then the bride-groom, not flown with wine nor enfeebled by excesses, but com-posed and sober, after supping at his public mess-table as usual, slipped stealthily into the room where the bride lay, loosed her virgin's zone, and bore her

p251 in his arms to the marriage-bound. [4]Then, after spending a short time with his bride, he went away composedly to his usual quarters, there to sleep with the other young men. And so he continued to do from that time on, spending his days with his comrades, and sleeping with them at night, but visiting his bride by stealth and with every precaution, full of dread and fear lest any of her household should be aware of his visits, his bride also contriving and conspiring with him that they might have stolen interviews as occasion offered. [5]And this they did not for a short time only, but long enough for some of them to become fathers before they had looked upon their own wives by daylight. Such interviews not only brought into exercise self-restraint and moderation, but united husbands and wives when their bodies were full of creative energy and their affections new and fresh, not when they were sated and dulled by unrestricted intercourse; and there was always left behind in their hearts some residual spark of longing and delight.

496 After giving marriage such traits of reserve and decorum, he none the less freed men from the empty and womanish passion of jealous possession, by making it honourable for them, while keeping the marriage relation free from all wanton irregularities, to share with other worthy men in the begetting of children, laughing to scorn those who regard such common privileges as intolerable, and resort to murder and war rather than grant them. [7]For example, an elderly man with a young wife, if he looked with favour and esteem on some fair and noble young man, might introduce him to her, and adopt her offspring by such a noble father as his p253 own. And again, a worthy man who admired some woman for the fine children that she bore her husband and the modesty of her behaviour as a wife, might enjoy her favours, if her husband would consent, thus planting, as it were, in a soil of bountiful fruitage, and begetting for himself noble sons, who would have the blood of noble men in their veins. [8]For in the first place, Lycurgus did not regard sons as the peculiar property of their fathers, but rather as the common property of the state, and therefore would not have his citizens spring from random parentage, but from the best there was. In the second place, he saw much folly and vanity in what other peoples enacted for the regulation of these matters; in the breeding of dogs and horses they insist on having the best sires which money or favour can secure, but they keep their wives under lock and key, demanding that they have children by none but themselves, even though they be foolish, or infirm, or diseased; [9]as though children of bad stock did not show their badness to those first who possessed and reared them, and children of good stock, contrariwise, their goodness. The freedom which thus prevailed at that time in marriage relations was aimed at physical and political well-being, and was far removed from the licentiousness which was afterwards attributed to their women, so much so that adultery was wholly unknown among them. [10]And a saying is reported of one Geradas,[15] a Spartan of very ancient type, who, on being asked by a stranger what the punishment for adulterers was among them, answered: "Stranger, p255 there is no adulterer among us." "Suppose, then," replied the stranger, "there should be one." "A bull," said Geradas, "would be his forfeit, a bull so large that it could stretch over Mount Taÿgetus and drink from the river Eurotas." Then the stranger was astonished and said: "But how could there be a bull so large?" To which Geradas replied, with a smile: "But how could there be an adulterer in Sparta?" Such, then, are the accounts we find of their marriages.

16 [1]Offspring was not reared at the will of the father, but was taken and carried by him to a place called Lesche,[b1] where the elders of the tribes officially examined the infant, and if it was well-built and sturdy, they ordered the father to rear it, and assigned it one of the nine thousand lots of land; but if it was ill-born and deformed, they sent it to the so-called Apothetae, a chasm-like place at the foot of Mount Taÿgetus, [2]in the conviction that the life of that which nature had not well equipped at the very beginning for health and strength, was of no advantage either to itself or the state. On the same principle, the women used to bathe their new-born babes not with water, but with wine, thus making a sort of test of their constitutions. For it is said that epileptic and sickly infants are thrown into convulsions by the strong wine and loose their senses, while the healthy ones are rather tempered by it, like steel, and given a firm habit of body. [3]Their nurses, too, exercised great care and skill; they reared infants without

swaddling-bands, and thus left their limbs and figures free to develop; besides, they taught them to be contented and happy, not dainty about their food, nor fearful of the dark, nor afraid to be left alone, p257 nor given to contemptible peevishness and whimpering. This is the reason why foreigners sometimes brought Spartan nurses for their children. Amycla, for instance, the nurse of the Athenian Alcibiades, is said to have been a Spartan.[16]

[4]And yet Alcibiades, as Plato says,[17] had for a tutor, set over him by Pericles, one Zopyrus, who was just a common slave. 50But Lycurgus would not put the sons of Spartans in charge of purchased or hired tutors, nor was it lawful for every father to rear or train his son as he pleased, but as soon as they were seven years old, Lycurgus ordered them all to be taken by the state and enrolled in companies, where they were put under the same discipline and nurture, and so became accustomed to share one another's sports and studies. [5]The boy who excelled in judgement and was most courageous in fighting, was made captain of his company; on him the rest all kept their eyes, obeying his orders, and submitting to his punishments, so that their boyish training was a practice of obedience. Besides, the elderly men used to watch their sports, and by ever and anon egging them on to mimic battles and disputes, learned accurately how each one of them was naturally disposed when it was a question of boldness and aggressiveness in their struggles.

[6]Of reading and writing, they learned only enough to serve their turn; all the rest of their training was calculated to make them obey commands well, endure hardships, and conquer in battle. Therefore, as they grew in age, their bodily exercise was increased; their heads were close-clipped, and they p259 were accustomed to going bare-foot, and to playing for the most part without clothes. When they were twelve years old, they no longer had tunics to wear, received one cloak a year, had hard, dry flesh, and knew little of baths and ointments; only on certain days of the year, and few at that, did they indulge in such amenities. [7]They slept together, in troops and companies, on pallet-beds which they collected for themselves, breaking off with their hands — no knives

allowed — the tops of the rushes which grew along the river Eurotas. In the winter-time, they added to the stuff of these pallets the so-called "lycophon," or *thistle-down*, which was thought to have warmth in it.

17 [1]When the boys reached this age, they were favoured with the society of lovers from among the reputable young men. The elderly men also kept close watch of them, coming more frequently to their places of exercises, and observing their contests of strength and wit, not cursorily, but with the idea that they were all in a sense the fathers and tutors and governors of all the boys. In this way, at every fitting time and in every place, the boy who went wrong had someone to admonish and chastise him. Nor was this all; [2]one of the noblest and best men of the city was appointed paedonome, or inspector of the boys, and under his directions the boys, in their several companies, put themselves under the command of the most prudent and warlike of the so-called Eirens. This was the name given to those who had been for two years out of the class of boys, and Melleirens, or *Would-be Eirens*, was the name for the oldest of the boys. This eiren, then, a youth of twenty years, commands his subordinates in their p261 mimic battles, and in doors makes them serve him at his meals. [3]He commissions the larger ones to fetch wood, and the smaller ones potherbs. And they steal what they fetch, some of them entering the gardens, and others creeping right slyly and cautiously into the public messes of the men; but if a boy is caught stealing, he is soundly flogged, as a careless and unskilful thief. They steal, too, whatever food they can, and learn to be adept in setting upon people when asleep or off their guard. [4]But the boy who is caught gets a flogging and must go hungry. For the meals allowed them are scanty, in order that they may take into their own hands the fight against hunger, and so be forced into boldness and cunning.

This is the main object of their spare diet; a secondary one is to make them grow tall. For it contributes to height of stature when the vitality is not impeded and hindered by a mass of nourishment which forces it into thickness and width, 51but ascends of its own lightness, and when the body grows freely and easily. [5]The same thing seems also to conduce to beauty of form; for lean and meagre habits yield more readily to the force of articulation, whereas the gross and over-fed are so heavy as to resist it. Just so, we may be sure, women who take physic while they are pregnant, bear children which are lean, it may be, but well-shaped and fine, because the lightness of the parent matter makes it more susceptible to moulding. However, the reason for this I must leave for others to investigate.

18 ¹à e boys make such a serious matter of their stealing, that one of them, as the story goes, p263 who was carrying concealed under his cloak a young fox which he had stolen,ᶜ suffered the animal to tear out his bowels with its teeth and claws, and died rather than have his theft detected. And even this story gains credence from what their youths now endure, many of whom I have seen expiring under the lash at the altar of Artemis Orthia.ᵈ

²The eiren, as he reclined after supper, would order one of the boys to sing a song, and to another would put a question requiring a careful and deliberate answer, as, for instance, "Who is the best man in the city?" or, "What thinkest thou of this man's conduct?" In this way the boys were accustomed to pass right judgements and interest themselves at the very outset in the conduct of the citizens. For if one of them was asked who was a good citizen, or who an infamous one, and had no answer to make, he was judged to have a torpid spirit, and one that would not aspire to excellence. ³And the answer must not only have reasons and proof given for it, but also be couched in very brief and concise language, and the one who gave a faulty answer was punished with a bite in the thumb from the eiren. Often-times, too, the eiren punished the boys in the presence of the elders and magistrates, thus showing whether his punishments were reasonable and proper or not. While he was punishing them, he suffered no restraint, but after the boys were gone, he was brought to an account if his punishments were harsher than was necessary, or, on the other hand, too mild and gentle.

524 The boys' lovers also shared with them in their honour or disgrace; and it is said that one of them p265 was once fined by the magistrates because his favourite boy had let an ungenerous cry escape him

while he was fighting. Moreover, though this sort of love was so approved among them that even the maidens found lovers in good and noble women, still, there was no jealous rivalry in it, but those who fixed their attentions on the same boys made this rather a foundation for friendship with one another, and persevered in common efforts to make their loved one as noble as possible.

19 ¹The boys were also taught to use a discourse which combined pungency with grace, and condensed much observation into a few words. His iron money, indeed, Lycurgus made of large weight and small value, as I have observed,¹⁸ but the current coin of discourse he adapted to the expression of deep and abundant meaning with simple and brief diction, by contriving that the general habit of silence should make the boys sententious and correct in their answers. For as sexual incontinence generally produces unfruitfulness and sterility, so intemperance in talking makes discourse empty and vapid. ²King Agis, accordingly, when a certain Athenian decried the Spartan swords for being so short, and said that jugglers on the stage easily swallowed them, replied: "And yet we certainly reach our enemies with these daggers." And I observe that although the speech also of the Spartans seems short, yet it certainly reaches the point, and arrests the thought of the listener.

³And indeed Lycurgus himself seems to have been p267 short and sententious in his speech, if we may judge from his recorded sayings; that, for instance, on forms of self-government, to one who demanded the establishment of democracy in the city: "Go thou," said he, "and first establish democracy in thy household." That, again, to one who inquired why he ordained such small and inexpensive sacrifices: "That we may never omit," said he, "to honour the gods." ⁴Again, in the matter of athletic contests, he allowed the citizens to engage only in those where there was no stretching forth of hands. ¹⁹There are also handed down similar answers which he made by letter to his fellow-citizens. When they asked how they could ward off an invasion of enemies, he answered: "By remaining poor, and by not desiring to be greater the one than the other." And when they asked about fortifying their city, he answered: "A city will be well

fortified which is surrounded by brave men and not by bricks." Now regarding these and similar letters, belief and scepticism are alike difficult.

20 [1]Of their aversion to long speeches, the following apophthegms are proof. King Leonidas, when a certain one discoursed with him out of all season on matters of great concern, said: "My friend, the matter urges, but not the time." Charilaüs, the nephew of Lycurgus, when asked why his uncle had made so few laws, answered: "Men of few words need few laws." [2]Archidamidas, when certain ones found fault with Hecataeus the Sophist for saying nothing after being admitted to their public mess, answered: "He who knows how, knows also when to speak." Instances of the pungent sayings p269 not devoid of grace, of which I spoke,[20] are the following. Demaratus, when a troublesome fellow was pestering him with ill-timed questions, and especially with the oft repeated query who was the best of the Spartans, answered at last: "He who is least like thee." [3]And Agis, when certain ones were praising the Eleians for their just and honourable conduct of the Olympic games, said: "And what great matter is it for the Eleians to practise righteousness one day in five years?"[e] And Theopompus, when a stranger kept saying, as he showed him kindness, that in his own city he was called a lover of Sparta, remarked: "My good Sir, it were better for thee to be called a lover of thine own city." [4]And Pleistoanax, the son of Pausanias, when an Athenian orator declared that the Lacedaemonians had no learning, said: "True, we are indeed the only Hellenes who have learned no evil from you." And Archidamus, when some one asked him how many Spartans there were, replied: "Enough, good Sir, to keep evil men away."

[5]And even from their jests it is possible to judge of their character. For it was their wont never to talk at random, and to let slip no speech which did not have some thought or other worth serious attention. For instance, when one of them was invited to hear a man imitate the nightingale, he said: "I have heard the bird herself." And another, on reading the epitaph:—

> "Tyranny's fires they were trying to quench when panoplied Ares Slew them; Selinus looked down from her gates on their death,"

p271 said: "The men deserved to die; they should have let the fires burn out entirely." [6]And a youth, when some one promised to give him game-cocks that would die fighting, said, "Don't do that, but give me some of the kind that kill fighting." Another, seeing men seated on stools in a privy, said: "May I never sit where I cannot give place to an elder." The character of their apophthegms, then, was such as to justify the remark that love of wisdom rather than love of bodily exercise was the special characteristic of a Spartan.

21 [1]Nor was their training in music and poetry any less serious a concern than the emulous purity of their speech, nay, their very songs had a stimulus that roused the spirit and awoke enthusiastic and effectual effort; the style of them was simple and unaffected, and their themes were serious and edifying. They were for the most part praises of men who had died for Sparta, calling them blessed and happy; censure of men who had played the coward, picturing their grievous and ill-starred life; and such promises and boasts of valour as befitted the different ages. [2]Of the last, it may not be amiss to cite one, by way of illustration. They had three choirs at their festivals, corresponding to the three ages, and the choir of old men would sing first:—

> "We once did deeds of prowess and were strong young men."

Then the choir of young men would respond:—

> "We are so now, and if you wish, behold and see."

And then the third choir, that of the boys, would sing:—

> "We shall be sometime mightier men by far than both."

[3]In short, if one studies the poetry of Sparta, of which some specimens were still extant in my time, and makes himself familiar with the marching songs which they used, to the accompaniment of the flute, when charging upon their foes, he will conclude that Terpander and Pindar were right in associating valour with music. The former writes thus of the Lacedaemonians:—

> "Flourish there both the spear of the brave and the Muse's clear message, Justice, too, walks the broad streets —."

[4]And Pindar says:—[21]

> "There are councils of Elders, And young men's conquering spears, And dances, the Muse, and joyousness."

The Spartans are thus shown to be at the same time most musical and most warlike;

> "In equal poise to match the sword hangs the sweet art of the harpist,"

as their poet says. For just before their battles, the king sacrificed to the Muses, reminding his warriors, as it would seem, of their training, and of the firm p275 decisions they had made, in order that they might be prompt to face the dread issue, and might perform such martial deeds as would be worthy of some record.[22]

22 [1]In time of war, too, they relaxed the severity of the young men's discipline, and permitted them to beautify their hair and ornament their arms and clothing, rejoicing to see them, like horses, prance and neigh for the contest. Therefore they wore their hair long as soon as they ceased to be youths, and particularly in times of danger they took pains to have it glossy and well-combed, remembering a certain saying of Lycurgus, that a fine head of hair made the handsome more comely still, and the ugly more terrible. [2]Their bodily exercises, too, were less rigorous during their campaigns, and in other ways their young warriors were allowed a regimen which was less curtailed and rigid, so that they were the only men in the world with whom war brought a respite in the training for war. And when at last they were drawn up in battle array and the enemy was at hand, the king sacrificed the customary she-goat, commanded all the warriors to set garlands upon their heads, and ordered the pipers to pipe the strains of the hymn to Castor; [3]then he himself led off in a marching paean, and it was a sight equally grand and terrifying when they marched in step with the rhythm of the flute, without any gap in their line of battle, and with no confusion in their souls, but calmly and cheerfully moving with the strains of their hymn into the deadly fight. Neither fear nor excessive fury is likely to possess men so disposed, p277 but rather a firm purpose full of hope and courage, believing as they do that Heaven is their ally.

[4]The king marched against the enemy in close companionship with one who had been crowned victor in the great games. 54And they tell of a certain Spartan who refused to be bought off from a contest at Olympia by large sums of money, and after a long struggle outwrestled his antagonist. When some one said to him then: "What advantage, O Spartan, hast thou got from thy victory? he answered, with a smile: "I shall stand in front of my king when I fight our enemies." [5]When they had conquered and routed an enemy, they pursued him far enough to make their victory secure by his flight, and then at once retired, thinking it ignoble and unworthy of a Hellene to hew men to pieces who had given up the fight and abandoned the field. And this was not only a noble and magnanimous policy, but it was also useful. For their antagonists, knowing that they slew those who resisted them, but showed mercy to those who yielded to them, were apt to think flight more advantageous than resistance.

23 [1]Hippias the Sophist says that Lycurgus himself was very well versed in war and took part in many campaigns, and Philostephanus attributes to him the arrangement of the Spartan cavalry by "oulamoi," explaining that the "oulamos," as constituted by him, was a troop of fifty horsemen in a square formation. But Demetrius the Phalerean says he engaged in no warlike undertakings, and established his constitution in a time of peace. [2]And indeed the design of the Olympic truce would seem to bespeak a man of gentleness, and predisposed to peace. And yet there are some who say, as Hermippus reminds us, that at the outset Lycurgus had nothing whatever to do with Iphitus and his enterprise, but happened to come that way by chance, and be a spectator at the games; that he heard behind him, however, what seemed to be a human voice, chiding him and expressing amazement that he did not urge his fellow-citizens to take part in the great festival; and since, on turning round, he did not see the speaker anywhere, he concluded that the voice was from heaven, and therefore betook himself to Iphitus, and assisted him in giving

the festival a more notable arrangement and a more enduring basis.

24 [1]The training of the Spartans lasted into the years of full maturity. No man was allowed to live as he pleased, but in their city, as in a military encampment, they always had a prescribed regimen and employment in public service, considering that they belonged entirely to their country and not to themselves, watching over the boys, if no other duty was laid upon them, and either teaching them some useful thing, or learning it themselves from their elders. [2]For one of the noble and blessed privileges which Lycurgus provided for his fellow-citizens, was abundance of leisure, since he forbade their engaging in any mechanical art whatsoever, and as for money-making, with its laborious efforts to amass wealth, there was no need of it at all, since wealth awakened no envy and brought no honour. [3]Besides, the Helots tilled their ground for them, and paid them the produce mentioned above.[23] Therefore it was that one of them who was sojourning at Athens when the courts were in session, and learned that a certain p281 Athenian had been fined for idleness and was going home in great distress of mind and attended on his way by sympathetic and sorrowing friends, begged the bystanders to show him the man who had been fined for living like a freeman. So servile a thing did they regard the devotion to the mechanical arts and to money-making. [4]And law-suits, of course, vanished from among them with their gold and silver coinage, for they knew neither greed nor want, but equality in well-being was established there, and easy living based on simple wants. Choral dances and feasts and festivals and hunting and bodily exercise and social converse occupied their whole time, when they were not on a military expedition.

25 [1]Those who were under thirty years of age did not go into the market-place at all,55but had their household wants supplied at the hands of their kinsfolk and lovers. And it was disreputable for the elderly men to be continually seen loitering there, instead of spending the greater part of the day in the places of exercise that are called "leschai."[24]For if they gathered in these, they spent their time suitably with one another, making no allusions to the problems of money-making or of exchange, [2]nay, they were chiefly occupied there in praising some noble action or censuring some base one, with jesting and laughter which made the path to instruction and correction easy and natural. For not even Lycurgus himself was immoderately severe; indeed, Sosibius tells us that he actually dedicated a little statue of Laughter, and introduced seasonable jesting into their drinking parties and like p283 diversions, to sweeten, as it were, their hardships and meagre fare.

[3]In a word, he trained his fellow-citizens to have neither the wish nor the ability to live for themselves; but like bees they were to make themselves always integral parts of the whole community, clustering together about their leader, almost beside themselves with enthusiasm and noble ambition, and to belong wholly to their country. This idea can be traced also in some of their utterances. [4]For instance, Paedaretus, when he failed to be chosen among the three hundred best men, went away with a very glad countenance, as if rejoicing that the city had three hundred better men than himself. And again, Polycratidas, one of an embassy to the generals of the Persian king, on being asked by them whether the embassy was there in a private or a public capacity, replied: "If we succeed, in a public capacity; if we fail, in a private." [5]Again, Argileonis, the mother of Brasidas, when some Amphipolitans who had come to Sparta paid her a visit, asked them if Brasidas had died nobly and in a manner worthy of Sparta. Then they greatly extolled the man and said that Sparta had not such another, to which she answered: "Say not so, Strangers; Brasidas was noble and brave, but Sparta has many better men than he."

26 [1]The senators were at first appointed by Lycurgus himself, as I have said,[25] from those who shared his counsels; but afterwards he arranged that any vacancy caused by death should be filled by the man elected as most deserving out of those above sixty years of age. And of all the contests in p285 the world this would seem to have been the greatest and the most hotly disputed. For it was not the swiftest of the swift, nor the strongest of the strong, but the best and wisest of the good and wise who was to be elected, and have for the rest of his life, as a victor's prize for excellence, what I may call the supreme power in the state, lord as he was of life and death,

honour and dishonour, and all the greatest issues of life. ²The election was made in the following manner. An assembly of the people having been convened, chosen men were shut up in a room near by so that they could neither see nor be seen, but only hear the shouts of the assembly. For as in other matters, so here, the cries of the assembly decided between the competitors. These did not appear in a body, but each one was introduced separately, as the lot fell, and passed silently through the assembly. ³Then the secluded judges, who had writing-tablets with them, recorded in each case the loudness of the shouting, not knowing for whom it was given, but only that he was introduced first, second, or third, and so on. Whoever was greeted with the most and loudest shouting, him they declared elected. The victor then set a wreath upon his head and visited in order the temples of the gods. He was followed by great numbers of young men, who praised and extolled him, as well as by many women, who celebrated his excellence in songs, and dwelt on the happiness of his life. 564 Each of his relations and friend set a repast before him, saying: "The city honours thee with this table." When he had finished his circuit, he went off to his mess-table. Here he fared in other ways as usual, but a second portion of food was set before him, p287 which he took and put by. After the supper was over, the women who were related to him being now assembled at the door of the mess-hall, he called to him the one whom he most esteemed and gave her the portion he had saved, saying that he had received it as a meed of excellence, and as such gave it to her. Upon this, she too was lauded by the rest of the women and escorted by them to her home.

27 ¹Furthermore, Lycurgus made most excellent regulations in the matter of their burials. To begin with, he did away with all superstitious terror by allowing them to bury their dead within the city, and to have memorials of them near the sacred places, thus making the youth familiar with such sights and accustomed to them, so that they were not confounded by them, and had no horror of death as polluting those who touched a corpse or walked among graves. In the second place, he permitted nothing to be buried with the dead; they simply covered the body with a scarlet robe and olive leaves when they laid it away. ²To inscribe the name of the dead upon the tomb was not allowed, unless it were that of a man who had fallen in war, or that of a woman who had died in sacred office. He set apart only a short time for mourning, eleven days; on the twelfth, they were to sacrifice to Demeter and cease their sorrowing. Indeed, nothing was left untouched and neglected, but with all the necessary details of life he blended some commendation of virtue or rebuke of vice; and he filled the city full of good examples, whose continual presence and society must of necessity exercise a controlling and moulding influence upon those who were walking the path of honour.

³This was the reason why he did not permit them to live abroad at their pleasure and wander in strange lands, assuming foreign habits and imitating the lives of peoples who were without training and lived under different forms of government. Nay more, he actually drove away from the city the multitudes which streamed in there for no useful purpose, not because he feared they might become imitators of his form of government and learn useful lessons in virtue, as Thucydides says,²⁶ but rather that they might not become in any wise teachers of evil. ⁴For along with strange people, strange doctrines must come in; and novel doctrines bring novel decisions, from which there must arise many feelings and resolutions which destroy the harmony of the existing political order. Therefore he thought it more necessary to keep bad manners and customs from invading and filling the city than it was to keep out infectious diseases.

28 ¹Now in all this there is no trace of injustice or arrogance, which some attribute to the laws of Lycurgus, declaring them efficacious in producing valour, but defective in producing righteousness. The so-called "krupteia," or *secret service*, of the Spartans, if this be really one of the institutions of Lycurgus, as Aristotle says it was, may have given Plato also²⁷ this opinion of the man and his civil polity. ²This secret service was of the following nature. The magistrates from time to time sent out into the country at large the most discreet of the young warriors, equipped only with daggers and

such supplies as were necessary. In the day time they scattered into obscure and out of the way places, p291 where they hid themselves and lay quiet; but in the night they came down into the highways and killed every Helot whom they caught. ³Oftentimes, too, they actually traversed the fields where Helots were working and slew the sturdiest and best of them. So, too, Thucydides, in his history of the Peloponnesian war,²⁸ tells us that the Helots who had been judged by the Spartans to be superior in bravery, 57set wreaths upon their heads in token of their emancipation, and visited the temples of the gods in procession, but a little afterwards all disappeared, more than two thousand of them, in such a way that no man was able to say, either then or afterwards, how they came by their deaths. ⁴And Aristotle in particular says also that the ephors, as soon as they came into office, made formal declaration of war upon the Helots, in order that there might be no impiety in slaying them.

And in other ways also they were harsh and cruel to the Helots. For instance, they would force them to drink too much strong wine, and then introduce them into their public messes, to show the young men what a thing drunkenness was. They also ordered them to sing songs and dance dances that were low and ridiculous, but to let the nobler kind alone. ⁵And therefore in later times, they say, when the Thebans made their expedition into Laconia,²⁹ they ordered the Helots whom they captured to sing the songs of Terpander, Alcman, and Spendon the Spartan; but they declined to do so, on the plea that their masters did not allow it, thus proving the correctness of the saying: "In Sparta the freeman is more a freeman than anywhere else in the world, p293 and the slave more a slave." ⁶However, in my opinion, such cruelties were first practised by the Spartans in later times, particularly after the great earthquake,³⁰ when the Helots and Messenians together rose up against them, wrought the widest devastation in their territory, and brought their city into the greatest peril. I certainly cannot ascribe to Lycurgus so abominable a measure as the "krupteia," judging of his character from his mildness and justice in all other instances. To this the voice of the god also bore witness.³¹

29 ¹When his principal institutions were at last firmly fixed in the customs of the people, and his civil polity

had sufficient growth and strength to support and preserve itself, just as Plato says³² that Deity was rejoiced to see His universe come into being and make its first motion, so Lycurgus was filled with joyful satisfaction in the magnitude and beauty of his system of laws, now that it was in operation and moving along its pathway. He therefore ardently desired, so far as human forethought could accomplish the task, to make it immortal, and let it go down unchanged to future ages. ²Accordingly, he assembled the whole people, and told them that the provisions already made were sufficiently adapted to promote the prosperity and virtue of the state, but that something of the greatest weight and importance remained, which he could not lay before them until he had consulted the god at Delphi. They must therefore abide by the established laws and make no change nor alteration in them until he came back from Delphi in person; p295 then he would do whatsoever the god thought best. ³When they all agreed to this and bade him set out on his journey, he exacted an oath from the kings and the senators, and afterwards from the rest of the citizens, that they would abide by the established polity and observe it until Lycurgus should come back; then he set out for Delphi.

On reaching the oracle, he sacrificed to the god, and asked if the laws which he had established were good, and sufficient to promote a city's prosperity and virtue. ⁴Apollo answered that the laws which he had established were good, and that the city would continue to be held in highest honour while it kept to the polity of Lycurgus. This oracle Lycurgus wrote down, and sent it to Sparta. But for his own part, he sacrificed again to the god, took affectionate leave of his friends and of his son, and resolved never to release his fellow-citizens from their oath, but of his own accord to put an end to his life where he was. He had reached an age in which life was not yet a burden, and death no longer a terror; when he and his friends, moreover, appeared to be sufficiently prosperous and happy. ⁵He therefore abstained from food till he died, considering that even the death of a statesman should be of service to the state, and the ending of his life not void of effect, but recognized as a virtuous deed. As for himself, since he had wrought out fully the noblest tasks, the end of life would actually be a consummation of his good fortune and happiness; and as for his fellow-citizens, he would make his death the guardian, as it were, of all the blessings he had secured for them during his life, since they had sworn to observe and maintain his polity until he should return. [6]And he was not p297 deceived in his expectations, so long did his city have the first rank in Hellas for good government and reputation, observing as she did for five hundred years the laws of Lycurgus, in which no one of the fourteen kings who followed him made any change, down to Agis the son of Archidamus. For the institution of the ephors did not weaken, but rather strengthened the civil polity, and though it was thought to have been done in the interests of the people, it really made the aristocracy more powerful.

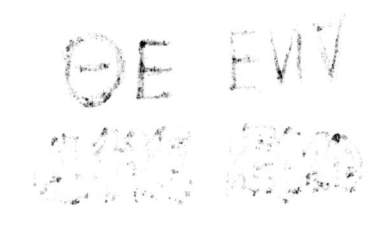

CHAPTER THREE

Ancient Rome

Rome did not achieve mastery of the ancient world quickly or easily. Founded by Latin tribesmen in the eighth century BCE in the hills of the Tiber River Valley, Rome's beginnings were inauspicious. A turning point occurred in the sixth century when Rome was conquered by the Etruscans. Under the rule of these kings, Rome's political and social institutions began to take shape. When, in 509 BCE, the Romans grew weary of despotic Etruscan rule and carried out a *coup d'etat*, the Roman Republic was born. The monarchy was abolished, but vestiges of the old order remained including the Senate and a desire for conquest. Over the next two centuries, the Romans fought endlessly against those who posed a threat—the Etruscans, Latins, Gauls, Samnites, and Greeks among others. Rome was not always victorious in these battles. Pyrrhus, a Greek warlord, defeated the Romans in two great battles, but lost so many men in the process that he was eventually forced to leave Italy with a "Pyrrhic victory."

By the mid-third century, Rome was supreme throughout the Italian peninsula and was now ready to step abroad. Continued expansion, though, brought Rome into conflict with Carthage, an old Phoenician colony situated on the northern coast of Africa. With its powerful navy, Carthage had extensive territorial interests throughout the Western Mediterranean area. Conflict between the two was inevitable. Between 264 and 146 BCE, Rome and Carthage fought three great wars for supremacy. There were many ups and downs in the so-called Punic Wars with success and failure on both sides. At one point during the Second Punic War, it appeared that Hannibal's victory at Cannae in 216 BCE would bring about the collapse of the Roman war effort. Rome, however, persevered, and found a capable war leader in the person of Scipio Africanus who defeated Hannibal at Zama in 202 BCE. With the destruction of Carthage in 146 BCE by Scipio's adopted grandson, Scipio Aemilianus, Rome was able to bring the conflict to a successful conclusion. As a result of its victories, Rome was now supreme in the ancient world. According to the Greek historian Polybius, Rome's political and military success during this period was attributable to a system of checks and balances in its unique constitution.

However, in the years that followed, Rome experienced many problems which brought about the decline of the Republic. The task of defending, administering, and supplying such a huge kingdom was both difficult and expensive. Moreover, the influx of great wealth and thousands of slaves caused serious economic problems, especially within Italy. There were attempts to fix these problems, most notably by the brothers Gracchi who, between 131 and 123 BCE, were elected tribunes of the people. Their bold efforts to effect remedial legislation, however, antagonized the Senate and cost them their lives. In the years that followed, the differences between the Senate and its supporters, called the Optimates, and those who favored reform, the Populares, oftentimes erupted into bloody confrontation. The volatile political climate favored the rise of political opportunists—military leaders who, by virtue of battlefield victories, captured the hearts and minds of the Roman people. Chief among these was Gaius Marius, leader of the Populares. Marius reorganized the army, defeated the Numidian usurper Jurgurtha, and repelled several Germanic tribes that threatened to enter Italy. For his noble efforts, Marius was elected consul an unprecedented seven times.

By the early years of the first century, though, the Senate had found a champion of its own in the person of Cornelius Sulla. After a number of battlefield successes, in 83 BCE Sulla broke from Roman custom, seized Rome, and boldly assumed the position of dictator. Over the next few years, Sulla routed the political opposition, including those who had supported Marius, and implemented reforms that guaranteed the ascendancy of the Optimates. Their victory, though, was short-lived. In the years that followed Sulla's death in 78 BCE, new charismatic leaders emerged to challenge the Senate's authority including the veteran general Pompey, the wealthy aristocrat Marcus Crassus, and a young political upstart named Julius Caesar. Cicero, the most influential of the Senators, lashed out at men of this ilk who ignored or trampled on the hallowed Republican traditions of the past. In 60 BCE, Caesar, Crassus, and Pompey, all of whom had an axe to grind with the Senate, formed the First Triumvirate through which they were able to gain important political concessions. The alliance enabled Caesar to become a consul and later governor of Gaul. In the latter capacity, Caesar gained much needed military experience fighting the Gallic tribes while pushing Rome's northern boundary all the way to the English Channel.

In the meantime, the political *amicitia* formed with Pompey and Crassus had begun to deteriorate. Crassus, trying to emulate Caesar's success in Gaul, was killed fighting the Parthians in Mesopotamia, whereas Pompey, out of necessity, formed an alliance with the Senate. When Pompey and the Senate attempted to remove Caesar from his Gallic command, a civil war ensued. Between 49 and 47 BCE, Caesar defeated Pompey and his supporters, established a strong Roman presence in Cleopatra's Egypt, and scored a decisive victory over the king of Pontus in Asia Minor prompting the famous declaration: "*Veni, vidi, vici!*" Caesar was now the uncontested master of the Roman world. Although Caesar held a number of titles and powers, he ruled Rome as a benevolent dictator. Even so, there were many who saw Caesar as nothing more than a dangerous tyrant, a man who, if given the opportunity, might make himself king. On the Ides of March in 44 BCE, Caesar was stabbed to death in the Senate and the Roman world was plunged yet again into chaos.

Caesar's death brought new leaders to the fore. To restore order, Caesar's nineteen-year old nephew and heir, Octavian, formed the Second Triumvirate with two other politically prominent figures, Mark Antony and Lepidus. Many of their political opponents, including Cicero, were put to death, while the assassins were routed at the Battle of Philippi in 42 BCE. The victors then divided the Empire among themselves which, for all practical purposes, brought the Republic and the alliance to an end. Lepidus was forced into retirement. Thereafter, only Mark Antony, who had become politically and romantically involved with Cleopatra, stood between Octavian and the position he envisioned for himself in the Roman world. In the struggle that followed, Octavian prevailed in a great naval battle at Actium in 31 BCE. As a result of his victory and the subsequent suicides of Antony and Cleopatra, Octavian was now *Imperator*.

In the years that followed Actium, Octavian took steps to consolidate his authority, steps which most historians believe brought one period of Roman history to an end and, in turn, inaugurated another—the Empire. While the Senate and the old offices of State remained, virtually all power was conferred on the *Imperator* who now came to be known by the godlike title of *Augustus*. Over the next two centuries, a time in Roman history known as the Principate (from *Princeps*, one of Augustus' many titles), the Empire grew and prospered. Sometimes growth was achieved even during periods of impotent leadership. The Roman historian Suetonius, from his vantage point in the second century, could find little good in the sexually depraved, egomaniacal, and ostentatious Julio-Claudians (14–68 CE). Nero, one of these rulers, had his mother and aunt killed, persecuted the Christians, and attempted to burn Rome to the ground. The infant Empire, though, weathered the storm. Between 69 and 180 CE, under the much improved leadership of the Flavian and Antonine emperors, Rome reached its greatest territorial extent. Now in possession of all lands touching the Mediterranean Sea, Rome could proudly refer to that body of water as *Mare Nostrum.*

By the latter years of the second century, though, forces were at work which would bring about a final, unhappy chapter in Roman history. During this period, the army became the most important factor in Roman politics. Indeed, between 235 and 284 CE, the Empire was ruled by the so-called "Barracks Emperors," approximately thirty professional soldiers who fought their way to the purple. Of this number, only one died a natural death, stark testimony to the strife and violence of the era. Rome's enemies—the Germans to the north, the Persians to the east among others—hammered the border fortifications. In addition to Rome's political and military problems, not surprisingly, Rome's world economy began to break down. The roads and maritime lanes were now filled with bandits and pirates. There was also a spiritual crisis. As their world collapsed about them, many Romans turned away from the State and its time-honored traditions to embrace new ideas and beliefs, including the religion known as Christianity. Although the Christians suffered terribly during the State-led persecutions of the era, their beliefs survived, and under the patronage of Constantine the Great (306–337 CE) and Theodosius I (379–395 CE) Christianity became the official religion of the Roman Empire.

It was against this chaotic backdrop that Diocletian, another army general, came to power in 284 CE. No ordinary "Barracks Emperor," Diocletian was determined to restore the strength of the Empire. Unlike Augustus who had ruled as *Princeps* or "first citizen of the state," Diocletian would rule as *Dominus or* "lord." For this reason, many historians refer to the latter phase of the Empire's history as the Dominate. To achieve stability, Diocletian was forced to implement far-reaching reforms. Chief among these was the creation of a Tetrarchy or the rule of four. The Empire was divided into two halves, each ruled by an Augustus and his subordinate called a Caesar. Although it might be argued that the Empire had reached a point where one-person rule was not feasible, it is also undeniable that the Tetrarchy accelerated the decline by pitting one Augustus against another in great power struggles. With the exception of a period of about sixty years in the fourth century when the Empire was reunited under the rule of Constantine, his sons, and Theodosius I, the Roman world remained divided. The Eastern Empire, centered on its capital at Constantinople, would endure until 1453. The Western Empire, however, was at an end. Faced with insurmountable problems and lacking competent leadership, the Empire collapsed in the last years of the fifth century from the weight of numerous Germanic tribes that marched practically unimpeded across Europe, sacked Rome on two occasions, and then in 476 CE deposed the last Western emperor.

RECOMMENDED READINGS

Boatwright, Mary T., Daniel J. Gargola, and Richard J. A. Talbert. *The Romans: From Village to Empire.* 2004.

Campbell, Brian. *War and Society in Imperial Rome, 31 BC–AD 284.* 2002.

Crawford, Michael. *The Roman Republic.* 1993. 2nd edition

Ferrell, Arthur. *The Fall of the Roman Empire, The Military Explanation.* 1986.

Holland, Tom. *Rubicon: The Last Years of the Roman Republic.* 2004.

Scullard, Howard H. *A History of the Roman World 753–146 B.C.E.* 1980. 4th edition.

Woolf, Greg. *Rome: An Empire's Story.* 2012.

QUESTIONS

1. According to Polybius, how did the system of checks and balances in Rome's government contribute to its success in building a strong, unified state?
2. What was Polybius' opinion of the Carthaginian general Hannibal?
3. According to Cicero, what were the benefits of growing older?
4. What prompted Julius Caesar to invade Britain in 55 and 54 BCE?
5. In what ways did Rome suffer from the rule of Nero?
6. What did Tacitus find admirable about the Germanic tribes of Western Europe?

THE HISTORIES OF POLYBIUS
Polybius

BOOK VI

As for the Roman constitution, it had three elements, each of them possessing sovereign powers: Triple element in the Roman Constitution.and their respective share of power in the whole state had been regulated with such a scrupulous regard to equality and equilibrium, that no one could say for certain, not even a native, whether the constitution as a whole were an aristocracy or democracy or despotism. And no wonder: for if we confine our observation to the power of the Consuls we should be inclined to regard it as despotic; if on that of the Senate, as aristocratic; and if finally one looks at the power possessed by the people it would seem a clear case of a democracy. What the exact powers of these several parts were, and still, with slight modifications, are, I will now state.

469

12. The Consuls, before leading out the legions, remain in Rome and are supreme masters of the administration. The Consuls.All other magistrates, except the Tribunes, are under them and take their orders. They introduce foreign ambassadors to the Senate; bring matters requiring deliberation before it; and see to the execution of its decrees. If, again, there are any matters of state which require the authorisation of the people, it is their business to see to them, to summon the popular meetings, to bring the proposals before them, and to carry out the decrees of the majority. In the preparations for war also, and in a word in the entire administration of a campaign, they have all but absolute power. It is competent to them to impose on the allies such levies as they think good, to appoint the Military Tribunes, to make up the roll for soldiers and select those that are suitable. Besides they have absolute power of inflicting punishment on all who are under their command

while on active service and they have authority to expend as much of the public money as they choose, being accompanied by a quaestor who is entirely at their orders. A survey of these powers would in fact justify our describing the constitution as despotic,— a clear case of royal government. Nor will it affect the truth of my description, if any of the institutions I have described are changed in our time, or in that of our posterity: and the same remarks apply to what follows.

13. The Senate has first of all the control of the treasury, and regulates the receipts and disbursements alike. The Senate.For the Quaestors cannot issue any public money for the various departments of the state without a decree of the Senate, except for the service of the Consuls. The Senate controls also what is by far the largest and most important expenditure, that, namely, which is made by the censors every *lustrum* for the repair or construction of public buildings; this money cannot be obtained by the censors except by the grant of the Senate. Similarly all crimes committed in Italy requiring a public investigation, such as treason, conspiracy, poisoning, or wilful murder, are in the hands of the Senate. Besides, if any individual or state470 among the Italian allies requires a controversy to be settled, a penalty to be assessed, help or protection to be afforded,—all this is the province of the Senate. Or again, outside Italy, if it is necessary to send an embassy to reconcile warring communities, or to remind them of their duty, or sometimes to impose requisitions upon them, or to receive their submission, or finally to proclaim war against them,—this too is the business of the Senate. In like manner the reception to be given to foreign ambassadors in Rome, and the answers to be returned to them, are decided by the Senate. With such business the people have nothing to do. Consequently, if one were staying at Rome when the

Consuls were not in town, one would imagine the constitution to be a complete aristocracy: and this has been the idea entertained by many Greeks, and by many kings as well, from the fact that nearly all the business they had with Rome was settled by the Senate.

14. After this one would naturally be inclined to ask what part is left for the people in the constitution, The people.when the Senate has these various functions, especially the control of the receipts and expenditure of the exchequer; and when the Consuls, again, have absolute power over the details of military preparation, and an absolute authority in the field? There is, however, a part left the people, and it is a most important one. For the people is the sole fountain of honour and of punishment; and it is by these two things and these alone that dynasties and constitutions and, in a word, human society are held together: for where the distinction between them is not sharply drawn both in theory and practice, there no undertaking can be properly administered,—as indeed we might expect when good and bad are held in exactly the same honour. The people then are the only court to decide matters of life and death; and even in cases where the penalty is money, if the sum to be assessed is sufficiently serious, and especially when the accused have held the higher magistracies. And in regard to this arrangement there is one point deserving especial commendation and record. Men who are on trial for their lives at Rome, while sentence is in process of being voted,—if even only one of the tribes whose votes are needed to ratify the471 sentence has not voted,—have the privilege at Rome of openly departing and condemning themselves to a voluntary exile. Such men are safe at Naples or Praeneste or at Tibur, and at other towns with which this arrangement has been duly ratified on oath.

Again, it is the people who bestow offices on the deserving, which are the most honourable rewards of virtue. It has also the absolute power of passing or repealing laws; and, most important of all, it is the people who deliberate on the question of peace or war. And when provisional terms are made for alliance, suspension of hostilities, or treaties, it is the people who ratify them or the reverse.

These considerations again would lead one to say that the chief power in the state was the people's, and that the constitution was a democracy.

15. Such, then, is the distribution of power between the several parts of the state. The mutual relation of the three.I must now show how each of these several parts can, when they choose, oppose or support each other.

The Consul, then, when he has started on an expedition with the powers I have described, is to all The Consul dependent on the Senate,appearance absolute in the administration of the business in hand; still he has need of the support both of people and Senate, and, without them, is quite unable to bring the matter to a successful conclusion. For it is plain that he must have supplies sent to his legions from time to time; but without a decree of the Senate they can be supplied neither with corn, nor clothes, nor pay, so that all the plans of a commander must be futile, if the Senate is resolved either to shrink from danger or hamper his plans. And again, whether a Consul shall bring any undertaking to a conclusion or no depends entirely upon the Senate: for it has absolute authority at the end of a year to send another Consul to supersede him, or to continue the existing one in his command. Again, even to the successes of the generals the Senate has the power to add distinction and glory, and on the other hand to obscure their merits and lower their credit. For these high achievements are brought in tangible form before the eyes of the citizens by what are called "triumphs."

472

But these triumphs the commanders cannot celebrate with proper pomp, or in some cases celebrate at all, unless the Senate concurs and grants the necessary money. and on the people.As for the people, the Consuls are pre-eminently obliged to court their favour, however distant from home may be the field of their operations; for it is the people, as I have said before, that ratifies, or refuses to ratify, terms of peace and treaties; but most of all because when laying down their office they have to give an account[291] of their administration before it. Therefore in no case is it safe for the Consuls to neglect either the Senate or the goodwill of the people.

16. As for the Senate, which possesses the immense power I have described, in the first place it is obliged in public affairs to take the multitude into account, The Senate controlled by the people.and respect the wishes of the people; and it cannot put into execution the penalty for offences against the republic, which are punishable with death, unless the people first ratify its decrees. Similarly even in matters which directly affect the senators,—for instance, in the case of a law diminishing the Senate's traditional authority, or depriving senators of certain dignities and offices, or even actually cutting down their property,—even in such cases the people have the sole power of passing or rejecting the law. But most important of all is the fact that, if the Tribunes interpose their veto, the Senate not only are unable to pass a decree, but cannot even hold a meeting at all, whether formal or informal. Now, the Tribunes are always bound to carry out the decree of the people, and above all things to have regard to their wishes: therefore, for all these reasons the Senate stands in awe of the multitude, and cannot neglect the feelings of the people.

17. In like manner the people on its part is far from being independent of the Senate, and is bound to take its wishes into account both collectively and individually. For 473 contracts, too numerous to count, are given out by the censors in all parts of Italy for the repairs or construction of public buildings; The people dependent on the Senate.there is also the collection of revenue from many rivers, harbours, gardens, mines, and land—everything, in a word, that comes under the control of the Roman government: and in all these the people at large are engaged; so that there is scarcely a man, so to speak, who is not interested either as a contractor or as being employed in the works. For some purchase the contracts from the censors for themselves; and others go partners with them; while others again go security for these contractors, or actually pledge their property to the treasury for them. Now over all these transactions the Senate has absolute control. It can grant an extension of time; and in case of unforeseen accident can relieve the contractors from a portion of their obligation, or release them from it altogether, if they are absolutely unable to fulfil it.

And there are many details in which the Senate can inflict great hardships, or, on the other hand, grant great indulgences to the contractors: for in every case the appeal is to it. But the most important point of all is that the judges are taken from its members in the majority of trials, whether public or private, in which the charges are heavy.[292] Consequently, all citizens are much at its mercy; and being alarmed at the uncertainty as to when they may need its aid, are cautious about resisting or actively opposing its will. and Consul.And for a similar reason men do not rashly resist the wishes of the Consuls, because one and all may become subject to their absolute authority on a campaign.

18. The result of this power of the several estates for mutual help or harm is a union sufficiently firm for all emergencies, and a constitution than which it is impossible to find a better. For whenever any danger from without compels 474 them to unite and work together, the strength which is developed by the State is so extraordinary, that everything required is unfailingly carried out by the eager rivalry shown by all classes to devote their whole minds to the need of the hour, and to secure that any determination come to should not fail for want of promptitude; while each individual works, privately and publicly alike, for the accomplishment of the business in hand. Accordingly, the peculiar constitution of the State makes it irresistible, and certain of obtaining whatever it determines to attempt. Nay, even when these external alarms are past, and the people are enjoying their good fortune and the fruits of their victories, and, as usually happens, growing corrupted by flattery and idleness, show a tendency to violence and arrogance,—it is in these circumstances, more than ever, that the constitution is seen to possess within itself the power of correcting abuses. For when any one of the three classes becomes puffed up, and manifests an inclination to be contentious and unduly encroaching, the mutual interdependency of all the three, and the possibility of the pretensions of any one being checked and thwarted by the others, must plainly check this tendency: and so the proper equilibrium is maintained by the impulsiveness of the one part being checked by its fear of the other....

BOOK IX

THE CHARACTER OF HANNIBAL

22. Of all that befell the Romans and Carthaginians, good or bad, the cause was one man and one mind,—Hannibal.

583

For it is notorious that he managed the Italian campaigns in person, and the Spanish by the agency of the elder of his brothers, Hasdrubal, and subsequently by that of Mago, the leaders who killed the two Roman generals in Spain about the same time. Again, he conducted the Sicilian campaign at first through Hippocrates and afterwards through Myttonus[330] the Libyan. So also in Greece and Illyria: and, by brandishing before their faces the dangers arising from these latter places, he was enabled to distract the attention of the Romans, thanks to his understanding with Philip. So great and wonderful is the influence of a Man, and a mind duly fitted by original constitution for any undertaking within the reach of human powers.

But since the position of affairs has brought us to an inquiry into the genius of Hannibal, the occasion seems to me to demand that I should explain in regard to him the peculiarities of his character which have been especially the subject of controversy. Some regard him as having been extraordinarily cruel, some exceedingly grasping of money. But to speak the truth of him, or of any person engaged in public affairs, is not easy. Some maintain that men's real natures are brought out by their circumstances, and that they are detected when in office, ἀρχὴ ἄνδρα δείξει. Bias, in Aristot. Eth. 5, 1.or as some say when in misfortunes, though they have up to that time completely maintained their secrecy. I, on the contrary, do not regard this as a sound dictum. For I think that men in these circumstances are compelled, not only occasionally but frequently, either by the suggestions of friends or the complexity of affairs, to speak and act contrary to their real principles.

23. And there are many proofs of this to be found in past history if any one will give the necessary attention. Examples to the contrary. 1. Agathocles. Is it not universally stated by the historians that Agathocles, tyrant of Sicily, after having the reputation of extreme cruelty in his original measures for the establishment of his dynasty, when he had once become convinced that his power over the Siceliots was firmly established, is considered to have become 584 the most humane and mild of rulers? 2. Cleomenes.Again, was not Cleomenes of Sparta a most excellent king, a most cruel tyrant, and then again as a private individual most obliging and benevolent? And yet it is not reasonable to suppose the most opposite dispositions to exist in the same nature. They are compelled to change with the changes of circumstances: and so some rulers often display to the world a disposition as opposite as possible to their true nature. Therefore the natures of men not only are not brought out by such things, but on the contrary are rather obscured. The same effect is produced also not only in commanders, despots, and kings, but in states also, by the suggestions of friends. 3. Athens.For instance, you will find the Athenians responsible for very few tyrannical acts, and of many kindly and noble ones, while Aristeides and Pericles were at the head of the state: but quite the reverse when Cleon and Chares were so. 4. Sparta.And when the Lacedaemonians were supreme in Greece, all the measures taken by King Cleombrotus were conceived in the interests of their allies, but those by Agesilaus not so.5. Philip V.The characters of states therefore vary with the variations of their leaders. King Philip again, when Taurion and Demetrius were acting with him, was most impious in his conduct, but when Aratus or Chrysogonus, most humane.

24. The case of Hannibal seems to me to be on a par with these. His circumstances were so extraordinary and shifting,Hannibal mastered by circumstances.his closest friends so widely different, that it is exceedingly difficult to estimate his character from his proceedings in Italy. What those circumstances suggested to him may easily be understood from what I have already said, and what is immediately to follow; but it is not right to omit the suggestions made by his friends either, especially as this matter may be rendered sufficiently clear by one instance of the advice offered him. At the time that Hannibal was meditating the march from Iberia to Italy with his army, he was confronted with the extreme difficulty of providing food and securing provisions, both because the journey 585 was thought to be of insuperable length, and because the barbarians that lived in the intervening country were so numerous and savage. His cruelty. It appears that at that time this difficulty frequently came on for discussion at the council; and that one of his friends, called Hannibal Monomachus, gave it as his opinion that there was one and only one way by which it was possible to get as far as Italy. Upon Hannibal bidding him speak out, he said that they must teach the army to eat human flesh, and make them accustomed to it. Hannibal could say nothing against the boldness and effectiveness of the idea, but was unable to persuade himself or his friends to entertain it. It is this man's acts in Italy that they say were attributed to Hannibal, to maintain the accusation of cruelty, as well as such as were the result of circumstances.

25. Fond of money indeed he does seem to have been to a conspicuous degree, and to have had a friend of the same character—Mago, His avarice.who commanded in Bruttium. That account I got from the Carthaginians themselves; for natives know best not only which way the wind lies, as the proverb has it, but the characters also of their fellow-countrymen. But I heard a still more detailed story from Massanissa, who maintained the charge of money-loving against all Carthaginians generally, but especially against Hannibal and Mago called the Samnite. Among other stories, he told me that these two men had arranged a most generous subdivision of operations between each other from their earliest youth; and though they had each taken a very large number of cities in Iberia and Italy by force or fraud, they had never taken part in the same operation together; but had always schemed against each other, more than against the enemy, in order to prevent the one being with the other at the taking of a city: that they might neither quarrel in consequence of things of this sort,

nor have to divide the profit on the ground of their equality of rank.

26. The influence of friends then, and still more that of circumstances, in doing violence to and changing the natural character of Hannibal, is shown by what I have narrated and 586 will be shown by what I have to narrate. For as soon as Capua fell into the hands of the Romans the other cities naturally became restless, Effect of the fall of Capua,B.C. 211.and began to look round for opportunities and pretexts for revolting back again to Rome. It was then that Hannibal seems to have been at his lowest point of distress and despair. For neither was he able to keep a watch upon all the cities so widely removed from each other,—while he remained entrenched at one spot, and the enemy were manœuvering against him with several armies,—nor could he divide his force into many parts; for he would have put an easy victory into the hands of the enemy by becoming inferior to them in numbers, and finding it impossible to be personally present at all points. Wherefore he was obliged to completely abandon some of the cities, and withdraw his garrisons from others: being afraid lest, in the course of the revolutions which might occur, he should lose his own soldiers as well. Some cities again he made up his mind to treat with treacherous violence, removing their inhabitants to other cities, and giving their property up to plunder; in consequence of which many were enraged with him, and accused him of impiety or cruelty. For the fact was that these movements were accompanied by robberies of money, murders, and violence, on various pretexts at the hands of the outgoing or incoming soldiers in the cities, because they always supposed that the inhabitants that were left behind were on the verge of turning over to the enemy. It is, therefore, very difficult to express an opinion on the natural character of Hannibal, owing to the influence exercised on it by the counsel of friends and the force of circumstances. The prevailing notion about him, however, at Carthage was that he was greedy of money, at Rome that he was cruel.[331]...

COMMENTARIES ON THE GALLIC WARS
Julius Caesar
Book 4, 20–38 (Caesar invades Britain)

XX.—During the short part of summer which remained, Caesar, although in these countries, as all Gaul lies towards the north, the winters are early, nevertheless resolved to proceed into Britain, because he discovered that in almost all the wars with the Gauls succours had been furnished to our enemy from that country; and even if the time of year should be insufficient for carrying on the war, yet he thought it would be of great service to him if he only entered the island, and saw into the character of the people, and got knowledge of their localities, harbours, and landing-places, all which were for the most part unknown to the Gauls. For neither does any one except merchants generally go thither, nor even to them was any portion of it known, except the sea-coast and those parts which are opposite to Gaul. Therefore, after having called up to him the merchants from all parts, he could learn neither what was the size of the island, nor what or how numerous were the nations which inhabited it, nor what system of war they followed, nor what customs they used, nor what harbours were convenient for a great number of large ships.

XXI.—He sends before him Caius Volusenus with a ship of war, to acquire a knowledge of these particulars before he in person should make a descent into the island, as he was convinced that this was a judicious measure. He commissioned him to thoroughly examine into all matters, and then return to him as soon as possible. He himself proceeds to the Morini with all his forces. He orders ships from all parts of the neighbouring countries, and the fleet which the preceding summer he had built for the war with the Veneti, to assemble in this place. In the meantime, his purpose having been discovered, and reported to the Britons by merchants, ambassadors come to him from several states of the island, to promise that they will give hostages, and submit to the government of the Roman people. Having given them an audience, he after promising liberally, and exhorting them to continue in that purpose, sends them back to their own country, and [despatches] with them Commius, whom, upon subduing the Atrebates, he had created king there, a man whose courage and conduct he esteemed, and who he thought would be faithful to him, and whose influence ranked highly in those countries. He orders him to visit as many states as he could, and persuade them to embrace the protection of the Roman people, and apprise them that he would shortly come thither. Volusenus, having viewed the localities as far as means could be afforded one who dared not leave his ship and trust himself to barbarians, returns to Caesar on the fifth day, and reports what he had there observed.

XXII.—While Caesar remains in these parts for the purpose of procuring ships, ambassadors come to him from a great portion of the Morini, to plead their excuse respecting their conduct on the late occasion; alleging that it was as men uncivilised, and as those who were unacquainted with our custom, that they had made war upon the Roman people, and promising to perform what he should command. Caesar, thinking that this had happened fortunately enough for him, because he neither wished to leave an enemy behind him, nor had an opportunity for carrying on a war, by reason of the time of year, nor considered that employment in such trifling matters was to be preferred to his enterprise on Britain, imposes a large number of hostages; and when these were brought, he received them to his protection. Having collected together and provided about eighty transport ships, as many as he thought necessary for conveying over two legions, he assigned such [ships] of war as he had besides to the quaestor, his lieutenants, and officers of cavalry. There were in addition to these eighteen ships of burden which were prevented, eight miles from that place, by winds, from being able to reach the same port. These he distributed amongst the horse; the rest of the army he delivered to Q. Titurius Sabinus and L. Aurunculeius Cotta, his lieutenants, to lead into the territories of the Menapii and those cantons of the Morini from which ambassadors had not come to him. He ordered P. Sulpicius Rufus, his lieutenant, to hold possession of the harbour, with such a garrison as he thought sufficient.

XXIII.—These matters being arranged, finding the weather favourable for his voyage, he set sail about the third watch, and ordered the horse to march forward to the farther port, and there embark and follow him. As this was performed rather tardily by them, he himself reached Britain with the first squadron of ships, about the fourth hour of the day, and there saw the forces of the enemy drawn up in arms on all the hills. The nature of the place was this: the sea was confined by mountains so close to it that a dart could be thrown from their summit upon the shore. Considering this by no means a fit place for disembarking, he remained at anchor till the ninth hour, for the other ships to arrive there. Having in the meantime assembled the lieutenants and military tribunes, he told them both what he had learnt from Volusenus, and what he wished to be done; and enjoined them (as the principle of military matters, and especially as maritime affairs, which have a precipitate and uncertain action, required) that all things should be performed by them at a nod and at the instant. Having dismissed them, meeting both with wind and tide favourable at the same time, the signal being given and the anchor weighed, he advanced about seven miles from that place, and stationed his fleet over against an open and level shore.

XXIV.—But the barbarians, upon perceiving the design of the Romans, sent forward their cavalry and charioteers, a class of warriors of whom it is their practice to make great use in their battles, and following with the rest of their forces, endeavoured to prevent our men landing. In this was the greatest difficulty, for the following reasons, namely, because our ships, on account of their great size, could be stationed only in deep water; and our soldiers, in places unknown to them, with their hands embarrassed, oppressed with a large and heavy weight of armour, had at the same time to leap from the ships, stand amidst the waves, and encounter the enemy; whereas they, either on dry ground, or advancing

a little way into the water, free in all their limbs, in places thoroughly known to them, could confidently throw their weapons and spur on their horses, which were accustomed to this kind of service. Dismayed by these circumstances and altogether untrained in this mode of battle, our men did not all exert the same vigour and eagerness which they had been wont to exert in engagements on dry ground.

XXV.—When Caesar observed this, he ordered the ships of war, the appearance of which was somewhat strange to the barbarians and the motion more ready for service, to be withdrawn a little from the transport vessels, and to be propelled by their oars, and be stationed towards the open flank of the enemy, and the enemy to be beaten off and driven away with slings, arrows, and engines: which plan was of great service to our men; for the barbarians being startled by the form of our ships and the motions of our oars and the nature of our engines, which was strange to them, stopped, and shortly after retreated a little. And while our men were hesitating [whether they should advance to the shore], chiefly on account of the depth of the sea, he who carried the eagle of the tenth legion, after supplicating the gods that the matter might turn out favourably to the legion, exclaimed, "Leap, fellow soldiers, unless you wish to betray your eagle to the enemy. I, for my part, will perform my duty to the commonwealth and my general." When he had said this with a loud voice, he leaped from the ship and proceeded to bear the eagle toward the enemy. Then our men, exhorting one another that so great a disgrace should not be incurred, all leaped from the ship. When those in the nearest vessels saw them, they speedily followed and approached the enemy.

XXVI.—The battle was maintained vigorously on both sides. Our men, however, as they could neither keep their ranks, nor get firm footing, nor follow their standards, and as one from one ship and another from another assembled around whatever standards they met, were thrown into great confusion. But the enemy, who were acquainted with all the shallows, when from the shore they saw any coming from a ship one by one, spurred on their horses, and attacked them while embarrassed; many surrounded a few, others threw their weapons upon our collected forces on their exposed flank. When Caesar observed this, he ordered the boats of the ships of war and the spy sloops to be filled with soldiers, and sent them up to the succour of those whom he had observed in distress. Our men, as soon as they made good their footing on dry ground, and all their comrades had joined them, made an attack upon the enemy, and put them to flight, but could not pursue them very far, because the horse had not been able to maintain their course at sea and reach the island. This alone was wanting to Caesar's accustomed success.

XXVII.—The enemy being thus vanquished in battle, as soon as they recovered after their flight, instantly sent ambassadors to Caesar to negotiate about peace. They promised to give hostages and perform what he should command. Together with these ambassadors came Commius the Atrebatian, who, as I have above said, had been sent by Caesar into Britain. Him they had seized upon when leaving his ship, although in the character of ambassador he bore the general's commission to them, and thrown into chains: then after the battle was fought, they sent him back, and in suing for peace cast the blame of that act upon the common people, and entreated that it might be pardoned on account of their indiscretion. Caesar, complaining that after they had sued for peace, and had voluntarily sent ambassadors into the continent for that purpose, they had made war without a reason, said that he would pardon their indiscretion, and imposed hostages, a part of whom they gave immediately; the rest they said they would give in a few days, since they were sent for from remote places. In the meantime they ordered their people to return to the country parts, and the chiefs assembled from all quarters, and proceeded to surrender themselves and their states to Caesar.

XXVIII.—A peace being established by these proceedings four days after we had come into Britain, the eighteen ships, to which reference has been made above, and which conveyed the cavalry, set sail from the upper port with a gentle gale; when, however, they were approaching Britain and were seen from the camp, so great a storm suddenly arose that none of them could maintain their course at sea; and

some were taken back to the same port from which they had started;—others, to their great danger, were driven to the lower part of the island, nearer to the west; which, however, after having cast anchor, as they were getting filled with water, put out to sea through necessity in a stormy night, and made for the continent.

XXIX.—It happened that night to be full moon, which usually occasions very high tides in that ocean; and that circumstance was unknown to our men. Thus, at the same time, the tide began to fill the ships of war which Caesar had provided to convey over his army, and which he had drawn up on the strand; and the storm began to dash the ships of burden which were riding at anchor against each other; nor was any means afforded our men of either managing them or of rendering any service. A great many ships having been wrecked, inasmuch as the rest, having lost their cables, anchors, and other tackling, were unfit for sailing, a great confusion, as would necessarily happen, arose throughout the army; for there were no other ships in which they could be conveyed back, and all things which are of service in repairing vessels were wanting, and corn for the winter had not been provided in those places, because it was understood by all that they would certainly winter in Gaul.

XXX.—On discovering these things the chiefs of Britain, who had come up after the battle was fought to perform those conditions which Caesar had imposed, held a conference, when they perceived that cavalry, and ships, and corn were wanting to the Romans, and discovered the small number of our soldiers from the small extent of the camp (which, too, was on this account more limited than ordinary because Caesar had conveyed over his legions without baggage), and thought that the best plan was to renew the war, and cut off our men from corn and provisions and protract the affair till winter; because they felt confident that, if they were vanquished or cut off from a return, no one would afterwards pass over into Britain for the purpose of making war. Therefore, again entering into a conspiracy, they began to depart from the camp by degrees and secretly bring up their people from the country parts.

XXXI.—But Caesar, although he had not as yet discovered their measures, yet, both from what had occurred to his ships, and from the circumstance that they had neglected to give the promised hostages, suspected that the thing would come to pass which really did happen. He therefore provided remedies against all contingencies; for he daily conveyed corn from the country parts into the camp, used the timber and brass of such ships as were most seriously damaged for repairing the rest, and ordered whatever things besides were necessary for this object to be brought to him from the continent. And thus, since that business was executed by the soldiers with the greatest energy, he effected that, after the loss of twelve ships, a voyage could be made well enough in the rest.

XXXII.—While these things are being transacted, one legion had been sent to forage, according to custom, and no suspicion of war had arisen as yet, and some of the people remained in the country parts, others went backwards and forwards to the camp, they who were on duty at the gates of the camp reported to Caesar that a greater dust than was usual was seen in that direction in which the legion had marched. Caesar, suspecting that which was [really the case],—that some new enterprise was undertaken by the barbarians, ordered the two cohorts which were on duty to march into that quarter with him, and two other cohorts to relieve them on duty; the rest to be armed and follow him immediately. When he had advanced some little way from the camp, he saw that his men were overpowered by the enemy and scarcely able to stand their ground, and that, the legion being crowded together, weapons were being cast on them from all sides. For as all the corn was reaped in every part with the exception of one, the enemy, suspecting that our men would repair to that, had concealed themselves in the woods during the night. Then attacking them suddenly, scattered as they were, and when they had laid aside their arms, and were engaged in reaping, they killed a small number, threw the rest into confusion, and surrounded them with their cavalry and chariots.

XXXIII.—Their mode of fighting with their chariots is this: firstly, they drive about in all directions and throw their weapons and generally break the ranks of the enemy with the very dread of their horses and the noise of their wheels; and when they have worked themselves in between the troops of horse, leap from their chariots and engage on foot. The charioteers in the meantime withdraw some little distance from the battle, and so place themselves with the chariots that, if their masters are overpowered by the number of the enemy, they may have a ready retreat to their own troops. Thus they display in battle the speed of horse, [together with] the firmness of infantry; and by daily practice and exercise attain to such expertness that they are accustomed, even on a declining and steep place, to check their horses at full speed, and manage and turn them in an instant and run along the pole, and stand on the yoke, and thence betake themselves with the greatest celerity to their chariots again.

XXXIV.—Under these circumstances, our men being dismayed by the novelty of this mode of battle, Caesar most seasonably brought assistance; for upon his arrival the enemy paused, and our men recovered from their fear; upon which, thinking the time unfavourable for provoking the enemy and coming to an action, he kept himself in his own quarter, and, a short time having intervened, drew back the legions into the camp. While these things were going on, and all our men engaged, the rest of the Britons, who were in the fields, departed. Storms then set in for several successive days, which both confined our men to camp and hindered the enemy from attacking us. In the meantime the barbarians despatched messengers to all parts and reported to their people the small number of our soldiers, and how good an opportunity was given for obtaining spoil and for liberating themselves for ever, if they should only drive the Romans from their camp. Having by these means speedily got together a large force of infantry and of cavalry, they came up to the camp.

XXXV.—Although Caesar anticipated that the same thing which had happened on former occasions would then occur—that, if the enemy were routed, they would escape from danger by their speed; still, having got about thirty horse, which Commius the Atrebatian, of whom mention has been made, had brought over with him [from Gaul], he drew up the legions in order of battle before the camp. When the action commenced, the enemy were unable to sustain the attack of our men long, and turned their backs; our men pursued them as far as their speed and strength permitted, and slew a great number of them; then, having destroyed and burnt everything far and wide, they retreated to their camp.

XXXVI.—The same day, ambassadors sent by the enemy came to Caesar to negotiate a peace. Caesar doubled the number of hostages which he had before demanded; and ordered that they should be brought over to the continent, because, since the time of the equinox was near, he did not consider that, with his ships out of repair, the voyage ought to be deferred till winter. Having met with favourable weather he set sail a little after midnight, and all his fleet arrived safe at the continent, except two of the ships of burden which could not make the same port which the other ships did, and were carried a little lower down.

XXXVII.—When our soldiers, about 300 in number, had been drawn out of these two ships, and were marching to the camp, the Morini, whom Caesar, when setting forth for Britain, had left in a state of peace, excited by the hope of spoil, at first surrounded them with a small number of men, and ordered them to lay down their arms, if they did not wish to be slain; afterwards however, when they, forming a circle, stood on their defence, a shout was raised and about 6000 of the enemy soon assembled; which being reported, Caesar sent all the cavalry in the camp as a relief to his men. In the meantime our soldiers sustained the attack of the enemy, and fought most valiantly for more than four hours, and, receiving but few wounds themselves, slew several of them. But after our cavalry came in sight, the enemy, throwing away their arms, turned their backs, and a great number of them were killed.

XXXVIII.—The day following Caesar sent Labienus, his lieutenant, with those legions which he had brought back from Britain, against the Morini, who had revolted; who, as they had no place to which they might retreat, on account of the drying up of their marshes (which they had availed themselves of as a place of refuge the preceding year), almost all fell into the power of Labienus. In the meantime Caesar's lieutenants, Q. Titurius and L. Cotta, who had led the legions into the territories of the Menapii, having laid waste all their lands, cut down their corn and burnt their houses, returned to Caesar because the Menapii had all concealed themselves in their thickest woods. Caesar fixed the winter quarters of all the legions amongst the Belgae. Thither only two British states sent hostages; the rest omitted to do so. For these successes, a thanksgiving of twenty days was decreed by the senate upon receiving Caesar's letter.

TREATISES ON FRIENDSHIP AND OLD AGE
Marcus Tullius Cicero
Translated by E. S. Shuckburgh

ON OLD AGE

1. And should my service, Titus, ease the weight
Of care that wrings your heart, and draw the sting
Which rankles there, what guerdon shall there he?

FOR I may address you, Atticus, in the lines in which Flamininus was addressed by the man,

who, poor in wealth, was rich in honour's gold,

though I am well assured that you are not, as Flamininus was,

kept on the rack of care by night and day.

For I know how well ordered and equable your mind is, and am fully aware that it was not a surname alone which you brought home with you from Athens, but its culture and good sense. And yet I have an idea that you are at times stirred to the heart by the same circumstances as myself. To console you for these is a more serious matter, and must be put off to another time. For the present I have resolved to dedicate to you an essay on Old Age. For from the burden of impending or at least advancing age, common to us both, I would do something to relieve us both though as to yourself I am fully aware that you support and will support it, as you do everything else, with calmness and philosophy. But directly I resolved to write on old age, you at once occurred to me as deserving a gift of which both of us might take advantage. To myself, indeed, the composition of this book has been so delightful, that it has not only wiped away all the disagreeables of old age, but has even made it luxurious and delightful too. Never, therefore, can philosophy be praised as highly as it deserves considering that its faithful disciple is able to spend every period of his life with unruffled feelings. However, on other subjects I have spoken at large, and shall often speak again: this hook which I herewith send you is on Old Age. I have put the whole discourse not, as Alisto of Cos did, in the mouth of Tithonus—for a mere fable would have lacked conviction—but in that of Marcus Cato when he was an old man, to give my essay greater weight. I represent Laelius and Scipio at his house expressing surprise at his carrying his years so lightly, and Cato answering them. If he shall seem to shew somewhat more learning in this discourse than he generally did in his own books, put it down to the Greek literature of which it is known that he became an eager student in his old age. But what need of more? Cato's own words will at once explain all I feel about old age.

M. Cato. Publius Cornelius Scipio Africanus (the younger). Gaius Laelius.

2. Scipio. Many a time have I in conversation with my friend Gaius Laelius here expressed my admiration, Marcus Cato, of the eminent, nay perfect, wisdom displayed by you indeed at all points, but above everything because I have noticed that old age never seemed a burden to you, while to most old men it is so hateful that they declare themselves under a weight heavier than Aetna.

Cato. Your admiration is easily excited, it seems, my dear Scipio and Laelius. Men, of course, who have no resources in themselves for securing a good and happy life find every age burdensome. But those who look for all happiness from within can never think anything had which nature makes inevitable. In that category before anything else comes old age, to which all wish to attain, and at which all grumble when attained. Such is Folly's inconsistency and unreasonableness! They say that it is stealing upon them faster than they expected. In the first place, who compelled them to hug an illusion? For in what respect did old age steal upon manhood faster than manhood upon childhood? In the next place, in what way would old age have been less disagreeable to them if they were in their eight-hundredth year than in their eightieth? For their past, however long, when once it was past, would have no consolation for a stupid old age. Wherefore, if it is your wont to admire my wisdom—and I would that it were worthy of your good opinion and of my own surname of Sapiens—it really consists in the fact that I follow Nature, the best of guides, as I would a god, and am loyal to her commands. It is not likely, if she has written the rest of the play well, that she has been careless about the last act like some idle poet. But after all some "last" was inevitable, just as to the berries of a tree and the fruits of the earth there comes in the fulness of time a period of decay and fall. A wise man will not make a grievance of this. To rebel against nature—is not that to fight like the giants with the gods?

Laelius. And yet, Cato, you will do us a very great favour (I venture to speak for Scipio as for myself) if—since we all hope, or at least wish, to become old men—you would allow us to learn from you in good time before it arrives, by what methods we may most easily acquire the strength to support the burden of advancing age.

Cato. I will do so without doubt, Laelius, especially if, as you say, it will be agreeable to you both.

Laelius We do wish very much, Cato, if it is no trouble to you, to be allowed to see the nature of the bourne which you have reached after completing a long journey, as it were, upon which we too are bound to embark.

3. *Cato.* I will do the best I can, Laelius. It has often been my fortune to bear the complaints of my contemporaries—like will to like, you know, according to the old proverb—complaints to which men like C. Salinator and Sp. Albinus, who were of consular rank and about my time, used to give vent. They were, first, that they had lost the pleasures of the senses, without which they did not regard life as life at all; and, secondly, that they were neglected by those from whom they had been used to receive attentions. Such men appear to me to lay the blame on the wrong thing. For if it had been the fault of old age, then these same misfortunes would have

befallen me and all other men of advanced years. But I have known many of them who never said a word of complaint against old age; for they were only too glad to be freed from the bondage of passion, and were not at all looked down upon by their friends. The fact is that the blame for all complaints of that kind is to be charged to character, not to a particular time of life. For old men who are reasonable and neither cross-grained nor churlish find old age tolerable enough: whereas unreason and churlishness cause uneasiness at every time of life.

Laelius It is as you say, Cato. But perhaps some one may suggest that it is your large means, wealth, and high position that make you think old age tolerable: whereas such good fortune only falls to few.

Cato. There is something in that, Laelius, but by no means all. For instance, the story is told of the answer of Themistocles in a wrangle with a certain Seriphian, who asserted that he owed his brilliant position to the reputation of his country, not to his own. "If I had been a Seriphian," said he, "even I should never have been famous, nor would you if you had been an Athenian." Something like this may be said of old age. For the philosopher himself could not find old age easy to bear in the depths of poverty, nor the fool feel it anything but a burden though he were a millionaire. You may be sure, my dear Scipio and Laelius, that the arms best adapted to old age are culture and the active exercise of the virtues. For if they have been maintained at every period—if one has lived much as well as long—the harvest they produce is wonderful, not only because they never fail us even in our last days (though that in itself is supremely important), but also because the consciousness of a well-spent life and the recollection of many virtuous actions are exceedingly delightful.

4. Take the case of Q. Fabius Maximus, the man, 1 mean, who recovered Tarentum. When I was a young man and he an old one, I was as much attached to him as if he had been my contemporary. For that great man 5 serious dignity was tempered by courteous manners, nor had old age made any change in his character. True, he was not exactly an

old man when my devotion to him began, yet he was nevertheless well on in life; for his first consulship fell in the year after my birth. When quite a stripling I went with him in his fourth consulship as a soldier in the ranks, on the expedition against Capua, and in the fifth year after that against Tarentum. Four years after that I was elected Quaestor, holding office in the consulship of Tuditanus and Cethegus, in which year, indeed, he as a very old man spoke in favour of the Cincian law "on gifts and fees."

Now this man conducted wars with all the spirit of youth when he was far advanced in life, and by his persistence gradually wearied out Hannibal, when rioting in all the confidence of youth. How brilliant are those lines of my friend Ennius on him!

> For us, down beaten by the storms of fate,
> One man by wise delays restored the State.
> Praise or dispraise moved not his constant mood,
> True to his purpose, to his country's good!
> Down ever-lengthening avenues of fame
> Thus shines and shall shine still his glorious name.

Again what vigilance, what profound skill did he show in the capture of Tarentum! It was indeed in my hearing that he made the famous retort to Salinator, who had retreated into the citadel after losing the town: "It was owing to me, Quintus Fabius, that you retook Tarentum." "Quite so," he replied with a laugh; "for had you not lost it, I should never have recovered it." Nor was he less eminent in civil life than in war. In his second consulship, though his colleague would not move in the matter, he resisted as long as he could the proposal of the tribune C. Flaminius to divide the territory of the Picenians and Gauls in free allotments in defiance of a resolution of the Senate. Again, though he was an augur, he ventured to say that whatever was done in the interests of the State was done with the best possible auspices, that any laws proposed against its interest were proposed against the auspices. I was cognisant of much that was admirable in that great man, but nothing struck me with greater astonishment than the way in which he bore the death of his son—a man of brilliant character and who had been consul. His funeral speech over him is in wide circulation, and when we read it, is there any philosopher of whom we do not think

meanly? Nor in truth was he only great in the light of day and in the sight of his fellow-citizens; he was still more eminent in private and at home. What a wealth of conversation! What weighty maxims! What a wide acquaintance with ancient history! What an accurate knowledge of the science of augury! For a Roman, too, he had a great tincture of letters. He had a tenacious memory for military history of every sort, whether of Roman or foreign wars. And I used at that time to enjoy his conversation with a passionate eagerness, as though I already divined, what actually turned out to be the case, that when he died there would be no one to teach me anything.

5. What then is the purpose of such a long disquisition on Maximus? It is because you now see that an old age like his cannot conscientiously be called unhappy. Yet it is after all true that everybody cannot be a Scipio or a Maximus, with stormings of cities, with battles by land and sea, with wars in which they themselves commanded, and with triumphs to recall. Besides this there is a quiet, pure, and cultivated life which produces a calm and gentle old age, such as we have been told Plato's was, who died at his writing-desk in his eighty-first year; or like that of Isocrates, who says that he wrote the book called The Panegyric in his ninety-fourth year, and who lived for five years afterwards; while his master Gorgias of Leontini completed a hundred and seven years without ever relaxing his diligence or giving up work. When some one asked him why he consented to remain so long alive—"I have no fault," said he, "to find with old age." That was a noble answer, and worthy of a scholar. For fools impute their own frailties and guilt to old age, contrary to the practice of Ennui, whom I mentioned just now. In the lines—

> Like some brave steed that oft before
> The Olympic wreath of victory bore,
> Now by the weight of years oppressed,
> Forgets the race, and takes his rest—

he compares his own old age to that of a high-spirited and successful race-horse. And him indeed you may very well remember. For the present consuls Titus Flamininus and Manius Acilius were elected in the nineteenth year after his death; and his death occurred in the consulship of Caepio and Philippus, the latter consul for the second time: in which year I, then sixty-six years old, spoke in favour of the Voconian law in a voice that was still strong and with lungs still sound; while be, though seventy years old, supported two burdens considered the heaviest of all—poverty and old age—in such a way as to be all but fond of them.

The fact is that when I come to think it over, I find that there are four reasons for old age being thought unhappy: First, that it withdraws us from active employments; second, that it enfeebles the body; third, that it deprives us of nearly all physical pleasures; fourth, that it is the next step to death. Of each of these reasons, if you will allow me, let us examine the force and justice separately.

6. OLD AGE WITHDRAWS US FROM ACTIVE EMPLOYMENTS. From which of them? Do you mean from those carried on by youth and bodily strength? Are there then no old men's employments to be after all conducted by the intellect, even when bodies are weak? So then Q. Maximus did nothing; nor L. Aemilius—our father, Scipio, and my excellent son's father-in-law! So with other old men—the Fabricii, the Guru and Coruncanii—when they were supporting the State by their advice and influence, they were doing nothing! To old age Appius Claudius had the additional disadvantage of being blind; yet it was he who, when the Senate was inclining towards a peace with Pyrrhus and was for making a treaty, did not hesitate to say what Ennius has embalmed in the verses:

Whither have swerved the souls so firm of yore?
Is sense grown senseless? Can feet stand no more?

And so on in a tone of the most passionate vehemence. You know the poem, and the speech of Appius himself is extant. Now, he delivered it seventeen years after his second consulship, there having been an interval of ten years between the two consulships, and he having been censor before his previous consulship. This will show you that at the time of the war with Pyrrhus he was a very old man. Yet this is the story handed down to us.

There is therefore nothing in the arguments of those who say that old age takes no part in public business.

They are like men who would say that a steersman does nothing in sailing a ship, because, while some of the crew are climbing the masts, others hurrying up and down the gangways, others pumping out the bilge water, he sits quietly in the stern holding the tiller. He does not do what young men do; nevertheless he does what is much more important and better. The great affairs of life are not performed by physical strength, or activity, or nimbleness of body, but by deliberation, character, expression of opinion. Of these old age is not only not deprived, but, as a rule, has them in a greater degree. Unless by any chance I, who as a soldier in the ranks, as military tribune, as legate, and as consul have been employed in various kinds of war, now appear to you to be idle because not actively engaged in war. But I enjoin upon the Senate what is to be done, and how. Carthage has long been harbouring evil designs, and I accordingly proclaim war against her in good time. I shall never cease to entertain fears about her till I hear of her having been levelled with the ground. The glory of doing that I pray that the immortal gods may reserve for you, Scipio, so that you may complete the task begun by your grand-father, now dead more than thirty-two years ago; though all years to come will keep that great man's memory green. He died in the year before my censorship, nine years after my consulship, having been returned consul for the second time in my own consulship. If then he had lived to his hundredth year, would he have regretted having lived to be old? For he would of course not have been practising rapid marches, nor dashing on a foe, nor hurling spears from a distance, nor using swords at close quarters—but only counsel, reason, and senatorial eloquence. And if those qualities had not resided in us *seniors*, our ancestors would never have called their supreme council a Senate. At Sparta, indeed, those who hold the highest magistracies are in accordance with the fact actually called "elders." But if you will take the trouble to read or listen to foreign history, you will find that the mightiest States have been brought into peril by young men, have been supported and restored by old. The question occurs in the poet Naevius's *Sport*:

Pray, who are those who brought your State
With such despatch to meet its fate?

There is a long answer, but this is the chief point:

A crop of brand-new orators we grew,
And foolish, paltry lads who thought they knew.

For of course rashness is the note of youth, prudence of old age.

7. But, it is said, memory dwindles. No doubt, unless you keep it in practice, or if you happen to be somewhat dull by nature. Themistocles had the names of all his fellow-citizens by heart. Do you imagine that in his old age he used to address Aristides as Lysimachus? For my part, I know not only the present generation, but their fathers also, and their grandfathers. Nor have I any fear of losing my memory by reading tombstones, according to the vulgar superstition. On the contrary, by reading them I renew my memory of those who are dead and gone. Nor, in point of fact, have I ever heard of any old man forgetting where he had hidden his money. They remember everything that interests them: when to answer to their bail, business appointments, who owes them money, and to whom they owe it. What about lawyers, pontiffs, augurs, philosophers, when old? What a multitude of things they remember! Old men retain their intellects well enough, if only they keep their minds active and fully employed. Nor is that the case only with men of high position and great office: it applies equally to private life and peaceful pursuits. Sophocles composed tragedies to extreme old age; and being believed to neglect the care of his property owing to his devotion to his art, his sons brought him into court to get a judicial decision depriving him of the management of his property on the ground of weak intellect—just as in our law it is customary to deprive a paterfamilias of the management of his property if he is squandering it. There—upon the old poet is said to have read to the judges the play he had on hand and had just composed—the *Oedipus Coloneus*—and to have asked them whether they thought that the work of a man of weak intellect. After the reading he was acquitted by the jury. Did old age then compel this man to become silent in his particular art, or Homer, Hesiod, Simonides, or Isocrates and Gorgias whom I mentioned before, or the founders of schools of philosophy, Pythagoras, Democritus, Plato, Xenocrates, or later Zeno and Cleanthus, or Diogenes the Stoic, whom you too saw at Rome? Is it not rather the case with all these that the active pursuit of study only ended with life?

But, to pass over these sublime studies, I can name some rustic Romans from the Sabine district, neighbours and friends of my own, without whose presence farm work of importance is scarcely ever performed—whether sowing, or harvesting or storing crops. And yet in other things this is less surprising; for no one is so old as to think that he may not live a year. But they bestow their labour on what they know does not affect them in any case:

He plants his trees to serve a race to come,

as our poet Statius says in his Comrades. Nor indeed would a farmer, however old, hesitate to answer any one who asked him for whom he was planting: "For the immortal gods, whose will it was that I should not merely receive these things from my ancestors, but should also hand them on to the next generation."

8. That remark about the old man is better than the following:

If age brought nothing worse than this,
It were enough to mar our bliss,
That he who bides for many years
Sees much to shun and much for tears.

Yes, and perhaps much that gives him pleasure too. Besides, as to subjects for tears, he often comes upon them in youth as well.

A still more questionable sentiment in the same Caecilius is:

No greater misery can of age be told
Than this: be sure, the young dislike the old.

Delight in them is nearer the mark than dislike. For just as old men, if they are wise, take pleasure in the society of young men of good parts, and as old age is rendered less dreary for those who are courted and liked by the youth, so also do young men find pleasure in the maxims of the old, by which they are drawn to the pursuit of excellence. Nor do I perceive that you find my society less pleasant than I do yours. But this is enough to show you how, so far from being listless and sluggish, old age is even a busy time, always doing and attempting something, of course of the same nature as each man's taste had been in the previous part of his life. Nay, do not some even add to their stock of learning? We see Solon, for instance, boasting in his poems that he grows old "daily learning something new." Or again in my own case, it was only when an old man that I became acquainted with Greek literature, which in fact I absorbed with such avidity—in my yearning to quench, as it were, a long-continued thirst—that I became acquainted with the very facts which you see me now using as precedents. When I heard what Socrates had done about the lyre I should have liked for my part to have done that too, for the ancients used to learn the lyre but, at any rate, I worked hard at literature.

9. Nor, again, do I now MISS THE BODILY STRENGTH OF A YOUNG MAN (for that was the second point as to the disadvantages of old age) any more than as a young man I missed the strength of a bull or an elephant. You should use what you have, and whatever you may chance to be doing, do it with all your might. What could be weaker than Milo of Croton's exclamation? When in his old age he was watching some athletes practising in the course, he is said to have looked at his arms and to have exclaimed with tears in his eyes: "Ah well! these are now as good as dead." Not a bit more so than yourself, you trifler! For at no time were you made famous by your real self, but by chest and biceps. Sext. Aelius never gave vent to such a remark, nor, many years before him, Titus Coruncanius, nor, more recently, P. Crassus—all of them learned jurisconsults in active practice, whose knowledge of their profession was maintained to their last breath. I am afraid an orator does lose vigour by old age, for his art is not a matter of the intellect alone, but of lungs and bodily strength. Though as a rule that musical ring in the voice even gains in brilliance in a certain way as one grows old—certainly I have not yet lost it, and you see my years. Yet after all the style of speech suitable to an old man is the quiet and unemotional, and it often happens that the chastened and calm delivery of an old man eloquent secures

a hearing. If you cannot attain to that yourself, you might still instruct a Scipio and a Laelius. For what is more charming than old age surrounded by the enthusiasm of youth? Shall we not allow old age even the strength to teach the young, to train and equip them for all the duties of life? And what can be a nobler employment? For my part, I used to think Publius and Gnaeus Scipio and your two grandfathers, L. Aemilius and P. Africanus, fortunate men when I saw them with a company of young nobles about them. Nor should we think any teachers of the fine arts otherwise than happy, however much their bodily forces may have decayed and failed. And yet that same failure of the bodily forces is more often brought about by the vices of youth than of old age; for a dissolute and intemperate youth hands down the body to old age in a worn-out state. Xenophon's Cyrus, for instance, in his discourse delivered on his death-bed and at a very advanced age, says that he never perceived his old age to have become weaker than his youth had been. I remember as a boy Lucius Metellus, who having been created Pontifex Maximus four years after his second consulship, held that office twenty-two years, enjoying such excellent strength of body in the very last hours of his life as not to miss his youth. I need not speak of myself; though that indeed is an old man's way and is generally allowed to my time of life. Don't you see in Homer how frequently Nestor talks of his own good qualities? For he was living through a third generation; nor had he any reason to fear that upon saying what was true about himself he should appear either over vain or talkative. For, as Homer says, "from his lips flowed discourse sweeter than honey," for which sweet breath he wanted no bodily strength. And yet, after all, the famous leader of the Greeks nowhere wishes to have ten men like Ajax, but like Nestor: if he could get them, he feels no doubt of Troy shortly falling.

10. But to return to my own case: I am in my eighty-fourth year. I could wish that I had been able to make the same boast as Cyrus; but, after all, I can say this: I am not indeed as vigorous as I was as a private soldier in the Punic war, or as quaestor in the same war, or as consul in Spain, and four years later when as a military tribune I took part

in the engagement at Thermopylae under the consul Manius Acilius Glabrio; but yet, as you see, old age has not entirely destroyed my muscles, has not quite brought me to the ground. The Senate-house does not find all my vigour gone, nor the rostra, nor my friends, nor my clients, nor my foreign guests. For I have never given in to that ancient and much-praised proverb:

Old when young
Is old for long.

For myself, I had rather be an old man a somewhat shorter time than an old man *before* my time. Accordingly, no one up to the present has wished to see me, to whom I have been denied as engaged. But, it may be said, I have less strength than either of you. Neither have you the strength of the centurion T. Pontius: is he the more eminent man on that account? Let there be only a proper husbanding of strength, and let each man proportion his efforts to his powers. Such an one will assuredly not be possessed with any great regret for his loss of strength. At Olympia Milo is said to have stepped into the course carrying a live ox on his shoulders. Which then of the two would you prefer to have given to you—bodily strength like that, or intellectual strength like that of Pythagoras? In fine, enjoy that blessing when you have it; when it is gone, don't wish it back—unless we are to think that young men should wish their childhood back, and those somewhat older their youth! The course of life is fixed, and nature admits of its being run but in one way, and only once; and to each part of our life there is something specially seasonable; so that the feebleness of children, as well as the high spirit of youth, the soberness of maturer years, and the ripe wisdom of old age—all have a certain natural advantage which should be secured in its proper season. I think you are informed, Scipio, what your grandfather's foreign friend Masinissa does to this day, though ninety years old. When he has once begun a journey on foot he does not mount his horse at all; when on horseback he never gets off his horse. By no rain or cold can he be induced to cover his head. His body is absolutely free from unhealthy humours, and so he still performs all the duties and functions of a king. Active exercise, therefore, and

temperance can preserve some part of one's former strength even in old age.

11. Bodily strength is wanting to old age; but neither is bodily strength demanded from old men. Therefore, both by law and custom, men of my time of life are exempt from those duties which cannot be supported without bodily strength. Accordingly not only are we not forced to do what we cannot do; we are not even obliged to do as much as we can. But, it will be said, many old men are so feeble that they cannot perform any duty in life of any sort or kind. That is not a weakness to be set down as peculiar to old age: it is one shared by ill health. How feeble was the son of P. Africanus, who adopted you! What weak health he had, or rather no health at all! If that had not been the case, we should have had in him a second brilliant light in the political horizon; for he had added a wider cultivation to his father's greatness of spirit. What wonder, then, that old men are eventually feeble, when even young men cannot escape it? My dear Laelius and Scipio, we must stand up against old age and make up for its drawbacks by taking pains. We must fight it as we should an illness. We must look after our health, use moderate exercise, take just enough food and drink to recruit, but not to overload, our strength. Nor is it the body alone that must be supported, but the intellect and soul much more. For they are like lamps: unless you feed them with oil, they too go out from old age. Again, the body is apt to get gross from exercise; but the intellect becomes nimbler by exercising itself. For what Caecilius means by "old dotards of the comic stage" are the credulous, the forgetful, and the slipshod. These are faults that do not attach to old age as such, but to a sluggish, spiritless, and sleepy old age. Young men are more frequently wanton and dissolute than old men; but yet, as it is not all young men that are so, but the bad set among them, even so senile folly—usually called imbecility—applies to old men of unsound character, not to all. Appius governed four sturdy sons, five daughters, that great establishment, and all those clients, though he was both old and blind. For he kept his mind at full stretch like a how, and never gave in to old age by growing slack. He maintained not merely an influence, but an absolute command over his

family: his slaves feared him, his sons were in awe of him, all loved him. In that family, indeed, ancestral custom and discipline were in full vigour. The fact is that old age is respectable just as long as it asserts itself, maintains its proper rights, and is not enslaved to any one. For as I admire a young man who has something of the old man in him, so do I an old one who has something of a young man. The man who aims at this may possibly become old in body—in mind he never will. I am now engaged in composing the seventh book of my *Origins*. I collect all the records of antiquity. The speeches delivered in all the celebrated cases which I have defended I am at this particular time getting into shape for publication. I am writing treatises on augural, pontifical, and civil law. I am, besides, studying hard at Greek, and after the manner of the Pythagoreans—to keep my memory in working order—I repeat in the evening whatever I have said, heard, or done in the course of each day. These are the exercises of the intellect, these the training grounds of the mind: while I sweat and labour on these I don't much feel the loss of bodily strength. I appear in court for my friends; I frequently attend the Senate and bring motions before it on my own responsibility, prepared after deep and long reflection. And these I support by my intellectual, not my bodily forces. And if I were not strong enough to do these things, yet I should enjoy my sofa—imagining the very operations which I was now unable to perform. But what makes me capable of doing this is my past life. For a man who is always living in the midst of these studies and labours does not perceive when old age creeps upon him. Thus, by slow and imperceptible degrees life draws to its end. There is no sudden breakage; it just slowly goes out.

12. The third charge against old age is that it LACKS SENSUAL PLEASURES. What a splendid service does old age render, if it takes from us the greatest blot of youth! Listen, my dear young friends, to a speech of Archytas of Tarentum, among the greatest and most illustrious of men, which was put into my hands when as a young man I was at Tarentum with Q. Maximus. "No more deadly curse than sensual pleasure has been inflicted on mankind by nature, to gratify which our wanton appetites are roused beyond all prudence or restraint. It is a fruitful source

of treasons, revolutions, secret communications with the enemy. In fact, there is no crime, no evil deed, to which the appetite for sensual pleasures does not impel us. Fornications and adulteries, and every abomination of that kind, are brought about by the enticements of pleasure and by them alone. Intellect is the best gift of nature or God: to this divine gift and endowment there is nothing so inimical as pleasure. For when appetite is our master, there is no place for self-control; nor where pleasure reigns supreme can virtue hold its ground. To see this more vividly, imagine a man excited to the highest conceivable pitch of sensual pleasure. It can be doubtful to no one that such a person, so long as he is under the influence of such excitation of the senses, will be unable to use to any purpose either intellect, reason, or thought. Therefore nothing can be so execrable and so fatal as pleasure; since, when more than ordinarily violent and lasting, it darkens all the light of the soul."

These were the words addressed by Archytas to the Samnite Caius Pontius, father of the man by whom the consuls Spurius Postumius and Titus Veturius were beaten in the battle of Caudium. My friend Nearchus of Tarentum, who had remained loyal to Rome, told me that he had heard them repeated by some old men; and that Plato the Athenian was present, who visited Tarentum, I find, in the consulship of L. Camillus and Appius Claudius.

What is the point of all this? It is to show you that, if we were unable to scorn pleasure by the aid of reason and philosophy, we ought to have been very grateful to old age for depriving us of all inclination for that which it was wrong to do. For pleasure hinders thought, is a foe to reason, and, so to speak, blinds the eyes of the mind. It is, moreover, entirely alien to virtue. I was sorry to have to expel Lucius, brother of the gallant Titus Flamininus, from the Senate seven years after his consulship; but I thought it imperative to affix a stigma on an act of gross sensuality. For when he was in Gaul as consul, he had yielded to the entreaties of his paramour at a dinner-party to behead a man who happened to be in prison condemned on a capital charge. When his brother Titus was Censor, who preceded me, he escaped; but I and Flaccus could not countenance an act of such criminal and abandoned lust, especially as, besides the personal dishonour, it brought disgrace on the Government.

13. I have often been told by men older than myself, who said that they had heard it as boys from old men, that Gaius Fabricius was in the habit of expressing astonishment at having heard, when envoy at the headquarters of king Pyrrhus, from the Thessalian Cineas, that there was a man of Athens who professed to be a "philosopher," and affirmed that everything we did was to be referred to pleasure. When he told this to Manius Curius and Publius Decius, they used to remark that they wished that the Samnites and Pyrrhus himself would hold the same opinion. It would be much easier to conquer them, if they had once given themselves over to sensual indulgences. Manius Curius had been intimate with P. Decius, who four years before the former's consulship had devoted himself to death for the Republic. Both Fabricius and Coruncanius knew him also, and from the experience of their own lives, as well as from the action of P. Decius, they were of opinion that there did exist something intrinsically noble and great, which was sought for its own sake, and at which all the best men aimed, to the contempt and neglect of pleasure. Why then do I spend so many words on the subject of pleasure? Why, because, far from being a charge against old age, that it does not much feel the want of any pleasures, it is its highest praise.

But, you will say, it is deprived of the pleasures of the table, the heaped up board, the rapid passing of the wine-cup. Well, then, it is also free from headache, disordered digestion, broken sleep. But if we must grant pleasure something, since we do not find it easy to resist its charms,—for Plato, with happy inspiration, calls pleasure "vice's bait," because of course men are caught by it as fish by a hook,—yet, although old age has to abstain from extravagant banquets, it is still capable of enjoying modest festivities. As a boy I often used to see Gaius Duilius the son of Marcus, then an old mali, returning from a dinner-party. He thoroughly enjoyed the frequent use of torch and flute-player, distinctions which he had assumed though unprecedented in the case of a private person. It was the privilege of his glory. But why mention others? I will come back to my own

case. To begin with, I have always remained a member of a "club"—clubs, you know, were established in my quaestorship on the reception of the Magna Mater from Ida. So I used to dine at their feast with the members of my club—on the whole with moderation, though there was a certain warmth of temperament natural to my time of life; but as that advances there is a daily decrease of all excitement. Nor was I, in fact, ever wont to measure my enjoyment even of these banquets by the physical pleasures they gave more than by the gathering and conversation of friends. For it was a good idea of our ancestors to style the presence of guests at a dinner-table—seeing that it implied a community of enjoyment—a *convivium*, "a living together." It is a better term than the Greek words which mean "a drinking together," or, "an eating together." For they would seem to give the preference to what is really the least important part of it.

14. For myself, owing to the pleasure I take in conversation, I enjoy even banquets that begin early in the afternoon, and not only in company with my contemporaries—of whom very few survive—but also with men of your age and with yourselves. I am thankful to old age, which has increased my avidity for conversation, while it has removed that for eating and drinking. But if anyone does enjoy these—not to seem to have proclaimed war against all pleasure without exception, which is perhaps a feeling inspired by nature—I fail to perceive even in these very pleasures that old age is entirely without the power of appreciation. For myself, I take delight even in the old-fashioned appointment of master of the feast; and in the arrangement of the conversation, which according to ancestral custom is begun from the last place on the left-hand couch when the wine is brought in; as also in the cups which, as in Xenophon's banquet, are small and filled by driblets; and in the contrivance for cooling in summer, and for warming by the winter sun or winter fire. These things I keep up even among my Sabine countrymen, and every day have a full dinner-party of neighbours, which we prolong as far into the night as we can with varied conversation.

But you may urge—there is not the same tingling sensation of pleasure in old men. No doubt; but neither do they miss it so much. For nothing gives you uneasiness which you do not miss. That was a fine answer of Sophocles to a man who asked him, when in extreme old age, whether he was still a lover. "Heaven forbid!" he replied; "I was only too glad to escape from that, as though from a boorish and insane master." To men indeed who are keen after such things it may possibly appear disagreeable and uncomfortable to be without them; but to jaded appetites it is pleasanter to lack than to enjoy. However, he cannot be said to lack who does not want: my contention is that not to want is the pleasanter thing.

But even granting that youth enjoys these pleasures with more zest; in the first place, they are insignificant things to enjoy, as I have said; and in the second place, such as age is not entirely without, if it does not possess them in profusion. Just as a man gets greater pleasure from Ambivius Turpio if seated in the front row at the theatre than if he was in the last, yet, after all, the man in the last row does get pleasure; so youth, because it looks at pleasures at closer quarters, perhaps enjoys itself more, yet even old age, looking at them from a distance, does enjoy itself well enough. Why, what blessings are these—that the soul, having served its time, so to speak, in the campaigns of desire and ambition, rivalry and hatred, and all the passions, should live in its own thoughts, and, as the expression goes, should dwell apart! Indeed, if it has in store any of what I may call the food of study and philosophy, nothing can be pleasanter than an old age of leisure. We were witnesses to C. Gallus—a friend of your father's, Scipio—intent to the day of his death on mapping out the sky and land. How often did the light surprise him while still working out a problem begun during the night! How often did night find him busy on what he had begun at dawn! How he delighted in predicting for us solar and lunar eclipses long before they occurred! Or again in studies of a lighter nature, though still requiring keenness of intellect, what pleasure Naevius took in his *Punic War*! Plautus in his *Truculentus* and *Pseudolus*! I even saw Livius Andronicus, who, having produced a play six years before I was born—in the consulship of Cento and Tuditanus—lived till I had become a young man. Why speak of Publius Licinius Crassus's

devotion to pontifical and civil law, or of the Publius Scipio of the present time, who within these last few days has been created Pontifex Maximus? And yet I have seen all whom I have mentioned ardent in these pursuits when old men. Then there is Marcus Cethegus, whom Ennius justly called "Persuasion's Marrow"—with what enthusiasm did we see him exert himself in oratory even when quite old! What pleasures are there in feasts, games, or mistresses comparable to pleasures such as these? And they are all tastes, too, connected with learning, which in men of sense and good education grow with their growth. It is indeed an honourable sentiment which Solon expresses in a verse which I have quoted before—that he grew old learning many a fresh lesson every day. Than that intellectual pleasure none certainly can be greater.

15. I come now to the pleasures of the farmer, in which I take amazing delight. These are not hindered by any extent of old age, and seem to me to approach nearest to' the ideal wise man's life. For he has to deal with the earth, which never refuses its obedience, nor ever returns what it has received without usury; sometimes, indeed, with less, but generally with greater interest. For my part, however, it is not merely the thing produced, but the earth's own force and natural productiveness that delight me. For received in its bosom the seed scattered broadcast upon it, softened and broken up, she first keeps it concealed therein (hence the harrowing which accomplishes this gets its name from a word meaning "to hide"); next, when it has been warmed by her heat and close pressure, she splits it open and draws from it the greenery of the blade. This, supported by the fibres of the root, little by little grows up, and held upright by its jointed stalk is enclosed in sheaths, as being still immature. When it has emerged from them it produces an ear of corn arranged in order, and is defended against the pecking of the smaller birds by a regular palisade of spikes.

Need I mention the starting, planting, and growth of vines? I can never have too much of this pleasure—to let you into the secret of what gives my old age repose and amusement. For I say nothing here of the natural force which all things propagated from the earth possess—the earth which from that tiny grain in a fig, or the grape-stone in a grape, or the most minute seeds of the other cereals and plants, produces such huge trunks and boughs. Mallet-shoots, slips, cuttings, quicksets, layers—are they not enough to fill anyone with delight and astonishment? The vine by nature is apt to fall, and unless supported drops down to the earth; yet in order to keep itself upright it embraces whatever it reaches with its tendrils as though they were hands. Then as it creeps on, spreading itself in intricate and wild profusion, the dresser's art prunes it with the knife and prevents it growing a forest of shoots and expanding to excess in every direction. Accordingly at the beginning of spring in the shoots which have been left there protrudes at each of the joints what is termed an From this the grape emerges and shows itself; which, swollen by the juice of the earth and the heat of the sun, is at first very bitter to the taste, but afterwards grows sweet as it matures; and being covered with tendrils is never without a moderate warmth, and yet is able to ward off the fiery heat of the sun. Can anything be richer in product or more beautiful to contemplate? It is not its utility only, as I said before, that charms me, but the method of its cultivation and the natural process of its growth: the rows of uprights, the cross-pieces for the tops of the plants, the tying up of the vines and their propagation by layers, the pruning, to which I have already referred, of some shoots, the setting of others. I need hardly mention irrigation, or trenching and digging the soil, which much increase its fertility. As to the advantages of manuring I have spoken in my book on agriculture. The learned Hesiod did not say a single word on this subject, though he was writing on the cultivation of the soil; yet Homer, who in my opinion was many generations earlier, represents Laertes as softening his regret for his son by cultivating and manuring his farm. Nor is it only in cornfields and meadows and vineyards and plantations that a farmer's life is made cheerful. There are the garden and the orchard, the feeding of sheep, the swarms of bees, endless varieties of flowers. Nor is it only planting out that charms: there is also grafting—surely the most ingenious invention ever made by husbandmen.

16. I might continue my list of the delights of country life; but even what I have said I think is somewhat over long. However, you must pardon me; for farming is a very favourite hobby of mine, and old age is naturally rather garrulous—for I would not be thought to acquit it of all faults.

Well, it was in a life of this sort that Manius Curius, after celebrating triumphs over the Samnites, the Sabines, and Pyrrhus, spent his last days. When I look at his villa—for it is not far from my own—I never can enough admire the man's own frugality or the spirit of the age. As Curius was sitting at his hearth the Samnites, who brought him a large sum of gold, were repulsed by him; for it was not, lie said, a fine thing in his eyes to possess gold, but to rule those who possessed it. Could such a high spirit fail to make old age pleasant?

But to return to farmers—not to wander from my own metier. Tn those days there were senators, *i. e.* old men, on their farms. For L. Quinctius Cincinnatus was actually at the plough when word was brought him that he had been named Dictator. It was by his order as Dictator, by the way, that C. Servilius Ahala, the Master of the Horse, seized and put to death Spurius Maelius when attempting to obtain royal power. Curius as well as other old men used to receive their summonses to attend the Senate in their farm-houses, from which circumstance the summoners were called *viatores* or "travellers." Was these men's old age an object of pity who found their pleasure in the cultivation of the land? In my opinion, scarcely any life can be more blessed, not alone from its utility (for agriculture is beneficial to the whole human race), but also as much from the mere pleasure of the thing, to which I have already alluded, and from the rich abundance and supply of all things necessary for the food of man and for the worship of the gods above. So, as these are objects of desire to certain people, let us make our peace with pleasure. For the good and hard-working farmer's wine-cellar and oil-store, as well as his larder, are always well filled, and his whole farm-house is richly furnished. It abounds in pigs, goats, lambs, fowls, milk, cheese, and honey. Then there is the garden, which the farmers themselves call their "second flitch." A zest and flavour is added to all these by hunting and fowling in spare hours. Need I mention the greenery of meadows, the rows of trees, the beauty of vineyard and olive-grove? I 'will put it briefly: nothing can either furnish necessaries more richly, or present a fairer spectacle, than well-cultivated land. And to the enjoyment of that, old age does not merely present no hindrance—it actually invites and allures to it. For where else can it better warm itself, either by basking in the sun or by sitting by the fire, or at the proper time cool itself more wholesomely by the help of shade or water? Let the young keep their arms then to themselves, their horses, spears, their foils and ball, their swimming baths and running path. To us old men let them, out of the many forms of sport, leave dice and counters; but even that as they choose, since old age can be quite happy without them.

17. Xenophon's books are very useful for many purposes. Pray go on reading them with attention, as you have ever done. In what ample terms is agriculture lauded by him in the book about husbanding one's property, which is called *Oceonomicus*! But to show you that he thought nothing so worthy of a prince as the taste for cultivating the soil, I will translate what Socrates says to Critobulus in that book:

"When that most gallant Lacedaemonian Lysander came to visit the Persian prince Cyrus at Sardis, so eminent for his character and the glory of his rule, bringing him presents from his allies, he treated Lysander in all ways with courteous familiarity and kindness, and, among other things, took him to see a certain park carefully planted. Lysander expressed admiration of the height of the trees and the exact arrangement of their rows in the quincunx, the careful cultivation of the soil, its freedom from weeds, and the sweetness of the odours exhaled from the flowers, and went on to say that what he admired was not the industry only, but also the skill of the man by whom this had been planned and laid out. Cyrus replied: 'Well, it was I who planned the whole thing these rows are my doing, the laying out is all mine; many of the trees were even planted by own hand.' Then Lysander, looking at his purple robe, the brilliance of his person, and his adornment Persian fashion with gold and many jewels, said: 'People are quite right, Cyrus, to call you happy, since the advantages of high fortune have been joined to an excellence like yours.'"

This kind of good fortune, then, it is in the power of old men to enjoy; nor is age any bar to our maintaining pursuits of every other kind, and especially of agriculture, to the very extreme verge of old age. For instance, we have it on record that M. Valerius Corvus kept it up to his hundredth year, living on his land and cultivating it after his active career was over, though between his first and sixth consulships there was an interval of six and forty years. So that he had an official career lasting the number of years which our ancestors defined as coming between birth and the beginning of old age. Moreover, that last period of his old age was more blessed than that of his middle life, inasmuch as he had greater influence and less labour. For the crowning grace of old age is influence.

How great was that of L. Caecilius Metellus! How great that of Atilius Calatinus, over whom the famous epitaph was placed, "Very many classes agree in deeming this to have been the very first man of the nation"! The line cut on his tomb is well known. It is natural, then, that a man should have had influence, in whose praise the verdict of history is unanimous. Again, in recent times, what a great man was Publius Crassus, Pontifex Maximus, and his successor in the same office, M. Lepidus! I need scarcely mention Paulus or Africanus, or, as I did before, Maximus. It was not only their senatorial utterances that had weight: their least gesture had it also. In fact, old age, especially when it has enjoyed honours, has an influence worth all the pleasures of youth put together.

18. But throughout my discourse remember that my panegyric applies to an old age that has been established on foundations laid by youth. From which may be deduced what I once said with universal applause, that it was a wretched old age that had to defend itself by speech. Neither white hairs nor wrinkles can at once claim influence in themselves: it is the honourable conduct of earlier days that is rewarded by possessing influence at the last. Even things generally regarded as trifling and matters of course—being saluted, being courted, having way made for one, people rising when one approaches,

being escorted to and from the forum, being referred to for advice—all these are marks of respect, observed among us and in other States—always most sedulously where the moral tone is highest. They say that Lysander the Spartan, whom I have mentioned before, used to remark that Sparta was the most dignified home for old age; for that nowhere was more respect paid to years, no-where was old age held in higher honour. Nay, the story is told of how when a man of advanced years came into the theatre at Athens when the games were going on, no place was given him anywhere in that large assembly by his own countrymen; but when he came near the Lacedaemonians, who as ambassadors had a fixed place assigned to them, they rose as one man out of respect for him, and gave the veteran a seat. When they were greeted with rounds of applause from the whole audience, one of them remarked:

"The Athenians know what is right, but will not do it." There are many excellent rules in our augural college, but among the best is one which affects our subject—that precedence in speech goes by seniority; and augurs who are older are preferred only to those who have held higher office, but even to those who are actually in possession of imperium. What then are the physical pleasures to be compared with the reward of influence? Those who have employed it with distinction appear to me to have played the drama of life to its end, and not to have broken down in the last act like unpractised players.

But, it will be said, old men are fretful, fidgety, ill-tempered, and disagreeable. If you come to that, they are also avaricious. But these are faults of character, not of the time of life. And, after all, fretfulness and the other faults I mentioned admit of some excuse—not, indeed, a complete one, but one that may possibly pass muster: they think themselves neglected, looked down upon, mocked, Besides with bodily weakness every rub is a source of pain. Yet all these faults are softened both by good character and good education. Illustrations of this may be found in real life, as also on the stage in the case of the brothers in the *Adeiphi*. What harshness in the one, what gracious manners in the other The fact is that, just as it is not every wine, so it is not every life, that turns sour from keeping, Serious gravity I approve of in

old age, but, as in other things, it must be within due limits: bitterness I can in no case approve. What the object of senile avarice may be I cannot conceive. For can there be anything more absurd than to seek more journey money, the less there remains of the journey?

19. There remains the fourth reason, which more than anything else appears to torment men of my age and keep them in a flutter—THE NEARNESS OF DEATH, which, it must be allowed, cannot be far from an old man. But what a poor dotard must he be who has not learnt in the course of so long a life that death is not a thing to be feared? Death, that is either to be totally disregarded, if it entirely extinguishes the soul, or is even to be desired, if it brings him where he is to exist forever. A third alternative, at any rate, cannot possibly be discovered. Why then should I be afraid if I am destined either not to be miserable after death or even to be happy? After all, who is such a fool as to feel certain—however young he may be—that he will be alive in the evening? Nay, that time of life has many more chances of death than ours, Young men more easily contract diseases; their illnesses are more serious; their treatment has to be more severe. Accordingly, only a few arrive at old age. If that were not so, life would be conducted better and more wisely; for it is in old men that thought, reason, and prudence are to be found; and if there had been no old men, States would never have existed at all. But I return to the subject of the imminence of death. What sort of charge is this against old age, when you see that it is shared by youth? I had reason in the case of my excellent son—as you had, Scipio, in that of your brothers, who were expected to attain the highest honours—to realise that death is common to every time of life. Yes, you will say; but a young man expects to live long; an old man cannot expect to do so. Well, he is a fool to expect it. For what can be more foolish than to regard the uncertain as certain, the false as true? "An old man has nothing even to hope." Ah, but it is just there that he is in a better position than a young man, since what the latter only hopes he has obtained. The one wishes to live long; the other has lived long.

And yet, good heaven! what is "long" in a man's life? For grant the utmost limit: let us expect an age like that of the King of the Tartessi. For there was, as I find recorded, a certain Agathonius at Gades who reigned eighty years and lived a hundred and twenty. But to my mind nothing seems even long in which there is any "last," for when that arrives, then all the past has slipped away—only that remains to which you have attained by virtue and righteous actions. Hours indeed, and days and months and years depart, nor does past time ever return, nor can the future be known. Whatever time each is granted for life, with that he is bound to be content. An actor, in order to earn approval, is not bound to perform the play from beginning to end; let him only satisfy the audience in whatever act he appears. Nor need a wise man go on to the concluding "plaudite." For a short term of life is long enough for living well and honourably. But if you go farther, you have no more right to grumble than farmers do because the charm of the spring season is past and the summer and autumn have come. For the word "spring" in a way suggests youth, and points to the harvest to be: the other seasons are suited for the reaping and storing of the crops. Now the harvest of old age is, as I have often said, the memory and rich store of blessings laid up in easier life. Again, all things that accord with nature are to be counted as good. But what can be more in accordance with nature than for old men to die? A thing, indeed, which also beliefs young men, though nature revolts and fights against it. Accordingly, the death of young men seems to me like putting out a great fire with a deluge of water; but old men die like a fire going out because it has burnt down of its own nature without artificial means. Again, just as apples when unripe are torn from trees, but when ripe and mellow drop down, so it is violence that takes life from young men, ripeness from old. This ripeness is so delightful to me, that, as I approach nearer to death, I seem as it were to be sighting land, and to be coming to port at last after a long voyage.

20. Again, there is no fixed borderline for old age, and you are making a good and proper use of it as long as you can satisfy the call of duty and disregard death. The result of this is, that old age is even more confident and courageous than youth. That is the meaning of Solon's answer to the tyrant Pisistratus. When the latter asked him what he relied upon in opposing him with such boldness, he is said to have replied, "On my old age." But that end of life is the best, when, without the intellect or senses being impaired, Nature herself takes to pieces her own handiwork which she also put together. Just as the builder of a ship or a house can break them up more easily than any one else, so the nature that knit together the human frame can also best unfasten it. Moreover, a thing freshly glued together is always difficult to pull asunder; if old, this is easily done.

The result is that the short time of life left to them is not to be grasped at by old men with greedy eagerness, or abandoned without cause. Pythagoras forbids us, without an order from our commander, that is God, to desert life's fortress and outpost. Solon's epitaph, indeed, is that of a wise man, in which he says that he does not wish his death to be unaccompanied by the sorrow and lamentations of his friends. He wants, I suppose, to be beloved by them. But I rather think Ennius says better:

None grace me with their tears, nor weeping loud
Make sad my funeral rites!

He holds that a death is not a subject for mourning when it is followed by immortality.

Again, there may possibly be some sensation of dying and that only for a short time, especially in the case of an old man: after death, indeed, sensation is either what one would desire, or it disappears altogether. But to disregard death is a lesson which must be studied from our youth up; for unless that is learnt, no one can have a quiet mind. For die we certainly must, and that too without being certain whether it may not be this very day. As death, therefore, is hanging over our head every hour, how can a man ever be unshaken in soul if he fears it?

But on this theme I don't think I need much enlarge: when I remember what Lucius Brutus did, who was killed while defending his country; or the two Decii, who spurred their horses to a gallop and met a voluntary death; or M. Atilius Regulus, who left his home to confront a death of torture, rather than break the word which lie had pledged to the enemy; or the two Scipios, who determined to block the Carthaginian advance even with their own bodies;

or your grandfather Lucius Paulus, who paid with his life for the rashness of his colleague in the disgrace at Cannae; or M. Marcellus, whose death not even the most bloodthirsty of enemies would allow to go without the honour of burial. It is enough to recall that our legions (as I have recorded in my *Origins*) have often marched with cheerful and lofty spirit to ground from which they believed that they would never return. That, therefore, which young men—not only uninstructed, but absolutely ignorant—treat as of no account, shall men who are neither young nor ignorant shrink from in terror? As a general truth, as it seems to me, it is weariness of all pursuits that creates weariness of life. There are certain pursuits adapted to childhood: do young men miss them? There are others suited to early manhood: does that settled time of life called "middle age" ask for them? There are others, again, suited to that age, but not looked for in old age. There are, finally, some which belong to Old age. Therefore, as the pursuits of the earlier ages have their time for disappearing, so also have those of old age. And when that takes place, a satiety of life brings on the ripe time for death.

21. For I do not see why I should not venture to tell you my personal opinion as to death, of which I seem to myself to have a clearer vision in proportion as I am nearer to it. I believe, Scipio and Laelius, that your fathers—those illustrious men and my dearest friends—are still alive, and that too with a life which alone deserves the name. For as long as we are imprisoned in this framework of the body, we perform a certain function and laborious work assigned us by fate. The soul, in fact, is of heavenly origin, forced down from its home in the highest, and, so to speak, buried in earth, a place quite opposed to its divine nature and its immortality. But I suppose the immortal gods to have sown souls broadcast in human bodies, that there might be some to survey the world, and while contemplating the order of the heavenly bodies to imitate it in the unvarying regularity of their life. Nor is it only reason and arguments that have brought me to this belief, but the great fame and authority of the most distinguished philosophers. I used to be told that Pythagoras and the Pythagoreans—almost natives of our country, who in old times had been called the Italian school of philosophers—never doubted that we had souls

drafted from the universal Divine intelligence. I used besides to have pointed out to me the discourse delivered by Socrates on the last day of his life upon the immortality of the soul—Socrates who was pronounced by the oracle at Delphi to be the wisest of men. I need say no more. I have convinced myself, and I hold—in view of the rapid movement of the soul, its vivid memory of the past and its prophetic knowledge of the future, its many accomplishments, its vast range of knowledge, its numerous discoveries —that a nature embracing such varied gifts cannot itself be mortal. And since the soul is always in motion and yet has no external source of motion, for it is self-moved, I conclude that it will also have no end to its motion, because it is not likely ever to abandon itself. Again, since the nature of the soul is not composite, nor has in it any admixture that is not homogeneous and similar, I conclude that it is indivisible, and, if indivisible, that it cannot perish. It is again a strong proof of men knowing most things before birth, that when mere children they grasp innumerable facts with such speed as to show that they are not then taking them in for the first time, but remembering and recalling them. This is roughly Plato's argument.

22. Once more in Xenophon we have the elder Cyrus on his deathbed speaking as follows:—

"Do not suppose, my dearest sons, that when I have left you I shall be nowhere and no one. Even when I was with you, you did not see my soul, but knew that it was in this body of mine from what I did. Believe then that it is still the same, even though you see it not. The honours paid to illustrious men had not continued to exist after their death, had the souls of these very men not done something to make us retain our recollection of them beyond the ordinary time. For myself, I never could be persuaded that souls while in mortal bodies were alive, and died directly they left them; nor, in fact, that the soul only lost all intelligence when it left the unintelligent body. I believe rather that when, by being liberated from all corporeal admixture, it has begun to be pure and undefiled, it is then that it becomes wise. And again, when man's natural frame is resolved into its elements by death, it is clearly seen whither each of the other elements departs: for they all go to the place from which they came: but the soul alone is invisible alike when present and when departing. Once more, you see that nothing is so like death as sleep. And yet it is in sleepers that souls most clearly reveal their divine nature; for they foresee many events when they are allowed to escape and are left free. This shows what they are likely to be when they have completely freed themselves from the fetters of the body. Wherefore, if these things are so, obey me as a god. But if my soul is to perish with my body,

nevertheless do you from awe of the gods, who guard and govern this fair universe, preserve my memory by the loyalty and piety of your lives."

THE LIVES OF THE TWELVE CAESARS

C. Suetonius Tranquillus;
The Translation of Alexander Thomson, M.D.
revised and corrected by T. Forester, Esq., A.M.

NERO CLAUDIUS CAESAR

(337)

I. Two celebrated families, the Calvini and Aenobarbi, sprung from the race of the Domitii. The Aenobarbi derive both their extraction and their cognomen from one Lucius Domitius, of whom we have this tradition:—As he was returning out of the country to Rome, he was met by two young men of a most august appearance, who desired him to announce to the senate and people a victory, of which no certain intelligence had yet reached the city. To prove that they were more than mortals, they stroked his cheeks, and thus changed his hair, which was black, to a bright colour, resembling that of brass; which mark of distinction descended to his posterity, for they had generally red beards. This family had the honour of seven consulships [548], one triumph [549], and two censorships [550]; and being admitted into the patrician order, they continued the use of the same cognomen, with no other praenomina [551] than those of Cneius and Lucius. These, however, they assumed with singular irregularity; three persons in succession sometimes adhering to one of them, and then they were changed alternately. For the first, second, and third of the Aenobarbi had the praenomen of Lucius, and again the three following, successively, that of Cneius, while those who came after were called, by turns, one, Lucius, and the other, Cneius. It appears to me proper to give a short account of several of the family, to show that Nero so far degenerated from the noble qualities of his ancestors, that he retained only their vices; as if those alone had been transmitted to him by his descent.

II. To begin, therefore, at a remote period, his great-grandfather's grandfather, Cneius Domitius, when he was tribune of the people, being offended with the high priests for electing another than himself in the room of his father, obtained the (338) transfer of the right of election from the colleges of the priests to the people. In his consulship [552], having conquered the Allobroges and the Arverni [553], he made a progress through the province, mounted upon an elephant, with a body of soldiers attending him, in a sort of triumphal pomp. Of this person the orator Licinius Crassus said, "It was no wonder he had a brazen beard, who had a face of iron, and a heart of lead." His son, during his praetorship [554], proposed that Cneius Caesar, upon the expiration of his consulship, should be called to account before the senate for his administration of that office, which was supposed to be contrary both to the omens and the laws. Afterwards, when he was consul himself [555], he tried to deprive Cneius of the command of the army, and having been, by intrigue and cabal, appointed his successor, he was made prisoner at Corsinium, in the beginning of the civil war. Being set at liberty, he went to Marseilles, which was then besieged; where having, by his presence, animated the people to hold out, he suddenly deserted them, and at last was slain in the battle of Pharsalia. He was a man of little constancy, and of a sullen temper. In despair of his fortunes, he had recourse to poison, but was so terrified at the thoughts of death, that, immediately repenting, he took a vomit to throw it up again, and gave freedom to his physician for having, with great prudence and wisdom, given him only a gentle dose of the poison. When Cneius Pompey was consulting with his friends in what manner he should conduct himself towards those who were neuter and took no part in the contest, he was the only one who proposed that they should be treated as enemies.

III. He left a son, who was, without doubt, the best of the family. By the Pedian law, he was condemned, although innocent, amongst others who were concerned in the death of Caesar [556]. Upon this, he went over to Brutus and Cassius, his near relations; and, after their death, not only kept together the fleet, the command of which had been given him some time before, but even increased it. At last, when the party had everywhere been defeated, he voluntarily surrendered it to (339) Mark Antony; considering it as a piece of service for which the latter owed him no small obligations. Of all those who were condemned by the law above-mentioned, he was the only man who was restored to his country, and filled the highest offices. When the civil war again broke out, he was appointed lieutenant under the same Antony, and offered the chief command by those who were ashamed of Cleopatra; but not daring, on account of a sudden indisposition with which he was seized, either to accept or refuse it, he went over to Augustus [557], and died a few days after, not without an aspersion cast upon his memory. For Antony gave out, that he was induced to change sides by his impatience to be with his mistress, Servilia Nais. [558]

IV. This Cneius had a son, named Domitius, who was afterwards well known as the nominal purchaser of the family property left by Augustus's will [559]; and no less famous in his youth for his dexterity in chariot-driving, than he was afterwards for the triumphal ornaments which he obtained in the German war. But he was a man of great arrogance, prodigality, and cruelty. When he was aedile, he obliged Lucius Plancus, the censor, to give him the way; and in his praetorship, and consulship, he made Roman knights and married women act on the stage. He gave hunts of wild beasts, both in the Circus and in all the wards of the city; as also a show of gladiators; but with such barbarity, that Augustus, after privately reprimanding him, to no purpose, was obliged to restrain him by a public edict.

V. By the elder Antonia he had Nero's father, a man of execrable character in every part of his life. During his attendance upon Caius Caesar in the East, he killed a freedman of his own, for refusing to drink as much as he ordered him. Being dismissed for this from Caesar's society, he did not mend his habits; for, in a village upon the Appian road, he suddenly whipped his horses, and drove his chariot, on purpose, (340) over a poor boy, crushing him to pieces. At Rome, he struck out the eye of a Roman knight in the Forum, only for some free language in a dispute between them. He was likewise so fraudulent, that he not only cheated some silversmiths [560] of the price of goods he had bought of them, but, during his praetorship, defrauded the owners of chariots in the Circensian games of the prizes due to them for their victory. His sister, jeering him for the complaints made by the leaders of the several parties, he agreed to sanction a law, "That, for the future, the prizes should be immediately paid." A little before the death of Tiberius, he was prosecuted for treason, adulteries, and incest with his sister Lepida, but escaped in the timely change of affairs, and died of a dropsy, at Pyrgi [561]; leaving behind him his son, Nero, whom he had by Agrippina, the daughter of Germanicus.

VI. Nero was born at Antium, nine months after the death of Tiberius [562], upon the eighteenth of the calends of January [15th December], just as the sun rose, so that its beams touched him before they could well reach the earth. While many fearful conjectures, in respect to his future fortune, were formed by different persons, from the circumstances of his nativity, a saying of his father, Domitius, was regarded as an ill presage, who told his friends who were congratulating him upon the occasion, "That nothing but what was detestable, and pernicious to the public, could ever be produced of him and Agrippina." Another manifest prognostic of his future infelicity occurred upon his lustration day [563]. For Caius Caesar being requested by his sister to give the child what name he thought proper—looking at his uncle, Claudius, who (341) afterwards, when emperor, adopted Nero, he gave his: and this not seriously, but only in jest; Agrippina treating it with contempt, because Claudius at that time was a mere laughing-stock at the palace. He lost his father when he was three years old, being left heir to a third part of his estate; of which he never got possession, the whole being seized by his co-heir, Caius. His mother being soon after banished, he lived with his aunt Lepida, in a very necessitous condition, under the care of two tutors, a dancing-master and a barber. After Claudius came to the empire, he not only recovered his father's estate, but was enriched with the additional inheritance of that of his step-father, Crispus Passienus. Upon his mother's recall from banishment, he was advanced to such favour, through Nero's powerful interest with the emperor, that it was reported, assassins were employed by Messalina, Claudius's wife, to strangle him, as Britannicus's rival, whilst he was taking his noon-day repose. In addition to the story, it was said that they were frightened by a serpent, which crept from under his cushion, and ran away. The tale was occasioned by finding on his couch, near the pillow, the skin of a snake, which, by his mother's order, he wore for some time upon his right arm, inclosed in a bracelet of gold. This amulet, at last, he laid aside, from aversion to her memory; but he sought for it again, in vain, in the time of his extremity.

VII. When he was yet a mere boy, before he arrived at the age of puberty, during the celebration of the Circensian games [564], he performed his part in the Trojan play with a degree of firmness which gained him great applause. In the eleventh year of his age, he was adopted by Claudius, and placed under the tuition of Annaeus Seneca [565], who had been made a senator. It is said, that Seneca dreamt the night after, that he was giving a lesson to Caius Caesar [566]. Nero soon verified his dream, betraying the cruelty of his disposition in every way he could. For he attempted to persuade his father that his brother, Britannicus, was nothing but a changeling, because the latter had (342) saluted him, notwithstanding his adoption, by the name of Aenobarbus, as usual. When his aunt, Lepida, was brought to trial, he appeared in court as a witness against her, to gratify his mother, who persecuted the accused. On his introduction into the Forum, at the age of manhood, he gave a largess to the people and a donative to the soldiers: for the pretorian cohorts, he appointed a solemn procession under arms, and marched at the head of them with a shield in his hand; after which he went to return thanks to his father in the senate. Before Claudius, likewise, at the time he was consul, he made a speech for the Bolognese, in Latin, and for the Rhodians and people of Ilium, in Greek. He had the jurisdiction of praefect of the city, for the first time, during the Latin festival; during which the most celebrated advocates brought before him, not short and trifling causes, as is usual in that case, but trials of importance, notwithstanding they had instructions from Claudius himself to the contrary.

Soon afterwards, he married Octavia, and exhibited the Circensian games, and hunting of wild beasts, in honour of Claudius.

VIII. He was seventeen years of age at the death of that prince [567], and as soon as that event was made public, he went out to the cohort on guard between the hours of six and seven; for the omens were so disastrous, that no earlier time of the day was judged proper. On the steps before the palace gate, he was unanimously saluted by the soldiers as their emperor, and then carried in a litter to the camp; thence, after making a short speech to the troops, into the senate-house, where he continued until the evening; of all the immense honours which were heaped upon him, refusing none but the title of FATHER OF HIS COUNTRY, on account of his youth.

IX. He began his reign with an ostentation of dutiful regard to the memory of Claudius, whom he buried with the utmost pomp and magnificence, pronouncing the funeral oration himself, and then had him enrolled amongst the gods. He paid likewise the highest honours to the memory of his father Domitius. He left the management of affairs, both public and private, to his mother. The word which he gave the first day of his reign to the tribune on guard, was, "The (343) Best of Mothers," and afterwards he frequently appeared with her in the streets of Rome in her litter. He settled a colony at Antium, in which he placed the veteran soldiers belonging to the guards; and obliged several of the richest centurions of the first rank to transfer their residence to that place; where he likewise made a noble harbour at a prodigious expense. [568]

X. To establish still further his character, he declared, "that he designed to govern according to the model of Augustus;" and omitted no opportunity of showing his generosity, clemency, and complaisance. The more burthensome taxes he either entirely took off, or diminished. The rewards appointed for informers by the Papian law, he reduced to a fourth part, and distributed to the people four hundred sesterces a man. To the noblest of the senators who were much reduced in their circumstances, he granted annual allowances, in some cases as much as five hundred thousand sesterces; and to the pretorian cohorts a monthly allowance of corn gratis. When called upon to subscribe the sentence, according to custom, of a criminal condemned to die, "I wish," said he, "I had never learnt to read and write." He continually saluted people of the several orders by name, without a prompter. When the senate returned him their thanks for his good government, he replied to them, "It will be time enough to do so when I shall have deserved it." He admitted the common people to see him perform his exercises in the Campus Martius. He frequently declaimed in public, and recited verses of his own composing, not only at home, but in the theatre; so much to the joy of all the people, that public prayers were appointed to be put up to the gods upon that account; and the verses which had been publicly read, were, after being written in gold letters, consecrated to Jupiter Capitolinus.

(344) XI. He presented the people with a great number and variety of spectacles, as the Juvenal and Circensian games, stage-plays, and an exhibition of gladiators. In the Juvenal, he even admitted senators and aged matrons to perform parts. In the Circensian games, he assigned the equestrian order seats apart from the rest of the people, and had races performed by chariots drawn each by four camels. In the games which he instituted for the eternal duration of the empire, and therefore ordered to be called Maximi, many of the senatorian and equestrian order, of both sexes, performed. A distinguished Roman knight descended on the stage by a rope, mounted on an elephant. A Roman play, likewise, composed by Afranius, was brought upon the stage. It was entitled, "The Fire;" and in it the performers were allowed to carry off, and to keep to themselves, the furniture of the house, which, as the plot of the play required, was burnt down in the theatre. Every day during the solemnity, many thousand articles of all descriptions were thrown amongst the people to scramble for; such as fowls of different kinds, tickets for corn, clothes, gold, silver, gems, pearls, pictures, slaves, beasts of burden, wild beasts that had been tamed; at last, ships, lots of houses, and lands, were offered as prizes in a lottery.

XII. These games he beheld from the front of the proscenium. In the show of gladiators, which he exhibited in a wooden amphitheatre, built within a year in the district of the Campus Martius [569], he ordered that none should be slain, not even the condemned criminals employed in the combats. He secured four hundred senators, and six hundred Roman knights, amongst whom were some of unbroken fortunes and unblemished reputation, to act as gladiators. From the same orders, he engaged persons to encounter wild beasts, and for various other services in the theatre. He presented the public with the representation of a naval fight, upon sea-water, with huge fishes swimming in it; as also with the Pyrrhic dance, performed by certain youths, to each of whom, after the performance was over, he granted the freedom of Rome. During this diversion, a bull covered Pasiphae, concealed within a wooden statue of a cow, as many of the spectators believed. Icarus, upon his first attempt to fly, fell on the stage close to (345) the emperor's pavilion, and bespattered him with blood. For he very seldom presided in the games, but used to view them reclining on a couch, at first through some narrow apertures, but afterwards with the Podium [570] quite open. He was the first who instituted [571], in imitation of the Greeks, a trial of skill in the three several exercises of music, wrestling, and horse-racing, to be performed at Rome every five years, and which he called Neronia. Upon the dedication of his bath [572] and gymnasium, he furnished the senate and the equestrian order with oil. He appointed as judges of the trial men of consular rank, chosen by lot, who sat with the praetors. At this time he went down into the orchestra amongst the senators, and received the crown for the best performance in Latin prose and verse, for which several persons of the greatest merit contended, but they unanimously yielded to him. The crown for the best performer on the harp, being likewise awarded to him by the judges, he devoutly saluted it, and ordered it to be carried to the statue of Augustus. In the gymnastic exercises, which he presented in the Septa, while they were preparing the great sacrifice of an ox, he shaved his beard for the first time [573], and putting it up in a casket of gold studded with pearls of great price, consecrated it to Jupiter Capitolinus. He invited the Vestal Virgins to see the (346) wrestlers perform, because, at Olympia, the priestesses of Ceres are allowed the privilege of witnessing that exhibition.

XIII. Amongst the spectacles presented by him, the solemn entrance of Tiridates [574] into the city deserves to be mentioned. This personage, who was king of Armenia, he invited to Rome by very liberal promises. But being prevented by unfavourable weather from showing him to the people upon the day fixed by proclamation, he took the first opportunity which occurred; several cohorts being drawn up under arms, about the temples in the forum, while he was seated on a curule chair on the rostra, in a triumphal dress, amidst the military standards and ensigns. Upon Tiridates advancing towards him, on a stage made shelving for the purpose, he permitted him to throw himself at his feet, but quickly raised him with his right hand, and kissed him. The emperor then, at the king's request, took the turban from his head, and replaced it by a crown, whilst a person of pretorian rank proclaimed in Latin the words in which the prince addressed the emperor as a suppliant. After this ceremony, the king was conducted to the theatre, where, after renewing his obeisance, Nero seated him on his right hand. Being then greeted by universal acclamation with the title of Emperor, and sending his laurel crown to the Capitol, Nero shut the temple of the two-faced Janus, as though there now existed no war throughout the Roman empire.

XIV. He filled the consulship four times [575]: the first for two months, the second and last for six, and the third for four; the two intermediate ones he held successively, but the others after an interval of some years between them.

XV. In the administration of justice, he scarcely ever gave his decision on the pleadings before the next day, and then in writing. His manner of hearing causes was not to allow any adjournment, but to dispatch them in order as they stood. When he withdrew to consult his assessors, he did not debate the matter openly with them; but silently and privately reading over their opinions, which they gave separately in writing, (347) he pronounced sentence from the tribunal according to his own view of the case, as if it was the opinion of the majority. For a long time he would not admit the sons of freedmen into the senate; and those who had been admitted by former princes, he excluded from all public offices. To supernumerary candidates he

gave command in the legions, to comfort them under the delay of their hopes. The consulship he commonly conferred for six months; and one of the two consuls dying a little before the first of January, he substituted no one in his place; disliking what had been formerly done for Caninius Rebilus on such an occasion, who was consul for one day only. He allowed the triumphal honours only to those who were of quaestorian rank, and to some of the equestrian order; and bestowed them without regard to military service. And instead of the quaestors, whose office it properly was, he frequently ordered that the addresses, which he sent to the senate on certain occasions, should be read by the consuls.

XVI. He devised a new style of building in the city, ordering piazzas to be erected before all houses, both in the streets and detached, to give facilities from their terraces, in case of fire, for preventing it from spreading; and these he built at his own expense. He likewise designed to extend the city walls as far as Ostia, and bring the sea from thence by a canal into the old city. Many severe regulations and new orders were made in his time. A sumptuary law was enacted. Public suppers were limited to the Sportulae [576]; and victualling-houses restrained from selling any dressed victuals, except pulse and herbs, whereas before they sold all kinds of meat. He likewise inflicted punishments on the Christians, a sort of people who held a new and impious [577] superstition.

(348) He forbad the revels of the charioteers, who had long assumed a licence to stroll about, and established for themselves a kind of prescriptive right to cheat and thieve, making a jest of it. The partisans of the rival theatrical performers were banished, as well as the actors themselves.

XVII. To prevent forgery, a method was then first invented, of having writings bored, run through three times with a thread, and then sealed. It was likewise provided that in wills, the two first pages, with only the testator's name upon them, should be presented blank to those who were to sign them as witnesses; and that no one who wrote a will for another, should insert any legacy for himself. It was likewise ordained that clients should pay their advocates a certain reasonable fee, but nothing for the court, which was to be gratuitous, the charges for it being paid out of the public treasury; that causes, the cognizance of which before belonged to the judges of the exchequer, should be transferred to the forum, and the ordinary tribunals; and that all appeals from the judges should be made to the senate.

XVIII. He never entertained the least ambition or hope of augmenting and extending the frontiers of the empire. On the contrary, he had thoughts of withdrawing the troops from Britain, and was only restrained from so doing by the fear of appearing to detract from the glory of his father [578]. All (349) that he did was to reduce the kingdom of Pontus, which was ceded to him by Polemon, and also the Alps [579], upon the death of Cottius, into the form of a province.

XIX. Twice only he undertook any foreign expeditions, one to Alexandria, and the other to Achaia; but he abandoned the prosecution of the former on the very day fixed for his departure, by being deterred both by ill omens, and the hazard of the voyage. For while he was making the circuit of the temples, having seated himself in that of Vesta, when he attempted to rise, the skirt of his robe stuck fast; and he was instantly seized with such a dimness in his eyes, that he could not see a yard before him. In Achaia, he attempted to make a cut through the Isthmus [580]; and, having made a speech encouraging his pretorians to set about the work, on a signal given by sound of trumpet, he first broke ground with a spade, and carried off a basket full of earth upon his shoulders. He made preparations for an expedition to the Pass of the Caspian mountains [581]; forming a new legion out of his late levies in Italy, of men all six feet high, which he called the phalanx of Alexander the Great. These transactions, in part unexceptionable, and in part highly commendable, I have brought into one view, in order to separate them from the scandalous and criminal part of his conduct, of which I shall now give an account.

XX. Among the other liberal arts which he was taught in his youth, he was instructed in music; and immediately after (350) his advancement to the empire, he sent for Terpnus, a performer upon the harp [582], who flourished at that time with the highest reputation. Sitting with him for several days following, as he sang and played after supper, until late at night, he began by degrees to practise upon the instrument himself. Nor did he omit any of those expedients which artists in music adopt, for the preservation and improvement of their voices. He would lie upon his back with a sheet of lead upon his breast, clear his stomach and bowels by vomits and clysters, and forbear the eating of fruits, or food prejudicial to the voice. Encouraged by his proficiency, though his voice was naturally neither loud nor clear, he was desirous of appearing upon the stage, frequently repeating amongst his friends a Greek proverb to this effect: "that no one had any regard for music which they never heard." Accordingly, he made his first public appearance at Naples; and although the theatre quivered with the sudden shock of an earthquake, he did not desist, until he had finished the piece of music he had begun. He played and sung in the same place several times, and for several days together; taking only now and then a little respite to refresh his voice. Impatient of retirement, it was his custom to go from the bath to the theatre; and after dining in the orchestra, amidst a crowded assembly of the people, he promised them in Greek [583], "that after he had drank a little, he would give them a tune which would make their ears tingle." Being highly pleased with the songs that were sung in his praise by some Alexandrians belonging to the fleet just arrived at Naples [584], he sent for more of the like singers from Alexandria. At the same time, he chose young men of the equestrian order, and above five thousand robust young fellows from the common people, on purpose to learn various kinds of applause, called bombi, imbrices, and testae [585], which they were to practise in his favour, whenever he performed. They were (351) divided into several parties, and were remarkable for their fine heads of hair, and were extremely well dressed, with rings upon their left hands. The leaders of these bands had salaries of forty thousand sesterces allowed them.

XXI. At Rome also, being extremely proud of his singing, he ordered the games called Neronia to be celebrated before the time fixed for their return. All now becoming importunate to hear "his heavenly voice," he informed them, "that he would gratify those who desired it at the gardens." But the soldiers then on guard seconding the voice of the people, he promised to comply with their request immediately, and with all his heart. He instantly ordered his name to be entered upon the list of musicians who proposed to contend, and having thrown his lot into the urn among the rest, took his turn, and entered, attended by the prefects of the pretorian cohorts bearing his harp, and followed by the military tribunes, and several of his intimate friends. After he had taken his station, and made the usual prelude, he commanded Cluvius Rufus, a man of consular rank, to proclaim in the theatre, that he intended to sing the story of Niobe. This he accordingly did, and continued it until nearly ten o'clock, but deferred the disposal of the crown, and the remaining part of the solemnity, until the next year; that he might have more frequent opportunities of performing. But that being too long, he could not refrain from often appearing as a public performer during the interval. He made no scruple of exhibiting on the stage, even in the spectacles presented to the people by private persons, and was offered by one of the praetors, no less than a million of sesterces for his services. He likewise sang tragedies in a mask; the visors of the heroes and gods, as also of the heroines and goddesses, being formed into a resemblance of his own face, and that of any woman he was in love with. Amongst the rest, he sung "Canace in Labour," [586] "Orestes the Murderer of his Mother," "Oedipus (352) Blinded," and "Hercules Mad." In the last tragedy, it is said that a young sentinel, posted at the entrance of the stage, seeing him in a prison dress and bound with fetters, as the fable of the play required, ran to his assistance.

XXII. He had from his childhood an extravagant passion for horses; and his constant talk was of the Circensian races, notwithstanding it was prohibited him. Lamenting once, among his fellow-pupils, the case of a charioteer of the green party, who was dragged round the circus at the tail of his chariot, and being reprimanded by his tutor for it, he pretended that he was talking of Hector. In the beginning of his reign, he used to amuse himself daily with chariots drawn by four horses, made of ivory, upon

a table. He attended at all the lesser exhibitions in the circus, at first privately, but at last openly; so that nobody ever doubted of his presence on any particular day. Nor did he conceal his desire to have the number of the prizes doubled; so that the races being increased accordingly, the diversion continued until a late hour; the leaders of parties refusing now to bring out their companies for any time less than the whole day. Upon this, he took a fancy for driving the chariot himself, and that even publicly. Having made his first experiment in the gardens, amidst crowds of slaves and other rabble, he at length performed in the view of all the people, in the Circus Maximus, whilst one of his freedmen dropped the napkin in the place where the magistrates used to give the signal. Not satisfied with exhibiting various specimens of his skill in those arts at Rome, he went over to Achaia, as has been already said, principally for this purpose. The several cities, in which solemn trials of musical skill used to be publicly held, had resolved to send him the crowns belonging to those who bore away the prize. These he accepted so graciously, that he not only gave the deputies who brought them an immediate audience, but even invited them to his table. Being requested by some of them to sing at supper, and prodigiously applauded, he said, "the Greeks were the only people who has an ear for music, and were the only good judges of him and his attainments." Without delay he commenced his journey, and on his arrival at Cassiope [587], (352) exhibited his first musical performance before the altar of Jupiter Cassius.

XXIII. He afterwards appeared at the celebration of all public games in Greece: for such as fell in different years, he brought within the compass of one, and some he ordered to be celebrated a second time in the same year. At Olympia, likewise, contrary to custom, he appointed a public performance in music: and that he might meet with no interruption in this employment, when he was informed by his freedman Helius, that affairs at Rome required his presence, he wrote to him in these words: "Though now all your hopes and wishes are for my speedy return, yet you ought rather to advise and hope that I may come back with a character worthy of Nero." During the time of his musical performance, nobody was allowed to stir out of the theatre upon any account, however necessary; insomuch, that it is said some women with child were delivered there. Many of the spectators being quite wearied with hearing and applauding him, because the town gates were shut, slipped privately over the walls; or counterfeiting themselves dead, were carried out for their funeral. With what extreme anxiety he engaged in these contests, with what keen desire to bear away the prize, and with how much awe of the judges, is scarcely to be believed. As if his adversaries had been on a level with himself, he would watch them narrowly, defame them privately, and sometimes, upon meeting them, rail at them in very scurrilous language; or bribe them, if they were better performers than himself. He always addressed the judges with the most profound reverence before he began, telling them, "he had done all things that were necessary, by way of preparation, but that the issue of the approaching trial was in the hand of fortune; and that they, as wise and skilful men, ought to exclude from their judgment things merely accidental." Upon their encouraging him to have a good heart, he went off with more assurance, but not entirely free from anxiety; interpreting the silence and modesty of some of them into sourness and ill-nature, and saying that he was suspicious of them.

XXIV. In these contests, he adhered so strictly to the rules, (354) that he never durst spit, nor wipe the sweat from his forehead in any other way than with his sleeve. Having, in the performance of a tragedy, dropped his sceptre, and not quickly recovering it, he was in a great fright, lest he should be set aside for the miscarriage, and could not regain his assurance, until an actor who stood by swore he was certain it had not been observed in the midst of the acclamations and exultations of the people. When the prize was adjudged to him, he always proclaimed it himself; and even entered the lists with the heralds. That no memory or the least monument might remain of any other victor in the sacred Grecian games, he ordered all their statues and pictures to be pulled down, dragged away with hooks, and thrown into the common sewers. He drove the chariot with various numbers of horses, and at the Olympic games with no fewer than ten; though, in a poem of his,

he had reflected upon Mithridates for that innovation. Being thrown out of his chariot, he was again replaced, but could not retain his seat, and was obliged to give up, before he reached the goal, but was crowned notwithstanding. On his departure, he declared the whole province a free country, and conferred upon the judges in the several games the freedom of Rome, with large sums of money. All these favours he proclaimed himself with his own voice, from the middle of the Stadium, during the solemnity of the Isthmian games.

XXV. On his return from Greece, arriving at Naples, because he had commenced his career as a public performer in that city, he made his entrance in a chariot drawn by white horses through a breach in the city-wall, according to the practice of those who were victorious in the sacred Grecian games. In the same manner he entered Antium, Alba, and Rome. He made his entry into the city riding in the same chariot in which Augustus had triumphed, in a purple tunic, and a cloak embroidered with golden stars, having on his head the crown won at Olympia, and in his right hand that which was given him at the Parthian games: the rest being carried in a procession before him, with inscriptions denoting the places where they had been won, from whom, and in what plays or musical performances; whilst a train followed him with loud acclamations, crying out, that "they (355) were the emperor's attendants, and the soldiers of his triumph." Having then caused an arch of the Circus Maximus [588] to be taken down, he passed through the breach, as also through the Velabrum [589] and the forum, to the Palatine hill and the temple of Apollo. Everywhere as he marched along, victims were slain, whilst the streets were strewed with saffron, and birds, chaplets, and sweetmeats scattered abroad. He suspended the sacred crowns in his chamber, about his beds, and caused statues of himself to be erected in the attire of a harper, and had his likeness stamped upon the coin in the same dress. After this period, he was so far from abating any thing of his application to music, that, for the preservation of his voice, he never addressed the soldiers but by messages, or with some person to deliver his speeches for him, when he thought fit to make his appearance amongst them. Nor did he ever do any thing either in jest or earnest, without a voice-master standing by him to caution him against overstraining his vocal organs, and to apply a handkerchief to his mouth when he did. He offered his friendship, or avowed (356) open enmity to many, according as they were lavish or sparing in giving him their applause.

XXVI. Petulancy, lewdness, luxury, avarice, and cruelty, he practised at first with reserve and in private, as if prompted to them only by the folly of youth; but, even then, the world was of opinion that they were the faults of his nature, and not of his age. After it was dark, he used to enter the taverns disguised in a cap or a wig, and ramble about the streets in sport, which was not void of mischief. He used to beat those he met coming home from supper; and, if they made any resistance, would wound them, and throw them into the common sewer. He broke open and robbed shops; establishing an auction at home for selling his booty. In the scuffles which took place on those occasions, he often ran the hazard of losing his eyes, and even his life; being beaten almost to death by a senator, for handling his wife indecently. After this adventure, he never again ventured abroad at that time of night, without some tribunes following him at a little distance. In the day-time he would be carried to the theatre incognito in a litter, placing himself upon the upper part of the proscenium, where he not only witnessed the quarrels which arose on account of the performances, but also encouraged them. When they came to blows, and stones and pieces of broken benches began to fly about, he threw them plentifully amongst the people, and once even broke a praetor's head.

XXVII. His vices gaining strength by degrees, he laid aside his jocular amusements, and all disguise; breaking out into enormous crimes, without the least attempt to conceal them. His revels were prolonged from mid-day to midnight, while he was frequently refreshed by warm baths, and, in the summer time, by such as were cooled with snow. He often supped in public, in the Naumachia, with the sluices shut, or in the Campus Martius, or the Circus Maximus, being waited upon at table by common prostitutes of the town, and Syrian strumpets and glee-girls. As often as he went down the Tiber to Ostia, or coasted

through the gulf of Baiae, booths furnished as brothels and eating-houses, were erected along the shore and river banks; before which stood matrons, who, like bawds and hostesses, allured him to land. It was also his custom to invite (357) himself to supper with his friends; at one of which was expended no less than four millions of sesterces in chaplets, and at another something more in roses.

XXVIII. Besides the abuse of free-born lads, and the debauch of married women, he committed a rape upon Rubria, a Vestal Virgin. He was upon the point of marrying Acte [590], his freedwoman, having suborned some men of consular rank to swear that she was of royal descent. He gelded the boy Sporus, and endeavoured to transform him into a woman. He even went so far as to marry him, with all the usual formalities of a marriage settlement, the rose-coloured nuptial veil, and a numerous company at the wedding. When the ceremony was over, he had him conducted like a bride to his own house, and treated him as his wife [591]. It was jocularly observed by some person, "that it would have been well for mankind, had such a wife fallen to the lot of his father Domitius." This Sporus he carried about with him in a litter round the solemn assemblies and fairs of Greece, and afterwards at Rome through the Sigillaria [592], dressed in the rich attire of an empress; kissing him from time to time as they rode together. That he entertained an incestuous passion for his mother [593], but was deterred by her enemies, for fear that this haughty and overbearing woman should, by her compliance, get him entirely into her power, and govern in every thing, was universally believed; especially after he had introduced amongst his concubines a strumpet, who was reported to have a strong resemblance to Agrippina [594].————

XXIX. He prostituted his own chastity to such a degree, that (358) after he had defiled every part of his person with some unnatural pollution, he at last invented an extraordinary kind of diversion; which was, to be let out of a den in the arena, covered with the skin of a wild beast, and then assail with violence the private parts both of men and women, while they were bound to stakes. After he had vented his furious passion upon them, he finished the play in the embraces of his freedman Doryphorus [595], to whom he was married in the same way that Sporus had been married to himself; imitating the cries and shrieks of young virgins, when they are ravished. I have been informed from numerous sources, that he firmly believed, no man in the world to be chaste, or any part of his person undefiled; but that most men concealed that vice, and were cunning enough to keep it secret. To those, therefore, who frankly owned their unnatural lewdness, he forgave all other crimes.

XXX. He thought there was no other use of riches and money than to squander them away profusely; regarding all those as sordid wretches who kept their expenses within due bounds; and extolling those as truly noble and generous souls, who lavished away and wasted all they possessed. He praised and admired his uncle Caius [596], upon no account more, than for squandering in a short time the vast treasure left him by Tiberius. Accordingly, he was himself extravagant and profuse, beyond all bounds. He spent upon Tiridates eight hundred thousand sesterces a day, a sum almost incredible; and at his departure, presented him with upwards of a million [597]. He likewise bestowed upon Menecrates the harper, and Spicillus a gladiator, the estates and houses of men who had received the honour of a triumph. He enriched the usurer Cercopithecus Panerotes with estates both in town and country; and gave him a funeral, in pomp and magnificence little inferior to that of princes. He never wore the same garment twice. He (359) has been known to stake four hundred thousand sesterces on a throw of the dice. It was his custom to fish with a golden net, drawn by silken cords of purple and scarlet. It is said, that he never travelled with less than a thousand baggage-carts; the mules being all shod with silver, and the drivers dressed in scarlet jackets of the finest Canusian cloth [598], with a numerous train of footmen, and troops of Mazacans [599], with bracelets on their arms, and mounted upon horses in splendid trappings.

XXXI. In nothing was he more prodigal than in his buildings. He completed his palace by continuing it from the Palatine to the Esquiline hill, calling the building at first only "The Passage," but, after it was burnt down and rebuilt, "The Golden House." [600] Of its dimensions and furniture, it may be sufficient to say thus much: the porch was so high that there stood in it a colossal statue of himself a hundred and twenty feet in height; and the space included in it was so ample, that it had triple porticos a mile in length, and a lake like a sea, surrounded with buildings which had the appearance of a city. Within its area were corn fields, vineyards, pastures, and woods, containing a vast number of animals of various kinds, both wild and tame. In other parts it was entirely over-laid with gold, and adorned with jewels and mother of pearl. The supper rooms were vaulted, and compartments of the ceilings, inlaid with ivory, were made to revolve, and scatter flowers; while they contained pipes which (360) shed unguents upon the guests. The chief banqueting room was circular, and revolved perpetually, night and day, in imitation of the motion of the celestial bodies. The baths were supplied with water from the sea and the Albula. Upon the dedication of this magnificent house after it was finished, all he said in approval of it was, "that he had now a dwelling fit for a man." He commenced making a pond for the reception of all the hot streams from Baiae, which he designed to have continued from Misenum to the Avernian lake, in a conduit, enclosed in galleries; and also a canal from Avernum to Ostia, that ships might pass from one to the other, without a sea voyage. The length of the proposed canal was one hundred and sixty miles; and it was intended to be of breadth sufficient to permit ships with five banks of oars to pass each other. For the execution of these designs, he ordered all prisoners, in every part of the empire, to be brought to Italy; and that even those who were convicted of the most heinous crimes, in lieu of any other sentence, should be condemned to work at them. He was encouraged to all this wild and enormous profusion, not only by the great revenue of the empire, but by the sudden hopes given him of an immense hidden treasure, which queen Dido, upon her flight from Tyre, had brought with her to Africa. This, a Roman knight pretended to assure him, upon good grounds, was still hid there in some deep caverns, and might with a little labour be recovered.

XXXII. But being disappointed in his expectations of this resource, and reduced to such difficulties, for want of money, that he was obliged to defer paying his troops, and the rewards due to the veterans; he resolved upon supplying his necessities by means of false accusations and plunder. In the first place, he ordered, that if any freedman, without sufficient reason, bore the name of the family to which he belonged; the half, instead of three fourths, of his estate should be brought into the exchequer at his decease: also that the estates of all such persons as had not in their wills been mindful of their prince, should be confiscated; and that the lawyers who had drawn or dictated such wills, should be liable to a fine. He ordained likewise, that all words and actions, upon which any informer could ground a prosecution, should be deemed treason. He demanded an equivalent for the crowns which the cities of (361) Greece had at any time offered him in the solemn games. Having forbad any one to use the colours of amethyst and Tyrian purple, he privately sent a person to sell a few ounces of them upon the day of the Nundinae, and then shut up all the merchants' shops, on the pretext that his edict had been violated. It is said, that, as he was playing and singing in the theatre, observing a married lady dressed in the purple which he had prohibited, he pointed her out to his procurators; upon which she was immediately dragged out of her seat, and not only stripped of her clothes, but her property. He never nominated a person to any office without saying to him, "You know what I want; and let us take care that nobody has any thing he can call his own." At last he rifled many temples of the rich offerings with which they were stored, and melted down all the gold and silver statues, and amongst them those of the penates [601], which Galba afterwards restored.

XXXIII. He began the practice of parricide and murder with Claudius himself; for although he was not the contriver of his death, he was privy to the plot. Nor did he make any secret of it; but used afterwards to commend, in a Greek proverb, mushrooms as food fit for the gods, because Claudius had been poisoned with them. He traduced his memory both by word and deed in the grossest manner; one while charging him with folly, another while with cruelty.

For he used to say by way of jest, that he had ceased morari [602] amongst men, pronouncing the first syllable long; and treated as null many of his decrees and ordinances, as made by a doting old blockhead. He enclosed the place where his body was burnt with only a low wall of rough masonry. He attempted to poison (362) Britannicus, as much out of envy because he had a sweeter voice, as from apprehension of what might ensue from the respect which the people entertained for his father's memory. He employed for this purpose a woman named Locusta, who had been a witness against some persons guilty of like practices. But the poison she gave him, working more slowly than he expected, and only causing a purge, he sent for the woman, and beat her with his own hand, charging her with administering an antidote instead of poison; and upon her alleging in excuse, that she had given Britannicus but a gentle mixture in order to prevent suspicion, "Think you," said he, "that I am afraid of the Julian law;" and obliged her to prepare, in his own chamber and before his eyes, as quick and strong a dose as possible. This he tried upon a kid: but the animal lingering for five hours before it expired, he ordered her to go to work again; and when she had done, he gave the poison to a pig, which dying immediately, he commanded the potion to be brought into the eating-room and given to Britannicus, while he was at supper with him. The prince had no sooner tasted it than he sunk on the floor, Nero meanwhile, pretending to the guests, that it was only a fit of the falling sickness, to which, he said, he was subject. He buried him the following day, in a mean and hurried way, during violent storms of rain. He gave Locusta a pardon, and rewarded her with a great estate in land, placing some disciples with her, to be instructed in her trade.

XXXIV. His mother being used to make strict inquiry into what he said or did, and to reprimand him with the freedom of a parent, he was so much offended, that he endeavoured to expose her to public resentment, by frequently pretending a resolution to quit the government, and retire to Rhodes. Soon afterwards, he deprived her of all honour and power, took from her the guard of Roman and German soldiers, banished her from the palace and from his society, and persecuted her in every way he could contrive; employing persons to harass her when at Rome with law-suits, and to disturb her in her retirement from town with the most scurrilous and abusive language, following her about by land and sea. But being terrified with her menaces and violent spirit, he resolved upon her destruction, and thrice attempted it by poison. Finding, however, (363) that she had previously secured herself by antidotes, he contrived machinery, by which the floor over her bed-chamber might be made to fall upon her while she was asleep in the night. This design miscarrying likewise, through the little caution used by those who were in the secret, his next stratagem was to construct a ship which could be easily shivered, in hopes of destroying her either by drowning, or by the deck above her cabin crushing her in its fall. Accordingly, under colour of a pretended reconciliation, he wrote her an extremely affectionate letter, inviting her to Baiae, to celebrate with him the festival of Minerva. He had given private orders to the captains of the galleys which were to attend her, to shatter to pieces the ship in which she had come, by falling foul of it, but in such manner that it might appear to be done accidentally. He prolonged the entertainment, for the more convenient opportunity of executing the plot in the night; and at her return for Bauli [603], instead of the old ship which had conveyed her to Baiae, he offered that which he had contrived for her destruction. He attended her to the vessel in a very cheerful mood, and, at parting with her, kissed her breasts; after which he sat up very late in the night, waiting with great anxiety to learn the issue of his project. But receiving information that every thing had fallen out contrary to his wish, and that she had saved herself by swimming,—not knowing what course to take, upon her freedman, Lucius Agerinus bringing word, with great joy, that she was safe and well, he privately dropped a poniard by him. He then commanded the freedman to be seized and put in chains, under pretence of his having been employed by his mother to assassinate him; at the same time ordering her to be put to death, and giving out, that, to avoid punishment for her intended crime, she had laid violent hands upon herself. Other circumstances, still more horrible, are related on good authority; as that he went to view her corpse, and handling her limbs, pointed out some blemishes, and commended other points; and that, growing thirsty during the survey, he called for drink. Yet he was never afterwards able to bear the stings of his own conscience for this atrocious act, although encouraged by the congratulatory addresses of the army, the senate, and people. He frequently affirmed that he was haunted by his mother's ghost, and persecuted with the whips (364) and burning torches of the Furies. Nay, he attempted by magical rites to bring up her ghost from below, and soften her rage against him. When he was in Greece, he durst not attend the celebration of the Eleusinian mysteries, at the initiation of which, impious and wicked persons are warned by the voice of the herald from approaching the rites [604]. Besides the murder of his mother, he had been guilty of that of his aunt; for, being obliged to keep her bed in consequence of a complaint in her bowels, he paid her a visit, and she, being then advanced in years, stroking his downy chin, in the tenderness of affection, said to him: "May I but live to see the day when this is shaved for the first time [605], and I shall then die contented." He turned, however, to those about him, made a jest of it, saying, that he would have his beard immediately taken off, and ordered the physicians to give her more violent purgatives. He seized upon her estate before she had expired; suppressing her will, that he might enjoy the whole himself.

XXXV. He had, besides Octavia, two other wives: Poppaea Sabina, whose father had borne the office of quaestor, and who had been married before to a Roman knight: and, after her, Statilia Messalina, great-grand-daughter of Taurus [606] who was twice consul, and received the honour of a triumph. To obtain possession of her, he put to death her husband, Atticus Vestinus, who was then consul. He soon became disgusted with Octavia, and ceased from having any intercourse with her; and being censured by his friends for it, he replied, "She ought to be satisfied with having the rank and appendages of his wife." Soon afterwards, he made several attempts, but in vain, to strangle her, and then divorced her for barrenness. But the people, disapproving of the divorce, and making severe comments upon it, he also banished her [607]. At last he (365) put her to death, upon a charge of adultery, so impudent and false, that, when all those who were put to the torture positively denied their knowledge of it, he suborned his pedagogue, Anicetus, to affirm, that he had secretly intrigued with and debauched her. He married Poppaea twelve days after the divorce of Octavia [608], and entertained a great affection for her; but, nevertheless, killed her with a kick which he gave her when she was big with child, and in bad health, only because she found fault with him for returning late from driving his chariot. He had by her a daughter, Claudia Augusta, who died an infant. There was no person at all connected with him who escaped his deadly and unjust cruelty. Under pretence of her being engaged in a plot against him, he put to death Antonia, Claudius's daughter, who refused to marry him after the death of Poppaea. In the same way, he destroyed all who were allied to him either by blood or marriage; amongst whom was young Aulus Plautinus. He first compelled him to submit to his unnatural lust, and then ordered him to be executed, crying out, "Let my mother bestow her kisses on my successor thus defiled;" pretending that he had been his mothers paramour, and by her encouraged to aspire to the empire. His step-son, Rufinus Crispinus, Poppaea's son, though a minor, he ordered to be drowned in the sea, while he was fishing, by his own slaves, because he was reported to act frequently amongst his play-fellows the part of a general or an emperor. He banished Tuscus, his nurse's son, for presuming, when he was procurator of Egypt, to wash in the baths which had been constructed in expectation of his own coming. Seneca, his preceptor, he forced to kill himself [609], though, upon his desiring leave to retire, and offering to surrender his estate, he solemnly swore, "that there was no foundation for his suspicions, and that he would perish himself sooner than hurt him." Having promised Burrhus, the pretorian prefect, a remedy for a swelling in his throat, he sent him poison. Some old rich freedmen of Claudius, who had formerly not only promoted (366) his adoption, but were also instrumental to his advancement to the empire, and had been his governors, he took off by poison given them in their meat or drink.

XXXVI. Nor did he proceed with less cruelty against those who were not of his family. A blazing star, which is vulgarly supposed to portend destruction to kings and princes, appeared above the horizon several nights successively [610]. He felt great anxiety on account of this phenomenon, and being informed by one Babilus, an astrologer, that princes were used to expiate such omens by the sacrifice of illustrious persons, and so avert the danger foreboded to their own persons, by bringing it on the heads of their chief men, he resolved on the destruction of the principal nobility in Rome. He was the more encouraged to this, because he had some plausible pretence for carrying it into execution, from the discovery of two conspiracies against him; the former and more dangerous of which was that formed by Piso [611], and discovered at Rome; the other was that of Vinicius [612], at Beneventum. The conspirators were brought to their trials loaded with triple fetters. Some ingenuously confessed the charge; others avowed that they thought the design against his life an act of favour for which he was obliged to them, as it was impossible in any other way than by death to relieve a person rendered infamous by crimes of the greatest enormity. The children of those who had been condemned, were banished the city, and afterwards either poisoned or starved to death. It is asserted that some of them, with their tutors, and the slaves who carried their satchels, were all poisoned together at one dinner; and others not suffered to seek their daily bread.

XXXVII. From this period he butchered, without distinction or quarter, all whom his caprice suggested as objects for his cruelty; and upon the most frivolous pretences. To mention only a few: Salvidienus Orfitus was accused of letting (367) out three taverns attached to his house in the Forum to some cities for the use of their deputies at Rome. The charge against Cassius Longinus, a lawyer who had lost his sight, was, that he kept amongst the busts of his ancestors that of Caius Cassius, who was concerned in the death of Julius Caesar. The only charge objected against Paetus Thrasea was, that he had a melancholy cast of features, and looked like a schoolmaster. He allowed but one hour to those whom he obliged to kill themselves; and, to prevent delay, he sent them physicians "to cure them immediately, if they lingered beyond that time;" for so he called bleeding them to death. There was at that time an Egyptian of a most voracious appetite, who would digest raw flesh, or any thing else that was given him. It was credibly reported, that the emperor was extremely desirous of furnishing him with living men to tear and devour. Being elated with his great success in the perpetration of crimes, he declared, "that no prince before himself ever knew the extent of his power." He threw out strong intimations that he would not even spare the senators who survived, but would entirely extirpate that order, and put the provinces and armies into the hands of the Roman knights and his own freedmen. It is certain that he never gave or vouchsafed to allow any one the customary kiss, either on entering or departing, or even returned a salute. And at the inauguration of a work, the cut through the Isthmus [613], he, with a loud voice, amidst the assembled multitude, uttered a prayer, that "the undertaking might prove fortunate for himself and the Roman people," without taking the smallest notice of the senate.

XXXVIII. He spared, moreover, neither the people of Rome, nor the capital of his country. Somebody in conversation saying—

Emou thanontos gaia michthaeto pyri
When I am dead let fire devour the world—

"Nay," said he, "let it be while I am living" [emou xontos]. And he acted accordingly: for, pretending to be disgusted with the old buildings, and the narrow and winding streets, he set the city on fire so openly, that many of consular rank caught his own household servants on their property with tow, and (368) torches in their hands, but durst not meddle with them. There being near his Golden House some granaries, the site of which he exceedingly coveted, they were battered as if with machines of war, and set on fire, the walls being built of stone. During six days and seven nights this terrible devastation continued, the people being obliged to fly to the tombs and monuments for lodging and shelter. Meanwhile, a vast number of stately buildings, the houses of generals celebrated in former times, and even then still decorated with the spoils of war, were laid in ashes; as well as the temples of the gods, which had been vowed and

dedicated by the kings of Rome, and afterwards in the Punic and Gallic wars: in short, everything that was remarkable and worthy to be seen which time had spared [614]. This fire he beheld from a tower in the house of Mecaenas, and "being greatly delighted," as he said, "with the beautiful effects of the conflagration," he sung a poem on the ruin of Troy, in the tragic dress he used on the stage. To turn this calamity to his own advantage by plunder and rapine, he promised to remove the bodies of those who had perished in the fire, and clear the rubbish at his own expense; suffering no one to meddle with the remains of their property. But he not only received, but exacted contributions on account of the loss, until he had exhausted the means both of the provinces and private persons.

XXXIX. To these terrible and shameful calamities brought upon the people by their prince, were added some proceeding from misfortune. Such were a pestilence, by which, within the space of one autumn, there died no less than thirty thousand persons, as appeared from the registers in the temple of Libitina; a great disaster in Britain [615], where two of the principal towns belonging to the Romans were plundered; and a (369) dreadful havoc made both amongst our troops and allies; a shameful discomfiture of the army of the East; where, in Armenia, the legions were obliged to pass under the yoke, and it was with great difficulty that Syria was retained. Amidst all these disasters, it was strange, and, indeed, particularly remarkable, that he bore nothing more patiently than the scurrilous language and railing abuse which was in every one's mouth; treating no class of persons with more gentleness, than those who assailed him with invective and lampoons. Many things of that kind were posted up about the city, or otherwise published, both in Greek and Latin: such as these,

Neron, Orestaes, Alkmaion, maetroktonai.
Neonymphon [616] Neron, idian maeter apekteinen.
Orestes and Alcaeon—Nero too,
The lustful Nero, worst of all the crew,
Fresh from his bridal—their own mothers slew.
Quis neget Aeneae magna de stirpe Neronem?
Sustulit hic matrem: sustulit [617] ille patrem.

Sprung from Aeneas, pious, wise and great,
Who says that Nero is degenerate?
Safe through the flames, one bore his sire; the other,
To save himself, took off his loving mother.
Dum tendit citharam noster, dum cornua Parthus,
Noster erit Paean, ille Ekataebeletaes.
His lyre to harmony our Nero strings;
His arrows o'er the plain the Parthian wings:
Ours call the tuneful Paean,—famed in war,
The other Phoebus name, the god who shoots afar.
[618]
Roma domus fiet: Vejos migrate, Quirites,
Si non et Vejos occupat ista domus.
All Rome will be one house: to Veii fly,
Should it not stretch to Veii, by and by. [619]

(370) But he neither made any inquiry after the authors, nor when information was laid before the senate against some of them, would he allow a severe sentence to be passed. Isidorus, the Cynic philosopher, said to him aloud, as he was passing along the streets, "You sing the misfortunes of Nauplius well, but behave badly yourself." And Datus, a comic actor, when repeating these words in the piece, "Farewell, father! Farewell mother!" mimicked the gestures of persons drinking and swimming, significantly alluding to the deaths of Claudius and Agrippina: and on uttering the last clause,

Orcus vobis ducit pedes;
You stand this moment on the brink of Orcus;

he plainly intimated his application of it to the precarious position of the senate. Yet Nero only banished the player and philosopher from the city and Italy; either because he was insensible to shame, or from apprehension that if he discovered his vexation, still keener things might be said of him.

XL. The world, after tolerating such an emperor for little less than fourteen years, at length forsook him; the Gauls, headed by Julius Vindex, who at that time governed the province as pro-praetor, being the first to revolt. Nero had been formerly told by astrologers, that it would be his fortune to be at last deserted by all the world; and this occasioned that celebrated saying of his, "An artist can live in any country;" by which he meant to offer as an excuse for his practice

of music, that it was not only his amusement as a prince, but might be his support when reduced to a private station. Yet some of the astrologers promised him, in his forlorn state, the rule of the East, and some in express words the kingdom of Jerusalem. But the greater part of them flattered him with assurances of his being restored to his former fortune. And being most inclined to believe the latter prediction, upon losing Britain and Armenia, he imagined he had run through all the misfortunes which the fates had decreed him. But when, upon consulting the oracle of Apollo at Delphi, he was advised to beware of the seventy-third year, as if he were not to die till then, never thinking of Galba's age, he conceived such hopes, not only of living to advanced years, but of constant and singular good fortune, that having lost some things of great value by shipwreck, he scrupled not to say amongst his friends, that (371) "the fishes would bring them back to him." At Naples he heard of the insurrection in Gaul, on the anniversary of the day on which he killed his mother, and bore it with so much unconcern, as to excite a suspicion that he was really glad of it, since he had now a fair opportunity of plundering those wealthy provinces by the right of war. Immediately going to the gymnasium, he witnessed the exercise of the wrestlers with the greatest delight. Being interrupted at supper with letters which brought yet worse news, he expressed no greater resentment, than only to threaten the rebels. For eight days together, he never attempted to answer any letters, nor give any orders, but buried the whole affair in profound silence.

XLI. Being roused at last by numerous proclamations of Vindex, treating him with reproaches and contempt, he in a letter to the senate exhorted them to avenge his wrongs and those of the republic; desiring them to excuse his not appearing in the senate-house, because he had got cold. But nothing so much galled him, as to find himself railed at as a pitiful harper, and, instead of Nero, styled Aenobarbus: which being his family name, since he was upbraided with it, he declared that he would resume it, and lay aside the name he had taken by adoption. Passing by the other accusations as wholly groundless, he earnestly refuted that of his want of skill in an art upon which he had bestowed so much pains, and in which he had arrived at such perfection; asking frequently those about him, "if they knew any one who was a more accomplished musician?" But being alarmed by messengers after messengers of ill news from Gaul, he returned in great consternation to Rome. On the road, his mind was somewhat relieved, by observing the frivolous omen of a Gaulish soldier defeated and dragged by the hair by a Roman knight, which was sculptured on a monument; so that he leaped for joy, and adored the heavens. Even then he made no appeal either to the senate or people, but calling together some of the leading men at his own house, he held a hasty consultation upon the present state of affairs, and then, during the remainder of the day, carried them about with him to view some musical instruments, of a new invention, which were played by water [620] (372) exhibiting all the parts, and discoursing upon the principles and difficulties of the contrivance; which, he told them, he intended to produce in the theatre, if Vindex would give him leave.

XLII. Soon afterwards, he received intelligence that Galba and the Spaniards had declared against him; upon which, he fainted, and losing his reason, lay a long time speechless, apparently dead. As soon as recovered from this state stupefaction he tore his clothes, and beat his head, crying out, "It is all over with me!" His nurse endeavouring to comfort him, and telling him that the like things had happened to other princes before him, he replied, "I am beyond all example wretched, for I have lost an empire whilst I am still living." He, nevertheless, abated nothing of his luxury and inattention to business. Nay, on the arrival of good news from the provinces, he, at a sumptuous entertainment, sung with an air of merriment, some jovial verses upon the leaders of the revolt, which were made public; and accompanied them with suitable gestures. Being carried privately to the theatre, he sent word to an actor who was applauded by the spectators, "that he had it all his own way, now that he himself did not appear on the stage."

XLIII. At the first breaking out of these troubles, it is believed that he had formed many designs of a monstrous nature, although conformable enough to his natural disposition. These were to send new governors and commanders to the provinces and the armies, and employ assassins to butcher all the former governors and commanders, as men unanimously engaged in a conspiracy against him; to massacre the exiles in every quarter, and all the Gaulish population in Rome; the former lest they should join the insurrection; the latter as privy to the designs of their countrymen, and ready to support (373) them; to abandon Gaul itself, to be wasted and plundered by his armies; to poison the whole senate at a feast; to fire the city, and then let loose the wild beasts upon the people, in order to impede their stopping the progress of the flames. But being deterred from the execution of these designs not so much by remorse of conscience, as by despair of being able to effect them, and judging an expedition into Gaul necessary, he removed the consuls from their office, before the time of its expiration was arrived; and in their room assumed the consulship himself without a colleague, as if the fates had decreed that Gaul should not be conquered, but by a consul. Upon assuming the fasces, after an entertainment at the palace, as he walked out of the room leaning on the arms of some of his friends, he declared, that as soon as he arrived in the province, he would make his appearance amongst the troops, unarmed, and do nothing but weep: and that, after he had brought the mutineers to repentance, he would, the next day, in the public rejoicings, sing songs of triumph, which he must now, without loss of time, apply himself to compose.

XLIV. In preparing for this expedition, his first care was to provide carriages for his musical instruments and machinery to be used upon the stage; to have the hair of the concubines he carried with him dressed in the fashion of men; and to supply them with battle-axes, and Amazonian bucklers. He summoned the city-tribes to enlist; but no qualified persons appearing, he ordered all masters to send a certain number of slaves, the best they had, not excepting their stewards and secretaries. He commanded the several orders of the people to bring in a fixed proportion of their estates, as they stood in the censor's books; all tenants of houses and mansions to pay one year's rent forthwith into the exchequer; and, with unheard-of strictness, would receive only new coin of the purest silver and the finest gold; insomuch that most people refused to pay, crying out unanimously that he ought to squeeze the informers, and oblige them to surrender their gains.

XLV. The general odium in which he was held received an increase by the great scarcity of corn, and an occurrence connected with it. For, as it happened just at that time, there arrived from Alexandria a ship, which was said to be freighted (374) with dust for the wrestlers belonging to the emperor [621]. This so much inflamed the public rage, that he was treated with the utmost abuse and scurrility. Upon the top of one of his statues was placed the figure of a chariot with a Greek inscription, that "Now indeed he had a race to run; let him be gone." A little bag was tied about another, with a ticket containing these words; "What could I do?"—"Truly thou hast merited the sack." [622] Some person likewise wrote on the pillars in the forum, "that he had even woke the cocks [623] with his singing." And many, in the night-time, pretending to find fault with their servants, frequently called for a Vindex. [624]

XLVI. He was also terrified with manifest warnings, both old and new, arising from dreams, auspices, and omens. He had never been used to dream before the murder of his mother. After that event, he fancied in his sleep that he was steering a ship, and that the rudder was forced from him: that he was dragged by his wife Octavia into a prodigiously dark place; and was at one time covered over with a vast swarm of winged ants, and at another, surrounded by the national images which were set up near Pompey's theatre, and hindered from advancing farther; that a Spanish jennet he was fond of, had his hinder parts so changed, as to resemble those of an ape; and having his head only left unaltered, neighed very harmoniously. The doors of the mausoleum of Augustus flying open of themselves, there issued from it a voice, calling on him by name. The Lares being adorned with fresh garlands on the calends (the first) of January, fell down during the preparations for sacrificing to them. While he was taking (375) the omens, Sporus presented him with a ring, the stone of which had carved upon it the Rape of Proserpine. When a great multitude of the several orders was assembled, to attend at the solemnity of making vows to the gods, it was a long time before the keys of the

Capitol could be found. And when, in a speech of his to the senate against Vindex, these words were read, "that the miscreants should be punished and soon make the end they merited," they all cried out, "You will do it, Augustus." It was likewise remarked, that the last tragic piece which he sung, was Oedipus in Exile, and that he fell as he was repeating this verse:

Thanein m' anoge syngamos, maetaer, pataer.
Wife, mother, father, force me to my end.

XLVII. Meanwhile, on the arrival of the news, that the rest of the armies had declared against him, he tore to pieces the letters which were delivered to him at dinner, overthrew the table, and dashed with violence against the ground two favourite cups, which he called Homer's, because some of that poet's verses were cut upon them. Then taking from Locusta a dose of poison, which he put up in a golden box, he went into the Servilian gardens, and thence dispatching a trusty freedman to Ostia, with orders to make ready a fleet, he endeavoured to prevail with some tribunes and centurions of the pretorian guards to attend him in his flight; but part of them showing no great inclination to comply, others absolutely refusing, and one of them crying out aloud,

Usque adeone mori miserum est?
Say, is it then so sad a thing to die? [625]

he was in great perplexity whether he should submit himself to Galba, or apply to the Parthians for protection, or else appear before the people dressed in mourning, and, upon the rostra, in the most piteous manner, beg pardon for his past misdemeanors, and, if he could not prevail, request of them to grant him at least the government of Egypt. A speech to this purpose was afterwards found in his writing-case. But it is conjectured that he durst not venture upon this project, for fear of being torn to pieces, before he could get to the Forum. Deferring, therefore, his resolution until the next (376) day, he awoke about midnight, and finding the guards withdrawn, he leaped out of bed, and sent round for his friends. But none of them vouchsafing any message in reply, he went with a few attendants to their houses. The doors being every where shut, and no one giving him any answer, he returned to his bed-chamber; whence those who had the charge of it had all now eloped;

some having gone one way, and some another, carrying off with them his bedding and box of poison. He then endeavoured to find Spicillus, the gladiator, or some one to kill him; but not being able to procure any one, "What!" said he, "have I then neither friend nor foe?" and immediately ran out, as if he would throw himself into the Tiber.

XLVIII. But this furious impulse subsiding, he wished for some place of privacy, where he might collect his thoughts; and his freedman Phaon offering him his country-house, between the Salarian [626] and Nomentan [627] roads, about four miles from the city, he mounted a horse, barefoot as he was, and in his tunic, only slipping over it an old soiled cloak; with his head muffled up, and an handkerchief before his face, and four persons only to attend him, of whom Sporus was one. He was suddenly struck with horror by an earthquake, and by a flash of lightning which darted full in his face, and heard from the neighbouring camp [628] the shouts of the soldiers, wishing his destruction, and prosperity to Galba. He also heard a traveller they met on the road, say, "They are (377) in pursuit of Nero:" and another ask, "Is there any news in the city about Nero?" Uncovering his face when his horse was started by the scent of a carcase which lay in the road, he was recognized and saluted by an old soldier who had been discharged from the guards. When they came to the lane which turned up to the house, they quitted their horses, and with much difficulty he wound among bushes, and briars, and along a track through a bed of rushes, over which they spread their cloaks for him to walk on. Having reached a wall at the back of the villa, Phaon advised him to hide himself awhile in a sand-pit; when he replied, "I will not go under-ground alive." Staying there some little time, while preparations were made for bringing him privately into the villa, he took up some water out of a neighbouring tank in his hand, to drink, saying, "This is Nero's distilled water." [629] Then his cloak having been torn by the brambles, he pulled out the thorns which stuck in it. At last, being admitted, creeping upon his hands and knees, through a hole made for him in the wall, he lay down in the first closet he came to, upon a miserable pallet, with an old coverlet thrown over it; and being both hungry and thirsty, though he refused some coarse bread that was brought him, he drank a little warm water.

XLIX. All who surrounded him now pressing him to save himself from the indignities which were ready to befall him, he ordered a pit to be sunk before his eyes, of the size of his body, and the bottom to be covered with pieces of marble put together, if any could be found about the house; and water and wood [630], to be got ready for immediate use about his corpse; weeping at every thing that was done, and frequently saying, "What an artist is now about to perish!" Meanwhile, letters being brought in by a servant belonging to Phaon, he snatched them out of his hand, and there read, "That he had been declared an enemy by the senate, and that search was making for him, that he might be punished according to the ancient custom of the Romans." He then inquired what kind of punishment that was; and being told, that the (378) practice was to strip the criminal naked, and scourge him to death, while his neck was fastened within a forked stake, he was so terrified that he took up two daggers which he had brought with him, and after feeling the points of both, put them up again, saying, "The fatal hour is not yet come." One while, he begged of Sporus to begin to wail and lament; another while, he entreated that one of them would set him an example by killing himself; and then again, he condemned his own want of resolution in these words: "I yet live to my shame and disgrace: this is not becoming for Nero: it is not becoming. Thou oughtest in such circumstances to have a good heart: Come, then: courage, man!" [631] The horsemen who had received orders to bring him away alive, were now approaching the house. As soon as he heard them coming, he uttered with a trembling voice the following verse,

> Hippon m' okupodon amphi ktupos ouata ballei; [632]
> The noise of swift-heel'd steeds assails my ears;

he drove a dagger into his throat, being assisted in the act by Epaphroditus, his secretary. A centurion bursting in just as he was half-dead, and applying his cloak to the wound, pretending that he was come to his assistance, he made no other reply but this, "'Tis too late;" and "Is this your loyalty?" Immediately after pronouncing these words, he expired, with his eyes fixed and starting out of his head, to the terror of all who beheld him. He had requested of his attendants, as the most essential favour, that they would let no one have his head, but that by all means his body might be burnt entire. And this, Icelus, Galba's freedman, granted. He had but a little before been discharged from the prison into which he had been thrown, when the disturbances first broke out.

L. The expenses of his funeral amounted to two hundred thousand sesterces; the bed upon which his body was carried to the pile and burnt, being covered with the white robes, interwoven with gold, which he had worn upon the calends of January preceding. His nurses, Ecloge and Alexandra, with his concubine Acte, deposited his remains in the tomb belonging (379) to the family of the Domitii, which stands upon the top of the Hill of the Gardens [633], and is to be seen from the Campus Martius. In that monument, a coffin of porphyry, with an altar of marble of Luna over it, is enclosed by a wall built of stone brought from Thasos. [634]

LI. In stature he was a little below the common height; his skin was foul and spotted; his hair inclined to yellow; his features were agreeable, rather than handsome; his eyes grey and dull, his neck was thick, his belly prominent, his legs very slender, his constitution sound. For, though excessively luxurious in his mode of living, he had, in the course of fourteen years, only three fits of sickness; which were so slight, that he neither forbore the use of wine, nor made any alteration in his usual diet. In his dress, and the care of his person, he was so careless, that he had his hair cut in rings, one above another; and when in Achaia, he let it grow long behind; and he generally appeared in public in the loose dress which he used at table, with a handkerchief about his neck, and without either a girdle or shoes.

LII. He was instructed, when a boy, in the rudiments of almost all the liberal sciences; but his mother diverted him from the study of philosophy, as unsuited to one destined to be an emperor; and his preceptor, Seneca, discouraged him from reading the ancient orators, that he might longer secure his devotion to himself. Therefore, having a turn for poetry, (380) he composed verses both with pleasure and ease; nor did he, as some think, publish those of other writers as his own. Several little pocket-books and loose sheets have cone into my possession, which contain some well-known verses in his own hand, and written in such a manner, that it was very evident, from the blotting and interlining, that they had not been transcribed from a copy, nor dictated by another, but were written by the composer of them.

LIII. He had likewise great taste for drawing and painting, as well as for moulding statues in plaster. But, above all things, he most eagerly coveted popularity, being the rival of every man who obtained the applause of the people for any thing he did. It was the general belief, that, after the crowns he won by his performances on the stage, he would the next lustrum have taken his place among the wrestlers at the Olympic games. For he was continually practising that art; nor did he witness the gymnastic games in any part of Greece otherwise than sitting upon the ground in the stadium, as the umpires do. And if a pair of wrestlers happened to break the bounds, he would with his own hands drag them back into the centre of the circle. Because he was thought to equal Apollo in music, and the sun in chariot-driving, he resolved also to imitate the achievements of Hercules. And they say that a lion was got ready for him to kill, either with a club, or with a close hug, in view of the people in the amphitheatre; which he was to perform naked.

LIV. Towards the end of his life, he publicly vowed, that if his power in the state was securely re-established, he would, in the spectacles which he intended to exhibit in honour of his success, include a performance upon organs [635], as well as upon flutes and bagpipes, and, on the last day of the games, would act in the play, and take the part of Turnus, as we find it in Virgil. And there are some who say, that he put to death the player Paris as a dangerous rival.

LV. He had an insatiable desire to immortalize his name, and acquire a reputation which should last through all succeeding ages; but it was capriciously directed. He therefore (381) took from several things and places their former appellations, and gave them new names derived from his own. He called the month of April, Neroneus, and designed changing the name of Rome into that of Neropolis.

LVI. He held all religious rites in contempt, except those of the Syrian Goddess [636]; but at last he paid her so little reverence, that he made water upon her; being now engaged in another superstition, in which only he obstinately persisted. For having received from some obscure plebeian a little image of a girl, as a preservative against plots, and discovering a conspiracy immediately after, he constantly worshipped his imaginary protectress as the greatest amongst the gods, offering to her three sacrifices daily. He was also desirous to have it supposed that he had, by revelations from this deity, a knowledge of future events. A few months before he died, he attended a sacrifice, according to the Etruscan rites, but the omens were not favourable.

LVII. He died in the thirty-second year of his age [637], upon the same day on which he had formerly put Octavia to death; and the public joy was so great upon the occasion, that the common people ran about the city with caps upon their heads. Some, however, were not wanting, who for a long time decked his tomb with spring and summer flowers. Sometimes they placed his image upon the rostra, dressed in robes of state; at another, they published proclamations in his name, as if he were still alive, and would shortly return to Rome, and take vengeance on all his enemies. Vologesus, king of the Parthians, when he sent ambassadors to the senate to renew his alliance with the Roman people, earnestly requested that due honour should be paid to the memory of Nero; and, to conclude, when, twenty years afterwards, at which time I was a young man [638], some person of obscure birth gave himself out for Nero, that name secured him so favourable a reception (382) from the Parthians, that he was very zealously supported, and it was with much difficulty that they were prevailed upon to give him up.

TACITUS ON GERMANY

Translated by Thomas Gordon

The whole of Germany is thus bounded; separated from Gaul, from Rhoetia and Pannonia, by the rivers Rhine and Danube; from Sarmatia and Dacia by mutual fear, or by high mountains: the rest is encompassed by the ocean, which forms huge bays, and comprehends a tract of islands immense in extent: for we have lately known certain nations and kingdoms there, such as the war discovered. The Rhine rising in the Rhoetian Alps from a summit altogether rocky and perpendicular, after a small winding towards the west, is lost in the Northern Ocean. The Danube issues out of the mountain Abnoba, one very high but very easy of ascent, and traversing several nations, falls by six streams into the Euxine Sea; for its seventh channel is absorbed in the Fenns.

The Germans, I am apt to believe, derive their original from no other people; and are nowise mixed with different nations arriving amongst them: since anciently those who went in search of new dwellings, travelled not by land, but were carried in fleets; and into that mighty ocean so boundless, and, as I may call it, so repugnant and forbidding, ships from our world rarely enter. Moreover, besides the dangers from a sea tempestuous, horrid and unknown, who would relinquish Asia, or Africa, or Italy, to repair to Germany, a region hideous and rude, under a rigorous climate, dismal to behold or to manure [to cultivate] unless the same were his native country? In their old ballads (which amongst them are the only sort of registers and history) they celebrate *Tuisto*, a God sprung from the earth, and *Mannus* his son, as the fathers and founders of the nation. To *Mannus* they assign three sons, after whose names so many people are called; the Ingaevones, dwelling next the ocean; the Herminones, in the middle country; and all the rest, Instaevones. Some, borrowing a warrant from the darkness of antiquity, maintain that the God had more sons, that thence came

more denominations of people, the Marsians, Gambrians, Suevians, and Vandalians, and that these are the names truly genuine and original. For the rest, they affirm Germany to be a recent word, lately bestowed: for that those who first passed the Rhine and expulsed the Gauls, and are now named Tungrians, were then called Germans: and thus by degrees the name of a tribe prevailed, not that of the nation; so that by an appellation at first occasioned by terror and conquest, they afterwards chose to be distinguished, and assuming a name lately invented were universally called *Germans*.

They have a tradition that Hercules also had been in their country, and him above all other heroes they extol in their songs when they advance to battle. Amongst them too are found that kind of verses by the recital of which (by them called *Barding*) they inspire bravery; nay, by such chanting itself they divine the success of the approaching fight. For, according to the different din of the battle they urge furiously, or shrink timorously. Nor does what they utter, so much seem to be singing as the voice and exertion of valour. They chiefly study a tone fierce and harsh, with a broken and unequal murmur, and therefore apply their shields to their mouths, whence the voice may by rebounding swell with greater fulness and force. Besides there are some of opinion, that Ulysses, whilst he wandered about in his long and fabulous voyages, was carried into this ocean and entered Germany, and that by him Asciburgium was founded and named, a city at this day standing and inhabited upon the bank of the Rhine: nay, that in the same place was formerly found an altar dedicated to Ulysses, with the name of his father Laertes added to his own, and that upon the confines of Germany and Rhoetia are still extant certain monuments and tombs inscribed with Greek characters. Traditions these which I mean not either to confirm with arguments of my own or to refute. Let every one believe or deny the same according to his own bent.

For myself, I concur in opinion with such as suppose the people of Germany never to have mingled by inter-marriages with other nations, but to have remained a people pure, and independent, and resembling none but themselves. Hence amongst such a mighty multitude of men, the same make and form is found in all, eyes stern and blue, yellow hair, huge bodies, but vigorous only in the first onset. Of pains and labour they are not equally patient, nor can they at all endure thrift and heat. To bear hunger and cold they are hardened by their climate and soil.

Their lands, however somewhat different in aspect, yet taken all together consist of gloomy forests or nasty marshes; lower and moister towards Noricum and Pannonia; very apt to bear grain, but altogether unkindly to fruit trees; abounding in flocks and herds, but generally small of growth. Nor even in their oxen is found the usual stateliness, no more than the natural ornaments and grandeur of head. In the number of their herds they rejoice; and these are their only, these their most desirable riches. Silver and gold the Gods have denied them, whether in mercy or in wrath, I am unable to determine. Yet I would not venture to aver that in Germany no vein of gold or silver is produced; for who has ever searched? For the use and possession, it is certain they care not. Amongst them indeed are to be seen vessels of silver, such as have been presented to their Princes and Ambassadors, but holden in no other esteem than vessels made of earth. The Germans however adjoining to our frontiers value gold and silver for the purposes of commerce, and are wont to distinguish and prefer certain of our coins. They who live more remote are more primitive and simple in their dealings, and exchange one commodity for another. The money which they like is the old and long known, that indented [with milled edges], or that impressed with a chariot and two horses. Silver too is what they seek more than gold, from no fondness or preference, but because small pieces are more ready in purchasing things cheap and common.

Neither in truth do they abound in iron, as from the fashion of their weapons may be gathered. Swords they rarely use, or the larger spear. They carry javelins or, in their own language, *framms*, pointed with a piece of iron short and narrow, but so sharp and manageable, that with the same weapon they can fight at a distance or hand to hand, just as need requires. Nay, the horsemen also are content with a shield and a javelin. The foot throw likewise weapons missive, each particular is armed with many, and hurls them a mighty space, all naked or only wearing a light cassock. In their equipment they show no ostentation; only that their shields are diversified and adorned with curious colours. With coats of mail very few are furnished, and hardly upon any is seen a headpiece or helmet. Their horses are nowise signal either in fashion or in fleetness; nor taught to wheel and bound, according to the practice of the Romans: they only move them forward in a line, or turn them right about, with such compactness and equality that no one is ever behind the rest. To one who considers the whole it is manifest, that in their foot their principal strength lies, and therefore they fight intermixed with the motions and engagements of the cavalry. So that the infantry are elected from amongst the most robust of their youth, and placed in front of the army. The number to be sent is also ascertained, out of every village *an hundred*, and by this very name they continue to be called at home, *those of the hundred band*: thus what was at first no more than a number, becomes thenceforth a title and distinction of honour. In arraying their army, they divide the whole into distinct battalions formed sharp in front. To recoil in battle, provided you return again to the attack, passes with them rather for policy than fear. Even when the combat is no more than doubtful, they bear away the bodies of their slain. The most glaring disgrace that can befall them, is to have quitted their shield; nor to one branded with such ignominy is it lawful to join in their sacrifices, or to enter into their assemblies; and many who had escaped in the day of battle, have hanged themselves to put an end to this their infamy.

In the choice of kings they are determined by the splendour of their race, in that of generals by their bravery. Neither is the power of their kings unbounded or arbitrary: and their generals procure obedience not so much by the force of their authority as by that of their example, when they appear enterprising and brave, when they signalise themselves by courage and prowess; and if they surpass all in admiration and pre-eminence, if they surpass all at the head of an army. But to none else but the Priests is it allowed to exercise correction, or to inflict bonds or stripes. Nor when the Priests do this, is the same considered as a punishment, or arising from the orders of the general, but from the immediate command of the Deity, Him whom they believe to accompany them in war. They therefore carry with them when going to fight, certain images and figures taken out of their holy groves. What proves the principal incentive to their valour is, that it is not at random nor by the fortuitous conflux of men that their troops and pointed battalions are formed, but by the conjunction of whole families, and tribes of relations. Moreover, close to the field of battle are lodged all the nearest and most interesting pledges of nature. Hence they hear the doleful howlings of their wives, hence the cries of their tender infants. These are to each particular the witnesses whom he most reverences and dreads; these yield him the praise which affect him most. Their wounds and maims they carry to their mothers, or to their wives, neither are their mothers or wives shocked in telling, or in sucking their bleeding sores. Nay, to their husbands and sons whilst engaged in battle, they administer meat and encouragement.

In history we find, that some armies already yielding and ready to fly, have been by women restored, through their inflexible importunity and entreaties, presenting their breasts, and showing their impending captivity; an evil to the Germans then by far most dreadful when it befalls their women. So that the spirit of such cities as amongst their hostages are enjoined to send their damsels of quality, is always engaged more effectually than that of others. They even believe them endowed with something celestial and the spirit of prophecy. Neither do they disdain to consult them, nor neglect the responses which they return. In the reign of the deified Vespasian, we have seen *Veleda* for a long time, and by many nations, esteemed and adored as a divinity. In times past they likewise worshipped *Aurinia* and several more, from no complaisance or effort of flattery, nor as Deities of their own creating.

Of all the Gods, Mercury is he whom they worship most. To him on certain stated days it is lawful to offer even human victims. Hercules and Mars they appease with beasts usually allowed for sacrifice. Some of the Suevians make likewise immolations to *Isis*. Concerning the cause and original of this foreign sacrifice I have found small light; unless the figure of her image formed like a galley, show that such devotion arrived from abroad. For the rest, from the grandeur and majesty of beings celestial, they judge it altogether unsuitable to hold the Gods enclosed within walls, or to represent them under any human likeness. They consecrate whole woods and groves, and by the names of the Gods they call these recesses; divinities these, which only in contemplation and mental reverence they behold.

To the use of lots and auguries, they are addicted beyond all other nations. Their method of divining by lots is exceeding simple. From a tree which bears fruit they cut a twig, and divide it into two small pieces. These they distinguish by so many several marks, and throw them at random and without order upon a white garment. Then the Priest of the community, if for the public the lots are consulted, or the father of a family if about a private concern, after he has solemnly invoked the Gods, with eyes lifted up to heaven, takes up every piece thrice, and having done thus forms a judgment according to the marks before made. If the chances have proved forbidding, they are no more consulted upon the same affair during the same day; even when they are inviting, yet, for confirmation, the faith of auguries too is tried. Yea, here also is the known practice of divining events from the voices and flight of birds. But to this nation it is peculiar, to learn presages and admonitions divine from horses also. These are nourished by the State in the same sacred woods and grooves, all milk-white and employed in no earthly labour. These yoked in the holy chariot, are accompanied by the Priest and the King, or the Chief of the community, who both carefully observed his actions and neighing. Nor in any sort of augury is more faith and assurance reposed, not by the populace only, but even by the nobles, even by the Priests. These account themselves the ministers of the Gods, and the horses privy to his will. They have likewise another method of divination, whence to learn the issue of great and mighty wars. From the nation with whom they are at war they contrive, it avails not how, to gain a captive: him they engage in combat with one selected from amongst themselves, each armed after the manner of his country, and according as the victory falls to this or to the other, gather a presage of the whole.

Affairs of smaller moment the chiefs determine: about matters of higher consequence the whole nation deliberates; yet in such sort, that whatever depends upon the pleasure and decision of the people, is examined and discussed by the chiefs. Where no accident or emergency intervenes, they assemble upon stated days, either, when the moon changes, or is full: since they believe such seasons to be the most fortunate for beginning all transactions. Neither in reckoning of time do they count, like us, the number of days but that of nights. In this style their ordinances are framed, in this style their diets appointed; and with them the night seems to lead and govern the day. From their extensive liberty this evil and default flows, that they meet not at once, nor as men commanded and afraid to disobey; so that often the second day, nay often the third, is consumed through the slowness of the members in assembling. They sit down as they list, promiscuously, like a crowd, and all armed. It is by the Priests that silence is enjoined, and with the power of correction the Priests are then invested. Then the King or Chief is heard, as are others, each according to his precedence in age, or in nobility, or in warlike renown, or in eloquence; and the influence of every speaker proceeds rather from his ability to persuade than from any authority to command. If the proposition displease, they reject it by an inarticulate murmur: if it be pleasing, they brandish their javelins. The most honourable manner of signifying their assent, is to express their applause by the sound of their arms.

In the assembly it is allowed to present accusations, and to prosecute capital offences. Punishments vary according to the quality of the crime. Traitors and deserters they hang upon trees. Cowards, and sluggards, and unnatural prostitutes they smother in mud and bogs under an heap of hurdles. Such diversity in their executions has this view, that in punishing of glaring iniquities, it behooves likewise to display them to sight; but effeminacy and pollution must be buried and concealed. In lighter transgressions too the penalty is measured by the fault, and the delinquents upon conviction are condemned to pay a certain number of horses or cattle. Part of this mulct accrues to the King or to the community, part to him whose wrongs are vindicated, or to his next kindred. In the same assemblies are also chosen their chiefs or rulers, such as administer justice in their villages and boroughs. To each of these are assigned an hundred persons chosen from amongst the populace, to accompany and assist him, men who help him at once with their authority and their counsel.

Without being armed they transact nothing, whether of public or private concernment. But it is repugnant to their custom for any man to use arms, before the community has attested his capacity to wield them. Upon such testimonial, either one of the rulers, or his father, or some kinsman dignify the young man in the midst of the assembly, with a shield and javelin. This amongst them is the *manly robe*, this first degree of honour conferred upon their youth. Before this they seem no more than part of a private family, but thenceforward part of the Commonweal. The princely dignity they confer even upon striplings, whose race is eminently noble, or whose fathers have done great and signal services to the State. For about the rest, who are more vigorous and long since tried, they crowd to attend; nor is it any shame to be seen amongst the followers of these. Nay, there are likewise degrees of followers, higher or lower, just as he whom they follow judges fit. Mighty too is the emulation amongst these followers, of each to be first in favour with his Prince; mighty also the emulation of the Princes, to excel in the number and valour of followers. This is their principal state, this their chief force, to be at all times surrounded with a huge band of chosen young men, for ornament and glory in peace, for security and defence in war. Nor is it amongst his own people only, but even from the neighbouring communities, that any of their Princes reaps so much renown and a name so great, when he surpasses in the number and magnanimity of his followers. For such are courted by Embassies, and distinguished with presents, and by the terror of their fame alone often dissipate wars.

In the day of battle, it is scandalous to the Prince to be surpassed in feats of bravery, scandalous to his followers to fail in matching the bravery of the Prince. But it is infamy during life, and indelible reproach, to return alive from a battle where their Prince was slain. To preserve their Prince, to defend him, and to ascribe to his glory all their own valorous deeds, is the sum and most sacred part of their oath. The Princes fight for victory; for the Prince his followers fight. Many of the young nobility, when their own community comes to languish in its vigour by long peace and inactivity, betake themselves through impatience in other States which then prove to be in war. For, besides that this people cannot brook repose, besides that by perilous adventures they more quickly blazon their fame, they cannot otherwise than by violence and war support their huge train of retainers. For from the liberality of their Prince, they demand and enjoy that *war-horse* of theirs, with that *victorious javelin* dyed in the blood of their enemies. In the place of pay, they are supplied with a daily table and repasts; though grossly prepared, yet very profuse. For maintaining such liberality and munificence, a fund is furnished by continual wars and plunder. Nor could you so easily persuade them to cultivate the ground, or to await the return of the seasons and produce of the year, as to provoke the foe and to risk wounds and death: since stupid and spiritless they account it, to acquire by their sweat what they can gain by their blood.

Upon any recess from war, they do not much attend the chase. Much more of their time they pass in indolence, resigned to sleep and repasts. All the most brave, all the most warlike, apply to nothing at all; but to their wives, to the ancient men, and to even the most impotent domestic, trust all the care of their house, and of their lands and possessions. They themselves loiter. Such is the amazing diversity of their nature, that in the same men is found so much delight in sloth, with so much enmity to tranquillity and repose. The communities are wont, of their own accord and man by man, to bestow upon

their Princes a certain number of beasts, or a certain portion of grain; a contribution which passes indeed for a mark of reverence and honour, but serves also to supply their necessities. They chiefly rejoice in the gifts which come from the bordering countries, such as are sent not only by particulars but in the name of the State; curious horses, splendid armour, rich harness, with collars of silver and gold. Now too they have learnt, what we have taught them, to receive money.

That none of the several people in Germany live together in cities, is abundantly known; nay, that amongst them none of their dwellings are suffered to be contiguous. They inhabit apart and distinct, just as a fountain, or a field, or a wood happened to invite them to settle. They raise their villages in opposite rows, but not in our manner with the houses joined one to another. Every man has a vacant space quite round his own, whether for security against accidents from fire, or that they want the art of building. With them in truth, is unknown even the use of mortar and of tiles. In all their structures they employ materials quite gross and unhewn, void of fashion and comeliness. Some parts they besmear with an earth so pure and resplendent, that it resembles painting and colours. They are likewise wont to scoop caves deep in the ground, and over them to lay great heaps of dung. Thither they retire for shelter in the winter, and thither convey their grain: for by such close places they mollify the rigorous and excessive cold. Besides when at any time their enemy invades them, he can only ravage the open country, but either knows not such recesses as are invisible and subterraneous; or must suffer them to escape him, on this very account that he is uncertain where to find them.

For their covering a mantle is what they all wear, fastened with a clasp or, for want of it, with a thorn. As far as this reaches not they are naked, and lie whole days before the fire. The most wealthy are distinguished with a vest, not one large and flowing like those of Sarmatians and Parthians, but girt close about them and expressing the proportion of every limb. They likewise wear the skins of savage beasts, a dress which those bordering upon the Rhine use without any fondness or delicacy, but about which such who live further in the country are more curious, as void of all apparel introduced by commerce. They choose certain wild beasts, and, having flayed them, diversify their hides with many spots, as also with the skins of monsters from the deep, such as are engendered in the distant ocean and in seas unknown. Neither does the dress of the women differ from that of the men, save that the women are orderly attired in linen embroidered with purple, and use no sleeves, so that all their arms are bare. The upper part of their breast is withal exposed.

Yet the laws of matrimony are severely observed there; for in the whole of their manners is aught more praiseworthy than this: for they are almost the only Barbarians contented with one wife, excepting a very few amongst them; men of dignity who marry divers wives, from no wantonness or lubricity, but courted for the lustre of their family into many alliances.

To the husband, the wife tenders no dowry; but the husband, to the wife. The parents and relations attend and declare their approbation of the presents, not presents adapted to feminine pomp and delicacy, nor such as serve to deck the new married woman; but oxen and horse accoutred, and a shield, with a javelin and sword. By virtue of these gifts, she is espoused. She too on her part brings her husband some arms. This they esteem the highest tie, these the holy mysteries, and matrimonial Gods. That the woman may not suppose herself free from the considerations of fortitude and fighting, or exempt from the casualties of war, the very first solemnities of her wedding serve to warn her, that she comes to her husband as a partner in his hazards and fatigues, that she is to suffer alike with him, to adventure alike, during peace or during war. This the oxen joined in the same yoke plainly indicate, this the horse ready equipped, this the present of arms. 'Tis thus she must be content to live, thus to resign life. The arms which she then receives she must preserve inviolate, and to her sons restore the same, as presents worthy of them, such as their wives may again receive, and still resign to her grandchildren.

They therefore live in a state of chastity well secured; corrupted by no seducing shows and public diversions, by no irritations from banqueting. Of learning and of any secret intercourse by letters, they are all equally ignorant, men and women. Amongst a people so numerous, adultery is exceeding rare; a crime instantly punished, and the punishment left to be inflicted by the husband. He, having cut off her hair, expells her from his house naked, in presence of her kindred, and pursues her with stripes throughout the village. For, to a woman who has prostituted her person, no pardon is ever granted. However beautiful she may be, however young, however abounding in wealth, a husband she can never find. In truth, nobody turns vices into mirth there, nor is the practice of corrupting and of yielding to corruption, called the custom of the Age. Better still do those communities, in which none but virgins marry, and where to a single marriage all their views and inclinations are at once confined. Thus, as they have but one body and one life, they take but one husband, that beyond him they may have no thought, no further wishes, nor love him only as their husband but as their marriage. To restrain generation and the increase of children, is esteemed an abominable sin, as also to kill infants newly born. And more powerful with them are good manners, than with other people are good laws.

In all their houses the children are reared naked and nasty; and thus grow into those limbs, into that bulk, which with marvel we behold. They are all nourished with the milk of their own mothers, and never surrendered to handmaids and nurses. The lord you cannot discern from the slave, by any superior delicacy in rearing. Amongst the same cattle they promiscuously live, upon the same ground they without distinction lie, till at a proper age the free-born are parted from the rest, and their bravery recommend them to notice. Slow and late do the young men come to the use of women, and thus very long preserve the vigour of youth. Neither are the virgins hastened to wed. They must both have the same sprightly youth, the like stature, and marry when equal and able-bodied. Thus the robustness of the parents is inherited by the children. Children are holden in the same estimation with their mother's brother, as with their father. Some hold this tie of blood to be most inviolable and binding, and in receiving of hostages, such pledges are most considered and claimed, as they who at once possess affections the most unalienable, and the most diffuse interest in their family. To every man, however, his own children are heirs and successors: wills they make none: for want of children his next akin inherits; his own brothers, those of his father, or those of his mother. To ancient men, the more they abound in descendants, in relations and affinities, so much the more favour and reverence accrues. From being childless, no advantage nor estimation is derived.

All the enmities of your house, whether of your father or of your kindred, you must necessarily adopt; as well as all their friendships. Neither are such enmities unappeasable and permanent: since even for so great a crime as homicide, compensation is made by a fixed number of sheep and cattle, and by it the whole family is pacified to content. A temper this, wholesome to the State; because to a free nation, animosities and faction are always more menacing and perilous. In social feasts, and deeds of hospitality, no nation upon earth was ever more liberal and abounding. To refuse admitting under your roof any man whatsoever, is held wicked and inhuman. Every man receives every comer, and treats him with repasts as large as his ability can possibly furnish. When the whole stock is consumed, he who has treated so hospitably guides and accompanies his guest to the next house, though neither of them invited. Nor avails it, that they were not; they are there received, with the same frankness and humanity. Between a stranger and an acquaintance, in dispensing the rules and benefits of hospitality, no difference is made. Upon your departure, if you ask anything, it is the custom to grant it; and with the same facility, they ask of you. In gifts they delight, but neither claim merit from what they give, nor own any obligation for what they receive. Their manner of entertaining their guests is familiar and kind.

The moment they rise from sleep, which they generally prolong till late in the day, they bathe, most frequently in warm water; as in a country where the winter is very long and severe. From bathing, they sit down to meat; every man apart, upon a particular seat, and at a separate table. They then proceed to their affairs, all in arms; as in arms, they no less frequently go to banquet. To continue drinking night and day without intermission, is a reproach to no man. Frequent then are their broils, as usual amongst men intoxicated with liquor; and such broils rarely terminate in angry words, but for the most part in maimings and slaughter. Moreover in these their feasts, they generally deliberate about reconciling parties at enmity, about forming affinities, choosing of Princes, and finally about peace and war. For they judge, that at no season is the soul more open to thoughts that are artless and upright, or more fired with such as are great and bold. This people, of themselves nowise subtile or politic, from the freedom of the place and occasion acquire still more frankness to disclose the most secret motions and purposes of their hearts. When therefore the minds of all have been once laid open and declared, on the day following the several sentiments are revised and canvassed; and to both conjectures of time, due regard is had. They consult, when they know not how to dissemble; they determine, when they cannot mistake.

For their drink, they draw a liquor from barley or other grain; and ferment the same so as to make it resemble wine. Nay, they who dwell upon the bank of the Rhine deal in wine. Their food is very simple; wild fruit, fresh venison, or coagulated milk. They banish hunger without formality, without curious dressing and curious fare. In extinguishing thirst, they use not equal temperance. If you will but humour their excess in drinking, and supply them with as much as they covet, it will be no less easy to vanquish them by vices than by arms.

Of public diversions they have but one sort, and in all their meetings the same is still exhibited. Young men, such as make it their pastime, fling themselves naked and dance amongst sharp swords and the deadly points of javelins. From habit they acquire their skill, and from their skill a graceful manner; yet from hence draw no gain or hire: though this adventurous gaiety has its reward, namely, that of pleasing the spectators. What is marvellous, playing at dice is one of their most serious employments; and even sober, they are gamesters: nay, so desperately do they venture upon the chance of winning or losing, that when their whole substance is played away, they stake their liberty and their persons upon one and the last throw. The loser goes calmly into voluntary bondage. However younger he be, however stronger, he tamely suffers himself to be bound and sold by the winner. Such is their perseverance in an evil course: they themselves call it honour.

Slaves of this class, they exchange in commerce, to free themselves too from the shame of such a victory. Of their other slaves they make not such use as we do of ours, by distributing amongst them the several offices and employments of the family. Each of them has a dwelling of his own, each a household to govern. His lord uses him like a tenant, and obliges him to pay a quantity of grain, or of cattle, or of cloth. Thus far only the subserviency of the slave extends. All the other duties in a family, not the slaves, but the wives and children discharge. To inflict stripes upon a slave, or to put him in chains, or to doom him to severe labour, are things rarely seen. To kill them they sometimes are wont, not through correction or government, but in heat and rage, as they would an enemy, save that no vengeance or penalty follows. The freedmen very little surpass the slaves, rarely are of moment in the house; in the community never, excepting only such nations where arbitrary dominion prevails. For there they bear higher sway than the free-born, nay, higher than the nobles. In other countries the inferior condition of freedmen is a proof of public liberty.

To the practice of usury and of increasing money by interest, they are strangers; and hence is found a better guard against it, than if it were forbidden. They shift from land to land; and, still appropriating a portion suitable to the number of hands for manuring, anon parcel out the whole amongst particulars according to the condition and quality of each. As the plains are very spacious, the allotments are easily assigned. Every year they change, and cultivate a fresh soil; yet still there is ground to spare. For they strive not to bestow labour proportionable to the fertility and compass of their lands, by planting orchards, by enclosing meadows, by watering gardens. From the earth, corn only is extracted. Hence they quarter not the year into so many seasons. Winter, Spring, and Summer, they understand; and for each have proper appellations. Of the name and blessings of Autumn, they are equally ignorant.

In performing their funerals, they show no state or vainglory. This only is carefully observed, that with the corpses of their signal men certain woods be burned. Upon the funeral pile they accumulate neither apparel nor perfumes. Into the fire, are always thrown the arms of the dead, and sometimes his horse. With sods of earth only the sepulchre is raised. The pomp of tedious and elaborate monuments they contemn, as things grievous to the deceased. Tears and wailings they soon dismiss: their affliction and woe they long retain. In women, it is reckoned becoming to bewail their loss; in men, to remember it. This is what in general we have learned, in the original and customs of the whole people of Germany. I shall now deduce the institutions and usages of the several people, as far as they vary one from another; as also an account of what nations from thence removed, to settle themselves in Gaul.

That the Gauls were in times past more puissant and formidable, is related by the Prince of authors, the deified Julius [Caesar]; and hence it is probable that they too have passed into Germany. For what a small obstacle must be a river, to restrain any nation, as each grew more potent, from seizing or changing habitations; when as yet all habitations were common, and not parted or appropriated by the founding and terror of Monarchies? The region therefore between the Hercynian Forest and the rivers Moenus and Rhine, was occupied by the Helvetians; as was that beyond it by the Boians, both nations of Gaul. There still remains a place called *Boiemum*, which denotes the primitive name and antiquity of the country, although the inhabitants have been changed. But whether the Araviscans are derived from the Osians, a nation of Germans passing into Pannonia, or the Osians from the Araviscans removing from thence into Germany, is a matter undecided; since they both still use the language, the same customs and the same laws. For, as of old they lived alike poor and alike free, equal proved the evils and advantages on each side the river, and common to both people. The Treverians and Nervians aspire passionately to the reputation of being descended from the Germans; since by the glory of this original, they would escape all imputation of resembling the Gauls in person and effeminacy. Such as dwell upon the bank of the Rhine, the Vangiones, the Tribocians, and the Nemetes, are without doubt all Germans. The Ubians are ashamed of their original; though they have a particular honour to boast, that of having merited an establishment as a Roman Colony, and still delight to be called *Agrippinensians*, after the name of their founder: they indeed formerly came from beyond the Rhine, and, for the many proofs of their fidelity, were settled upon the very bank of the river; not to be there confined or guarded themselves, but to guard and defend that boundary against the rest of the Germans.

Of all these nations, the Batavians are the most signal in bravery. They inhabit not much territory upon the Rhine, but possess an island in it. They were formerly part of the Cattans, and by means of feuds at home removed to these dwellings; whence they might become a portion of the Roman Empire. With them this honour still remains, as also the memorials of their ancient association with us: for they are not under the contempt of paying tribute, nor subject to be squeezed by the farmers of the revenue. Free from all impositions and payments, and only set apart for the purposes of fighting, they are reserved wholly for the wars, in the same manner as a magazine of weapons and armour. Under the same degree of homage are the nation of the Mattiacians. For such is the might and greatness of the Roman People, as to have carried the awe and esteem of their Empire beyond the Rhine and the ancient boundaries. Thus the Mattiacians, living upon the opposite banks, enjoy a settlement and limits of their own; yet in spirit and inclination are attached to us: in other things resembling the Batavians, save that as they still breathe their original air, still possess their primitive soil, they are thence inspired with superior vigour and keenness. Amongst the people of Germany I would not reckon those who occupy the lands which are under decimation, though they be such as dwell beyond the Rhine and the Danube. By several worthless and vagabond Gauls, and such as poverty rendered daring, that region was seized as one belonging to no certain possessor: afterwards it became a skirt of the Empire and part of a province, upon the enlargement of our bounds and the extending of our garrisons and frontier.

Beyond these are the Cattans, whose territories begin at the Hercynian Forest, and consist not of such wide and marshy plains, as those of the other communities contained within the vast compass of Germany; but produce ranges of hills, such as run lofty and contiguous for a long tract, then by degrees sink and decay. Moreover the Hercynian Forest attends for a while its native Cattans, then suddenly forsakes them. This people are distinguished with bodies more hardy and robust, compact limbs, stern countenances, and greater vigour of spirit. For Germans, they are men of much sense and address. They dignify chosen men, listen to such as are set over them, know how to preserve their post, to discern occasions, to rebate their own ardour and impatience; how to employ the day, how to entrench themselves by night. They account fortune amongst things slippery and uncertain, but bravery amongst such as are never-failing and secure; and, what is exceeding rare nor ever to be learnt but by a wholesome course of discipline, in the conduct of the general they repose more assurance than in the strength of the army. Their whole forces consist of foot, who besides their arms carry likewise instruments of iron and their provisions. You may see other Germans proceed equipped to battle, but the Cattans so as to conduct a war. They rarely venture upon excursions or casual encounters. It is in truth peculiar to cavalry, suddenly to conquer, or suddenly to fly. Such haste and velocity rather resembles fear. Patience and deliberation are more akin to intrepidity.

Moreover a custom, practised indeed in other nations of Germany, yet very rarely and confined only to particulars more daring than the rest, prevails amongst the Cattans by universal consent. As soon as they arrive to maturity of years, they let their hair and beards continue to grow, nor till they have slain an enemy do they ever lay aside this form of countenance by vow sacred to valour. Over the blood and spoil of a foe they make bare their face. They allege, that they have now acquitted themselves of the debt and duty contracted by their birth, and rendered themselves worthy of their country, worthy of their parents. Upon the spiritless, cowardly and unwarlike, such deformity of visage still remains. All the most brave likewise wear an iron ring (a mark of great dishonour this in that nation) and retain it as a chain; till by killing an enemy they become released. Many of the Cattans delight always to bear this terrible aspect; and, when grown white through age, become awful and conspicuous by such marks, both to the enemy and their own countrymen. By them in all engagements the first assault is made: of them the front of the battle is always composed, as men who in their looks are singular and tremendous. For even during peace they abate nothing in the grimness and horror of their countenance. They have no house to inhabit, no land to cultivate, nor any domestic charge or care. With whomsoever they come to sojourn, by him they are maintained; always very prodigal of the substance of others, always despising what is their own, till the feebleness of old age overtakes them, and renders them unequal to the efforts of such rigid bravery.

Next to the Cattans, dwell the Usipians and Tencterians; upon the Rhine now running in a channel uniform and certain, such as suffices for a boundary. The Tencterians, besides their wonted glory in war, surpass in the service and discipline of their cavalry. Nor do the Cattans derive higher applause from their foot, than the Tencterians from their horse. Such was the order established by their forefathers, and what their posterity still pursue. From riding and exercising of horse, their children borrow their pastimes; in this exercise the young men find matter for emulating one another, and in this the old men take pleasure to persevere. Horses are by the father bequeathed as part of his household and family, horses are conveyed amongst the rights of succession, and as such the son receives them; but not the eldest son, like other effects, by priority of birth, but he who continues to be signal in boldness and superior in war.

Contiguous to the Tencterians formerly dwelt the Bructerians, in whose room it is said the Chamavians and Angrivarians are now settled; they who expulsed and almost extirpated the Bructerians, with the concurrence of the neighbouring nations: whether in detestation of their arrogance, or allured by the love of spoil, or through the special favour of the Gods towards us Romans. They in truth even vouchsafed to gratify us with the sight of the battle. In it there fell above sixty thousand souls, without a blow struck by the Romans; but, what is a circumstance still more glorious, fell to furnish them with a spectacle of joy and recreation. May the Gods continue and perpetuate amongst these nations, if not any love for us, yet by all means this their animosity and hate towards each other: since whilst the destiny of the Empire thus urges it, fortune cannot more signally befriend us, than in sowing strife amongst our foes.

The Angrivarians and Chamavians are enclosed behind, by the Dulgibinians and Chasuarians; and by other nations not so much noted: before the Frisians face them. The country of Frisia is divided into two; called the greater and lesser, according to the measure of their strength. Both nations stretch along the Rhine, quite to the ocean; and surround vast lakes such as once have born Roman fleets. We have moreover even ventured out from thence into the ocean, and upon its coasts common fame has reported the pillars of Hercules to be still standing: whether it be that Hercules ever visited these parts, or that to his renowned name we are wont to ascribe whatever is grand and glorious everywhere. Neither did Drusus who made the attempt, want boldness to pursue it: but the roughness of the ocean withstood him, nor would suffer discoveries to be made about itself, no more than about Hercules. Thenceforward the enterprise was dropped: nay, more pious and reverential it seemed, to believe the marvellous feats of the Gods than to know and to prove them.

Hitherto, I have been describing Germany towards the west. To the northward, it winds away with an immense compass. And first of all occurs the nation of the Chaucians; who though they begin immediately at the confines of the Frisians, and occupy part of the shore, extend so far as to border upon all the several people whom I have already recounted; till at last, by a Circuit, they reach quite to the boundaries of the Cattans. A region so vast, the Chaucians do not only possess but fill; a people of all the Germans the most noble, such as would rather maintain their grandeur by justice than violence. They live in repose, retired from broils abroad, void of avidity to possess more, free from a spirit of domineering over others. They provoke no wars, they ravage no countries, they pursue no plunder. Of their bravery and power, the chief evidence arises from hence, that, without wronging or oppressing others, they are come to be superior to all. Yet they are all ready to arm, and if an exigency require, armies are presently raised, powerful and abounding as they are in men and horses; and even when they are quiet and their weapons laid aside, their credit and name continue equally high.

Along the side of the Chaucians and Cattans dwell the Cheruscans; a people who finding no enemy to rouse them, were enfeebled by a peace over lasting and uniform, but such as they failed not to nourish. A conduct which proved more pleasing than secure; since treacherous is that repose which you enjoy amongst neighbours that are very powerful and very fond of rule and mastership. When recourse is once had to the sword, modesty and fair dealing will be vainly pleaded by the weaker; names these which are always assumed by the stronger. Thus the Cheruscans, they who formerly bore the character of *good and upright*, are now called *cowards and fools*; and the fortune of the Cattans who subdued them, grew immediately to be wisdom. In the ruin of the Cheruscans, the Fosians, also their neighbours, were involved; and in their calamities bore an equal share, though in their prosperity they had been weaker and less considered.

In the same winding tract of Germany live the Cimbrians, close to the ocean; a community now very small, but great in fame. Nay, of their ancient renown, many and extensive are the traces and monuments still remaining; even their entrenchments upon either shore, so vast in compass that from thence you may even now measure the greatness and numerous bands of that people, and assent to the account of an army so mighty. It was on the six hundred and fortieth year of Rome, when of the arms of the Cimbrians the first mention was made, during the Consulship of Caecilius Metellus and Papirius Carbo. If from that time we count to the second Consulship of the Emperor Trajan, the interval comprehends near two hundred and ten years; so long have we been conquering Germany. In a course of time, so vast between these two periods, many have been the blows and disasters suffered on each side. In truth neither from the Samnites, nor from the Carthaginians, nor from both Spains, nor from all the nations of Gaul, have we received more frequent checks and alarms; nor even from the Parthians:

for, more vigorous and invincible is the liberty of the Germans than the monarchy of the Arsacides. Indeed, what has the power of the East to allege to our dishonour; but the fall of Crassus, that power which was itself overthrown and abased by Ventidius, with the loss of the great King Pacorus bereft of his life? But by the Germans the Roman People have been bereft of five armies, all commanded by Consuls; by the Germans, the commanders of these armies, Carbo, and Cassius, and Scaurus Aurelius, and Servilius Caepio, as also Marcus Manlius, were all routed or taken: by the Germans even the Emperor Augustus was bereft of Varus and three legions. Nor without difficulty and loss of men were they defeated by Caius Marius in Italy, or by the deified Julius in Gaul, or by Drusus or Tiberius or Germanicus in their native territories. Soon after, the mighty menaces of Caligula against them ended in mockery and derision. Thenceforward they continued quiet, till taking advantage of our domestic division and civil wars, they stormed and seized the winter entrenchments of the legions, and aimed at the dominion of Gaul; from whence they were once more expulsed, and in the times preceding the present, we gained a triumph over them rather than a victory.

I must now proceed to speak of the Suevians, who are not, like the Cattans and Tencterians, comprehended in a single people; but divided into several nations all bearing distinct names, though in general they are entitled Suevians, and occupy the larger share of Germany. This people are remarkable for a peculiar custom, that of twisting their hair and binding it up in a knot. It is thus the Suevians are distinguished from the other Germans, thus the free Suevians from their slaves. In other nations, whether from alliance of blood with the Suevians, or, as is usual from imitation, this practice is also found, yet rarely, and never exceeds the years of youth. The Suevians, even when their hair is white through age, continue to raise it backwards in a manner stern and staring; and often tie it upon the top of their head only. That of their Princes, is more accurately disposed, and so far they study to appear agreeable and comely; but without any culpable intention. For by it, they mean not to make love or to incite it: they thus dress when proceeding to war, and deck their heads so as to add to their height and terror in the eyes of the enemy.

Of all the Suevians, the Semnones recount themselves to be the most ancient and most noble. The belief of their antiquity is confirmed by religious mysteries. At a stated time of the year, all the several people descended from the same stock, assemble by their deputies in a wood; consecrated by the idolatries of their forefathers, and by superstitious awe in times of old. There by publicly sacrificing a man, they begin the horrible solemnity of their barbarous worship. To this grove another sort of reverence is also paid. No one enters it otherwise than bound with ligatures, thence professing his subordination and meanness, and power of the Deity there. If he fall down, he is not permitted to rise or be raised, but grovels along upon the ground. And of all their superstition, this is the drift and tendency; that from this place the nation drew their original, that here God, the supreme Governor of the world, resides, and that all things else whatsoever are subject to him and bound to obey him. The potent condition of the Semnones has increased their influence and authority, as they inhabit an hundred towns; and from the largeness of their community it comes, that they hold themselves for the head of the Suevians.

What on the contrary ennobles the Langobards is the smallness of their number, for that they, who are surrounded with very many and very powerful nations, derive their security from no obsequiousness or plying; but from the dint of battle and adventurous deeds. There follow in order the Reudignians, and Aviones, and Angles, and Varinians, and Eudoses, and Suardones and Nuithones; all defended by rivers or forests. Nor in one of these nations does aught remarkable occur, only that they universally join in the worship of *Herthum*; that is to say, the Mother Earth. Her they believe to interpose in the affairs of men, and to visit countries. In an island of the ocean stands the wood *Castum*: in it is a chariot dedicated to the Goddess covered over with a curtain, and permitted to be touched by none but the Priest. Whenever the Goddess enters this her holy vehicle, he perceives her; and with profound veneration attends the motion of the chariot, which is always drawn by yoked cows. Then it is that days of rejoicing always ensue, and in all places whatsoever which she descends to honour with a visit and her

company, feasts and recreation abound. They go not to war; they touch no arms; fast laid up is every hostile weapon; peace and repose are then only known, then only beloved, till to the temple the same priest reconducts the Goddess when well tired with the conversation of mortal beings. Anon the chariot is washed and purified in a secret lake, as also the curtain; nay, the Deity herself too, if you choose to believe it. In this office it is slaves who minister, and they are forthwith doomed to be swallowed up in the same lake. Hence all men are possessed with mysterious terror; as well as with a holy ignorance what that must be, which none see but such as are immediately to perish. Moreover this quarter of the Suevians stretches to the middle of Germany.

The community next adjoining, is that of the Hermondurians; (that I may now follow the course of the Danube, as a little before I did that of the Rhine) a people this, faithful to the Romans. So that to them alone of all the Germans, commerce is permitted; not barely upon the bank of the Rhine, but more extensively, and even in that glorious colony in the province of Rhoetia. They travel everywhere at their own discretion and without a guard; and when to other nations, we show no more than our arms and encampments, to this people we throw open our houses and dwellings, as to men who have no longing to possess them. In the territories of the Hermondurians rises the Elbe, a river very famous and formerly well known to us; at present we only hear it named.

Close by the Hermondurians reside the Nariscans, and next to them the Marcomanians and Quadians. Amongst these the Marcomanians are most signal in force and renown; nay, their habitation itself they acquired by their bravery, as from thence they formerly expulsed the Boians. Nor do the Nariscans or Quadians degenerate in spirit. Now this is as it were the frontier of Germany, as far as Germany is washed by the Danube. To the times within our memory the Marcomanians and Quadians were governed by kings, who were natives of their own, descended from the noble line of Maroboduus and Tudrus. At present they are even subject to such as are foreigners. But the whole strength and sway of their king is derived from the authority of the Romans. From our arms, they rarely receive any aid; from our money very frequently.

Nor less powerful are the several people beyond them; namely, the Marsignians, the Gothinians, the Osians and the Burians, who altogether enclose the Marcomanians and Quadians behind. Of those, the Marsignians and the Burians in speech and dress resemble the Suevians. From the Gallic language spoken by the Gothinians, and from that of Pannonia by the Osians, it is manifest that neither of these people are Germans; as it is also from their bearing to pay tribute. Upon them as upon aliens their tribute is imposed, partly by the Sarmatians, partly by the Quadians. The Gothinians, to heighten their disgrace, are forced to labour in the iron mines. By all these several nations but little level country is possessed: they are seated amongst forests, and upon the ridges and declivities of mountains. For, Suevia is parted by a continual ridge of mountains; beyond which, live many distinct nations. Of these the Lygians are most numerous and extensive, and spread into several communities. It will suffice to mention the most puissant; even the Arians, Helvicones, Manimians; Elysians and Naharvalians. Amongst the Naharvalians is shown a grove, sacred to devotion extremely ancient. Over it a Priest presides apparelled like a woman; but according to the explication of the Romans, 'tis *Castor* and *Pollux* who are here worshipped. This Divinity is named *Alcis*. There are indeed no images here, no traces of an extraneous superstition; yet their devotion is addressed to young men and to brothers. Now the Arians, besides their forces, in which they surpass the several nations just recounted, are in their persons stern and truculent; and even humour and improve their natural grimness and ferocity by art and time. They wear black shields, their bodies are painted black, they choose dark nights for engaging in battle; and by the very awe and ghastly hue of their army, strike the enemy with dread, as none can bear this their aspect so surprising and as it were quite infernal. For, in all battles the eyes are vanquished first.

Beyond the Lygians dwell the Gothones, under the rule of a King; and thence held in subjection somewhat stricter than the other German nations, yet not so strict as to extinguish all their liberty. Immediately adjoining are the Rugians and Lemovians upon the coast of the ocean, and of these several nations the characteristics are a round shield, a short sword and kingly government. Next occur the communities of the Suiones, situated in the ocean itself; and besides their strength in men and arms, very powerful at sea. The form of their vessels varies thus far from ours, that they have prows at each end, so as to be always ready to row to shore without turning nor are they moved by sails, nor on their sides have benches of oars placed, but the rowers ply here and there in all parts of the ship alike, as in some rivers is done, and change their oars from place to place, just as they shift their course hither or thither. To wealth also, amongst them, great veneration is paid, and thence a single ruler governs them, without all restriction of power, and exacting unlimited obedience. Neither here, as amongst other nations of Germany, are arms used indifferently by all, but shut up and warded under the care of a particular keeper, who in truth too is always a slave: since from all sudden invasions and attacks from their foes, the ocean protects them: besides that armed bands, when they are not employed, grow easily debauched and tumultuous. The truth is, it suits not the interest of an arbitrary Prince, to trust the care and power of arms either with a nobleman or with a freeman, or indeed with any man above the condition of a slave.

Beyond the Suiones is another sea, one very heavy and almost void of agitation; and by it the whole globe is thought to be bounded and environed, for that the reflection of the sun, after his setting, continues till his rising, so bright as to darken the stars. To this, popular opinion has added, that the tumult also of his emerging from the sea is heard, that forms divine are then seen, as likewise the rays about his head. Only thus far extend the limits of nature, if what fame says be true. Upon the right of the Suevian Sea the AEstyan nations reside, who use the same customs and attire with the Suevians; their language more resembles that of Britain. They worship the Mother of the Gods. As the characteristic of their national superstition, they wear the images of wild boars. This alone serves them for arms, this is the safeguard of all, and by this every worshipper of the goddess is secured even amidst his foes. Rare amongst them is the use of weapons of iron, but frequent that of clubs. In producing of grain and the other fruits of the earth, they labour with more assiduity and patience than is suitable to the usual laziness of Germans. Nay, they even search the deep, and of all the rest are the only people who gather *amber*. They call it *glasing*, and find it amongst the shallows and upon the very shore. But, according to the ordinary incuriosity and ignorance of Barbarians, they have neither learnt, nor do they inquire, what is its nature, or from what cause it is produced. In truth it lay long neglected amongst the other gross discharges of the sea; till from our luxury, it gained a name and value. To themselves it is of no use: they gather it rough, they expose it in pieces coarse and unpolished, and for it receive a price with wonder. You would however conceive it to be a liquor issuing from trees, for that in the transparent substance are often seen birds and other animals, such as at first stuck in the soft gum, and by it, as it hardened, became quite enclosed. I am apt to believe that, as in the recesses of the East are found woods and groves dropping frankincense and balms, so in the isles and continent of the West such gums are extracted by the force and proximity of the sun; at first liquid and flowing into the next sea, then thrown by the winds and waves upon the opposite shore. If you try the nature of amber by the application of fire, it kindles like a torch; and feeds a thick and unctuous flame very high scented, and presently becomes glutinous like pitch or rosin.

Upon the Suiones, border the people Sitones; and, agreeing with them in all other things, differ from them in one, that here the sovereignty is exercised by a woman. So notoriously do they degenerate not only from a state of liberty, but even below a state of bondage. Here end the territories of the Suevians.

Whether amongst the Sarmatians or the Germans I ought to account the Peucinians, the Venedians, and the Fennians, is what I cannot determine; though the Peucinians, whom some call Basstarnians, speak the same language with the Germans, use the same attire, build like them, and live like them, in that dirtiness and sloth so common to all. Somewhat they are corrupted into the fashion of the Sarmatians by the inter-marriages of the principal sort with that nation: from whence the Venedians have derived very many of their customs and a great resemblance. For they are continually traversing and infesting with robberies all the forests and mountains lying between the Peucinians and Fennians. Yet they are rather reckoned amongst the Germans, for that they have fixed houses, and carry shields, and prefer travelling on foot, and excel in swiftness. Usages these, all widely differing from those of the Sarmatians, who live on horseback and dwell in waggons. In wonderful savageness live the nation of the Fennians, and in beastly poverty, destitute of arms, of horses, and of homes; their food, the common herbs; their apparel, skins; their bed, the earth; their only hope in their arrows, which for want of iron they point with bones. Their common support they have from the chase, women as well as men; for with these the former wander up and down, and crave a portion of the prey. Nor other shelter have they even for their babes, against the violence of tempests and ravening beasts, than to cover them with the branches of trees twisted together; this a reception for the old men, and hither resort the young. Such a condition they judge more happy than the painful occupation of cultivating the ground, than the labour of rearing houses, than the agitations of hope and fear attending the defence of their own property or the seizing that of others. Secure against the designs of men, secure against the malignity of the Gods, they have accomplished a thing of infinite difficulty; that to them nothing remains even to be wished.

What further accounts we have are fabulous: as that the Hellusians and Oxiones have the countenances and aspect of men, with the bodies and limbs of savage beasts. This, as a thing about which I have no certain information, I shall leave untouched.

CHAPTER FOUR

The Middle Ages

With the collapse of the Western Roman Empire in the fifth century CE, Europe was plunged into a difficult era often called the "Dark Ages," but more properly known as the Early Middle Ages. During this period, Germanic tribes marched across the landscape carving out tribal kingdoms wherein bonds of loyalty were forged between warlords and their retainers. Herein are to be found the roots of later day feudalism, the governmental system, which prevailed for the better part of a thousand years. The peasantry, those who made it possible for the nobility to fight their wars, huddled together in villages on manors under the protection of some lord, whether lay or ecclesiastical. In return for their labor, these lords provided a relatively safe and secure environment within which the peasants could live and work. The third layer of society, the clergy, provided the rites and rituals by which all medieval groups lived in expectation of an eternal life at the end of their days. The stratified nature of medieval society was not lost on monkish historians who knew their world was composed of three groups: those whose business was to fight, those who worked the land, and those who prayed.

Against this rather depressing backdrop, a new empire eventually emerged in Western Europe, one which would have a tremendous impact on the political, economic, and religious fortunes of the era. The Franks, one of those Germanic tribes, which had overrun the Roman Empire, were shaped into a power by Carolingian rulers such as Clovis I, Pepin II of Heristal, Charles Martel, and Pepin the Short. Under Charlemagne, the greatest of these rulers, the Franks defeated the Saxons, Slavs, Lombards, and others en route to creating an empire that embraced most of Western Europe. Charlemagne was no ordinary Germanic king. According to Einhard, a contemporaneous source, Charlemagne was remarkably well educated by the standards of his day and worked hard to uplift his countrymen culturally and intellectually. Charlemagne's reign reached its peak when, on Christmas day in the year 800, while attending mass in Rome, he was crowned "King of the Romans" by Pope Leo III. Unfortunately, Charlemagne's successors were weaklings who could not hold the empire together. In 843, the sons of Louis the Pious, after much internal strife, agreed to the Treaty of Verdun, which divided Frankish Gaul into three kingdoms and began the shaping of Modern Europe.

The journey, though, was long and difficult. In the ninth and tenth centuries, Europe came under siege from the Vikings, Magyars, Muslims, and others. England survived the initial onslaught thanks to Alfred the Great (871–899) and his immediate successors, but eventually succumbed to the Danes under Canute in 1016 and later the Normans under William the Conqueror in 1066. The Norman Conquest signaled the beginning of a new period in England's history. Under a number of powerful kings—Henry II, Edward I, and Edward III in particular—a powerful monarchy was forged which, after a number of spectacular victories in the early stages of the Hundred Years War with France, left England as the most powerful country in Western Europe. In France, the nobility repudiated the Carolingians in 987 and threw their support to Hugh Capet who, although his reign was very brief, established a dynasty which would endure until 1328. The most powerful of the Capetian rulers was Philip II (1180–1223) who, through his wars with King John of England, was able to significantly increase the size of the royal domain. Germany, too, succeeded in throwing off Carolingian rule, but was never able to build a strong monarchy. Otto I, Henry III, and Frederick I called Barbarossa, enjoyed some measure of success, but the strong opposition of the nobility to political centralization and a militant papacy, which was determined to emancipate itself from German control ensured that the country would remain divided and weak for centuries to come.

The Eastern part of the Roman Empire survived the chaos that had engulfed the West in the fourth and fifth centuries. The Byzantine Empire, as it later came to be known, was founded in 330 when Constantine the Great finished building his new Rome, better known as Constantinople, on the strait which connected the Black Sea with the larger Mediterranean world. The Empire would endure for over eleven hundred years. The first truly important Byzantine emperor was Justinian (527–565) who, with the capable aid of the general Belisarius, worked to recapture the lost western provinces. Within Constantinople, Justinian constructed *Hagia Sophia*, the largest Christian cathedral in the world for over a thousand years. He also codified Roman law. The end result of his work, although he did not know it as such, was the *Corpus Juris Civilis or the Body of Civil Law.* The *Corpus* would have a profound impact on both the secular and ecclesiastical legal systems of medieval Europe. Lost, perhaps, in the story of Justinian's numerous accomplishments, is the influence of his queen Theodora. According to Procopius, a contemporaneous historian with a flair for the dramatic and salacious, Theodora was born and raised in the circus to become a prostitute. Although Theodora was an unlikely match, Justinian fell in love and made her his queen In 532, when the government was threatened by the *Nika* Riot, it was Theodora who dissuaded Justinian from flight. Justinian remained within the city, crushed the revolt, and subsequently became one of the Empire's great rulers. Following Justinian's day, the Empire endured many internal uprisings, much court intrigue, and assaults by numerous enemies including the Persians, Muslims, Avars, Bulgarians, and Turks. That the Empire was able to endure these problems until it fell to the Turks in 1453 was due in large part to a stable government, a flourishing economy, a capable army and navy with expert leadership, and the support of the Eastern Church.

One of those civilizations which benefitted immeasurably from the work of the Byzantines was that of the Muslims. Arabia before Mohammed was a primitive place filled with Bedouins who, in one way or another, had managed to create a highly polytheistic religion. According to tradition, Mohammed, after a vision on Mount Hira near Mecca, became convinced that there was only one god, Allah, and that he was Allah's prophet. Imbued with this new purpose in life, Mohammed had little success at first in Mecca where his fellow Arabs worshipped the many idols housed in the *Kaaba*. It was only after he had fled to Medina, an event called the *Hegira*, in 622, that he gained support. In 630 he returned to Mecca, purged the *Kaaba* of its many idols and then began the process of implementing his new religion. In the century following his death in 632, his followers spread his religion, called Islam, eastward to India, northward to the gates of Constantinople, and westward through North Africa, across the Strait of Gibraltar and up into Gaul where the Muslim advance was eventually stopped in a great battle at Tours in 732.

Although political unity was eventually lost amid the squabbles of Mohammed's successors, the Muslim world would long remain a threat to Western Christendom. It was this threat that induced the countries of Western Europe and the Byzantine Empire to set aside their petty differences and strive for a cause which they felt would produce both spiritual and material gain. Such was the case in 1095 when Pope Urban II, at the behest of the Byzantine emperor who needed help against the Turks, preached the First Crusade at Clermont, France. According to a Christian chronicler, the Crusade was a spectacular success. After a great slaughter of Muslim men, women, and children, Jerusalem was taken in 1099. Thereafter, a Christian kingdom was created, a king was enthroned, and fiefs were doled out in Western fashion. However, the Christian principalities were always surrounded by hostile Muslim forces. Future battles were inevitable. Indeed, between 1096 and 1291, many crusades were preached and launched in the ebb and flow of the struggle between the Christians and Muslims for control of the Holy Land. Most of these expeditions, from a military perspective, were abysmal failures and some, such as the Fourth Crusade and the ill-fated Children's Crusade, never even reached their destinations. The Crusades did, however, play a significant role in breaking down the economic and cultural barriers that had existed for centuries between the East and West. Trade, town life, and commerce, all of which had suffered in the wake of Rome's collapse, were now revived. Italy, of vital importance in the traffic between the East and West, benefitted immeasurably. Important also was the influx of knowledge from the East, especially in math, science, and medicine.

Although the impact of the crusades has been diminished somewhat by scholars in recent years, clearly there were forces at work between 1300 and 1500, which would forever alter the medieval landscape. Some of these forces—the Hundred Years' War, the Black Death and peasant uprisings—were quite destructive. Feudalism and the manor system withered away. The Church survived, but suffered in other ways. Scandals such as the Babylonian Captivity and the Great Schism, coupled with widespread dissatisfaction with the wealth and worldliness of the clergy paved the way for the Protestant Reformation of the sixteenth century. Despite these calamities, there were encouraging signs. France and England survived long wars and dynastic strife. In Spain, the marriage of Ferdinand and Isabella brought political unity and enabled the country to become a major participant in the exploration, conquest, and exploitation of the New World. In Germany, John Gutenberg introduced the idea of printing with movable type, arguably one of the most important technological developments in history. A new era, later known as the "Renaissance," was at hand.

RECOMMENDED READINGS

Allmand, Christopher. *The Hundred Years' War: England and France at War, c. 1300-c. 1450.* 1988. Revised edition.

Armstrong, Karen. *Muhammad: A Biography of the Prophet.* 1992.

Clanchy, M. T. England and Its Rulers 1066–1307. 2006. 3rd edition.

Collins, Roger. *Charlemagne.* 1998.

Gregory, Timothy E. *A History of Byzantium.* 2005.

Hallam, Elizabeth and Judith Everard, *Capetian France, 987–1328.* 2001. 2nd edition.

Mayer, Hans E. *The Crusades.* 1972.

Reilly, Bernard F. *The Medieval Spains.* 1993.

Swanson, R. N. *The Twelfth Century –Renaissance.* 1999.

QUESTIONS

1. According to Einhard, how did Charlemagne's personal qualities set him apart from other rulers of that day?

2. Why was Theodora an unlikely match for the Byzantine emperor Justinian? How did Theodora save Justinian's throne in the Nika Revolt of 532?

3. How did Peter Abelard benefit from the tragic love affair with Heloise?

4. What guarantees did the *Magna Carta* make to the nobles and the Church in 1215?

5. According to Boccaccio, to what degree did the Black Death affect life in the city of Florence, Italy?

EINHARD: THE LIFE OF CHARLEMAGNE

Translated by Samuel Epes Turner

(New York: Harper & Brothers, 1880)

15. EXTENT OF CHARLEMAGNE'S CONQUESTS

Such are the wars, most skillfully planned and successfully fought, which this most powerful king waged during the forty-seven years of his reign. He so largely increased the Frank kingdom, which was already great and strong when he received it at his father's hands, that more than double its former territory was added to it. The authority of the Franks was formerly confined to that part of Gaul included between the Rhine and the Loire, the Ocean and the Balearic Sea; to that part of Germany which is inhabited by the so-called Eastern Franks, and is bounded by Saxony and the Danube, the Rhine and the Saale-this stream separates the Thuringians from the Sorabians; and to the country of the Alemanni and Bavarians. By the wars above mentioned he first made tributary Aquitania, Gascony, and the whole of the region of the Pyrenees as far as the River Ebro, which rises in the land of the Navarrese, flows through the most fertile districts of Spain, and empties into the Balearic Sea, beneath the walls of the city of Tortosa. He next reduced and made tributary all Italy from Aosta to Lower Calabria, where the boundary line runs between the Beneventans and the Greeks, a territory more than a thousand miles" long; then Saxony, which constitutes no small part of Germany, and is reckoned to be twice as wide as the country inhabited by the Franks, while about equal to it in length; in addition, both Pannonias, Dacia beyond the Danube, and Istria, Liburnia, and Dalmatia, except the cities on the coast, which he left to the Greek Emperor for friendship's sake, and because of the treaty that he had made with him. In fine, he vanquished and made tributary all the wild and barbarous tribes dwelling in Germany between the Rhine and the Vistula, the Ocean and the Danube, all of which speak very much the same language, but differ widely from one another in customs and dress. The chief among them are the Welatabians, the Sorabians, the Abodriti, and the Bohemians, and he had to make war upon these; but the rest, by far the larger number, submitted to him of their own accord.

16. FOREIGN RELATIONS

H added to the glory of his reign by gaining the good will of several kings and nations; so close, indeed, was the alliance that he contracted with Alfonso [II 791–842] King of Galicia and Asturias, that the latter, when sending letters or ambassadors to Charles, invariably styled himself his man. His munificence won the kings of the Scots also to pay such deference to his wishes that they never gave him any other title than lord or themselves than subjects and slaves: there are letters from them extant in which these feelings in his regard are expressed. His relations with Aaron [ie Harun Al-Rashid, 786–809], King of the Persians, who ruled over almost the whole of the East, India excepted, were so friendly that this prince preferred his favor to that of all the kings and potentates of the earth, and considered that to him alone marks of honor and munificence were due. Accordingly, when the ambassadors sent by Charles to visit the most holy sepulcher and place of resurrection of our Lord and Savior presented themselves before him with gifts, and made known their master's wishes, he not only granted what was asked, but gave possession of that holy and blessed spot. When they returned, he dispatched his ambassadors with them, and sent magnificent gifts, besides stuffs, perfumes, and other rich products of the Eastern lands. A few years before this, Charles had asked him for an elephant, and he sent the only one that he had. The Emperors of Constantinople, Nicephorus [I 802–811], Michael [I, 811–813], and Leo [V, 813-820], made advances to Charles, and sought friendship and alliance with him by several embassies; and even when the Greeks suspected him of designing to wrest the empire from them, because of his assumption of the title Emperor, they made a close alliance with him, that he might have no cause of offense. In fact, the power of the Franks was always viewed by the Greeks and Romans with a jealous eye, whence the Greek proverb "Have the Frank for your friend, but not for your neighbor."

17. PUBLIC WORKS

This King, who showed himself so great in extending his empire and subduing foreign nations, and was constantly occupied with plans to that end, undertook also very many works calculated to adorn and benefit his kingdom, and brought several of them to completion. Among these, the most deserving of mention are the basilica of the Holy Mother of God at Aix-la-Chapelle, built in the most admirable manner, and a bridge over the Rhine at Mayence, half a mile long, the breadth of the river at this point. This bridge was destroyed by fire [May, 813] the year before Charles died, but, owing to his death so soon after, could not be repaired, although he had intended to rebuild it in stone. He began two palaces of beautiful workmanship - one near his manor called Ingelheim, not far from Mayence; the other at Nimeguen, on the Waal, the stream that washes the south side of the island of the Batavians. But, above all, sacred edifices were the object of his care throughout his whole kingdom; and whenever he found them falling to ruin from age, he commanded the priests and fathers who had charge of them to repair them, and made sure by commissioners that his instructions were obeyed. He also fitted out a fleet for the war with the Northmen; the vessels required for this purpose

were built on the rivers that flow from Gaul and Germany into the Northern Ocean. Moreover, since the Northmen continually overran and laid waste the Gallic and German coasts, he caused watch and ward to be kept in all the harbors, and at the mouths of rivers large enough to admit the entrance of vessels, to prevent the enemy from disembarking; and in the South, in Narbonensis and Septimania, and along the whole coast of Italy as far as Rome, he took the same precautions against the Moors, who had recently begun their piratical practices. Hence, Italy suffered no great harm in his time at the hands of the Moors, nor Gaul and Germany from the Northmen, save that the Moors got possession of the Etruscan town of Civita Vecchia by treachery, and sacked it, and the Northmen harried some of the islands in Frisia off the German coast.

18. PRIVATE LIFE

Thus did Charles defend and increase as well, as beautify his, kingdom, as is well known; and here let me express my admiration of his great qualities and his extraordinary constancy alike in good and evil fortune. I will now forthwith proceed to give the details of his private and family life.

After his father's death, while sharing the kingdom with his brother, he bore his unfriendliness and jealousy most patiently, and, to the wonder of all, could not be provoked to be angry with him. Later he married a daughter of Desiderius, King of the Lombards, at the instance of his mother; but he repudiated her at the end of a year for some reason unknown, and married Hildegard, a woman of high birth, of Suabian origin. He had three sons by her - Charles, Pepin and Louis -and as many daughters - Hruodrud, Bertha, and Gisela. He had three other daughters besides these- Theoderada, Hiltrud, and Ruodhaid - two by his third wife, Fastrada, a woman of East Frankish (that is to say, of German) origin, and the third by a concubine, whose name for the moment escapes me. At the death of Fastrada [794], he married Liutgard, an Alemannic woman, who bore him no children. After her death [Jun44, 800] he had three concubines - Gersuinda, a Saxon by whom he had Adaltrud; Regina, who was the mother of Drogo and Hugh; and Ethelind, by whom he lead Theodoric. Charles' mother, Berthrada, passed her old age with him in great honor; he entertained the greatest veneration for her; and there was never any disagreement between them except when he divorced the daughter of King Desiderius, whom he had married to please her. She died soon after Hildegard, after living to three grandsons and as many granddaughters in her son's house, and he buried her with great pomp in the Basilica of St. Denis, where his father lay. He had an only sister, Gisela, who had consecrated herself to a religious life from girlhood, and he cherished as much affection for her as for his mother. She also died a few years before him in the nunnery where she passed her life.

19. PRIVATE LIFE (CONTINUED) [CHARLES AND THE EDUCATION OF HIS CHILDREN]

The plan that he adopted for his children's education was, first of all, to have both boys and girls instructed in the liberal arts, to which he also turned his own attention. As soon as their years admitted, in accordance with the custom of the Franks, the boys had to learn horsemanship, and to practise war and the chase, and the girls to familiarize themselves with cloth-making, and to handle distaff and spindle, that they might not grow indolent through idleness, and he fostered in them every virtuous sentiment. He only lost three of all his children before his death, two sons and one daughter, Charles, who was the eldest, Pepin, whom he had made King of Italy, and Hruodrud, his oldest daughter. whom he had betrothed to Constantine [VI, 780–802], Emperor of the Greeks. Pepin left one son, named Bernard, and five daughters, Adelaide, Atula, Guntrada, Berthaid and Theoderada. The King gave a striking proof of his

fatherly affection at the time of Pepin's death [810]: he appointed the grandson to succeed Pepin, and had the granddaughters brought up with his own daughters. When his sons and his daughter died, he was not so calm as might have been expected from his remarkably strong mind, for his affections were no less strong, and moved him to tears. Again, when he was told of the death of Hadrian [796], the Roman Pontiff, whom he had loved most of all his friends, he wept as much as if he had lost a brother, or a very dear son. He was by nature most ready to contract friendships, and not only made friends easily, but clung to them persistently, and cherished most fondly those with whom he had formed such ties. He was so careful of the training of his sons and daughters that he never took his meals without them when he was at home, and never made a journey without them; his sons would ride at his side, and his daughters follow him, while a number of his body-guard, detailed for their protection, brought up the rear. Strange to say, although they were very handsome women, and he loved them very dearly, he was never willing to marry any of them to a man of their own nation or to a foreigner, but kept them all at home until his death, saying that he could not dispense with their society. Hence, though otherwise happy, he experienced the malignity of fortune as far as they were concerned; yet he concealed his knowledge of the rumors current in regard to them, and of the suspicions entertained of their honor.

20. CONSPIRACIES AGAINST CHARLEMAGNE

By one of his concubines he had a son, handsome in face, but hunchbacked, named Pepin, whom I omitted to mention in the list of his children. When Charles was at war with the Huns, and was wintering in Bavaria [792], this Pepin shammed sickness, and plotted against his father in company with some of the leading Franks, who seduced him with vain promises of the royal authority. When his deceit was discovered, and the conspirators were punished, his head was shaved, and he was suffered, in accordance with his wishes, to devote himself to a religious life in the monastery of Prüm. A formidable conspiracy against Charles had previously been set on foot in Germany, but all the traitors were banished, some of them without mutilation, others after their eyes had been put out. Three of them only lost their lives; they drew their swords and resisted arrest, and, after killing several men, were cut down, because they could not be otherwise overpowered. It is supposed that the cruelty of Queen Fastrada was the primary cause of these plots, and they were both due to Charles' apparent acquiescence in his wife's cruel conduct, and deviation from the usual kindness and gentleness of his disposition. All the rest of his life he was regarded by everyone with the utmost love and affection, so much so that not the least accusation of unjust rigor was ever made against him.

21. CHARLEMAGNE'S TREATMENT OF FOREIGNERS

He liked foreigners, and was at great pains to take them under his protection. There were often so many of them, both in the palace and the kingdom, that they might reasonably have been considered a nuisance; but he, with his broad humanity, was very little disturbed by such annoyances, because he felt himself compensated for these great inconveniences by the praises of his generosity and the reward of high renown.

22. PERSONAL APPEARANCE

Charles was large and strong, and of lofty stature, though not disproportionately tall (his height is well known to have been seven times the length of his foot); the upper part of his head was round, his eyes very large and animated, nose a little long, hair fair, and face laughing and merry. Thus his appearance was always stately and dignified, whether he was standing or sitting; although his neck was thick and somewhat short, and his belly rather prominent; but the symmetry of the rest of his body concealed these defects. His gait was firm, his whole carriage manly, and his voice clear, but not so strong as his size led one to expect.

His health was excellent, except during the four years preceding his death, when he was subject to frequent fevers; at the last he even limped a little with one foot. Even in those years he consulted rather his own inclinations than the advice of physicians, who were almost hateful to him, because they wanted him to give up roasts, to which he was accustomed, and to eat boiled meat instead. In accordance with the national custom, he took frequent exercise on horseback and in the chase, accomplishments in which scarcely any people in the world can equal the Franks. He enjoyed the exhalations from natural warm springs, and often practised swimming, in which he was such an adept that none could surpass him; and hence it was that he built his palace at Aixla-Chapelle, and lived there constantly during his latter years until his death. He used not only to invite his sons to his bath, but his nobles and friends, and now and then a troop of his retinue or body guard, so that a hundred or more persons sometimes bathed with him.

23. DRESS

He used to wear the national, that is to say, the Frank, dress-next his skin a linen shirt and linen breeches, and above these a tunic fringed with silk; while hose fastened by bands covered his lower limbs, and shoes his feet, and he protected his shoulders and chest in winter by a close-fitting coat of otter or marten skins. Over all he flung a blue cloak, and he always had a sword girt about him, usually one with a gold or silver hilt and belt; he sometimes carried a jewelled sword, but only on great feast-days or at the reception of ambassadors from foreign nations. He despised foreign costumes, however handsome, and never allowed himself to be robed in them, except twice in Rome, when he donned the Roman tunic, chlamys, and shoes; the first time at the request of Pope Hadrian, the second to gratify Leo, Hadrian's successor. On great feast-days he made use of embroidered clothes, and shoes bedecked with precious stones; his cloak was fastened by a golden buckle, and he appeared crowned with a diadem of gold and gems: but on other days his dress varied little from the common dress of the people.

24. HABITS

Charles was temperate in eating, and particularly so in drinking, for he abominated drunkenness in anybody, much more in himself and those of his household; but he could not easily abstain from food, and often complained that fasts injured his health. He very rarely gave entertainments, only on great feast-days, and then to large numbers of people. His meals ordinarily consisted of four courses, not counting the roast, which his huntsmen used to bring in on the spit; he was more fond of this than of any other dish. While at table, he listened to reading or music. The subjects of the readings were the stories and deeds of olden time: he was fond, too, of St. Augustine's books, and especially of the one entitled "The City of God."

He was so moderate in the use of wine and all sorts of drink that he rarely allowed himself more than three cups in the course of a meal. In summer after the midday meal, he would eat some fruit, drain a single cup, put off his clothes and shoes, just as he did for the night, and rest for two or three hours. He was in the habit of awaking and rising from bed four or five times during the night. While he was dressing and putting on his shoes, he not only gave audience to his friends, but if the Count of the Palace told him of any suit in which his judgment was necessary, he had the parties brought before him forthwith, took cognizance of the case, and gave his decision, just as if he were sitting on the Judgment-seat. This was not the only business that he transacted at this time, but he performed any duty of the day whatever, whether he had to attend to the matter himself, or to give commands concerning it to his officers.

25. STUDIES

Charles had the gift of ready and fluent speech, and could express whatever he had to say with the utmost clearness. He was not satisfied with command of his native language merely, but gave attention to the study of foreign ones, and in particular was such a master of Latin that he could speak it as well as his native tongue; but he could understand Greek better than he could speak it. He was so eloquent, indeed, that he might have passed for a teacher of eloquence. He most zealously cultivated the liberal arts, held those who taught them in great esteem, and conferred great honors upon them. He took lessons in grammar of the deacon Peter of Pisa, at that time an aged man. Another deacon, Albin of Britain, surnamed Alcuin, a man of Saxon extraction, who was the greatest scholar of the day, was his teacher in other branches of learning. The King spent much time and labour with him studying rhetoric, dialectics, and especially astronomy; he learned to reckon, and used to investigate the motions of the heavenly bodies most curiously, with an intelligent scrutiny. He also tried to write, and used to keep tablets and blanks in bed under his pillow, that at leisure hours he might accustom his hand to form the letters; however, as he did not begin his efforts in due season, but late in life, they met with ill success.

26. PIETY

He cherished with the greatest fervor and devotion the principles of the Christian religion, which had been instilled into him from infancy. Hence it was that he built the beautiful basilica at Aix-la-Chapelle, which he adorned with gold and silver and lamps, and with rails and doors of solid brass. He had the columns and marbles for this structure brought from Rome and Ravenna, for he could not find such as were suitable elsewhere. He was a constant worshipper at this church as long as his health permitted, going morning and evening, even after nightfall, besides attending mass; and he took care that all the services there conducted should be administered with the utmost possible propriety, very often warning the sextons not to let any improper or unclean thing be brought into the building or remain in it. He provided it with a great number of sacred vessels of gold and silver and with such a quantity of clerical robes that not even the doorkeepers who fill the humblest office in the church were obliged to wear their everyday clothes when in the exercise of their duties. He was at great pains to improve the church reading and psalmody, for he was well skilled in both although he neither read in public nor sang, except in a low tone and with others.

27. GENEROSITY [CHARLES AND THE ROMAN CHURCH]

He was very forward in succoring the poor, and in that gratuitous generosity which the Greeks call alms, so much so that he not only made a point of giving in his own country and his own kingdom, but when he discovered that there were Christians living in poverty in Syria, Egypt, and Africa, at Jerusalem, Alexandria, and Carthage, he had compassion on their wants, and used to send money over the seas to them. The reason that he zealously strove to make friends with the kings beyond seas was that he might get help and relief to the Christians living under their rule.

He cherished the Church of St. Peter the Apostle at Rome above all other holy and sacred places, and heaped its treasury with a vast wealth of gold, silver, and precious stones. He sent great and countless gifts to the popes; and throughout his whole reign the wish that he had nearest at heart was to re-establish the ancient authority of the city of Rome under his care and by his influence, and to defend and protect the Church of St. Peter, and to beautify and enrich it out of his own store above all other churches. Although he held it in such veneration, he only repaired to Rome to pay his vows and make his supplications four times during the whole forty-seven years that he reigned.

28. CHARLEMAGNE CROWNED EMPEROR

When he made his last journey thither, he also had other ends in view. The Romans had inflicted many injuries upon the Pontiff Leo, tearing out his eyes and cutting out his tongue, so that he had been comp lied to call upon the King for help [Nov 24, 800]. Charles accordingly went to Rome, to set in order the affairs of the Church, which were in great confusion, and passed the whole winter there. It was then that he received the titles of Emperor and Augustus [Dec 25, 800], to which he at first had such an aversion that he declared that he would not have set foot in the Church the day that they were conferred, although it was a great feast-day, if he could have foreseen the design of the Pope. He bore very patiently with the jealousy which the Roman emperors showed upon his assuming these titles, for they took this step very ill; and by dint of frequent embassies and letters, in which he addressed them as brothers, he made their haughtiness yield to his magnanimity, a quality in which he was unquestionably much their superior.

http://www.fordham.edu/halsall/basis/einhard.asp#Extent of Charlemagne's Conquests

HISTORY OF THE WARS, BOOK I
Procopius
Translated by H. B. Dewing

XXIV

Jan. 1, 532 At this same time an insurrection broke out unexpectedly in Byzantium among the populace, and, contrary to expectation, it proved to be a very serious affair, and ended in great harm to the people and to the senate, as the following account will shew. In every city the population has been divided for a long time past into the Blue and the Green factions; but within comparatively recent times it has come about that, for the sake of these names and the seats which the rival factions occupy in watching the games, they spend their money and abandon their bodies to the most cruel tortures, and even do not think it unworthy to die a most shameful death. And they fight against their opponents knowing not for what end they imperil themselves, but knowing well that, even if they overcome their enemy in the fight, the conclusion of the matter for them will be to be carried off straightway to the prison, and finally, after suffering extreme torture, to be destroyed. So there grows up in them against their fellow men a hostility which has no cause, and at no time does it cease or disappear, for it gives[4–8] place neither to the ties of marriage nor of relationship nor of friendship, and the case is the same even though those who differ with respect to these colours be brothers or any other kin. They care neither for things divine nor human in comparison with conquering in these struggles; and it matters not whether a sacrilege is committed by anyone at all against God, or whether the laws and the constitution are violated by friend or by foe; nay even when they are perhaps ill supplied with the necessities of life, and when their fatherland is in the most pressing need and suffering unjustly, they pay no heed if only it is likely to go well with their "faction"; for so they name the bands of partisans. And even women join with them in this unholy strife, and they not only follow the men, but even resist them if opportunity offers, although they neither go to the public exhibitions at all, nor are they impelled by any other cause; so that I, for my part, am unable to call this anything except a disease of the soul. This, then, is pretty well how matters stand among the people of each and every city.

But at this time the officers of the city administration in Byzantium were leading away to death some of the rioters. But the members of the two factions, conspiring together and declaring a truce with each other, seized the prisoners and then straightway entered the prison and released all those who were in confinement there, whether they had been condemned on a charge of stirring up sedition, or for any other unlawful act. And all the attendants in the service of the city government were killed indiscriminately; meanwhile, all of the citizens who were[8–13] sane-minded were fleeing to the opposite mainland, and fire was applied to the city as if it had fallen under the hand of an enemy. The sanctuary of Sophia and the baths of Zeuxippus, and the portion of the imperial residence from the propylaea as far as the so-called House of Ares were destroyed by fire, and besides these both the great colonnades which extended as far as the market place which bears the name of Constantine, in addition to many houses of wealthy men and a vast amount of treasure. During this time the emperor and his consort with a few members of the senate shut themselves up in the palace and remained quietly there. Now the watch-word which the populace passed around to one another was Nika,[31] and the insurrection has been called by this name up to the present time.

The praetorian prefect at that time was John the Cappadocian, and Tribunianus, a Pamphylian by birth, was counsellor to the emperor; this person the Romans call "quaestor." One of these two men, John, was entirely without the advantages of a liberal education; for he learned nothing while attending the elementary school except his letters, and these, too, poorly enough; but by his natural ability he became the most powerful man of whom we know. For he was most capable in deciding upon what was needful and in finding a solution for difficulties. But he became the basest of all men and employed his natural power to further his low designs; neither consideration for God nor any shame before man entered into his mind, but to destroy the lives of many men for the sake of gain and to wreck whole cities was his[13–18] constant concern. So within a short time indeed he had acquired vast sums of money, and he flung himself completely into the sordid life of a drunken scoundrel; for up to the time of lunch each day he would plunder the property of his subjects, and for the rest of the day occupy himself with drinking and with wanton deeds of lust. And he was utterly unable to control himself, for he ate food until he vomited, and he was always ready to steal money and more ready to bring it out and spend it. Such a man then was John. Tribunianus, on the other hand, both possessed natural ability and in educational attainments was inferior to none of his contemporaries; but he was extraordinarily fond of the pursuit of money and always ready to sell justice for gain; therefore every day, as a rule, he was repealing some laws and proposing others, selling off to those who requested it either favour according to their need.

Now as long as the people were waging this war with each other in behalf of the names of the colours, no attention was paid to the offences of these men against the constitution; but when the factions came to a mutual understanding, as has been said, and so began the sedition, then openly throughout the whole city they began to abuse the two and went about seeking them to kill. Accordingly the emperor, wishing to win the people to his side, instantly dismissed both these men from office. And Phocas, a patrician, he appointed praetorian prefect, a man of the greatest discretion and fitted by nature to be a guardian of justice; Basilides he commanded to fill the office of quaestor, a man known among the patricians for his agreeable qualities and a notable besides. However,[18–24] the insurrection continued no less violently under them. Now on the fifth day of the insurrection in the late afternoon the Emperor Justinian gave orders to Hypatius and Pompeius, nephews of the late emperor, Anastasius, to go home as quickly as possible, either because he suspected that some plot was being matured by them against his own person, or, it may be, because destiny brought them to this. But they feared that the people would force them to the throne (as in fact fell out), and they said that they would be doing wrong if they should abandon their sovereign when he found himself in such danger. When the Emperor Justinian heard this, he inclined still more to his suspicion, and he bade them quit the palace instantly. Thus, then, these two men betook themselves to their homes, and, as long as it was night, they remained there quietly.

But on the following day at sunrise it became known to the people that both men had quit the palace where they had been staying. So the whole population ran to them, and they declared Hypatius emperor and prepared to lead him to the market-place to assume the power. But the wife of Hypatius, Mary, a discreet woman, who had the greatest reputation for prudence, laid hold of her husband and would not let go, but cried out with loud lamentation and with entreaties to all her kinsmen that the people were leading him on the road to death. But since the throng overpowered her, she unwillingly released her husband, and he by no will of his own came to the Forum of Constantine, where they summoned him to the throne; then since they[24–30] had neither diadem nor anything else with which it is customary for a king to be clothed, they placed a golden necklace upon his head and proclaimed him Emperor of the Romans. By this time the members of the senate were assembling,—as many of them as had not been left in the emperor's residence,—and many expressed the opinion that they should go to the palace to fight. But Origenes, a man of the senate, came forward and spoke as follows: "Fellow Romans, it is impossible that the situation which is upon us be solved in any way except by war. Now war and royal power are agreed to be the greatest of all things in the world. But when action involves great issues, it refuses to be brought to a successful conclusion by the brief crisis of a moment, but this is accomplished only by wisdom of thought and energy of action, which men display for a length of time. Therefore if we should go out against the enemy, our cause will hang in the balance, and we shall be taking a risk which will decide everything in a brief space of time; and, as regards the consequences of such action, we shall either fall down and worship Fortune or reproach her altogether. For those things whose issue is most quickly decided, fall, as a rule, under the sway of fortune. But if we handle the present situation more deliberately, not even if we wish shall we be able to take Justinian in the palace, but he will very speedily be thankful if he is allowed to flee; for authority which is ignored always loses its power, since its strength ebbs away with each day. Moreover we have other palaces, both Placillianae and the palace named from Helen, which this emperor should[30–36] make his headquarters and from there he should carry on the war and attend to the ordering of all other matters in the best possible way." So spoke Origenes. But the rest, as a crowd is accustomed to do, insisted more excitedly and thought that the present moment was opportune, and not least of all Hypatius (for it was fated that evil should befall him) bade them lead the way to the hippodrome. But some say that he came there purposely, being well-disposed toward the emperor.

Now the emperor and his court were deliberating as to whether it would be better for them if they remained or if they took to flight in the ships. And many opinions were expressed favouring either course. And the Empress Theodora also spoke to the following effect: "As to the belief that a woman ought not to be daring among men or to assert herself boldly among those who are holding back from fear, I consider that the present crisis most certainly does not permit us to discuss whether the matter should be regarded in this or in some other way. For in the case of those whose interests have come into the greatest danger nothing else seems best except to settle the issue immediately before them in the best possible way. My opinion then is that the present time, above all others, is inopportune for flight, even though it bring safety. For while it is impossible for a man who has seen the light not also to die, for one who has been an emperor it is unendurable to be a fugitive. May I never be separated from this purple, and may I not live that day on which those who meet me shall not address me as mistress. If, now, it is your wish to save yourself, O Emperor, there is no difficulty. For[37–43] we have much money, and there is the sea, here the boats. However consider whether it will not come about after you have been saved that you would gladly exchange that safety for death. For as for myself, I approve a certain ancient saying that royalty is a good burial-shroud." When the queen had spoken thus, all were filled with boldness, and, turning their thoughts towards resistance, they began to consider how they might be able to defend themselves if any hostile force should come against them. Now the soldiers as a body, including those who were stationed about the emperor's court, were neither well disposed to the emperor nor willing openly to take an active part in fighting, but were waiting for what the future would bring forth. All the hopes of the emperor were centred upon Belisarius and Mundus, of whom the former, Belisarius, had recently returned from the Persian war bringing with him a following which was both powerful and imposing, and in particular he had a great number of spearmen and guards who had received their training in battles and the perils of warfare. Mundus had been appointed general of the Illyrians, and by mere chance had happened to come under summons to Byzantium on some necessary errand, bringing with him Erulian barbarians.

When Hypatius reached the hippodrome, he went up immediately to where the emperor is accustomed to take his place and seated himself on the royal throne from which the emperor was always accustomed to view the equestrian and athletic contests. And from the palace Mundus went out through the gate which, from the circling descent, has been given [44–50] the name of the Snail. Belisarius meanwhile began at first to go straight up toward Hypatius himself and the royal throne, and when he came to the adjoining structure where there has been a guard of soldiers from of old, he cried out to the soldiers commanding them to open the door for him as quickly as possible, in order that he might go against the tyrant. But since the soldiers had decided to support neither side, until one of them should be manifestly victorious, they pretended not to hear at all and thus put him off. So Belisarius returned to the emperor and declared that the day was lost for them, for the soldiers who guarded the palace were rebelling against him. The emperor therefore commanded him to go to the so-called Bronze Gate and the propylaea there. So Belisarius, with difficulty and not without danger and great exertion, made his way over ground covered by ruins and half-burned buildings, and ascended to the stadium. And when he had reached the Blue Colonnade which is on the right of the emperor's throne, he purposed to go against Hypatius himself first; but since there was a small door there which had been closed and was guarded by the soldiers of Hypatius who were inside, he feared lest while he was struggling in the narrow space the populace should fall upon him, and after destroying both himself and all his followers, should proceed with less trouble and difficulty against the emperor. Concluding, therefore, that he must go against the populace who had taken their stand in the hippodrome—a vast multitude crowding each other in great disorder—he drew his sword from its sheath and, commanding the others to do likewise, with a[50–56] shout he advanced upon them at a run. But the populace, who were standing in a mass and not in order, at the sight of armoured soldiers who had a great reputation for bravery and experience in war, and seeing that they struck out with their swords unsparingly, beat a hasty retreat. Then a great outcry arose, as was natural, and Mundus, who was standing not far away, was eager to join in the fight,—for he was a daring and energetic fellow—but he was at a loss as to what he should do under the circumstances; when, however, he observed that Belisarius was in the struggle, he straightway made a sally into the hippodrome through the entrance which they call the Gate of Death. Then indeed from both sides the partisans of Hypatius were assailed with might and main and destroyed. When the rout had become complete and there had already been great slaughter of the populace, Boraedes and Justus, nephews of the Emperor Justinian, without anyone daring to lift a hand against them, dragged Hypatius down from the throne, and, leading him in, handed him over together with Pompeius to the emperor. And there perished among the populace on that day more than thirty thousand. But the emperor commanded the two prisoners to be kept in severe confinement.

Then, while Pompeius was weeping and uttering pitiable words (for the man was wholly inexperienced in such misfortunes), Hypatius reproached him at length and said that those who were about to die unjustly should not lament. For in the beginning they had been forced by the people against their will, and afterwards they had come to the hippodrome with no thought of harming the emperor. And the soldiers killed both[56–4] of them on the following day and threw their bodies into the sea. The emperor confiscated all their property for the public treasury, and also that of all the other members of the senate who had sided with them. Later, however, he restored to the children of Hypatius and Pompeius and to all others the titles which they had formerly held, and as much of their property as he had not happened to bestow upon his friends. This was the end of the insurrection in Byzantium.

THE SECRET HISTORY OF THE COURT OF JUSTINIAN

Procopius

Chapter IX

As for Justinian's wife, I shall now describe her birth, how she was brought up, how she married him, and how in conjunction with him she utterly ruined the Roman Empire.

There was one Acacius at Byzantium, of the Green faction, who was keeper of the wild beasts used in the amphitheatre, and was called the Bear-keeper. This man died of some malady during the reign of Anastasius, and left three daughters, Comito, Theodora and Anastasia, the eldest of whom was not yet seven years of age. His widow married her husband's successor in his house and profession; but the chief dancer of the Green faction, named Asterius, was easily bribed into taking away the office from this man and giving it to one who paid him for it: for the dancers had the power to manage these matters as they pleased.

When Theodora's mother saw the whole populace assembled in the amphitheatre to see the show of the wild beasts, she placed fillets on her daughters' heads and hands, and made them sit in the attitude of suppliants. The Greens regarded their appeal with indifference, but the Blues, who had lately lost their own bear-keeper, bestowed the office upon them. As the children grew up, their mother straightway sent them on the stage, for they were handsome girls. She did not send them on all at once, but as each one arrived at a fit age so to do. The eldest girl, Comito, had already become one of the most celebrated prostitutes of her time.

Theodora, the next eldest, was dressed in a little sleeved tunic, such as a slave-girl would wear, and waited on her sister, carrying on her shoulders the stool in which she was wont to sit in public. Theodora was still too young to have intercourse with a man after the manner of women, but she satisfied the unnatural passions of certain wretches, even the vilest slaves, who followed their masters to the theatre and amused their leisure by this infamy. She remained for some time also in a brothel, where she practised this hateful form of vice.

As soon, however, as she reached the age of puberty, as she was handsome, her mother sent her into the theatrical troupe, and she straightway became a simple harlot, as old-fashioned people called it; for she was neither a musician nor a dancer, but merely prostituted herself to everyone whom she met, giving up every part of her body to debauchery. She associated chiefly with the theatrical "pantomimes," and took part in their performances, playing in comic scenes, for she was exceedingly witty and amusing; so that she soon became well known by her acting. She had no shame whatever, and no one ever saw her put out of countenance, but she lent herself to scandalous purposes without the least hesitation.

She excelled in raising a laugh by being slapped on her puffed-out cheeks, and used to uncover herself so far as to show the spectators everything before and behind which decency forbids to be shown to men. She stimulated her lovers by lascivious jests, and continually invented new postures of coition, by which means she completely won the hearts of all libertines; for she did not wait to be solicited by anyone whom she met, but herself, with joke and gestures, invited everyone whom she fell in with, especially beardless boys.

She never succumbed to these transports; for she often went to a supper at which each one paid his share, with ten or more young men, in the full vigour of their age and practised in debauchery, and would pass the whole night with all of them. When they were all exhausted, she would go to their servants, thirty in number, it may be, and fornicate with each one of them; and yet not even so did she quench her lust. Once she went to the house of some great man, and while the guests were drinking pulled up her clothes on the edge of the couch and did not blush to exhibit her wantonness without reserve. Though she received the male in three orifices she nevertheless complained of Nature for not having made the passage of her breasts wider, that she might contrive a new form of coition in that part of her person also.

She frequently became pregnant, but as she employed all known remedies without delay, she promptly procured abortion. Often, even on the stage, she stripped before the eyes of all the people, and stood naked in their midst, wearing only a girdle about her private parts and groin; not because she had any modesty about showing that also to the people, but because no one was allowed to go on the stage without a girdle about those parts. In this attitude she would throw herself down on the floor, and lie on her back. Slaves, whose duty it was, would then pour grains of barley upon her girdle, which trained geese would then pick up with their beaks one by one and eat. She did not blush or rise up, but appeared to glory in this performance; for she was not only without shame, but especially fond of encouraging others to be shameless, and often would strip naked in the midst of the actors, and swing herself backwards and forwards, explaining to those who had already enjoyed her and those who had not, the peculiar excellences of that exercise.

She proceeded to such extremities of abuse as to make her face become what most women's private parts are: wherefore her lovers became known at once by their unnatural tastes, and any respectable man who met her in the public streets turned away, and made haste to avoid her, lest his clothes should be soiled by contact with such an abandoned creature, for she was a bird of ill-omen, especially for those who saw her early in the day. As for her fellow-actresses, she always abused them most savagely, for she was exceedingly jealous.

Afterwards she accompanied Hecebolus, who had received the appointment of Governor of Pentapolis, to that country, to serve his basest passions, but quarrelled with him, and was straightway sent out of the country. In consequence of this she fell into want of common necessaries, with which she hereafter provided herself by prostitution, as she had been accustomed to do. She first went to Alexandria, and afterwards wandered all through the East, until she reached Byzantium, plying her trade in every city on her way—a trade which, I imagine, Heaven will not pardon a man for calling by its right name—as if the powers of evil would not allow any place on earth to be free from the debaucheries of Theodora. Such was the birth, and such the training of this woman, and her name became better known than that of any other prostitute of her time.

On her return to Byzantium, Justinian became excessively enamoured of her. At first he had intercourse with her merely as her lover, although he raised her to the position of a patrician. By this means Theodora was straightway enabled to gain very great influence and to amass considerable sums of money. She charmed Justinian beyond all the world, and, like most infatuated lovers, he delighted to show her all the favour and give her all the money that he could. This lavishness added fuel to the flame of passion. In concert with her he plundered the people more than ever, not only in the capital, but throughout the Roman Empire; for, as both of them had for a long time been members of the Blue faction, they had placed unlimited power in its hands, although the evil was subsequently somewhat checked, in the manner which I will now relate.

Justinian had for some time suffered from a dangerous illness; in fact, it was even reported that he was dead. The Blue faction were committing the crimes of which I have spoken, and slew Hypatius, a person of consequence, in the Church of St. Sophia, in broad daylight. When the murderer had accomplished his work, clamour was raised which reached the Emperor's ears, and all his courtiers seized upon the opportunity of pointing out the outrageous character of the offence which, owing to Justinian's

absence from public affairs, the murderer had been enabled to perpetrate, and enumerated all the crimes that had been committed from the outset. Hereupon the Emperor gave orders to the prefect of the city to punish these crimes. This man was named Theodotus, nick-named Colocynthius.[11] He instituted an inquiry into the whole matter, and had the courage to seize and put to death, according to the law, many of the malefactors, several of whom, however, hid themselves and so escaped, being destined to perish afterwards together with the Roman Empire. Justinian, who miraculously recovered, straightway began to plan the destruction of Theodotus, on the pretext that he was a magician and used philtres. However, as he found no proofs on which the man could be condemned, he flogged and tortured some of his intimates until he forced them to make most unfounded accusations against him. When no one dared to oppose Justinian, but silently bewailed the plot against Theodotus, Proclus, the Quaestor, alone declared that the man was innocent and did not deserve to die. Theodotus was therefore sentenced by the Emperor to banishment to Jerusalem. But, learning that certain men had been sent thither to assassinate him, he took sanctuary in the temple, where he spent the rest of his life in concealment until he died. Such was the end of Theodotus.

From this time forth, however, the Blue party behaved with the greatest moderation; they did not venture to perpetrate such crimes, although they had it in their power to abuse their authority more outrageously and with greater impunity than before. Here is a proof of this; when a few of them afterwards showed the same audacity in evil-doing, they were not punished in any way; for those who had the power to punish always gave malefactors an opportunity to escape, and by this indulgence encouraged them to trample upon the laws.

Chapter X

As long as the Empress Euphemia was alive, Justinian could not contrive to marry Theodora. Though she did not oppose him on any other point, she obstinately refused her consent to this one thing. She was altogether free from vice, although she was a homely person and of barbarian descent, as I have already said. She never cultivated any active virtues, but remained utterly ignorant of State affairs. She did not bear her own name, which was a ridiculous one, when she came to the palace, but was re-named Euphemia. Soon afterwards, however, she died.

Justin was in his second childhood and so sunk in senility that he was the laughing-stock of his subjects. All despised him utterly, and disregarded him because he was incompetent to control State affairs, but they paid their court to Justinian with awe, for he terrified them all by his love of disturbance and reckless innovations.

He then resolved to bring about his marriage with Theodora. It was forbidden by the most ancient laws of the State that anyone of the senatorial order should marry a courtesan; so he prevailed upon the Emperor to repeal the existing law and introduce a new one, whereby he was allowed to live with Theodora as his legitimate wife, and it became possible for anyone else to marry a courtesan. He also straightway assumed the demeanour of absolute despot, veiling his forcible seizure of power under the pretext of reasons of State. He was proclaimed Emperor of the Romans, as his uncle's colleague. Whether this was legal or not may be doubted, since he owed his election to the terror with which he inspired those who gave him their votes.

So Justinian and Theodora ascended the Imperial throne three days before Easter, at a time when it is forbidden to make visits or even to greet one's friends. A few days later Justin was carried off by disease, after a reign of nine years, and Justinian and Theodora reigned alone.

Thus did Theodora, as I have told you, in spite of her birth and bringing-up, reach the throne without finding any obstacle in her way. Justinian felt no shame at having wedded her, although he might have chosen the best born, the best educated, the most modest and virtuously nurtured virgin in all the Roman Empire, with outstanding breasts, as the saying is; whereas he preferred to take to himself the common refuse of all mankind, and without a thought of all that has been told, married a woman stained with the shame of many abortions

and many other crimes. Nothing more, I conceive, need be said about this creature's character, for all the vices of his heart are thoroughly displayed in the fact of so unworthy a marriage. When a man feels no shame at an act of this kind, and braves the loathing of the world, there is thereafter no path of wickedness which may not be trodden by him, but, with a face incapable of blushing, he plunges, utterly devoid of scruple, into the deepest baseness.

However, no one in the Senate had the courage to show dissatisfaction at seeing the State fasten this disgrace upon itself, but all were ready to worship Theodora as if she had been a goddess. Neither did any of the clergy show any indignation, but bestowed upon her the title of "Lady." The people who had formerly seen her upon the stage now declared themselves, with uplifted hands, to be her slaves, and made no secret of the name. None of the army showed irritation at having to face the dangers of war in the service of Theodora, nor did anyone of all mankind offer her the least opposition. All, I suppose, yielded to circumstances, and suffered this disgraceful act to take place, as though Fortune had wished to display her power by disposing human affairs so that events came about in utter defiance of reason, and human counsel seemed to have no share in directing them. Fortune does thus raise men suddenly to great heights of power, by means in which reason has no share, in spite of all obstacles that may bar the way, for nothing can check her course, but she proceeds straight on towards her goal, and everything makes way for her. But let all this be, and be represented as it pleases God.

Theodora was at this time handsome and of a graceful figure, but she was short, without much colour, but rather of a pale complexion, and with brilliant and piercing eyes. It would take a lifetime to tell of all her adventures during her theatrical life, but I think what little I have selected above will be sufficient to give an indication of her character. We must now briefly set forth what she and her husband did, for during their married life neither ever did anything without the other. For a long time they appeared to all to be at variance both in their characters and in their actions; but afterwards this disagreement was seen to have been purposely arranged between them, in order that their subjects might not come to an agreement and rise against them, but might all be divided in their opinion. First, they split up the Christians into two parties and brought them to ruin, as I shall tell you hereafter, by this plan of pretending to take different sides. Next they created divisions amongst the State factions. Theodora feigned to be an eager partisan of the Blues, and gave them permission to commit the greatest atrocities and deeds of violence against the opposite faction, while Justinian pretended to be grieved and annoyed in his secret soul, as though he could not oppose his wife's orders; and often they would pretend to act in opposition. The one would declare that the Blues must be punished because they were evil-doers, while the other pretended to be enraged, and angrily declared that she was overruled by her husband against her will. Yet, as I have said, the Blue faction seemed wondrously quiet, for they did not outrage their neighbours as much as they might have done.

In legal disputes, each of them would pretend to favour one of the litigants, and of necessity made the man with the worse case win; by this means they plundered both the parties of most of the disputed property. The Emperor received many persons into his intimacy, and gave them appointments with liberty to do what they pleased in the way of violent injustice and fraud against the State; but when they were seen to have amassed a considerable amount of wealth, they straightway fell into disgrace for having offended the Empress. At first Justinian would take upon himself to inquire kindly into their case, but soon he would drop the pretence of good-will, and his zeal on their behalf would throw the whole matter into confusion. Upon this, Theodora would treat them in the most shameful way, while he, pretending not to understand what was going on, would shamelessly confiscate their entire property. They used to carry on these machinations by appearing to be at variance, while really playing into each other's hands, and were thus able to set their subjects by their ears and firmly establish their own power.

HISTORIA CALAMITATUM
The Story of My Misfortunes
An Autobiography by Peter Abélard
Translated by Henry Adams Bellows

CHAPTER I
OF THE BIRTHPLACE OF PIERRE ABÉLARD AND OF HIS PARENTS

Know, then, that I am come from a certain town which was built on the way into lesser Brittany, distant some eight miles, as I think, eastward from the city of Nantes, and in its own tongue called Palets. Such is the nature of that country, or, it may be, of them who dwell there—for in truth they are quick in fancy—that my mind bent itself easily to the study of letters. Yet more, I had a father who had won some smattering of letters before he had girded on the soldier's belt. And so it came about that long afterwards his love thereof was so strong that he saw to it that each son of his should be taught in letters even earlier than in the management of arms. Thus indeed did it come to pass. And because I was his first born, and for that reason the more dear to him, he sought with double diligence to have me wisely taught. For my part, the more I went forward in the study of letters, and ever more easily, the greater became the ardour of my devotion to them, until in truth I was so enthralled by my passion for learning that, gladly leaving to my brothers the pomp of glory in arms, the right of heritage and all the honours that should have been mine as the eldest born, I fled utterly from the court of Mars that I might win learning in the bosom of Minerva. And since I found the armory of logical reasoning more to my liking than the other forms of philosophy, I exchanged all other weapons for these, and to the prizes of victory in war I preferred the battle of minds in disputation. Thenceforth, journeying through many provinces, and debating as I went, going whithersoever I heard that the study of my chosen art most flourished, I became such an one as the Peripatetics.

CHAPTER II
OF THE PERSECUTION HE HAD FROM HIS MASTER WILLIAM OF CHAMPEAUX— OF HIS ADVENTURES AT MELUN, AT CORBEIL AND AT PARIS—OF HIS WITHDRAWAL FROM THE CITY OF THE PARISIANS TO MELUN, AND HIS RETURN TO MONT STE. GENEVIÈVE—OF HIS JOURNEY TO HIS OLD HOME

I came at length to Paris, where above all in those days the art of dialectics was most flourishing, and there did I meet William of Champeaux, my teacher, a man most distinguished in his science both by his renown and by his true merit. With him I remained for some time, at first indeed well liked of him; but later I brought him great grief, because I undertook to refute certain of his opinions, not infrequently attacking him in disputation, and now and then in these debates I was adjudged victor. Now this, to those among my fellow students who were ranked foremost, seemed all the more insufferable because of my youth and the brief duration of my studies.

Out of this sprang the beginning of my misfortunes, which have followed me even to the present day; the more widely my fame was spread abroad, the more bitter was the envy that was kindled against me. It was given out that I, presuming on my gifts far beyond the warranty of my youth, was aspiring despite my tender, years to the leadership of a school; nay, more, that I was making read the very place in which I would undertake this task, the place being none other than the castle of Melun, at that time a royal seat. My teacher himself had some foreknowledge of this, and tried to remove my school as far as possible from his own. Working in secret, he sought in every way he could before I left his following to bring to nought the school I had planned and the place I had chosen for it. Since, however, in that very place he had many rivals, and some of them men of influence among the great ones of the land, relying on their aid I won to the fulfillment of my wish; the support of many was secured for me by reason of his own unconcealed envy. From this small inception of my school, my fame in the art of dialectics began to spread abroad, so that little by little the renown, not alone of those who had been my fellow students, but of our very teacher himself, grew dim and was like to die out altogether. Thus it came about that, still more confident in myself, I moved my school as soon as I well might to the castle of Corbeil, which is hard by the city of Paris, for there I knew there would be given more frequent chance for my assaults in our battle of disputation.

No long time thereafter I was smitten with a grievous illness, brought upon me by my immoderate zeal for study. This illness forced me to turn homeward to my native province, and thus for some years I was as if cut off from France. And yet, for that very reason, I was sought out all the more eagerly by those whose hearts were troubled by the lore of dialectics. But after a few years had passed, and I was whole again from my sickness, I learned that my teacher, that same William Archdeacon of Paris, had changed his former garb and joined an order of the regular clergy. This he had done, or so men said, in order that he might be deemed more deeply religious, and so might be elevated to a loftier rank in the prelacy, a thing which, in truth, very soon came to pass, for he was made bishop of Châlons. Nevertheless, the garb he had donned by reason of his

conversion did nought to keep him away either from the city of Paris or from his wonted study of philosophy; and in the very monastery wherein he had shut himself up for the sake of religion he straightway set to teaching again after the same fashion as before.

To him did I return, for I was eager to learn more of rhetoric from his lips; and in the course of our many arguments on various matters, I compelled him by most potent reasoning first to alter his former opinion on the subject of the universals, and finally to abandon it altogether. Now, the basis of this old concept of his regarding the reality of universal ideas was that the same quality formed the essence alike of the abstract whole and of the individuals which were its parts: in other words, that there could be no essential differences among these individuals, all being alike save for such variety as might grow out of the many accidents of existence. Thereafter, however, he corrected this opinion, no longer maintaining that the same quality was the essence of all things, but that, rather, it manifested itself in them through diverse ways. This problem of universals is ever the most vexed one among logicians, to such a degree, indeed, that even Porphyry, writing in his "Isagoge" regarding universals, dared not attempt a final pronouncement thereon, saying rather: "This is the deepest of all problems of its kind." Wherefore it followed that when William had first revised and then finally abandoned altogether his views on this one subject, his lecturing sank into such a state of negligent reasoning that it could scarce be called lecturing on the science of dialectics at all; it was as if all his science had been bound up in this one question of the nature of universals.

Thus it came about that my teaching won such strength and authority that even those who before had clung most vehemently to my former master, and most bitterly attacked my doctrines, now flocked to my school. The very man who had succeeded to my master's chair in the Paris school offered me his post, in order that he might put himself under my tutelage along with all the rest, and this in the very place where of old his master and mine had reigned. And when, in so short a time, my master saw me directing the study of dialectics there, it is not easy to find words to tell with what envy he was consumed or with what pain he was tormented. He could not long, in truth, bear the anguish of what he felt to be his wrongs, and shrewdly he attacked me that he might drive me forth. And because there was nought in my conduct whereby he could come at me openly, he tried to steal away the school by launching the vilest calumnies against him who had yielded his post to me, and by putting in his place a certain rival of mine. So then I returned to Melun, and set up my school there as before; and the more openly his envy pursued me, the greater was the authority it conferred upon me. Even so held the poet: "Jealousy aims at the peaks; the winds storm the loftiest summits." (Ovid: "Remedy for Love," I, 369.)

Not long thereafter, when William became aware of the fact that almost all his students were holding grave doubts as to his religion, and were whispering earnestly among themselves about his conversion, deeming that he had by no means abandoned this world, he withdrew himself and his brotherhood, together with his students, to a certain estate far distant from the city. Forthwith I returned from Melun to Paris, hoping for peace from him in the future. But since, as I have said, he had caused my place to be occupied by a rival of mine, I pitched the camp, as it were, of my school outside the city on Mont Ste. Geneviève. Thus I was as one laying siege to him who had taken possession of my post. No sooner had my master heard of this than he brazenly returned post haste to the city, bringing back with him such students as he could, and reinstating his brotherhood in their for mer monastery, much as if he would free his soldiery, whom he had deserted, from my blockade. In truth, though, if it was his purpose to bring them succour, he did nought but hurt them. Before that time my rival had indeed had a certain number of students, of one sort and another, chiefly by reason of his lectures on Priscian, in which he was considered of great authority. After our master had returned, however, he lost nearly all of these followers, and thus was compelled to give up the direction of the school. Not long thereafter, apparently despairing further of worldly fame, he was converted to the monastic life.

Following the return of our master to the city, the combats in disputation which my scholars waged both with him himself and with his pupils, and the successes

which fortune gave to us, and above all to me, in these wars, you have long since learned of through your own experience. The boast of Ajax, though I speak it more temperately, I still am bold enough to make:

"... if fain you would learn now
How victory crowned the battle, by him was
I never vanquished."
(Ovid, "Metamorphoses," XIII, 89.)

But even were I to be silent, the fact proclaims itself, and its outcome reveals the truth regarding it.

While these things were happening, it became needful for me again to repair to my old home, by reason of my dear mother, Lucia, for after the conversion of my father, Berengarius, to the monastic life, she so ordered her affairs as to do likewise. When all this had been completed, I returned to France, above all in order that I might study theology, since now my oft-mentioned teacher, William, was active in the episcopate of Châlons. In this held of learning Anselm of Laon, who was his teacher therein, had for long years enjoyed the greatest renown.

CHAPTER III
OF HOW HE CAME TO LAON TO SEEK ANSELM AS TEACHER

Sought out, therefore, this same venerable man, whose fame, in truth, was more the result of long-established custom than of the potency of his own talent or intellect. If any one came to him impelled by doubt on any subject, he went away more doubtful still. He was wonderful, indeed, in the eyes of these who only listened to him, but those who asked him questions perforce held him as nought. He had a miraculous flock of words, but they were contemptible in meaning and quite void of reason. When he kindled a fire, he filled his house with smoke and illumined it not at all. He was a tree which seemed noble to those who gazed upon its leaves from afar, but to those who came nearer and examined it more closely was revealed its barrenness. When, therefore, I had come to this tree that I might pluck the fruit thereof, I discovered that it was indeed the fig tree which Our Lord cursed (Matthew xxi, 19; Mark xi, 13), or that ancient oak to which Lucan likened Pompey, saying:

> "... he stands, the shade of a name once mighty,
> Like to the towering oak in the midst of the fruit-
> ful field."
> (Lucan, "Pharsalia," IV, 135.)

It was not long before I made this discovery, and stretched myself lazily in the shade of that same tree. I went to his lectures less and less often, a thing which some among his eminent followers took sorely to heart, because they interpreted it as a mark of contempt for so illustrious a teacher. Thenceforth they secretly sought to influence him against me, and by their vile insinuations made me hated of him. It chanced, moreover, that one day, after the exposition of certain texts, we scholars were jesting among ourselves, and one of them, seeking to draw me out, asked me what I thought of the lectures on the Books of Scripture. I, who had as yet studied only the sciences, replied that following such lectures seemed to me most useful in so far as the salvation of the soul was concerned, but that it appeared quite extraordinary to me that educated persons should not be able to understand the sacred books simply by studying them themselves, together with the glosses thereon, and without the aid of any teacher. Most of those who were present mocked at me, and asked whether I myself could do as I had said, or whether I would dare to undertake it. I answered that if they wished, I was ready to try it. Forthwith they cried out and jeered all the more. "Well and good," said they; "we agree to the test. Pick out and give us an exposition of some doubtful passage in the Scriptures, so that we can put this boast of yours to the proof." And they all chose that most obscure prophecy of Ezekiel.

I accepted the challenge, and invited them to attend a lecture on the very next day. Whereupon they undertook to give me good advice, saying that I should by no means make undue haste in so important a matter, but that I ought to devote a much loner space to working out my exposition and offsetting my inexperience by diligent toil. To this I replied indignantly that it was my wont to win success, not by routine, but by ability. I added that I would abandon the test altogether unless they would agree not to put off their attendance at my lecture. In truth at this first lecture of mine only a few were present, for it seemed quite absurd to all of them that I, hitherto so inexperienced in discussing the Scriptures, should attempt the thing so hastily. However, this lecture gave such satisfaction to all those who heard it that they spread its praises abroad with notable enthusiasm, and thus compelled me to continue my interpretation of the sacred text. When word of this was bruited about, those who had stayed away from the first lecture came eagerly, some to the second and more to the third, and all of them were eager to write down the glosses which I had begun on the first day, so as to have them from the very beginning.

CHAPTER IV
OF THE PERSECUTION HE HAD FROM HIS TEACHER ANSELM

Now this venerable man of whom I have spoken was acutely smitten with envy, and straightway incited, as I have already mentioned, by the insinuations of sundry persons, began to persecute me for my lecturing on the Scriptures no less bitterly than my former master, William, had done for my work in philosophy. At that time there were in this old man's school two who were considered far to excel all the others: Alberic of Rheims and Lotulphe the Lombard. The better opinion these two held of themselves, the more they were incensed against me. Chiefly at their suggestion, as it afterwards transpired, yonder venerable coward had the impudence to forbid me to carry on any further in his school the work of preparing glosses which I had thus begun. The pretext he alleged was that if by chance in the course of this work I should write anything containing blunders—as was likely enough in view of my lack of training—the thing might be imputed to him. When this came to the ears of his scholars, they were filled with indignation at so undisguised a manifestation of spite, the like of which had never been directed against any one before. The more obvious this rancour became, the more it redounded to my honour, and his persecution did nought save to make me more famous.

CHAPTER V
OF HOW HE RETURNED TO PARIS AND FINISHED THE GLOSSES WHICH HE HAD BEGUN AT LAON

And so, after a few days, I returned to Paris, and there for several years I peacefully directed the school which formerly had been destined for me, nay, even offered to me, but from which I had been driven out. At the very outset of my work there, I set about completing the glosses on Ezekiel which I had begun at Laon. These proved so satisfactory to all who read them that they came to believe me no less adept in lecturing on theology than I had proved myself to be in the held of philosophy. Thus my school was notably increased in size by reason of my lectures on subjects of both these kinds, and the amount of financial profit as well as glory which it brought me cannot be concealed from you, for the matter was widely talked of. But prosperity always puffs up the foolish, and worldly comfort enervates the soul, rendering it an easy prey to carnal temptations. Thus I, who by this time had come to regard myself as the only philosopher remaining in the whole world, and had ceased to fear any further disturbance of my peace, began to loosen the rein on my desires, although hitherto I had always lived in the utmost continence. And the greater progress I made in my lecturing on philosophy or theology, the more I departed alike from the practice of the philosophers and the spirit of the divines in the uncleanness of my life. For it is well known, methinks, that philosophers, and still more those who have devoted their lives to arousing the love of sacred study, have been strong above all else in the beauty of chastity.

Thus did it come to pass that while I was utterly absorbed in pride and sensuality, divine grace, the cure for both diseases, was forced upon me, even though I, forsooth, would fain have shunned it. First

was I punished for my sensuality, and then for my pride. For my sensuality I lost those things whereby I practiced it; for my pride, engendered in me by my knowledge of letters—and it is even as the Apostle said: "Knowledge puffeth itself up" (I Cor. viii, 1)—I knew the humiliation of seeing burned the very book in which I most gloried. And now it is my desire that you should know the stories of these two happenings, understanding them more truly from learning the very facts than from hearing what is spoken of them, and in the order in which they came about. Because I had ever held in abhorrence the foulness of prostitutes, because I had diligently kept myself from all excesses and from association with the women of noble birth who attended the school, because I knew so little of the common talk of ordinary people, perverse and subtly flattering chance gave birth to an occasion for casting me lightly down from the heights of my own exaltation. Nay, in such case not even divine goodness could redeem one who, having been so proud, was brought to such shame, were it not for the blessed gift of grace.

CHAPTER VI
OF HOW, BROUGHT LOW BY HIS LOVE FOR HÉLOISE, HE WAS WOUNDED IN BODY AND SOUL

Now there dwelt in that same city of Paris a certain young girl named Héloïse, the niece of a canon who was called Fulbert. Her uncle's love for her was equalled only by his desire that she should have the best education which he could possibly procure for her. Of no mean beauty, she stood out above all by reason of her abundant knowledge of letters. Now this virtue is rare among women, and for that very reason it doubly graced the maiden, and made her the most worthy of renown in the entire kingdom. It was this young girl whom I, after carefully considering all those qualities which are wont to attract lovers, determined to unite with myself in the bonds of love, and indeed the thing seemed to me very easy to be done. So distinguished was my name, and I possessed such advantages of youth and comeliness, that no matter what woman I might favour with my love, I dreaded rejection of none. Then, too, I believed that I could win the maiden's consent all the more easily by reason of her knowledge of letters and her zeal therefor; so, even if we were parted, we might yet be together in thought with the aid of written messages. Perchance, too, we might be able to write more boldly than we could speak, and thus at all times could we live in joyous intimacy.

Thus, utterly aflame with my passion for this maiden, I sought to discover means whereby I might have daily and familiar speech with her, thereby the more easily to win her consent. For this purpose I persuaded the girl's uncle, with the aid of some of his friends, to take me into his household—for he dwelt hard by my school—in return for the payment of a small sum. My pretext for this was that the care of my own household was a serious handicap to my studies, and likewise burdened me with an expense far greater than I could afford. Now, he was a man keen in avarice, and likewise he was most desirous for his niece that her study of letters should ever go forward, so, for these two reasons, I easily won his consent to the fulfillment of my wish, for he was fairly agape for my money, and at the same time believed that his niece would vastly benefit by my teaching. More even than this, by his own earnest entreaties he fell in with my desires beyond anything I had dared to hope, opening the way for my love; for he entrusted her wholly to my guidance, begging me to give her instruction whensoever I might be free from the duties of my school, no matter whether by day or by night, and to punish her sternly if ever I should find her negligent of her tasks. In all this the man's simplicity was nothing short of astounding to me; I should not have been more smitten with wonder if he had entrusted a tender lamb to the care of a ravenous wolf. When he had thus given her into my charge, not alone to be taught but even to be disciplined, what had he done save to give free scope to my desires, and to offer me every opportunity, even if I had not sought it, to bend her to my will with threats and blows if I failed to do so with caresses? There were, however, two things which particularly served to allay any foul suspicion: his own love for his niece, and my former reputation for continence.

Why should I say more: We were united first in the dwelling that sheltered our love, and then in the hearts that burned with it. Under the pretext of study we spent our hours in the happiness of love, and learning held out to us the secret opportunities that our passion craved. Our speech was more of love than of the book which lay open before us; our kisses far outnumbered our reasoned words. Our hands sought less the book than each other's bosoms; love drew our eyes together far more than the lesson drew them to the pages of our text. In order that there might be no suspicion, there were, indeed, sometimes blows, but love gave them, not anger; they were the marks, not of wrath, but of a tenderness surpassing the most fragrant balm in sweetness. What followed? No degree in love's progress was left untried by our passion, and if love itself could imagine any wonder as yet unknown, we discovered it. And our inexperience of such delights made us all the more ardent in our pursuit of them, so that our thirst for one another was still unquenched.

In measure as this passionate rapture absorbed me more and more, I devoted ever less time to philosophy and to the work of the school. Indeed it became loathsome to me to go to the school or to linger there; the labour, moreover, was very burdensome, since my nights were vigils of love and my days of study. My lecturing became utterly careless and lukewarm; I did nothing because of inspiration, but everything merely as a matter of habit. I had become nothing more than a reciter of my former discoveries, and though I still wrote poems, they dealt with love, not with the secrets of philosophy. Of these songs you yourself well know how some have become widely known and have been sung in many lands, chiefly, methinks, by those who delighted in the things of this world. As for the sorrow, the groans, the lamentations of my students when they perceived the preoccupation, nay, rather the chaos, of my mind, it is hard even to imagine them.

A thing so manifest could deceive only a few, no one, methinks, save him whose shame it chiefly bespoke, the girl's uncle, Fulbert. The truth was often enough hinted to him, and by many persons, but he could not believe it, partly, as I have said, by reason of his boundless love for his niece, and partly because of the well-known continence of my previous life. Indeed we do not easily suspect shame in those whom we most cherish, nor can there be the blot of foul suspicion on devoted love. Of this St. Jerome in his epistle to Sabinianus (Epist. 48) says: "We are wont to be the last to know the evils of our own households, and to be ignorant of the sins of our children and our wives, though our neighbours sing them aloud." But no matter how slow a matter may be in disclosing itself, it is sure to come forth at last, nor is it easy to hide from one what is known to all. So, after the lapse of several months, did it happen with us. Oh, how great was the uncle's grief when he learned the truth, and how bitter was the sorrow of the lovers when we were forced to part! With what shame was I overwhelmed, with what contrition smitten because of the blow which had fallen on her I loved, and what a tempest of misery burst over her by reason of my disgrace! Each grieved most, not for himself, but for the other. Each sought to allay, not his own sufferings, but those of the one he loved. The very sundering of our bodies served but to link our souls closer together; the plentitude of the love which was denied to us inflamed us more than ever. Once the first wildness of shame had passed, it left us more shameless than before, and as shame died within us the cause of it seemed to us ever more desirable. And so it chanced with us as, in the stories that the poets tell, it once happened with Mars and Venus when they were caught together.

It was not long after this that Héloïse found that she was pregnant, and of this she wrote to me in the utmost exultation, at the same time asking me to consider what had best be done. Accordingly, on a night when her uncle was absent, we carried out the plan we had determined on, and I stole her secretly away from her uncle's house, sending her without delay to my own country. She remained there with my sister until she gave birth to a son, whom she named Astrolabe. Meanwhile her uncle, after his return, was almost mad with grief; only one who had then seen him could rightly guess the burning agony of his sorrow and the bitterness of his shame. What steps to take against me, or what snares to set

for me, he did not know. If he should kill me or do me some bodily hurt, he feared greatly lest his dear-loved niece should be made to suffer for it among my kinsfolk. He had no power to seize me and imprison me somewhere against my will, though I make no doubt he would have done so quickly enough had he been able or dared, for I had taken measures to guard against any such attempt.

At length, however, in pity for his boundless grief, and bitterly blaming myself for the suffering which my love had brought upon him through the baseness of the deception I had practiced, I went to him to entreat his forgiveness, promising to make any amends that he himself might decree. I pointed out that what had happened could not seem incredible to any one who had ever felt the power of love, or who remembered how, from the very beginning of the human race, women had cast down even the noblest men to utter ruin. And in order to make amends even beyond his extremest hope, I offered to marry her whom I had seduced, provided only the thing could be kept secret, so that I might suffer no loss of reputation thereby. To this he gladly assented, pledging his own faith and that of his kindred, and sealing with kisses the pact which I had sought of him—and all this that he might the more easily betray me.

CHAPTER VII
OF THE ARGUMENTS OF HÉLOÏSE AGAINST WEDLOCK—OF HOW NONE THE LESS HE MADE HER HIS WIFE

Forthwith I repaired to my own country, and brought back thence my mistress, that I might make her my wife. She, however, most violently disapproved of this, and for two chief reasons: the danger thereof, and the disgrace which it would bring upon me. She swore that her uncle would never be appeased by such satisfaction as this, as, indeed, afterwards proved only too true. She asked how she could ever glory in me if she should make me thus inglorious, and should shame herself along with me.

What penalties, she said, would the world rightly demand of her if she should rob it of so shining a light! What curses would follow such a loss to the Church, what tears among the philosophers would result from such a marriage! How unfitting, how lamentable it would be for me, whom nature had made for the whole world, to devote myself to one woman solely, and to subject myself to such humiliation! She vehemently rejected this marriage, which she felt would be in every way ignominious and burdensome to me.

Besides dwelling thus on the disgrace to me, she reminded me of the hardships of married life, to the avoidance of which the Apostle exhorts us, saying: "Art thou loosed from a wife? seek not a wife. But and if thou marry, thou hast not sinned; and if a virgin marry, she hath not sinned. Nevertheless such shall have trouble in the flesh: but I spare you" (I Cor. vii, 27). And again: "But I would have you to be free from cares" (I Cor. vii, 32). But if I would heed neither the counsel of the Apostle nor the exhortations of the saints regarding this heavy yoke of matrimony, she bade me at least consider the advice of the philosophers, and weigh carefully what had been written on this subject either by them or concerning their lives. Even the saints themselves have often and earnestly spoken on this subject for the purpose of warning us. Thus St. Jerome, in his first book against Jovinianus, makes Theophrastus set forth in great detail the intolerable annoyances and the endless disturbances of married life, demonstrating with the most convincing arguments that no wise man should ever have a wife, and concluding his reasons for this philosophic exhortation with these words: "Who among Christians would not be overwhelmed by such arguments as these advanced by Theophrastus?"

Again, in the same work, St. Jerome tells how Cicero, asked by Hircius after his divorce of Terentia whether he would marry the sister of Hircius, replied that he would do no such thing, saying that he could not devote himself to a wife and to philosophy at the same time. Cicero does not, indeed, precisely speak of "devoting himself," but he does add that he did not wish to undertake anything which might rival his study of philosophy in its demands upon him.

Then, turning from the consideration of such hindrances to the study of philosophy, Héloïse bade me observe what were the conditions of honourable wedlock. What possible concord could there be between scholars and domestics, between authors and cradles, between books or tablets and distaffs, between the stylus or the pen and the spindle? What man, intent on his religious or philosophical meditations, can possibly endure the whining of children, the lullabies of the nurse seeking to quiet them, or the noisy confusion of family life? Who can endure the continual untidiness of children? The rich, you may reply, can do this, because they have palaces or houses containing many rooms, and because their wealth takes no thought of expense and protects them from daily worries. But to this the answer is that the condition of philosophers is by no means that of the wealthy, nor can those whose minds are occupied with riches and worldly cares find time for religious or philosophical study. For this reason the renowned philosophers of old utterly despised the world, fleeing from its perils rather than reluctantly giving them up, and denied themselves all its delights in order that they might repose in the embraces of philosophy alone. One of them, and the greatest of all, Seneca, in his advice to Lucilius, says: "Philosophy is not a thing to be studied only in hours of leisure; we must give up everything else to devote ourselves to it, for no amount of time is really sufficient thereto" (Epist. 73).

It matters little, she pointed out, whether one abandons the study of philosophy completely or merely interrupts it, for it can never remain at the point where it was thus interrupted. All other occupations must be resisted; it is vain to seek to adjust life to include them, and they must simply be eliminated. This view is maintained, for example, in the love of God by those among us who are truly called monastics, and in the love of wisdom by all those who have stood out among men as sincere philosophers. For in every race, gentiles or Jews or Christians, there have always been a few who excelled their fellows in faith or in the purity of their lives, and who were set apart from the multitude by their continence or by their abstinence from worldly pleasures.

Among the Jews of old there were the Nazarites, who consecrated themselves to the Lord, some of them the sons of the prophet Elias and others the followers of Eliseus, the monks of whom, on the authority of St. Jerome (Epist. 4 and 13), we read in the Old Testament. More recently there were the three philosophical sects which Josephus defines in his Book of Antiquities (xviii, 2), calling them the Pharisees, the Sadducees and the Essenes. In our times, furthermore, there are the monks who imitate either the communal life of the Apostles or the earlier and solitary life of John. Among the gentiles there are, as has been said, the philosophers. Did they not apply the name of wisdom or philosophy as much to the religion of life as to the pursuit of learning, as we find from the origin of the word itself, and likewise from the testimony of the saints?

There is a passage on this subject in the eighth book of St. Augustine's "City of God," wherein he distinguishes between the various schools of philosophy. "The Italian school," he says, "had as its founder Pythagoras of Samos, who, it is said, originated the very word 'philosophy.' Before his time those who were regarded as conspicuous for the praiseworthiness of their lives were called wise men, but he, on being asked of his profession, replied that he was a philosopher, that is to say a student or a lover of wisdom, because it seemed to him unduly boastful to call himself a wise man." In this passage, therefore, when the phrase "conspicuous for the praiseworthiness of their lives" is used, it is evident that the wise, in other words the philosophers, were so called less because of their erudition than by reason of their virtuous lives. In what sobriety and continence these men lived it is not for me to prove by illustration, lest I should seem to instruct Minerva herself.

Now, she added, if laymen and gentiles, bound by no profession of religion, lived after this fashion, what ought you, a cleric and a canon, to do in order not to prefer base voluptuousness to your sacred duties, to prevent this Charybdis from sucking you down headlong, and to save yourself from being plunged shamelessly and irrevocably into such filth as this? If you care nothing for your privileges as a cleric, at least uphold your dignity as a philosopher. If you

scorn the reverence due to God, let regard for your reputation temper your shamelessness. Remember that Socrates was chained to a wife, and by what a filthy accident he himself paid for this blot on philosophy, in order that others thereafter might be made more cautious by his example. Jerome thus mentions this affair, writing about Socrates in his first book against Jovinianus: "Once when he was withstanding a storm of reproaches which Xantippe was hurling at him from an upper story, he was suddenly drenched with foul slops; wiping his head, he said only, 'I knew there would be a shower after all that thunder.'"

Her final argument was that it would be dangerous for me to take her back to Paris, and that it would be far sweeter for her to be called my mistress than to be known as my wife; nay, too, that this would be more honourable for me as well. In such case, she said, love alone would hold me to her, and the strength of the marriage chain would not constrain us. Even if we should by chance be parted from time to time, the joy of our meetings would be all the sweeter by reason of its rarity. But when she found that she could not convince me or dissuade me from my folly by these and like arguments, and because she could not bear to offend me, with grievous sighs and tears she made an end of her resistance, saying: "Then there is no more left but this, that in our doom the sorrow yet to come shall be no less than the love we two have already known." Nor in this, as now the whole world knows, did she lack the spirit of prophecy.

So, after our little son was born, we left him in my sister's care, and secretly returned to Paris. A few days later, in the early morning, having kept our nocturnal vigil of prayer unknown to all in a certain church, we were united there in the benediction of wedlock, her uncle and a few friends of his and mine being present. We departed forthwith stealthily and by separate ways, nor thereafter did we see each other save rarely and in private, thus striving our utmost to conceal what we had done. But her uncle and those of his household, seeking solace for their disgrace, began to divulge the story of our marriage, and thereby to violate the pledge they had given me on this point. Héloïse, on the contrary, denounced her own kin and swore that they were speaking the most absolute lies. Her uncle, aroused to fury thereby, visited her repeatedly with punishments. No sooner had I learned this than I sent her to a convent of nuns at Argenteuil, not far from Paris, where she herself had been brought up and educated as a young girl. I had them make ready for her all the garments of a nun, suitable for the life of a convent, excepting only the veil, and these I bade her put on.

When her uncle and his kinsmen heard of this, they were convinced that now I had completely played them false and had rid myself forever of Héloïse by forcing her to become a nun. Violently incensed, they laid a plot against me, and one night, while I, all unsuspecting, was asleep in a secret room in my lodgings, they broke in with the help of one of my servants, whom they had bribed. There they had vengeance on me with a most cruel and most shameful punishment, such as astounded the whole world, for they cut off those parts of my body with which I had done that which was the cause of their sorrow. This done, straightway they fled, but two of them were captured, and suffered the loss of their eyes and their genital organs. One of these two was the aforesaid servant, who, even while he was still in my service, had been led by his avarice to betray me.

CHAPTER VIII
OF THE SUFFERING OF HIS BODY—OF HOW HE BECAME A MONK IN THE MONASTERY OF ST. DENIS AND HÉLOISE A NUN AT ARGENTEUIL

When morning came the whole city was assembled before my dwelling. It is difficult, nay, impossible, for words of mine to describe the amazement which bewildered them, the lamentations they uttered, the uproar with which they harassed me, or the grief with which they increased my own suffering. Chiefly the clerics, and above all my scholars, tortured me

with their intolerable lamentations and outcries, so that I suffered more intensely from their compassion than from the pain of my wound. In truth I felt the disgrace more than the hurt to my body, and was more afflicted with shame than with pain. My incessant thought was of the renown in which I had so much delighted, now brought low, nay, utterly blotted out, so swiftly by an evil chance. I saw, too, how justly God had punished me in that very part of my body whereby I had sinned. I perceived that there was indeed justice in my betrayal by him whom I had myself already betrayed; and then I thought how eagerly my rivals would seize upon this manifestation of justice, how this disgrace would bring bitter and enduring grief to my kindred and my friends, and how the tale of this amazing outrage would spread to the very ends of the earth.

What path lay open to me thereafter? How could I ever again hold up my head among men, when every finger should be pointed at me in scorn, every tongue speak my blistering shame, and when I should be a monstrous spectacle to all eyes? I was overwhelmed by the remembrance that, according to the dread letter of the law, God holds eunuchs in such abomination that men thus maimed are forbidden to enter a church, even as the unclean and filthy; nay, even beasts in such plight were not acceptable as sacrifices. Thus in Leviticus (xxii, 24) is it said: "Ye shall not offer unto the Lord that which hath its stones bruised, or crushed, or broken, or cut." And in Deuteronomy (xxiii, 1), "He that is wounded in the stones, or hath his privy member cut off, shall not enter into the congregation of the Lord."

I must confess that in my misery it was the overwhelming sense of my disgrace rather than any ardour for conversion to the religious life that drove me to seek the seclusion of the monastic cloister. Héloïse had already, at my bidding, taken the veil and entered a convent. Thus it was that we both put on the sacred garb, I in the abbey of St. Denis, and she in the convent of Argenteuil, of which I have already spoken. She, I remember well, when her fond friends sought vainly to deter her from submitting her fresh youth to the heavy and almost intolerable yoke of monastic life, sobbing and weeping replied in the words of Cornelia:

> "... O husband most noble,
> Who ne'er shouldst have shared my couch! Has fortune such power To smite so lofty a head? Why then was I wedded Only to bring thee to woe? Receive now my sorrow, The price I so gladly pay."
> (Lucan, "Pharsalia," viii, 94.)

With these words on her lips did she go forthwith to the altar, and lifted therefrom the veil, which had been blessed by the bishop, and before them all she took the vows of the religious life. For my part, scarcely had I recovered from my wound when clerics sought me in great numbers, endlessly beseeching both my abbot and me myself that now, since I was done with learning for the sake of gain or renown, I should turn to it for the sole love of God. They bade me care diligently for the talent which God had committed to my keeping (Matthew, xxv, 15), since surely He would demand it back from me with interest. It was their plea that, inasmuch as of old I had laboured chiefly in behalf of the rich, I should now devote myself to the teaching of the poor. Therein above all should I perceive how it was the hand of God that had touched me, when I should devote my life to the study of letters in freedom from the snares of the flesh and withdrawn from the tumultuous life of this world. Thus, in truth, should I become a philosopher less of this world than of God.

The abbey, however, to which I had betaken myself was utterly worldly and in its life quite scandalous. The abbot himself was as far below his fellows in his way of living and in the foulness of his reputation as he was above them in priestly rank. This intolerable state of things I often and vehemently denounced, sometimes in private talk and sometimes publicly, but the only result was that I made myself detested of them all. They gladly laid hold of the daily eagerness of my students to hear me as an excuse whereby they might be rid of me; and finally, at the insistent urging of the students themselves, and with the hearty consent of the abbot and the rest of the brotherhood, I departed thence to a certain hut, there to teach in my wonted way. To this place such a throng of students flocked that the neighbourhood could not afford shelter for them, nor the earth sufficient sustenance.

Here, as befitted my profession, I devoted myself chiefly to lectures on theology, but I did not wholly abandon the teaching of the secular arts, to which I was more accustomed, and which was particularly demanded of me. I used the latter, however, as a hook, luring my students by the bait of learning to the study of the true philosophy, even as the Ecclesiastical History tells of Origen, the greatest of all Christian philosophers. Since apparently the Lord had gifted me with no less persuasiveness in expounding the Scriptures than in lecturing on secular subjects, the number of my students in these two courses began to increase greatly, and the attendance at all the other schools was correspondingly diminished. Thus I aroused the envy and hatred of the other teachers. Those who sought to belittle me in every possible way took advantage of my absence to bring two principal charges against me: first, that it was contrary to the monastic profession to be concerned with the study of secular books; and, second, that I had presumed to teach theology without ever having been taught therein myself. This they did in order that my teaching of every kind might be prohibited, and to this end they continually stirred up bishops, archbishops, abbots and whatever other dignitaries of the Church they could reach.

THE MAGNA CARTA

Release Date: March, 2006 [eBook #10000] [Yes, we are more than one year ahead of schedule] [This file was first posted on October 15, 2003] [Date last updated: January 2, 2003]

Edition: 0.1 [1.0 should be posted by December 10, 2003] [The date of the 10th Anniversay of eBook #100]

Language: English

Magna Carta 1215 The Magna Carta (The Great Charter):

Preamble:

John, by the grace of God, king of England, lord of Ireland, duke of Normandy and Aquitaine, and count of Anjou, to the archbishop, bishops, abbots, earls, barons, justiciaries, foresters, sheriffs, stewards, servants, and to all his bailiffs and liege subjects, greetings.

Know that, having regard to God and for the salvation of our soul, and those of all our ancestors and heirs, and unto the honor of God and the advancement of his holy Church and for the rectifying of our realm, we have granted as underwritten by advice of our venerable fathers, Stephen, archbishop of Canterbury, primate of all England and cardinal of the holy Roman Church, Henry, archbishop of Dublin, William of London, Peter of Winchester, Jocelyn of Bath and Glastonbury, Hugh of Lincoln, Walter of Worcester, William of Coventry, Benedict of Rochester, bishops; of Master Pandulf, subdeacon and member of the household of our lord the Pope, of brother Aymeric (master of the Knights of the Temple in England), and of the illustrious men William Marshal, earl of Pembroke, William, earl of Salisbury, William, earl of Warenne, William, earl of Arundel, Alan of Galloway (constable of Scotland), Waren Fitz Gerold, Peter Fitz Herbert, Hubert De Burgh (seneschal of Poitou), Hugh de Neville, Matthew Fitz Herbert, Thomas Basset, Alan Basset, Philip d'Aubigny, Robert of Roppesley, John Marshal, John Fitz Hugh, and others, our liegemen.

1. In the first place we have granted to God, and by this our present charter confirmed for us and our heirs forever that the English Church shall be free, and shall have her rights entire, and her liberties inviolate; and we will that it be thus observed; which is apparent from this that the freedom of elections, which is reckoned most important and very essential to the English Church, we, of our pure and unconstrained will, did grant, and did by our charter confirm and did obtain the ratification of the same from our lord, Pope Innocent III, before the quarrel arose between us and our barons: and this we will observe, and our will is that it be observed in good faith by our heirs forever. We have also granted to all freemen of our kingdom, for us and our heirs forever, all the underwritten liberties, to be had and held by them and their heirs, of us and our heirs forever.

2. If any of our earls or barons, or others holding of us in chief by military service shall have died, and at the time of his death his heir shall be full of age and owe "relief", he shall have his inheritance by the old relief, to wit, the heir or heirs of an earl, for the whole baroncy of an earl by L100; the heir or heirs of a baron, L100 for a whole barony; the heir or heirs of a knight, 100s, at most, and whoever owes less let him give less, according to the ancient custom of fees.

3. If, however, the heir of any one of the aforesaid has been under age and in wardship, let him

have his inheritance without relief and without fine when he comes of age.

4. The guardian of the land of an heir who is thus under age, shall take from the land of the heir nothing but reasonable produce, reasonable customs, and reasonable services, and that without destruction or waste of men or goods; and if we have committed the wardship of the lands of any such minor to the sheriff, or to any other who is responsible to us for its issues, and he has made destruction or waster of what he holds in wardship, we will take of him amends, and the land shall be committed to two lawful and discreet men of that fee, who shall be responsible for the issues to us or to him to whom we shall assign them; and if we have given or sold the wardship of any such land to anyone and he has therein made destruction or waste, he shall lose that wardship, and it shall be transferred to two lawful and discreet men of that fief, who shall be responsible to us in like manner as aforesaid.

5. The guardian, moreover, so long as he has the wardship of the land, shall keep up the houses, parks, fishponds, stanks, mills, and other things pertaining to the land, out of the issues of the same land; and he shall restore to the heir, when he has come to full age, all his land, stocked with ploughs and wainage, according as the season of husbandry shall require, and the issues of the land can reasonable bear.

6. Heirs shall be married without disparagement, yet so that before the marriage takes place the nearest in blood to that heir shall have notice.

7. A widow, after the death of her husband, shall forthwith and without difficulty have her marriage portion and inheritance; nor shall she give anything for her dower, or for her marriage portion, or for the inheritance which her husband and she held on the day of the death of that husband; and she may remain in the house of her husband for forty days after his death, within which time her dower shall be assigned to her.

8. No widow shall be compelled to marry, so long as she prefers to live without a husband; provided always that she gives security not to marry without our consent, if she holds of us, or without the consent of the lord of whom she holds, if she holds of another.

9. Neither we nor our bailiffs will seize any land or rent for any debt, as long as the chattels of the debtor are sufficient to repay the debt; nor shall the sureties of the debtor be distrained so long as the principal debtor is able to satisfy the debt; and if the principal debtor shall fail to pay the debt, having nothing wherewith to pay it, then the sureties shall answer for the debt; and let them have the lands and rents of the debtor, if they desire them, until they are indemnified for the debt which they have paid for him, unless the principal debtor can show proof that he is discharged thereof as against the said sureties.

10. If one who has borrowed from the Jews any sum, great or small, die before that loan be repaid, the debt shall not bear interest while the heir is under age, of whomsoever he may hold; and if the debt fall into our hands, we will not take anything except the principal sum contained in the bond.

11. And if anyone die indebted to the Jews, his wife shall have her dower and pay nothing of that debt; and if any children of the deceased are left under age, necessaries shall be provided for them in keeping with the holding of the deceased; and out of the residue the debt shall be paid, reserving, however, service due to feudal lords; in like manner let it be done touching debts due to others than Jews.

12. No scutage not aid shall be imposed on our kingdom, unless by common counsel of our kingdom, except for ransoming our person, for making our eldest son a knight, and for once marrying our eldest daughter; and for these there shall not be levied more than a reasonable aid. In like manner it shall be done concerning aids from the city of London.

13. And the city of London shall have all it ancient liberties and free customs, as well by land as by water; furthermore, we decree and grant that all other cities, boroughs, towns, and ports shall have all their liberties and free customs.

14. And for obtaining the common counsel of the kingdom anent the assessing of an aid (except in the three cases aforesaid) or of a scutage, we will cause to be summoned the archbishops, bishops, abbots, earls, and greater barons, severally by our letters; and we will moveover cause to be summoned generally, through our sheriffs and bailiffs, and others who hold of us in chief, for a fixed date, namely, after the expiry of at least forty days, and at a fixed place; and in all letters of such summons we will specify the reason of the summons. And when the summons has thus been made, the business shall proceed on the day appointed, according to the counsel of such as are present, although not all who were summoned have come.

15. We will not for the future grant to anyone license to take an aid from his own free tenants, except to ransom his person, to make his eldest son a knight, and once to marry his eldest daughter; and on each of these occasions there shall be levied only a reasonable aid.

16. No one shall be distrained for performance of greater service for a knight's fee, or for any other free tenement, than is due therefrom.

17. Common pleas shall not follow our court, but shall be held in some fixed place.

18. Inquests of novel disseisin, of mort d'ancestor, and of darrein presentment shall not be held elsewhere than in their own county courts, and that in manner following; We, or, if we should be out of the realm, our chief justiciar, will send two justiciaries through every county four times a year, who shall alone with four knights of the county chosen by the county, hold the said assizes in the county court, on the day and in the place of meeting of that court.

19. And if any of the said assizes cannot be taken on the day of the county court, let there remain of the knights and freeholders, who were present at the county court on that day, as many as may be required for the efficient making of judgments, according as the business be more or less.

20. A freeman shall not be amerced for a slight offense, except in accordance with the degree of the offense; and for a grave offense he shall be amerced in accordance with the gravity of the offense, yet saving always his "contentment"; and a merchant in the same way, saving his "merchandise"; and a villein shall be amerced in the same way, saving his "wainage" if they have fallen into our mercy: and none of the aforesaid amercements shall be imposed except by the oath of honest men of the neighborhood.

21. Earls and barons shall not be amerced except through their peers, and only in accordance with the degree of the offense.

22. A clerk shall not be amerced in respect of his lay holding except after the manner of the others aforesaid; further, he shall not be amerced in accordance with the extent of his ecclesiastical benefice.

23. No village or individual shall be compelled to make bridges at river banks, except those who from of old were legally bound to do so.

24. No sheriff, constable, coroners, or others of our bailiffs, shall hold pleas of our Crown.

25. All counties, hundred, wapentakes, and trithings (except our demesne manors) shall remain at the old rents, and without any additional payment.

26. If anyone holding of us a lay fief shall die, and our sheriff or bailiff shall exhibit our letters patent of summons for a debt which the deceased owed us, it shall be lawful for our sheriff or bailiff to attach and enroll the chattels of the deceased, found upon the lay fief, to the value of that debt, at the sight of law worthy men, provided always that nothing whatever be thence removed until the debt which

is evident shall be fully paid to us; and the residue shall be left to the executors to fulfill the will of the deceased; and if there be nothing due from him to us, all the chattels shall go to the deceased, saving to his wife and children their reasonable shares.

27. If any freeman shall die intestate, his chattels shall be distributed by the hands of his nearest kinsfolk and friends, under supervision of the Church, saving to every one the debts which the deceased owed to him.

28. No constable or other bailiff of ours shall take corn or other provisions from anyone without immediately tendering money therefor, unless he can have postponement thereof by permission of the seller.

29. No constable shall compel any knight to give money in lieu of castle-guard, when he is willing to perform it in his own person, or (if he himself cannot do it from any reasonable cause) then by another responsible man. Further, if we have led or sent him upon military service, he shall be relieved from guard in proportion to the time during which he has been on service because of us.

30. No sheriff or bailiff of ours, or other person, shall take the horses or carts of any freeman for transport duty, against the will of the said freeman.

31. Neither we nor our bailiffs shall take, for our castles or for any other work of ours, wood which is not ours, against the will of the owner of that wood.

32. We will not retain beyond one year and one day, the lands those who have been convicted of felony, and the lands shall thereafter be handed over to the lords of the fiefs.

33. All kydells for the future shall be removed altogether from Thames and Medway, and throughout all England, except upon the seashore.

34. The writ which is called praecipe shall not for the future be issued to anyone, regarding any tenement whereby a freeman may lose his court.

35. Let there be one measure of wine throughout our whole realm; and one measure of ale; and one measure of corn, to wit, "the London quarter"; and one width of cloth (whether dyed, or russet, or "halberget"), to wit, two ells within the selvedges; of weights also let it be as of measures.

36. Nothing in future shall be given or taken for a writ of inquisition of life or limbs, but freely it shall be granted, and never denied.

37. If anyone holds of us by fee-farm, either by socage or by burage, or of any other land by knight's service, we will not (by reason of that fee-farm, socage, or burgage), have the wardship of the heir, or of such land of his as if of the fief of that other; nor shall we have wardship of that fee-farm, socage, or burgage, unless such fee-farm owes knight's service. We will not by reason of any small serjeancy which anyone may hold of us by the service of rendering to us knives, arrows, or the like, have wardship of his heir or of the land which he holds of another lord by knight's service.

38. No bailiff for the future shall, upon his own unsupported complaint, put anyone to his "law", without credible witnesses brought for this purposes.

39. No freemen shall be taken or imprisoned or disseised or exiled or in any way destroyed, nor will we go upon him nor send upon him, except by the lawful judgment of his peers or by the law of the land.

40. To no one will we sell, to no one will we refuse or delay, right or justice.

41. All merchants shall have safe and secure exit from England, and entry to England, with the right to tarry there and to move about as well by land as by water, for buying and selling by the ancient and right customs, quit from all evil tolls, except (in time of war) such merchants as are of the land at war with us. And if such are found in our land at the beginning of the war, they shall be detained, without injury to their bodies or goods, until information be received by us, or by our chief justiciar, how

the merchants of our land found in the land at war with us are treated; and if our men are safe there, the others shall be safe in our land.

42. It shall be lawful in future for anyone (excepting always those imprisoned or out-lawed in accordance with the law of the king-dom, and natives of any country at war with us, and merchants, who shall be treated as if above provided) to leave our kingdom and to return, safe and secure by land and water, except for a short period in time of war, on grounds of public policy- reserving always the allegiance due to us.

43. If anyone holding of some escheat (such as the honor of Wallingford, Nottingham, Boulogne, Lancaster, or of other escheats which are in our hands and are baronies) shall die, his heir shall give no other relief, and perform no other service to us than he would have done to the baron if that barony had been in the baron's hand; and we shall hold it in the same manner in which the baron held it.

44. Men who dwell without the forest need not henceforth come before our justiciaries of the forest upon a general summons, unless they are in plea, or sureties of one or more, who are attached for the forest.

45. We will appoint as justices, constables, sher-iffs, or bailiffs only such as know the law of the realm and mean to observe it well.

46. All barons who have founded abbeys, con-cerning which they hold charters from the kings of England, or of which they have long continued possession, shall have the wardship of them, when vacant, as they ought to have.

47. All forests that have been made such in our time shall forthwith be disafforsted; and a similar course shall be followed with regard to river banks that have been placed "in defense" by us in our time.

48. All evil customs connected with forests and warrens, foresters and warreners, sheriffs and their officers, river banks and their wardens, shall immediately by inquired into in each county by twelve sworn knights of the same county chosen by the honest men of the same county, and shall, within forty days of the said inquest, be utterly abolished, so as never to be restored, provided always that we previously have intimation thereof, or our justiciar, if we should not be in England.

49. We will immediately restore all hostages and charters delivered to us by Englishmen, as sureties of the peace of faithful service.

50. We will entirely remove from their bailiwicks, the relations of Gerard of Athee (so that in future they shall have no bailiwick in England); namely, Engelard of Cigogne, Peter, Guy, and Andrew of Chanceaux, Guy of Cigogne, Geoffrey of Martigny with his brothers, Philip Mark with his brothers and his nephew Geoffrey, and the whole brood of the same.

51. As soon as peace is restored, we will banish from the kingdom all foreign born knights, crossbowmen, serjeants, and mercenary sol-diers who have come with horses and arms to the kingdom's hurt.

52. If anyone has been dispossessed or removed by us, without the legal judgment of his peers, from his lands, castles, franchises, or from his right, we will immediately restore them to him; and if a dispute arise over this, then let it be decided by the five and twenty bar-ons of whom mention is made below in the clause for securing the peace. Moreover, for all those possessions, from which anyone has, without the lawful judgment of his peers, been disseised or removed, by our father, King Henry, or by our brother, King Richard, and which we retain in our hand (or which as possessed by others, to whom we are bound to warrant them) we shall have respite until the usual term of crusaders; excepting those things about which a plea has been raised, or an inquest made by our order, before our tak-ing of the cross; but as soon as we return from the expedition, we will immediately grant full justice therein.

53. We shall have, moreover, the same respite and in the same manner in rendering justice

concerning the disafforestation or retention of those forests which Henry our father and Richard our brother afforested, and concerning the wardship of lands which are of the fief of another (namely, such wardships as we have hitherto had by reason of a fief which anyone held of us by knight's service), and concerning abbeys founded on other fiefs than our own, in which the lord of the fee claims to have right; and when we have returned, or if we desist from our expedition, we will immediately grant full justice to all who complain of such things.

54. No one shall be arrested or imprisoned upon the appeal of a woman, for the death of any other than her husband.

55. All fines made with us unjustly and against the law of the land, and all amercements, imposed unjustly and against the law of the land, shall be entirely remitted, or else it shall be done concerning them according to the decision of the five and twenty barons whom mention is made below in the clause for securing the pease, or according to the judgment of the majority of the same, along with the aforesaid Stephen, archbishop of Canterbury, if he can be present, and such others as he may wish to bring with him for this purpose, and if he cannot be present the business shall nevertheless proceed without him, provided always that if any one or more of the aforesaid five and twenty barons are in a similar suit, they shall be removed as far as concerns this particular judgment, others being substituted in their places after having been selected by the rest of the same five and twenty for this purpose only, and after having been sworn.

56. If we have disseised or removed Welshmen from lands or liberties, or other things, without the legal judgment of their peers in England or in Wales, they shall be immediately restored to them; and if a dispute arise over this, then let it be decided in the marches by the judgment of their peers; for the tenements in England according to the law of England, for tenements in Wales according to the law of Wales, and for tenements in the marches according to the law of the marches. Welshmen shall do the same to us and ours.

57. Further, for all those possessions from which any Welshman has, without the lawful judgment of his peers, been disseised or removed by King Henry our father, or King Richard our brother, and which we retain in our hand (or which are possessed by others, and which we ought to warrant), we will have respite until the usual term of crusaders; excepting those things about which a plea has been raised or an inquest made by our order before we took the cross; but as soon as we return (or if perchance we desist from our expedition), we will immediately grant full justice in accordance with the laws of the Welsh and in relation to the foresaid regions.

58. We will immediately give up the son of Llywelyn and all the hostages of Wales, and the charters delivered to us as security for the peace.

59. We will do towards Alexander, king of Scots, concerning the return of his sisters and his hostages, and concerning his franchises, and his right, in the same manner as we shall do towards our other barons of England, unless it ought to be otherwise according to the charters which we hold from William his father, formerly king of Scots; and this shall be according to the judgment of his peers in our court.

60. Moreover, all these aforesaid customs and liberties, the observances of which we have granted in our kingdom as far as pertains to us towards our men, shall be observed b all of our kingdom, as well clergy as laymen, as far as pertains to them towards their men.

61. Since, moveover, for God and the amendment of our kingdom and for the better allaying of the quarrel that has arisen between us and our barons, we have granted all these concessions, desirous that they should enjoy them in complete and firm endurance forever, we give and grant to them the underwritten security, namely, that the barons choose five and twenty barons of the kingdom, whomsoever they

will, who shall be bound with all their might, to observe and hold, and cause to be observed, the peace and liberties we have granted and confirmed to them by this our present Charter, so that if we, or our justiciar, or our bailiffs or any one of our officers, shall in anything be at fault towards anyone, or shall have broken any one of the articles of this peace or of this security, and the offense be notified to four barons of the foresaid five and twenty, the said four barons shall repair to us (or our justiciar, if we are out of the realm) and, laying the transgression before us, petition to have that transgression redressed without delay. And if we shall not have corrected the transgression (or, in the event of our being out of the realm, if our justiciar shall not have corrected it) within forty days, reckoning from the time it has been intimated to us (or to our justiciar, if we should be out of the realm), the four barons aforesaid shall refer that matter to the rest of the five and twenty barons, and those five and twenty barons shall, together with the community of the whole realm, distrain and distress us in all possible ways, namely, by seizing our castles, lands, possessions, and in any other way they can, until redress has been obtained as they deem fit, saving harmless our own person, and the persons of our queen and children; and when redress has been obtained, they shall resume their old relations towards us. And let whoever in the country desires it, swear to obey the orders of the said five and twenty barons for the execution of all the aforesaid matters, and along with them, to molest us to the utmost of his power; and we publicly and freely grant leave to everyone who wishes to swear, and we shall never forbid anyone to swear.

All those, moveover, in the land who of themselves and of their own accord are unwilling to swear to the twenty five to help them in constraining and molesting us, we shall by our command compel the same to swear to the effect foresaid. And if any one of the five and twenty barons shall have died or departed from the land, or be incapacitated in any other manner which would prevent the foresaid provisions being carried out, those of the said twenty five barons who are left shall choose another in his place according to their own judgment, and he shall be sworn in the same way as the others. Further, in all matters, the execution of which is entrusted,to these twenty five barons, if perchance these twenty five are present and disagree about anything, or if some of them, after being summoned, are unwilling or unable to be present, that which the majority of those present ordain or command shall be held as fixed and established, exactly as if the whole twenty five had concurred in this; and the said twenty five shall swear that they will faithfully observe all that is aforesaid, and cause it to be observed with all their might. And we shall procure nothing from anyone, directly or indirectly, whereby any part of these concessions and liberties might be revoked or diminished; and if any such things has been procured, let it be void and null, and we shall never use it personally or by another.

62. And all the will, hatreds, and bitterness that have arisen between us and our men, clergy and lay, from the date of the quarrel, we have completely remitted and pardoned to everyone. Moreover, all trespasses occasioned by the said quarrel, from Easter in the sixteenth year of our reign till the restoration of peace, we have fully remitted to all, both clergy and laymen, and completely forgiven, as far as pertains to us. And on this head, we have caused to be made for them letters testimonial patent of the lord Stephen, archbishop of Canterbury, of the lord Henry, archbishop of Dublin, of the bishops aforesaid, and of Master Pandulf as touching this security and the concessions aforesaid.

63. Wherefore we will and firmly order that the English Church be free, and that the men in our kingdom have and hold all the aforesaid liberties, rights, and concessions, well and peaceably, freely and quietly, fully and wholly, for themselves and their heirs, of us and our heirs, in all respects and in all places forever,

as is aforesaid. An oath, moreover, has been taken, as well on our part as on the part of the barons, that all these conditions aforesaid shall be kept in good faith and without evil intent.

Given under our hand - the above named and many others being witnesses - in the meadow which is called Runnymede, between Windsor and Staines, on the fifteenth day of June, in the seventeenth year of our reign.

THE DECAMERON OF GIOVANNI BACCACCIO

Giovanni Boccaccio

DAY THE FIRST

Here Beginneth the First Day of the Decameron Wherein (After Demonstration Made by the Author of the Manner in Which it Came to Pass That the Persons Who Are Hereinafter Presented Foregathered for the Purpose of Devising Together) Under the Governance of Pampinea Is Discoursed of That Which Is Most Agreeable Unto Each

As often, most gracious ladies, as, taking thought in myself, I mind me how very pitiful you are all by nature, so often do I recognize that this present work will, to your thinking, have a grievous and a weariful beginning, inasmuch as the dolorous remembrance of the late pestiferous mortality, which it beareth on its forefront, is universally irksome to all who saw or otherwise knew it. But I would not therefore have this affright you from reading further, as if in the reading you were still to fare among sighs and tears. Let this grisly beginning be none other to you than is to wayfarers a rugged and steep mountain, beyond which is situate a most fair and delightful plain, which latter cometh so much the pleasanter to them as the greater was the hardship of the ascent and the descent; for, like as dolour occupieth the extreme of gladness, even so are miseries determined by imminent joyance. This brief annoy (I say brief, inasmuch as it is contained in few pages) is straightway succeeded by the pleasance and delight which I have already promised you and which, belike, were it not aforesaid, might not be looked for from such a beginning. And in truth, could I fairly have availed to bring you to my desire otherwise than by so rugged a path as this will be I had gladly done it; but being in a manner constrained thereto, for that, without this reminiscence of our past miseries, it might not be shown what was the occasion of the coming about of the things that will hereafter be read, I have brought myself to write them.[3]

I say, then, that the years [of the era] of the fruitful Incarnation of the Son of God had attained to the number of one thousand three hundred and forty-eight, when into the notable city of Florence, fair over every other of Italy, there came the death-dealing pestilence, which, through the operation of the heavenly bodies or of our own iniquitous dealings, being sent down upon mankind for our correction by the just wrath of God, had some years before appeared in the parts of the East and after having bereft these latter of an innumerable number of inhabitants, extending without cease from one place to another, had now unhappily spread towards the West. And thereagainst no wisdom availing nor human foresight (whereby the city was purged of many impurities by officers deputed to that end and it was forbidden unto any sick person to enter therein and many were the counsels given[4] for the preservation2 of health) nor yet humble supplications, not once but many times both in ordered processions and on other wise made unto God by devout persons,—about the coming in of the Spring of the aforesaid year, it began on horrible and miraculous wise to show forth its dolorous effects. Yet not as it had done in the East, where, if any bled at the nose, it was a manifest sign of inevitable death; nay, but in men and women alike there appeared, at the beginning of the malady, certain swellings, either on the groin or under the armpits, whereof some waxed of the bigness of a common apple, others like unto an egg, some more and some less, and these the vulgar named plague-boils. From these two parts the aforesaid death-bearing plague-boils proceeded, in brief space, to appear and come indifferently in every part of the body; wherefrom, after awhile, the fashion of the contagion began to change into black or livid blotches, which showed themselves in many [first] on the arms and about the thighs and [after spread to] every other part of the person, in some large and sparse and in others small and thick-sown; and like as the plague-boils had been first (and yet were) a very certain token of coming death, even so were these for every one to whom they came.

To the cure of these maladies nor counsel[5] of physician nor virtue of any medicine appeared to avail or profit aught; on the contrary,—whether it was that the nature of the infection suffered it not or that the ignorance of the physicians (of whom, over and above the men of art, the number, both men and women, who had never had any teaching of medicine, was become exceeding great,) availed not to know whence it arose and consequently took not due measures thereagainst,—not only did few recover thereof, but well nigh all died within the third day from the appearance of the aforesaid signs, this sooner and that later, and for the most part without fever or other accident.[6] And this pestilence was the more virulent for that, by communication with those who were sick thereof, it gat hold upon the sound, no otherwise than fire upon things dry or greasy, whenas they are brought very near thereunto. Nay, the mischief was yet greater; for that not only did converse and consortion with the sick give to the sound infection of cause of common death, but the mere touching of the clothes or of whatsoever other thing had been touched or used of the sick appeared of itself to communicate the malady to the toucher. A marvellous thing to hear is that which I have to tell and one which, had it not been seen of many men's eyes and of mine own, I had scarce dared credit, much less set down in writing, though I had heard it from one worthy of belief. I say, then, that of such efficience was the nature of the pestilence in question in communicating itself from one to another, that, not only did it pass from man to man, but this, which is much more, it many times visibly did;—to wit, a thing which had pertained to a man sick or dead of the aforesaid sickness, being touched by an animal foreign to the human species, not only3 infected this latter with the plague, but in a very brief

space of time killed it. Of this mine own eyes (as hath a little before been said) had one day, among others, experience on this wise; to wit, that the rags of a poor man, who had died of the plague, being cast out into the public way, two hogs came up to them and having first, after their wont, rooted amain among them with their snouts, took them in their mouths and tossed them about their jaws; then, in a little while, after turning round and round, they both, as if they had taken poison, fell down dead upon the rags with which they had in an ill hour intermeddled.

From these things and many others like unto them or yet stranger divers fears and conceits were begotten in those who abode alive, which well nigh all tended to a very barbarous conclusion, namely, to shun and flee from the sick and all that pertained to them, and thus doing, each thought to secure immunity for himself. Some there were who conceived that to live moderately and keep oneself from all excess was the best defence against such a danger; wherefore, making up their company, they lived removed from every other and shut themselves up in those houses where none had been sick and where living was best; and there, using very temperately of the most delicate viands and the finest wines and eschewing all incontinence, they abode with music and such other diversions as they might have, never suffering themselves to speak with any nor choosing to hear any news from without of death or sick folk. Others, inclining to the contrary opinion, maintained that to carouse and make merry and go about singing and frolicking and satisfy the appetite in everything possible and laugh and scoff at whatsoever befell was a very certain remedy for such an ill. That which they said they put in practice as best they might, going about day and night, now to this tavern, now to that, drinking without stint or measure; and on this wise they did yet more freely in other folk's houses, so but they scented there aught that liked or tempted them, as they might lightly do, for that every one—as he were to live no longer—had abandoned all care of his possessions, as of himself, wherefore the most part of the houses were become common good and strangers used them, whenas they happened upon them, like as the very owner might have done; and with all this bestial preoccupation, they still shunned the sick to the best of their power.

In this sore affliction and misery of our city, the reverend authority of the laws, both human and divine, was all in a manner dissolved and fallen into decay, for [lack of] the ministers and executors thereof, who, like other men, were all either dead or sick or else left so destitute of followers that they were unable to exercise any office, wherefore every one had license to do whatsoever pleased him] Many others held a middle course between the two aforesaid, not straitening themselves so exactly in the matter of diet as the first neither allowing themselves such license in drinking and other debauchery as the second, but using things in sufficiency, according to their appetites; nor did they seclude themselves, but went about, carrying in their hands, some flowers, some odoriferous herbs and other some4 divers kinds of spiceries,[7] which they set often to their noses, accounting it an excellent thing to fortify the brain with such odours, more by token that the air seemed all heavy and attainted with the stench of the dead bodies and that of the sick and of the remedies used.

Some were of a more barbarous, though, peradventure, a surer way of thinking, avouching that there was no remedy against pestilences better than—no, nor any so good as—to flee before them; wherefore, moved by this reasoning and recking of nought but themselves, very many, both men and women, abandoned their own city, their own houses and homes, their kinsfolk and possessions, and sought the country seats of others, or, at the least, their own, as if the wrath of God, being moved to punish the iniquity of mankind, would not proceed to do so wheresoever they might be, but would content itself with afflicting those only who were found within the walls of their city, or as if they were persuaded that no person was to remain therein and that its last hour was come] And albeit these, who opined thus variously, died not all, yet neither did they all escape; nay, many of each way of thinking and in every place sickened of the plague and languished on all sides, well nigh abandoned, having themselves, what while they were whole, set the example to those who abode in health.

Indeed, leaving be that townsman avoided townsman and that well nigh no neighbour took thought unto other and that kinsfolk seldom or never visited one another and held no converse together save from afar, this tribulation had stricken such terror to the hearts of all, men and women alike, that brother forsook brother, uncle nephew and sister brother and oftentimes wife husband; nay (what is yet more extraordinary and well nigh incredible) fathers and mothers refused to visit or tend their very children, as they had not been theirs] By reason whereof there remained unto those (and the number of them, both males and females, was incalculable) who fell sick, none other succour than that which they owed either to the charity of friends (and of these there were few) or the greed of servants, who tended them, allured by high and extravagant wage; albeit, for all this, these latter were not grown many, and those men and women of mean understanding and for the most part unused to such offices, who served for well nigh nought but to reach things called for by the sick or to note when they died; and in the doing of these services many of them perished with their gain.

Of this abandonment of the sick by neighbours, kinsfolk and friends and of the scarcity of servants arose an usage before well nigh unheard, to wit, that no woman, how fair or lovesome or well-born soever she might be, once fallen sick, recked aught of having a man to tend her, whatever he might be, or young or old, and without any shame discovered to him every part of her body, no otherwise than she would have done to a woman, so but the necessity of her sickness required it; the which belike, in those who recovered, was the occasion of lesser modesty in time to come. Moreover, there ensued of this abandonment the death of many who5 peradventure, had they been succoured, would have escaped alive; wherefore, as well for the lack of the opportune services which the sick availed not to have as for the virulence of the plague, such was the multitude of those who died in the city by day and by night that it was an astonishment to hear tell thereof, much more to see it; and thence, as it were of necessity, there sprang up among those who abode alive things contrary to the pristine manners of the townsfolk.

It was then (even as we yet see it used) a custom that the kinswomen and she-neighbours of the dead should assemble in his house and there condole with those who more nearly pertained unto him, whilst his neighbours and many other citizens foregathered with his next of kin before his house, whither, according to the dead man's quality, came the clergy, and he with funeral pomp of chants and candles was borne on the shoulders of his peers to the church chosen by himself before his death; which usages, after the virulence of the plague began to increase, were either altogether or for the most part laid aside, and other and strange customs sprang up in their stead. For that, not only did folk die without having a multitude of women about them, but many there were who departed this life without witness and few indeed were they to whom the pious plaints and bitter tears of their kinsfolk were vouchsafed; nay, in lieu of these things there obtained, for the most part, laughter and jests and gibes and feasting and merrymaking in company; which usance women, laying aside womanly pitifulness, had right well learned for their own safety.

Few, again, were they whose bodies were accompanied to the church by more than half a score or a dozen of their neighbours, and of these no worshipful and illustrious citizens, but a sort of bloodsuckers, sprung from the dregs of the people, who styled themselves *pickmen*[8] and did such offices for hire, shouldered the bier and bore it with hurried steps, not to that church which the dead man had chosen before his death, but most times to the nearest, behind five or six[9] priests, with little light[10] and whiles none at all, which latter, with the aid of the said pickmen, thrust him into what grave soever they first found unoccupied, without troubling themselves with too long or too formal a service.

The condition of the common people (and belike, in great part, of the middle class also) was yet more pitiable to behold, for that these, for the most part retained by hope[11] or poverty in their houses and abiding in their own quarters, sickened by the thousand daily and being altogether untended and unsuccoured, died well nigh all without recourse. Many breathed their last in the open street, whilst other many, for all they died in their houses, made it known to the neighbours that they were dead rather by the stench of their rot6ting bodies than otherwise; and of these and others who died all about the whole city was full. For the most part one same usance was observed by the neighbours, moved more by fear lest the corruption of the dead bodies should imperil themselves than by any charity they had for the departed; to wit, that either with their own hands or with the aid of certain bearers, whenas they might have any, they brought the bodies of those who had died forth of their houses and laid them before their doors, where, especially in the morning, those who went about might see corpses without number; then they fetched biers and some, in default thereof, they laid upon some board or other. Nor was it only one bier that carried two or three corpses, nor did this happen but once; nay, many might have been counted which contained husband and wife, two or three brothers, father and son or the like. And an infinite number of times it befell that, two priests going with one cross for some one, three or four biers, borne by bearers, ranged themselves behind the latter,[12] and whereas the priests thought to have but one dead man to bury, they had six or eight, and whiles more. Nor therefore were the dead honoured with aught of tears or candles or funeral train; nay, the thing was come to such a pass that folk recked no more of men that died than nowadays they would of goats; whereby it very manifestly appeared that that which the natural course of things had not availed, by dint of small and infrequent harms, to teach the wise to endure with patience, the very greatness of their ills had brought even the simple to expect and make no account of. The consecrated ground sufficing not to the burial of the vast multitude of corpses aforesaid, which daily and well nigh hourly came carried in crowds to every church,—especially if it were sought to give each his own place, according to ancient usance,—there were made throughout the churchyards, after every other part was full, vast trenches, wherein those who came after were laid by the hundred and being heaped up therein by layers, as goods are stowed aboard ship, were covered with a little earth, till such time as they reached the top of the trench.

Moreover,—not to go longer searching out and recalling every particular of our past miseries, as they befell throughout the city,—I say that, whilst so sinister a time prevailed in the latter, on no wise therefor was the surrounding country spared, wherein, (letting be the castles,[13] which in their littleness[14] were like unto the city,) throughout the scattered villages and in the fields, the poor and miserable husbandmen and their families, without succour of physician or aid of servitor, died, not like men, but well nigh like beasts, by the ways or in their tillages or about the houses, indifferently by day and night. By reason whereof, growing lax like the towns-folk in their manners and customs, they recked not of any thing or business of theirs; nay, all, as if they looked for death that very day, studied with all their wit, not to help to maturity the future produce of their cattle and their fields and the fruits of their own past toils, but to consume those which were7 ready to hand. Thus it came to pass that the oxen, the asses, the sheep, the goats, the swine, the fowls, nay, the very dogs, so faithful to mankind, being driven forth of their own houses, went straying at their pleasure about the fields, where the very corn was abandoned, without being cut, much less gathered in; and many, well nigh like reasonable creatures, after grazing all day, returned at night, glutted, to their houses, without the constraint of any herdsman.

To leave the country and return to the city, what more can be said save that such and so great was the cruelty of heaven (and in part, peradventure, that of men) that, between March and the following July, what with the virulence of that pestiferous sickness and the number of sick folk ill tended or forsaken in their need, through the fearfulness of those who were whole, it is believed for certain that upward of an hundred thousand human beings perished within the walls of the city of Florence, which, peradventure, before the advent of that death-dealing calamity, had not been accounted to hold so many? Alas, how many great palaces, how many goodly houses, how many noble mansions, once full of families, of lords and of ladies, abode empty even to the meanest servant! How many memorable families, how many ample heritages, how many famous fortunes were seen to remain without lawful heir! How

many valiant men, how many fair ladies, how many sprightly youths, whom, not others only, but Galen, Hippocrates or Æsculapius themselves would have judged most hale, breakfasted in the morning with their kinsfolk, comrades and friends and that same night supped with their ancestors in the other world!

I am myself weary of going wandering so long among such miseries; wherefore, purposing hence-forth to leave such part thereof as I can fitly, I say that,—our city being at this pass, well nigh void of inhabitants,—it chanced (as I afterward heard from a person worthy of credit) that there foregathered in the venerable church of Santa Maria Novella, one Tuesday morning when there was well nigh none else there, seven young ladies, all knit one to another by friendship or neighbourhood or kinship, who had heard divine service in mourning attire, as sorted with such a season. Not one of them had passed her eight-and-twentieth year nor was less than eighteen years old, and each was discreet and of noble blood, fair of favour and well-mannered and full of honest sprightliness. The names of these ladies I would in proper terms set out, did not just cause forbid me, to wit, that I would not have it possible that, in time to come, any of them should take shame by reason of the things hereinafter related as being told or heark-ened by them, the laws of disport being nowadays somewhat straitened, which at that time, for the rea-sons above shown, were of the largest, not only for persons of their years, but for those of a much riper age; nor yet would I give occasion to the envious, who are still ready to carp at every praiseworthy life, on anywise to disparage the fair fame of these hon-ourable ladies with unseemly talk. Wherefore, so that which each saith may hereafterward be apprehended without confusion, I purpose to denominate them by names altogether or in part sorting with each one's8 quality.[15] The first of them and her of ripest age I shall call Pampinea, the second Fiammetta, the third Filomena and the fourth Emilia. To the fifth we will give the name of Lauretta, to the sixth that of Neifile and the last, not without cause, we will style Elisa. [16] These, then, not drawn of any set purpose, but foregathering by chance in a corner of the church, having seated themselves in a ring, after divers sighs, let be the saying of paternosters and fell to devising with one another many and various things of the nature of the time. After awhile, the others being silent, Pampinea proceeded to speak thus:

"Dear my ladies, you may, like myself, have many times heard that whoso honestly useth his right doth no one wrong; and it is the natural right of every one who is born here below to succour, keep and defend his own life as best he may, and in so far is this allowed that it hath happened whiles that, for the preservation thereof, men9 have been slain without any fault. If this much be conceded of the laws, which have in view the well-being of all mortals, how much more is it lawful for us and whatsoever other, without offence unto any, to take such means as we may for the preservation of our lives? As often as I consider our fashions of this morning and those of many other mornings past and bethink me what and what manner discourses are ours, I feel, and you likewise must feel, that each of us is in fear for herself. Nor do I anywise wonder at this; but I wonder exceedingly, considering that we all have a woman's wit, that we take no steps to provide ourselves against that which each of us justly feareth. We abide here, to my seeming, no otherwise than as if we would or should be witness of how many dead bodies are brought hither for burial or to hearken if the friars of the place, whose number is come well nigh to nought, chant their offices at the due hours or by our apparel to show forth unto whosoever appeareth here the nature and extent of our distresses. If we depart hence, we either see dead bodies or sick persons carried about or those, whom for their misdeeds the authority of the public laws whilere condemned to exile, overrun the whole place with unseemly excesses, as if scoffing at the laws, for that they know the executors thereof to be either dead or sick; whilst the dregs of our city, fattened with our blood, style themselves *pickmen* and ruffle it everywhere in mockery of us, riding and running all about and flouting us with our distresses in ribald songs. We hear nothing here but 'Such an one is dead' or 'Such an one is at the point of death'; and were there any to make them, we should hear dolorous lamentations on all sides. And if we return to our houses, I know not if it is with you as with me, but, for my part, when I find none left therein of a

great household, save my serving-maid, I wax fearful and feel every hair of my body stand on end; and wherever I go or abide about the house, meseemeth I see the shades of those who are departed and who wear not those countenances that I was used to see, but terrify me with a horrid aspect, I know not whence newly come to them.

By reason of these things I feel myself alike ill at ease here and abroad and at home, more by token that meseemeth none, who hath, as we have, the power and whither to go, is left here, other than ourselves; or if any such there be, I have many a time both heard and perceived that, without making any distinction between things lawful and unlawful, so but appetite move them, whether alone or in company, both day and night, they do that which affordeth them most delight. Nor is it the laity alone who do thus; nay, even those who are shut in the monasteries, persuading themselves that what befitteth and is lawful to others alike sortable and unforbidden unto them,[17] have10 broken the laws of obedience and giving themselves to carnal delights, thinking thus to escape, are grown lewd and dissolute. If thus, then, it be, as is manifestly to be seen, what do we here? What look we for? What dream we? Why are we more sluggish and slower to provide for our safety than all the rest of the townsfolk? Deem we ourselves of less price than others, or do we hold our life to be bounden in our bodies with a stronger chain than is theirs and that therefore we need reck nothing of aught that hath power to harm it? We err, we are deceived; what folly is ours, if we think thus! As often as we choose to call to mind the number and quality of the youths and ladies overborne of this cruel pestilence, we may see a most manifest proof thereof.

Wherefore, in order that we may not, through wilfulness or nonchalance, fall into that wherefrom we may, peradventure, an we but will, by some means or other escape, I know not if it seem to you as it doth to me, but methinketh it were excellently well done that we, such as we are, depart this city, as many have done before us, and eschewing, as we would death, the dishonourable example of others, betake ourselves quietly to our places in the country, whereof each of us hath great plenty, and there take such diversion, such delight and such pleasance as we may, without anywise overpassing the bounds of reason. There may we hear the small birds sing, there may we see the hills and plains clad all in green and the fields full of corn wave even as doth the sea; there may we see trees, a thousand sorts, and there is the face of heaven more open to view, the which, angered against us though it be, nevertheless denieth not unto us its eternal beauties, far goodlier to look upon than the empty walls of our city. Moreover, there is the air far fresher[18] and there at this season is more plenty of that which behoveth unto life and less is the sum of annoys, for that, albeit the husbandmen die there, even as do the townsfolk here, the displeasance is there the less, insomuch as houses and inhabitants are rarer than in the city.

Here, on the other hand, if I deem aright, we abandon no one; nay, we may far rather say with truth that we ourselves are abandoned, seeing that our kinsfolk, either dying or fleeing from death, have left us alone in this great tribulation, as it were we pertained not unto them. No blame can therefore befall the ensuing of this counsel; nay, dolour and chagrin and belike death may betide us, an we ensue it not. Wherefore, an it please you, methinketh we should do well to take our maids and letting follow after us with the necessary gear, sojourn to-day in this place and to-morrow in that, taking such pleasance and diversion as the season may afford, and on this wise abide till such time (an we be not earlier overtaken of death) as we shall see what issue Heaven reserveth unto these things. And I would remind you that it is no more forbidden unto us honourably to depart than it is unto many others of our sex to abide in dishonour."

The other ladies, having hearkened to Pampinea, not only commended her counsel, but, eager to follow it, had already begun to devise more particularly among themselves of the manner,11 as if, arising from their session there, they were to set off out of hand. But Filomena, who was exceeding discreet, said, "Ladies, albeit that which Pampinea allegeth is excellently well said, yet is there no occasion for running, as meseemeth you would do. Remember that we are all women and none of us is child enough not to know how [little] reasonable women are among themselves and how [ill], without some man's

guidance, they know how to order themselves. We are fickle, wilful, suspicious, faint-hearted and timorous, for which reasons I misdoubt me sore, an we take not some other guidance than our own, that our company will be far too soon dissolved and with less honour to ourselves than were seemly; wherefore we should do well to provide ourselves, ere we begin."

"Verily," answered Elisa, "men are the head of women, and without their ordinance seldom cometh any emprise of ours to good end; but how may we come by these men? There is none of us but knoweth that of her kinsmen the most part are dead and those who abide alive are all gone fleeing that which we seek to flee, in divers companies, some here and some there, without our knowing where, and to invite strangers would not be seemly, seeing that, if we would endeavour after our welfare, it behoveth us find a means of so ordering ourselves that, wherever we go for diversion and repose, scandal nor annoy may ensue thereof."

Whilst such discourse was toward between the ladies, behold, there entered the church three young men,—yet not so young that the age of the youngest of them was less than five-and-twenty years,—in whom neither the perversity of the time nor loss of friends and kinsfolk, no, nor fear for themselves had availed to cool, much less to quench, the fire of love. Of these one was called Pamfilo,[19] another Filostrato[20] and the third Dioneo,[21] all very agreeable and well-bred, and they went seeking, for their supreme solace, in such a perturbation of things, to see their mistresses, who, as it chanced, were all three among the seven aforesaid; whilst certain of the other ladies were near kinswomen of one or other of the young men.

No sooner had their eyes fallen on the ladies than they were themselves espied of them; whereupon quoth Pampinea, smiling, "See, fortune is favourable to our beginnings and hath thrown in our way young men of worth and discretion, who will gladly be to us both12 guides and servitors, an we disdain not to accept of them in that capacity." But Neifile, whose face was grown all vermeil for shamefastness, for that it was she who was beloved of one of the young men, said, "For God's sake, Pampinea, look what thou sayest! I acknowledge most frankly that there can be nought but all good said of which one soever of them and I hold them sufficient unto a much greater thing than this, even as I opine that they would bear, not only ourselves, but far fairer and nobler dames than we, good and honourable company. But, for that it is a very manifest thing that they are enamoured of certain of us who are here, I fear lest, without our fault or theirs, scandal and blame ensue thereof, if we carry them with us." Quoth Filomena, "That skilleth nought; so but I live honestly and conscience prick me not of aught, let who will speak to the contrary; God and the truth will take up arms for me. Wherefore, if they be disposed to come, verily we may say with Pampinea that fortune is favourable to our going."

The other ladies, hearing her speak thus absolutely, not only held their peace, but all with one accord agreed that the young men should be called and acquainted with their project and bidden to be pleased bear them company in their expedition. Accordingly, without more words, Pampinea, who was knit by kinship to one of them, rising to her feet, made for the three young men, who stood fast, looking upon them, and saluting them with a cheerful countenance, discovered to them their intent and prayed them, on behalf of herself and her companions, that they would be pleased to bear them company in a pure and brotherly spirit. The young men at the first thought themselves bantered, but, seeing that the lady spoke in good earnest, they made answer joyfully that they were ready, and without losing time about the matter, forthright took order for that which they had to do against departure.

On the following morning, Wednesday to wit, towards break of day, having let orderly make ready all things needful and despatched them in advance whereas they purposed to go,[22] the ladies, with certain of their waiting-women, and the three young men, with as many of their serving-men, departing Florence, set out upon their way; nor had they gone more than two short miles from the city, when they came to the place fore-appointed of them, which was situate on a little hill, somewhat withdrawn on every side from the high way and full of various shrubs and plants, all green of leafage and pleasant to behold. On the summit of this hill was a palace, with a goodly and great courtyard in its midst and galleries[23] and saloons and bedchambers, each in itself most fair and adorned and notable with jocund paintings, with lawns and grassplots round about and wonder-goodly gardens and wells of very cold water and cellars full of wines of price, things more apt unto curious drinkers13 than unto sober and modest ladies. The new comers, to their no little pleasure, found the place all swept and the beds made in the chambers and every thing full of such flowers as might be had at that season and strewn with rushes.

As soon as they had seated themselves, Dioneo, who was the merriest springald in the world and full of quips and cranks, said, "Ladies, your wit, rather than our foresight, hath guided us hither, and I know not what you purpose to do with your cares; as for my own, I left them within the city gates, whenas I issued thence with you awhile agone; wherefore, do you either address yourselves to make merry and laugh and sing together with me (in so far, I mean, as pertaineth to your dignity) or give me leave to go back for my cares and abide in the afflicted city." Whereto Pampinea, no otherwise than as if in like manner she had banished all her own cares, answered blithely, "Dioneo, thou sayst well; it behoveth us live merrily, nor hath any other occasion caused us flee from yonder miseries. But, for that things which are without measure may not long endure, I, who began the discourse wherethrough this so goodly company came to be made, taking thought for the continuance of our gladness, hold it of necessity that we appoint some one to be principal among us, whom we may honour and obey as chief and whose especial care it shall be to dispose us to live joyously. And in order that each in turn may prove the burden of solicitude, together with the pleasure of headship; and that, the chief being thus drawn, in turn, from one and the other sex, there may be no cause for jealousy, as might happen, were any excluded from the sovranty, I say that unto each be attributed the burden and the honour for one day. Let who is to be our first chief be at the election of us all. For who shall follow, be it he or she whom it shall please the governor of the day to appoint, whenas the hour of vespers draweth near, and let each in turn, at his or her discretion, order and dispose of the place and manner wherein we are to live, for such time as his or her seignory shall endure."

Pampinea's words pleased mightily, and with one voice they elected her chief of the first day; whereupon Filomena, running nimbly to a laurel-tree—for that she had many a time heard speak of the honour due to the leaves of this plant and how worshipworth they made whoso was deservedly crowned withal—and plucking divers sprays therefrom, made her thereof a goodly and honourable wreath, which, being set upon her head, was thenceforth, what while their company lasted, a manifest sign unto every other of the royal office and seignory.

Pampinea, being made queen, commanded that every one should be silent; then, calling the servingmen of the three young gentlemen and her own and the other ladies' women, who were four in number, before herself and all being silent, she spoke thus: "In order that I may set you a first example, by which, proceeding from good to better, our company may live and last in order and pleasance and without reproach so long as it is agreeable to us, I constitute, firstly, Parmeno, Dioneo's servant, my seneschal and commit unto him the care and ordinance of all our household and [especially] that which pertaineth to the service of the saloon. Sirisco, Pamfilo's14 servant, I will shall be our purveyor and treasurer and ensue the commandments of Parmeno. Tindaro shall look to the service of Filostrato and the other two gentlemen in their bed chambers, what time the others, being occupied about their respective offices, cannot attend thereto. Misia, my woman, and Filomena's Licisca shall still abide in the kitchen and there diligently prepare such viands as shall be appointed them of Parmeno. Lauretta's Chimera and Fiammetta's Stratilia it is our pleasure shall occupy themselves with the ordinance of the ladies' chambers and the cleanliness of the places where we shall abide; and we will and command all and several, as they hold our favour dear, to have a care that, whithersoever they go or whencesoever they return and whatsoever they hear or see, they bring us from without no news other than joyous." These orders summarily given and commended of all, Pampinea,

rising blithely to her feet, said, "Here be gardens, here be meadows, here be store of other delectable places, wherein let each go a-pleasuring at will; and when tierce[24] soundeth, let all be here, so we may eat in the cool."

The merry company, being thus dismissed by the new queen, went straying with slow steps, young men and fair ladies together, about a garden, devising blithely and diverting themselves with weaving goodly garlands of various leaves and carolling amorously. After they had abidden there such time as had been appointed them of the queen, they returned to the house, where they found that Parmeno had made a diligent beginning with his office, for that, entering a saloon on the ground floor, they saw there the tables laid with the whitest of cloths and beakers that seemed of silver and everything covered with the flowers of the broom; whereupon, having washed their hands, they all, by command of the queen, seated themselves according to Parmeno's ordinance. Then came viands delicately drest and choicest wines were proffered and the three servingmen, without more, quietly tended the tables. All, being gladdened by these things, for that they were fair and orderly done, ate joyously and with store of merry talk, and the tables being cleared away,[25]15 the queen bade bring instruments of music, for that all the ladies knew how to dance, as also the young men, and some of them could both play and sing excellent well. Accordingly, by her commandment, Dioneo took a lute and Fiammetta a viol and began softly to sound a dance; whereupon the queen and the other ladies, together with the other two young men, having sent the serving-men to eat, struck up a round and began with a slow pace to dance a brawl; which ended, they fell to singing quaint and merry ditties. On this wise they abode till it seemed to the queen time to go to sleep,[26] and she accordingly dismissed them all; whereupon the young men retired to their chambers, which were withdrawn from the ladies' lodging, and finding them with the beds well made and as full of flowers as the saloon, put off their clothes and betook themselves to rest, whilst the ladies, on their part, did likewise.

None[27] had not long sounded when the queen, arising, made all the other ladies arise, and on like wise the three young men, alleging overmuch sleep to be harmful by day; and so they betook themselves to a little meadow, where the grass grew green and high nor there had the sun power on any side. There, feeling the waftings of a gentle breeze, they all, as their queen willed it, seated themselves in a ring on the green grass; while she bespoke them thus, "As ye see, the sun is high and the heat great, nor is aught heard save the crickets yonder among the olives; wherefore it were doubtless folly to go anywhither at this present. Here is the sojourn fair and cool, and here, as you see, are chess and tables,[28] and each can divert himself as is most to his mind. But, an my counsel be followed in this, we shall pass away this sultry part of the day, not in gaming,—wherein the mind of one of the players must of necessity be troubled, without any great pleasure of the other or of those who look on,—but in telling stories, which, one telling, may afford diversion to all the company who hearken; nor shall we have made an end of telling each his story but the sun will have declined and the heat be abated, and we can then go a-pleasuring whereas it may be most agreeable to us. Wherefore, if this that I say please you, (for I am disposed to follow your pleasure therein,) let us do it; and if it please you not, let each until the hour of vespers do what most liketh him." Ladies and men alike all approved the story-telling, whereupon, "Then," said the queen, "since this pleaseth you, I will that this first day each be free to tell of such matters as are most to his liking." Then, turning to Pamfilo, who sat on her right hand, she smilingly bade him give beginning to the story-telling with one of his; and he, hearing the commandment, forthright began thus, whilst all gave ear to him.

CPSIA information can be obtained at www.ICGtesting.com
Printed in the USA
LVOW09s0539110615

441966LV00001B/1/P